Things that Travelled

Things that Travelled

Mediterranean Glass in the First Millennium CE

Edited by Daniela Rosenow, Matt Phelps, Andrew Meek and Ian Freestone

UCLPRESS

First published in 2018 by
UCL Press
University College London
Gower Street
London WC1E 6BT

Available to download free: www.ucl.ac.uk/ucl-press

A CIP catalogue record for this book is available from The British Library.

ISBN: 978-1-78735-119-6 (Hbk.)
ISBN: 978-1-78735-118-9 (Pbk.)
ISBN: 978-1-78735-117-2 (PDF)
ISBN: 978-1-78735-120-2 (epub)
ISBN: 978-1-78735-164-6 (mobi)
ISBN: 978-1-78735-121-9 (html)
DOI: https://doi.org/10.14324/111.9781787351172

Foreword

Archaeological discoveries and scientific analysis have combined to bring about a revolution in our ability to understand ancient glass over the past 20 years, and arguably this new understanding has been most profoundly felt in investigation of the natron glass industry of the first millennium CE. The recognition that the majority of glass was made from sand and soda in the eastern Mediterranean, then shipped as unworked chunks to be shaped in glass workshops across the known world, has led to renewed interest in glass as an item of trade, and the ebb and flow of its manufacture and movement.

The present volume grew out of a symposium held to address issues around the movement of glass. In November 2014, 125 delegates from across the world attended a two-day conference held in the British Museum, the Wallace Collection and UCL's Institute of Archaeology. It was organised by UCL's Early Glass Technology Research Network (EGTRN), the Association for the History of Glass (AHG) and the British Museum. The success of the meeting and the high level of discussion prompted us to explore the possibility of a volume on the topic and number of participants agreed to prepare chapters related to their contributions.

The title, *Things that Travelled: Mediterranean Glass in the First Millennium CE*, references a 2004 article by the late David Whitehouse ('"Things That Travelled": The Surprising Case of Raw Glass', *Early Medieval Europe* 12 (3), 301–5). Whitehouse's article was intended to be 'an interim report on work in progress on glass' and was inspired by Michael McCormick's *Origins of the European Economy: Communications and Commerce, AD 300–900* (Cambridge University Press, 2001) who had expressed the hope that, in the near future, archaeologists would contribute fresh information on the movement of ceramics and glass. Ten years later, it seemed to be a fitting time for archaeologists and scientists to give an update on their progress.

The volume aims to contribute to our understanding of glass production, distribution, trade and technologies and to contextualise this material within the social, economic and cultural framework of ancient societies. Chapters encompass various glass artefact groups (jewellery, vessels, secondary and primary production remains) from a plethora of regions such as Greece (Antonaras), Bulgaria (Cholakova and Rehren), Cyprus (Cosyns and Ceglia), the Libyan Sahara (Duckworth and Mattingly), Egypt (Rosenow and Rehren), Italy (Maltoni et al., Silvestri et al.), Jordan (O'Hea), Israel (Phelps), Britain (Sainsbury, Davis and Freestone), covering the Roman, Late Antique and early Islamic periods. Aspects discussed include the place of origin and production of raw glass, technology, patterns of distribution and trade, raw glass ingredients, the usage and spread of specific object groups such as gold-glass (Cesarin, Walker et al.), gems (Antonaras) or objects made of emerald green glass (Cottam and Jackson), as well as the relationship between objects made of glass and other materials. Analytical chapters focus on the chemical definition, introduction and distribution of various raw glass groups such as HIMT glass (Freestone et al.), aspects such as glass recycling (Sainsbury), the supply and trade of natron and plant ash glass in Upper Egypt (Rosenow and Rehren), and the characterisation of new plant ash glass groups in early Islamic Palestine (Phelps).

We would like to thank all authors of the chapters included here as well as the other contributors to the conference for presenting their research. Further thanks are due to the British Museum, the Wallace Collection, and UCL's Institute of Archaeology for providing conference space; to UCL and the Association for the History of Glass for providing funding (grants for travel and accommodation for participants, print permissions for images); and to UCL Press. Finally, we would like to thank all those students of UCL who helped in the organisation of the conference, in particular Laura Adlington, Ana Franjić, Umberto Veronesi, Carlotta Farci, Nyree Manoukian, Martina Bertini and Jo Ahmet.

The Editors

Contents

List of figures

List of tables

List of contributors

Anastassios Ch. Antonaras, a specialist in the history of glass, jewellery and textiles, is an archaeologist and curator at the Museum of Byzantine Culture, Thessaloniki. Antonaras has organised numerous exhibitions and symposia, and has published numerous books and articles on objects from Thessaloniki. He currently serves on the board of the Christian Archaeological Association and is the secretary general of the International Association for the History of Glass.

Andrea Ceglia is a postdoctoral research fellow at the Photonics research group (B-PHOT) of the Free University Brussels (VUB). In 2015 he obtained his PhD in Engineering at the VUB developing a methodology to study ancient glasses with portable optical absorption spectroscopy and X-rays absorption spectroscopy on first–fifith century CE Roman black glass and fourth–seventh century CE Cypriot glass.

Giulia Cesarin attended the University of Padua from 2007 to 2012. For her master's thesis in Classical Archaeology, she studied the Hellenistic Sandwich gold-glass. Her PhD research (University of Cologne and University of Padua) focuses on gold-band glass, a category of luxury glassware produced in the late Hellenistic period and early empire.

Tania Chinni obtained her PhD in 2017 in History and Cultures at the University of Bologna with a dissertation on production, trade and consumption of glass objects in the south-eastern part of Emilia Romagna (Italy) during the Middle Ages (fifth–fifteenth century CE). Currently, she collaborates with the Department of History and Cultures as a glass specialist.

Anastasia Cholakova is a research fellow at the National Institute of Archaeology with Museum – Bulgarian Academy of Sciences in Sofia. Her doctoral project, conducted as a Marie Curie ESR at UCL's Institute of Archaeology, explored the archaeology and chemical composition of the Late Antique glass in the Lower Danube region.

Enrico Cirelli is Alexander von Humboldt Researcher and Adjunct Professor at the University of Bologna. His research topics are the economic transformation and commerce dynamics in the Late Antique and Medieval Mediterranean Sea region, using archaeological data.

Peter Cosyns obtained his PhD in 2012 at the Free University Brussels (VUB) with a dissertation on the production and consumption of black glass in the Roman empire through a multidisciplinary approach. Currently he is a postdoctoral research fellow working specifically on the consumption of Late Antique glass in Cyprus based on the material from early Christian basilicas.

Sally Cottam is a doctoral student in the Department of Classics at King's College, London, where she is undertaking research into glass vessel production during the first century CE in the western provinces of the Roman empire. She has published widely on glass from Roman Britain and France.

Mary Davis is the Science liaison Conservator at West Dean College, and additionally works as a freelance archaeological conservator and researcher based in Cardiff. She completed a PhD at Cardiff University, having previously worked in the National Museum of Wales for nearly 20 years. She is an accredited conservator/restorer and a fellow of the Society of Antiquaries.

Patrick Degryse is Professor of Archaeometry and head of the Centre for Archaeological Sciences at KU Leuven, and Leiden University. His main research efforts focus on the use of mineral raw materials in ancient ceramic, glass, metal and building stone production, using petrographical, mineralogical and isotope geochemical techniques.

Chloë N. Duckworth is a lecturer in Archaeological Materials Science at Newcastle University. She directs archaeological field projects investigating production at medieval sites including Madinat al-Zahra and the Alhambra, Spain. Prior to this she held a British Academy Postdoctoral Fellowship, investigating scientific evidence for glass recycling in the first millennium CE.

Ian C. Freestone is Professor of Archaeological Materials and Technology at the UCL Institute of Archaeology, London. A recipient of the Archaeological Institute of America's Pomerance Medal for Archaeological Science, he has worked extensively on the materials science of the early glass, ceramics and metals industries. He was previously Deputy Keeper of Conservation and Science at the British Museum, then Professor of Archaeological Science at Cardiff University.

Filomena Gallo studied Science for Cultural Heritage Conservation at the University of Florence. In 2012 she obtained a PhD from the University of Padova with a project investigating the production and provenance of Roman and late Roman Italian glasses through a geochemical and isotopic approach.

Monica Ganio is an assistant scientist at the Getty Conservation Institute, working primarily on the Antiquities collection. In 2013 she received her PhD in geology from the Katholieke Universiteit Leuven with a dissertation on the provenance of Roman glass from the Italian peninsula. Prior to the GCI, she was a postdoctoral fellow at NU-ACCESS involved in the technical study of Romano-Egyptian portraits, and investigation of Roman red opaque glass.

Bernard Gratuze is senior research fellow at Institut de Recherche sur les Archéomateriaux – Centre Ernest-Babelon (UMR 5060 CNRS/Univ. Orléans). His research fields are the development of analytical protocols using laser ablation ICP MS for ancient glass and lithic materials to study their production and trade from Protohistory to the Modern Period.

Julian Henderson is Professor of Archaeological Science at the University of Nottingham. His research concerns the archaeological and scientific characteristics of ancient materials, especially vitreous materials and ceramics. He has had visiting positions in Melbourne University, Oxford University and the University of Science and Technology, Beijing. He was editor of the *Journal of Archaeological Science* for 11 years.

Caroline Jackson is Professor of Archaeological Materials in the Department of Archaeology, University of Sheffield. Her research encompasses the study and scientific analysis of archaeological materials, specialising in glass and other vitreous materials.

James Lankton is an honorary senior research fellow at UCL's Institute of Archaeology, London, with a focus on how the scientific analysis of glass can help us learn about production and exchange in the ancient world.

Antonio Longinelli is retired Professor of Geochemistry from the University of Parma. His research work lasted for about 60 years and was mainly focused on stable isotope studies (oxygen, hydrogen, carbon, nitrogen, sulfur) in the fields of palaeoclimatology, ecology, hydrology, oceanography, biology, petrology and archaeometry with a focus on ancient glass and its raw materials.

Sarah Maltoni obtained her PhD in 2015 in Study and Conservation of Archaeological and Architectonic Heritage from the Department of Cultural Heritage of the University of Padova and continued her post-doctoral research at the Department of Geosciences of the same university. Her research focuses on the archaeometric characterisation of Roman and Byzantine glass and the experimental replica of ancient glass technologies.

Alessandra Marcante received her PhD in 2012 from the University of Siena (Italy) with a thesis on the morphometric approach to archaeological glass from Italy. Her main research topic is the archaeology of glass from Roman to modern times, with a morphometric and statistic approach. She cooperates with the University of Padova, Pisa and Trento as a glass specialist.

David J. Mattingly is Professor of Roman Archaeology at the University of Leicester. He specialises in landscape archaeology, and has published extensively on a range of subjects. He has led and collaborated on notable projects including the Trans-SAHARA Project and Endangered Archaeology in the Middle East and North Africa (EAMENA).

Andrew Meek is a scientist in the Department of Scientific Research at the British Museum. His specialism is the analysis of vitreous materials. He is a board member of the Early Glass Technology Research Network and The Association for the History of Glass, and co-editor of *Glass News*.

Gianmario Molin is retired Professor of Mineralogy at the University of Padova, Italy (2005–15) and director of the Centro per i Musei-Università di Padova. His research and teaching interests in the field of cultural heritage focused on characterisation of archaeological materials as glass and bones.

Margaret O'Hea is a senior lecturer at The University of Adelaide. Trained in both history and archaeology, her research uses ancient glass in the Levant as a means of understanding wider historical and socio-economic issues, focusing upon the relationship of consumer demand for glass with trade and technological change.

Matt Phelps completed a Physical Sciences degree at UCL in 2007 before moving into the field of archaeological science, gaining a master's degree in the Technology and Analysis of Archaeological Materials in 2010. After a placement at the Research Laboratory with English Heritage he went on to do a doctorate at UCL's Institute of Archaeology, finishing in 2017. His research interests lie in glass production, provenance and technology, particularly during the Roman, Byzantine and Islamic periods, with further interests in iron metallurgy. He is currently conducting freelance work as a material remains specialist analysing glass, metals and slag.

Thilo Rehren is Director of the Science and Technology in Archaeology Research Center of the Cyprus Institute. He studies the primary production of metals and glass from their raw materials, and the role of ceramics in this. He has previously worked for UCL (1999–2017) and the German Mining Museum (1990–99).

Daniela Rosenow gained her PhD in Egyptology from the Humboldt-University Berlin in 2008. Her research interests include Late Period and Greco-Roman Egypt with a specialisation in ancient glass. Over the past 16 years she has been involved in several German, UK and Austrian field projects in Egypt as well as exhibition and documentation projects in the UK and US. From 2012–14 she conducted a Marie Curie-funded postdoctoral research project at UCL's Institute of Archaeology on Roman and Late Antique glass from Egypt, and in 2015 joined the British Museum as a project curator for the exhibition 'Sunken Cities: Egypt's Lost Worlds'. Since 2017 she has been employed as an academic research fellow at the German Archaeological Institute, Cairo and responsible for excavations at Dahshur. Daniela is a coordinator of UCL's Early Glass Technology Research Network and The British Association for the History of Glass.

Victoria A. Sainsbury completed her bachelors and honours degrees at the University of Adelaide and an MSc in Archaeological Science at St. Catherine's College, Oxford. She focuses on analytically identifying and quantifying the place of recycling of glass in the Roman period, primarily throughout Roman Britain.

Andrew Shortland is Professor of Archaeological Science at Cranfield University and Director of Cranfield Forensic Institute. He specialises in the analysis of glass, glaze and ceramics from a range of periods and geographical regions, but especially the late Bronze Age of Egypt and the Near East.

Alberta Silvestri received her PhD in Earth Sciences from the University of Padova (Italy) in 2004 and is currently Assistant Professor at the Department of Geosciences of the same University. Her main research interest is the archaeometric characterisation of Roman and Medieval glass (vessels and mosaic tesserae) from various Italian sites, with the aims of identifying raw materials and production techniques by means of a multi-methodological approach.

Mariangela Vandini is Associate Professor of Physics Applied to Cultural Heritage at the University of Bologna. Her teaching and research activities include archaeometry with a special interest in glass studies and analyses. She has been the local team leader for the University of Bologna of the Italian National Research Project PRIN on the investigation of glass production technology in the Romagna area.

Susan Walker was Sackler Keeper of Antiquities at the Ashmolean Museum, Oxford, from 2004 until her retirement in 2014. She is now Honorary Curator at the Ashmolean and Emerita Fellow of Wolfson College, University of Oxford. She is the principal author of *Saints and Salvation: The Wilshere Collection of Gold-Glass, Sarcophagi and Inscriptions from Rome and Southern Italy* (Ashmolean Museum, Oxford 2017).

1

A special group of early Christian glass 'gems' from Greece

Anastassios Ch. Antonaras

Abstract

Semi-precious stones are frequently depicted in Roman and early Christian works of art, such as wall mosaics, paintings and textiles. These depictions present them as either parts of jewelled frames, or as decorations in buildings, architectural elements like columns, or other objects like thrones, wreaths, shields, tables, crosses, book bindings, etc. They appear usually as green, blue and red in colour, mostly of oblong and oval shapes. The prototypes of these gems, or rather the glass rendering of them, is the focus of this chapter. Only recently discovered and otherwise unknown, these large-size (7 × 4 × 0.5 cm) emerald green glass gems deriving from six early Christian excavations in northern Greece and a harbour site in Constantinople, will be presented. Their use will be discussed in relation to their symbolic meaning connected to theological texts and to their representations in contemporaneous mural paintings and mosaics and textiles. Furthermore, Thessaloniki is identified as the production site of at least one type of these gems according to relevant finds from a late sixth-century glass workshop, while the distribution pattern of these products in the wider region of Thessaloniki's hinterland will shed light on a facet of the circulation of glass objects on a regional trade level.

Introduction

Semi-precious stones are often depicted in Roman and early Christian works of art. They are presented either as part of the jewelled frame of a scene, or in the decoration of buildings, as architectural elements or other objects. They appear usually green, blue and in red colour, mostly oblong, circular and oval, and they are always plain and smooth. The glass replicas of semi-precious stones are the theme of the present chapter. Newly found emerald green smooth glass gems from six early Christian excavations in northern Greece and a port in Constantinople are discussed. These gems are far larger than any known ring bezel gems, nor are they found in association with jewellery. A discussion of early Byzantine glass ring gems is beyond the scope of this chapter. Thessaloniki is identified as the production site of at least one type of these gems as evidenced by finds from a late sixth-century CE glass workshop. The distribution pattern of these products in the wider region of Thessaloniki's hinterland is able to shed light on the circulation of these glass objects on a regional level.

Glass workshop in Vasileos Irakleiou 44, Thessaloniki

In the large and prosperous eastern Mediterranean port of Thessaloniki four early Christian secondary glass workshops are archaeologically attested. Only one workshop, that excavated from 44 Vasileos Irakleiou Street, is relatively well preserved. Parts of the building, the bases of several furnaces and substantial amounts of glass refuse have been unearthed (Antonaras 2014a, 95–113). The period of operation of the workshop is defined by a hoard of 50 small-denomination bronze coins, most of them of Justinian I (r. 527–65) and one of Tiberius II (r. 574–82), all of them struck in Thessaloniki's mint (Dr Evangelos Maladakis pers. Comms.). The workshop was operating in the late sixth century, mostly producing stemmed beakers, some of which bear stamped letters and ligatures/numerals, as well as stemmed lamps and probably some forms of flasks or bottles. Among the glass-working refuse were also a few oblong, dark green gems, they are relatively large and quite unusual. These and other identical or very similar finds from seven further sites, mostly associated with early Christian basilicas, are the topic of this chapter, with the aim of investigating their production and distribution in the wider region of Thessaloniki and beyond, as well as their use and their symbolic meaning.

The gems were unearthed within the glass workshop, in the same layer as the refuse and a late sixth-century hoard of bronze coins (Figure 1.1). Although none of the extant finds appears to be unfinished or otherwise deformed, which would prove that it was worked

Figure 1.1 Glass gems from Vasileos Irakleiou 44, Thessaloniki. Dating from the second half of the sixth century.

on that site, the fact that they were found within a glass workshop, among deformed vessels and other glass-working refuse, makes it probable that this type of gem was produced here as well. Scientific analyses, planned for 2017, will help to clarify the relation of the gems to raw glass unearthed in the workshop and also distorted vessels from the same pit. The excavations of the glass workshop at 45 Vasileos Irakleiou Street yielded three or possibly four oblong examples (measuring *c.*7 × 3 × 1.8 cm), all of them made of dark green translucent glass (Antonaras 2014a, 111, fig. 12.32).

The underside of the gems is rough, with many anomalies and small cavities, possibly echoing the relief of the surface on which firing took place, or more probably they are the result of the uneven change in temperature during the cooling of the mass of glass. Some of the oblong specimens have relatively anomalous ridges visible along the centre of the bottom side. The top is mildly convex, gradually sloping towards the edge of the undersurface. No tooling marks are visible in most of the gems, although this might simply indicate that the craftsman's handling was subtle enough not to leave any traces on the finished product. For instance, on the oblong gem from Louloudies, a scar is visible along its length, which is particularly straight, compared to the majority of objects with irregular sides. Furthermore, tooling marks are clearly visible along the long sides of the triangular find from Fourka (see Figure 1.4). It seems that the gems were originally discoid and were squeezed while hot into the oblong or triangular shape, probably by pinchers, the jaws of which left a scar along them.

A comparative examination of the examples under study indicates that the oblong gems have a length–width ratio of 2:1 (7 × 3 × 1.8 cm weighing *c.*27 grams). The almost square examples have a ratio of 1:1 (3 × 2 × 1.2 cm). The triangular measures 4.3 × 1.8–0.8 × 1 cm and it could have been shaped from an originally discoid piece. The oval example has a ratio of 1:1.5 (3.5 × 2.3 × 0.5 cm). While the circular specimen weighs *c.*6 grams and is larger than *c.*2.5 cm in diameter, being more than twice the size of usual ring gems.

Distribution range

Seven early Christian sites yielded the inlay gems discussed here; five from basilicas, and one each from a secular building and a port. Three of the sites were situated in Chalkidiki, the peninsula east of Thessaloniki; two of them in Pieria at the south-west of Thessaloniki at the foothill of Mount Olympos; one further to the south in Velika in Thessalian seashore, and one from Constantinople's harbour. Most of the sites are situated within the province of Macedonia, between 50 to 150 km from the capital Thessaloniki. All of the sites are on the seashore and thus are relatively easily accessible from Thessaloniki by sea, appearing to present a commercial hinterland and in a way defining the range of the regional trade.

Solinos

Solinos is located on the east coast of Cassandra, on the south-western part of the Chalkidiki peninsula, south of the modern village of Kalithea. The site includes an early Christian cemetery and a three-aisled basilica. The basilica was built in the early fifth century and was ruined probably in the seventh century (Papangelos 1989–90, 171–82; Papangelos 1995). The glass finds from the excavation of the basilica comprise mostly window glass made with the blown cylinder technique, and to a lesser degree vessel fragments, mostly lamps (stemmed lamps), stemmed beakers and bowls, and a few drinking (stemmed and conical beakers) and pouring tableware vessels. The context of the finds is to the destruction phase of the complex dating to the late sixth or seventh centuries (Antonaras

Figure 1.2 Glass gems, Solinos Basilica, *c.* sixth century.

2014b, 97–110). The production date of the glass objects themselves vary, some of them date as early as the fourth century, although most of them were produced in the fifth–sixth centuries. Finally, a few glass beads and glass gems for the embellishment of precious objects conclude the picture of the finds from this site.

Two small, blue, discoid plano-convex gems were found (diameter 0.8, height 0.5 cm) as well as a slender cylindrical element and a blue rectangular tile or *crusta*. These were all made of glass of various colours and they seem to be part of a different production time or workshop, unrelated to the workshop from 44 Vasileos Irakleiou Street. Regarding the topic of this chapter, five glass gems unearthed in the ruins of the basilica should be particularly mentioned: four oblong, dark green gems. They appeared in three sizes, the largest and smallest of which measured 6 × 2 × 1 cm and 4 × 2.5 × 0.8 cm respectively, and appear identical to the ones from Thessaloniki (see Figure 1.2 and compare with Figure 1.1).

Ierissos

At the eastern end of Chalkidiki, at the beginning of the eastern most peninsula known as Athos or *Aghion Oros*, lies the Byzantine and modern town of Ierissos. Near the cemetery of the medieval town a large, three-aisled basilica has been partly excavated. It was founded in the fourth or fifth century and destroyed some time in the sixth century. It was decorated with wall paintings, opus sectile and mosaics. A cemetery

Figure 1.3 Glass gems, Basilica in Ierisos, *c.* sixth century.

was formed in the late tenth and early eleventh century over the ruins of the basilica (Papangelos and Doukas 2008; 2011, 14–15).

The glass finds comprise loose tesserae, window panes made by the blown cylinder technique and fragments of lamps – handled bowls/lamps, a few stemmed lamps and a stemmed beaker. In addition, two similar examples of large gems were found (Figure 1.3). The first one is almost square, but otherwise quite similar to the finds from Thessaloniki, i.e. it is made of dark green translucent glass. It is slightly elongated, plano-convex, and half the length of the gems from Thessaloniki, measuring 3 × 2 × 1.2 cm. The second gem is made of dark amber or olive green glass, discoid with a diameter of 2.5 cm, identical to the discoid finds from Pieria (see *infra*, finds from Louloudies).

Fourka

In 2009 an early Christian basilica was excavated on the beach of the modern village of Fourka. This site was located on the west coast of Cassandra, on the south-western part of Chalkidiki. Apart from the usual anticipated object types – lamps, handled bowls, stemmed beakers and stemmed lamps – as well as a few flasks and jugs, one large triangular dark green glass gem was identified. It measures 4.3 × 1.8 – 0.8 × 1 cm (Figure 1.4). It appears to have been made using a discoid blank, which was squeezed and pulled out by pinchers. The scar of the jacks along its long sides is clearly visible, while the curved endings of the top and the base of the triangle bear all features of the free, natural shaping which is typical for objects shaped by firing.

Louloudies

An early Christian square fort was excavated a few kilometres south of Pydna at a site called Louloudies (Marki 1996, 239, 243). It was founded overtop of a Roman station/*mansio* in the fifth century, most probably by the local episcope of Pydna who moved there when the Arian Goths moved into Pydna. In the second half of the seventh century the site was abandoned and several workshops operated in the ruined complex. At least three distinct glass workshops, probably melting down window

Figure 1.4 Glass gem, Basilica in Fourka, *c.* sixth century.

Figure 1.5 Glass gems, Louloudies Kitrous, *c.* sixth century.

panes and mosaic tesserae to produce new vessels, have been found. Glass droplets and moils are identified on site and confirm the local production of vessels. Also, many pieces of glass 'cakes' – slabs for the production of glass tesserae – are also found there (Marki 2002, 65–6). Regarding the glass gems, one oblong dark green example was found (6.7 × 2.3 x1.3 cm, 26.5 grams) and two circular examples, one dark green and the other yellowish green (both measuring 2.8 × 0.8 cm, weighing 5.6 and 6.1 grams respectively (Figure 1.5).

Dion

Dion, a large Macedonian city, is another site that yielded relevant finds, namely, in the excavation of a house in which a dark green, plano-convex, oblong glass gem was found (Figure 1.6; Mentzos et al. forthcoming). In addition, a discoid gem of the same type was unearthed in the excavation of the early Christian basilica of Dion, currently unpublished (Dr Sapho Tambaki pers. comms.).

Velika

Parts of the castle and the city walls of the early Christian site have been excavated by the local Ephorate of Antiquities (Sdrolia 2013). A dark green, oblong glass gem (5 × 2 cm) which is evidently a product of

Figure 1.6 Glass gem, Dion, *c*. sixth century.
Source: photo by A. Mentzos

Figure 1.7 Glass gem, Velika, *c*. sixth century.
Source: photo by I. Varalis

the workshop of Thessaloniki was located in a sixth-century context in the 'Priest's house', a building connected to the early Christian basilica founded in the middle of the sixth century and abandoned either in the late sixth or in the first decades of the seventh century (Figure 1.7). The excavations are conducted by the University of Thessaly and the local Ephorate of Antiquities.

Figure 1.8 Glass gem, Yenikapi, *c.* fifth–sixth century.
Source: photo by S. Atik

Constantinople

These finds were the farthest from Thessaloniki, unearthed in south-western Constantinople in the excavations at Yenikapı of the port of Theodosius. It is a dark green, plano-convex, oblong glass gem (6.1 × 2.4 × 1 cm) found in a layer dating between the fifth and the seventh century, and evidently presents another product of the Thessaloniki workshop (Atik 2009, 1–15, fig. 71; Figure 1.8).

Other sites

In Corinth, among the finds of the old excavations of the American School of Classical Studies, an object in the same spirit to the Macedonian ones, but of different, more subtle craftsmanship, has been recorded. It is an oval dark blue gem (3.5 × 2.3 × 0.5 cm) ascribed to the Roman period without any particular chronological details (Davidson 1952, 226, no. 791, pl. 101; Figure 1.9). It should be noted that objects of the same form and size are quite often encountered on wall mosaics of the early Christian period.

A few more examples of gems of a similar size and shape are known from Arles in France. Green, oval, square and rectangular examples have been identified as tiles for inlays, mostly dated between the first and fourth centuries CE (Foy 2010, 462–3, nos 944–9).

Figure 1.9 Glass gem, Corinth, Roman period.

There is one object that contains 26 emerald green gems, seemingly identical to the ones we are researching, all in their original setting. It is an early fourth-century, silver-gilt, parade helmet from Berkasovo, which was decorated with 54 glass gems: 16 oblong and 10 lozenge emerald green gems, 10 circular and 8 lozenge undecorated glass nicolo gems and 10 oval agate-like glass gems (Manojlović-Marijanski 1964; Tijana Stanković-Pešterac and Stanko Trifunovic pers. comms). Furthermore, a late fourth-century parade helmet from Budapest contains more than 10 emerald green gems (Thomas 1973, 39–50).

Additional finds come from a church in Petra, Jordan, where there are indications of some similar rectangular and rounded finds. In one case, they are associated with one lock-plate of a chest or coffer. Fiema (2007, 616) describes them as 'dark yellowish green, too thick to be window panes, generally of rectangular shape'. Furthermore, in another spot of the same church, excavations yielded many rectangular and discoid glass objects that appear to be very similar to the finds from Macedonia, according to the description of the excavator, which were presumably originally associated with other objects, such as wooden boxes or chests, possibly as inlaid decoration' (Fiema 2007, 617). Finally, it should be noted that glass discs such as these, used for inlay work, were also reported from Byzantine levels at Jerash (Baur 1938, 546).

Uses

Gems were used from the earliest times in human history for their bright colours and their shiny appearance. Glass is thought to have been first invented in order to replicate precious and semi-precious stones, bearing the name *lithos chyte*, i.e. molten stone. Glass was used in the form of inlays and gems from the middle of the second millennium BCE in Elam and in Egypt (Stern and Schlick-Nolte 1994, 49, 142–9; Nenna 1995, 377–384; Ignatiadou 2007, 473–83). This was a tradition that was kept alive even in the Middle Ages, and this was particularly true for green, emerald-like, glass gems (Krueger 2011, 103–4 and references within). Furthermore, the production of glass substitutes of emeralds and other, yellow, white and blue semi-precious stones is well attested in the preserved alchemic recipes of Zosimos of Panopolis and Olympiodorus, who were active in the fourth–fifth century (Berthelot and Ruelle 1967 I: 83, II: 348).

In the Judaic tradition, semi-precious stones are chiefly mentioned in connection to the breastplate of the High-Priest (Exodus, xxviii, 17–20; xxxix, 10–13), the treasure of the King of Tyre (Ezekiel, xxviii, 13), and the foundations of the New Jerusalem (Tobit, xiii, 16–17), which was described in detail in the Book of Revelation (Rev, xxi, 18–21). Epiphanius of Salamis (Epiphanius, De duodecim qemmis in Migne 1886, vol. XLIII, col. 294–304) and Isidore of Seville (St. Isidore, De lapidibus in Migne 1857–66, vol. LXXXII, col. 570–80), both Christian writers, dealt with the stones and their magical features, classifying them according to Pliny's system.

John's description in Revelation of Heavenly Jerusalem as founded and built of precious stones is of great interest for our research because it is exactly this text and the overall picture of this realm that was illustrated in the mosaics of several early Christian churches. The interior of the church – especially the upper part of the building – renders Heavenly Jerusalem, and this is where we find the most realistic representations of our finds. This text offers the theoretical basis for the wide use of gems on ecclesiastical objects, as they were intended to reflect objects of Heavenly Jerusalem, which were imitated on profane objects of the imperial entourage and the highest social echelons. It should be mentioned that several gemmed gold imperial gifts have been recorded in written sources.

In the *Liber Pontificalis*, among the imperial and papal gifts alone, more than 28 gemmed objects are recorded in the period from the fourth to the seventh centuries. These are mostly vessels: calices and bowls (*calices, scyphi, patenae*), but also censers (*thymiamaterium*), crosses, altars and even the eyes of statues of angels (Duchesne 1886: Silvester. XIII 17, XVIII 12, 17, 22, 25; Xystus III 4; Hilarus III 3, VII 22,VIII 3, IX 1; Symmachus VII 1; Hormisdas X 5–6; Iohannes I, VII 15–16; Gregorius IV; Leo IV 46). Furthermore, fifth- to sixth-century imperial gifts to other important churches include gold gemmed crosses, an altar and a book (Kazhdan 1991, s.v. *Gems*, 828).

Further information referring to Byzantium and the imperial entourage can be found in the *De cerimoniis aulae byzantine*, a tenth-century compilation of several texts the earliest of which goes back to the sixth century (Kazhdan 1991, s.v. *De Ceremoniis*, 595–7). It is a book of ceremonial protocol at the court of the Byzantine emperor. In this work, at least 23 direct references to gemmed objects are recorded, most of them connected to the Emperor, or donated by the Emperor to dignitaries as symbol of their particular office. Gemmed gold crosses, swords, sceptres, cloths, belts, horse saddles and harnesses, batons and sticks, torques, whips and even a gemmed seat are mentioned (Constantinos and Reiske 1829, Batons: p. 10, l. 18, p. 81, l. 17–18, p. 91, l. 23, p. 100, l. 3, p. 105, l. 7, p. 167 1. 23–4, p. 172, l. 4, p. 574, l. 16–18, p. 640, l. 6–7, p. 721, l. 18–20; Cross: p. 25, l. 21–2; Sword: p. 80, l. 10–12, p. 167, l. 9–10, p. 188, l. 4, p. 188, l. 25. Sceptre: p. 187, l. 15. Dress-*kolovi:* p. 80, l. 10–12; Belts: p. 582, l. 10, p. 710, l. 21–2; Saddle and harness: p. 80, l. 25, p. 99, l. 15; Torques: p. 584, l. 4–5, p. 709, l. 20; Whip: p. 709, l. 1–2; Seat: p. 22, l. 23–4). Furthermore, the references to green and white crowns might also allude to a gemmed decoration (Constantinos and Reiske 1829, Crown: 188 1. 9–10, 190 l. 15–16, 581 l. 17–21). There are few surviving objects of this type, but apart from the silver gilt cross of Justin II (r. 565–78) donated to the Vatican, all the others were made or circulated outside the Byzantine empire's borders. They are Lombard and Visigoth royal gifts and include book covers and votive crowns (Kazhdan 1991, s.v. Gems, 828 and further references within).

There are other uses of glass in architectural decoration in the Roman and early Christian period that can help in the contextualisation of the glass gems under study, for example, opus sectile and inserts in marble sculptures. Square green gems set in a yellow frame, imitating emeralds set in gold are depicted in the glass inlays of the sumptuous *opera sectilia* from the early second-century villa of Lucius Verus (r. 161–9) (Whitehouse 1997, 34, no. 6, see references within).

In the fifth century, pieces of glass were used in the *opus sectile* intarsia decorations, e.g. the folds of the curtains of the heavenly tribelon of Hagios Demetrios in Thessaloniki (Antonaras 2013, 193, plate 13). The gold-glass tiles in all their variants, simple and elaborate, were also in use on wall revetments (Antonaras 2009, 301–6 and references within; Antonaras 2013, 192–3, plate 12). Furthermore, it has been convincingly proposed that features of the art of jewellery were infused in the innovative works of the Constantinopolitan sculptors of the Justinian era (Pittarakis 2007, 69–70). This tendency was particularly expressed in St Polyeuktos, where carved imitations of gem inlays are visible. For example, in the net-like arrangement of carved bands with rectangular gems carved at the intersections (Harrison 1986, figs 130–1; Pittarakis 2007, 69–70, figs 3 and 6). Furthermore, real inlays of colourful stones and pieces of glass is attested in the same monuments, for example, at St. Polyeuktos, where amethyst-coloured lozenges, inlayed with opaque green and gold-glass pieces, were inserted into the shafts of columns that probably belonged to a ciborium or baldachin (Harrison 1986, 168–81; Pittarakis 2007, 70–2); at St Euphemia, where a band of rectangular and circular cavities that might have originally contained inlays are carved at the base of the columns from the apse (Pittarakis 2007, 72–3, fig. 9); and at St. John the Forerunner in the Hebdomon where there are columns with lozenge-shaped and triangular cavities for inserts (Pittarakis 2007, 73–4, fig. 10). This technique was used later during the tenth century in other monuments as well, for example, marble elements with cavities and glass inlays are found at Boukoleon palace and in part of the imperial palace in Constantinople (ninth to early tenth century), and also from Lips Church in Constantinople and from Preslav (Mundell Mango 2001, 24–5). These sites demonstrate the distribution of this technique. This type of inlayed decoration was probably imitating the painted motifs on the polychrome clay tiles, some of which were made with blue-green glaze (Mundell Mango 2001, fig. 9; cat. nos II.3–II.5, VI.3, VI.4, XIII.2)

The use of the glass gems under study could be best interpreted within this artistic context, as inlays quite probably on metal or wooden objects but not on architectural stone.

All our finds bear no remains of plaster or mortar on them and thus it is improbable that they were used in wall mosaic or *opus sectile* decoration. It seems more likely that they were used in the embellishment of some sort of movable object. Furthermore, the sides of the gems are not bevelled but rather vertical and no signs of scratches on the top side of the gems are noticed, which would be indicative of a prong setting. Thus, we can assume that a bezel type of setting was used for the glass gems under discussion, similar to what we see in their representations on mosaics and textiles. The new Macedonian finds for the first time now offer clear archaeological evidence of the use of glass gems to create the sizable decoration on ecclesiastical objects. These glass gems had hitherto only been known through idealised representations on wall and floor mosaics, textiles, book illustrations and textual descriptions. These finds offer a new tool to perceive these depictions as actual objects from real life of the late Roman/early Christian world. For example, gem-stud thrones and borders are depicted on the woven decoration of extant opulent textiles, some of them clearly representing objects similar to our finds. Namely, red and green oblong gems are very clearly portrayed on a probably sixth-century textile in the collections of the Cleveland Museum of Art on the thrones of Christ and Virgin Mary (Weitzmann 1977, colour plate XIV, cat. no. 477; Fleigel 2012, 2). In addition, another textile in the same collection depicts two figures that are framed by a jewelled border comprised of blue ovals and green squares with the characteristic yellow rim forming the gold setting of the gems. This is also clearly visible on the previously mentioned textile (Cleveland Museum of Art 2016). In addition, some other Coptic textiles in the collections of the Museum of Byzantine Culture presents scenes of game with a mounted figure in the centre exhibiting a gem-studded harness (Antonaras 2004, 50–1) and the same decoration, supplemented with small gemstones is depicted on the emperor's mount on the Barberini diptych (Weitzmann 1977, 35, cat. no. 28).

Furthermore, the examination of the representations on early Christian wall mosaics in monuments from Thessaloniki, Ravenna, Constantinople, Cyprus and Sinai and floor mosaic from Palestine suggests that glass gems were used in the decoration of: architectural elements – shafts of columns, arches, ciboria and chain-like bands that were framing entire scenes; furniture – thrones and pedestals; movable objects – gospel bindings, ecclesiastical vessels, shields, crowns, wreaths; and vestments, such as Christ's halo, crosses and standards. Gems appear in these mosaics in six main shapes and three different colours (Table 1.1): large oblong (green and blue), large square (green, red), large and small oval (blue, red, green), large and small lozenge (green, blue), large and mainly small circular (green, blue) and small tear-shaped/triangular (green, red) ones. The most common among them are the green oblong examples, and blue oval and circular types (Figure 1.10).

Table 1.1 Colour, shape and size of glass gems in mosaics

	Green	*Red*	*Blue*
Oblong, large	•		•
Oblong, small			
Square, large	•	•	
Square, small			
Oval, large	•	•	•
Oval, small	•	•	•
Lozenge, large	•		•
Lozenge, small	•		•
Circular, large	•		•
Circular, small	•		•
Triangular, large			
Triangular, small	•	•	

Gemmed decorations are often represented on wall mosaics in Thessaloniki (Bakirtzis et al. 2012, particularly 48–237) and on wall mosaics in Ravenna (Bustacchini 1989; David 2013). In addition, they are found in the decoration on the *transenna* on the Apse of St Catherine in Sinai (Katz 2003) and in a sixth-century mosaic from Greater Syria, which belongs to Toledo Museum of Art (exhibited in the Metropolitan Museum of Art, NY, registration no. L. 2014–42).

It seems that there is a correlation in the frequency in which particular shapes and colours of gems appear in works of art and the quantities recorded among our finds. Oblong, circular and oval, blue and green gems are most numerous as finds and they are also the most frequently depicted on the mosaics and textiles. This hypothesis is quite logical, particularly if one takes into consideration that, as seen from most excavations, the colours of raw glass most easily accessible to glass workers were indeed predominantly green followed by dark blue. It is also interesting to note the tendency of the artists towards a realistic representation of their theme that urged them to avoid the use of the bright but single-coloured opaque glass – readily available in the area as preserved mosaics indicate – for these objects. Gems were made of transparent or translucent glass, depending on the thickness of the object, which would have created a far closer resemblance to actual semi-precious stones.

Figure 1.10 Forms of gems depicted on mosaics from Thessaloniki and Ravenna and their glass prototypes.

Conclusion

A new facet of the early Christian glass production has been unveiled and at least initially tackled. Several forms of large gems, which until now were perceived only as idealised depictions on sumptuous wall mosaics and textiles, have been found in archaeological excavations. Hopefully this brief discussion will lead to a further enrichment of this corpus with finds from other monuments and other regions and reveal the true extent of this practice, which presumably reach far beyond Thessaloniki and its hinterland.

Acknowledgements

I am very grateful to the Association for the History of Glass who provided a travel grant making it possible for me to attend this conference. I thank Dr Evangelos Maladakis for the information on the nature of the hoard of the Vasileos Irakleiou 44 workshop, Professor Aristotelis Mentzos for the information on the find from Dion and Dr Margaret O'Hea for the information on the finds from Petra. I also thank Dr Stavroula Sdrolia and Professor Ioannis Varalis for the information on the find from Velika.

References

Antonaras, A. 2004. *2004 Calendar: Textiles and Clothing in the Collections of the Museum of Byzantine Culture*. Thessaloniki: Museum of Byzantine Culture.

Antonaras, A. 2009. 'Gold-Glass Tile Decoration in the St. Demetrios Basilica, Thessaloniki'. In *18th Annales du 18e Congrès de l'Association Internationale pour l'Histoire du Verre*, edited by D. Ignatiadou and A. Antonaras, 301–6. Thessaloniki: Ziti Publications.

Antonaras, A. 2013. 'The Production and Uses of Glass in Byzantine Thessaloniki'. In *New Light on Old Glass: Recent Research on Byzantine Mosaics and Glass*, edited by C. Entwistle and L. James, 189–98. London: The British Museum Press.

Antonaras, A. 2014a. 'An Early Christian Glass Workshop at 45, Vasileos Irakleiou Street in the Centre of Thessaloniki'. In *Neighbours and Successors of Rome: Traditions of Glass Production and Use in Europe and the Middle East in the Later First Millennium AD*, edited by D. Keller, J. Price and C. Jackson, 95–113. Oxford and Philadelphia: Oxbow Books.

Antonaras, A. 2014b. 'The Glass Finds from a Provincial early Christian Balkan Basilica: The Solinos Basilica in Chalkidiki Greece'. *Nova Antička Duklja* V: 97–110.

Atik, S. 2009. 'Late Roman/Early Byzantine Glass from the Marmaray Rescue Excavations at Yenikapı in Istanbul'. In *Late Antique/Early Byzantine Glass in the Eastern Mediterranean*, edited by E. Laflı, 1–15. Izmir: Hürriyet Matbaası.

Bakirtzis, Ch., Kourkoutidou-Nikolaidou, E. and Mavropoulou-Tsioumi, Ch. 2012. *Mosaics of Thessaloniki 4th–14th Century*. Athens: Kapon editions.

Baur, P. V. C. 1938. 'Glassware'. In *Gerasa, City of Decapolis*, edited by C. H. Kraeling, 505–46, New Haven: American School of Oriental Research.

Berthelot, M. and C. É. Ruelle 1967. *Collection des anciens alchimistes grecs*. Osnabrück: Zeller.

Bustacchini, G. 1989. *Ravenna capital of mosaic*. Ravenna: Cartolibreria Salbaroli.

Cleveland Museum of Art online Catalogue. 2016. Last modified 7 March 2017. www.clevelandart.org/art/1979.58

Constantinos and Reiske, J. J. 1829. 'Constantini Porphyrogeniti imperatoris'. In *De cerimoniis aulae byzantinae: graece et latine. Libri duo Libri duo. Corpus Scriptorum Historiae Byzantina*, edited by Constantine, Johann Jacob Reiske, Hierocles, Peter Wesseling, Anselmo Banduri and Immanuel Bekker, 9–10. Bonnae: Impensis E. Weberi.

David, M. 2013. *Eternal Ravenna: From the Etruscans to the Venetians*. Turnhout: Brepols.

Davidson, G. 1952. *Corinth Volume XII: The Minor Objects*. Princeton: The American School of Classical Studies at Athens.

Duchesne, L. 1886. *Le Liber pontificalis; texte, introduction et commentaire par l'abbé L. Duchesne*. Paris: E. Thorin.

Fiema, Z. T. 2007. 'Storing in the Church: Artefacts in Room I of the Petra Church'. In *Objects in Context, Objects in Use, Material Spatiality in Late Antiquity*, edited by L. Lavan, E. Swift and T. Putzeys, 607–24. Leiden and Boston: Brill.

Fleigel, S. N. 2012. *A Higher Contemplation: Sacred Meaning in the Christian Art of the Middle Ages*. Kent, OH: Kent State University Press.

Foy, D. 2010. *Les Verres antiques d'Arles. La collection du Musée départemental Arles antique*. Paris: éditions errance/Musée départemental Arles Antique.

Harrison, R. M. 1986. *Excavations at Saraçhane in Istanbul*. Princeton: Princeton University Press; Washington, DC: Dumbarton Oaks Research Library and Collection.

Ignatiadou, D. 2007. 'Amber and Glass Inlays. A Chronological Sequence'. In *Ancient Macedonia VII. Macedonia from the Iron Age to the Death of Philip II*, 473–83. Thessaloniki: Idryma Meleton Chersonisou tou Aimou.

Katz, V. 2003. 'Philip Taaffe's Golden Days'. Last modified 7 March 2017. www.philiptaaffe.info/Critical_Commentary/vincentKatz/monastery.jpg

Kazhdan, A. P. (ed.) 1991. *Oxford Dictionary of Byzantium*. New York: Oxford University Press.

Krueger, I. 2011. 'Zu einigen grossen Smaragden aus Glas'. *Journal of Glass Studies* 53: 103–27.

Manojlović-Marijanski, M. 1964. 'Kasnorimski šlemovi iz Berkasova, Novi Sad, Vojvođanski muzej'. *Posebna izdanja*, 3: 9–11.

Marki, E. 1996. 'Conclusions from the Excavations Conducted by the 9th Ephorate in North Pieria'. *Archaiologiko Ergo stin Makedonia kai Thraki 10A*, 239–58 (in Greek with English summary). Thessaloniki: Archaeological Museum of Thessaloniki, Aristotle University of Thessaloniki.

Marki, E. 2002. 'Locating Productive and Workshop Activities in the Episcopal Complex at Louloudies, Pieria'. In *22nd Symposium of Byzantine and Post-Byzantine Archaeology and Art, Program and Abstracts, Athens, May 17, 18 and 19*, 65–6. Athens: Christianiki Archaiologiki Etaireia (in Greek).

Mentzos, A., Minasidis, D. and Frangoulis K. Forthcoming. 'Oikia opsimis arhaiotitas sto Dion: I anaskafi ton eton 2010–2014'. In *Archaiologiko Ergo stin Makedonia kai Thraki*.

Migne, J. P. 1857–66. *Patrologiae cursus completus/Patrologia Latina: sive bibliotheca universalis ... omnium ss. patrum, doctorum scriptorum que ecclesiasticorum qui ab aevo apostolico ad usque Innocentii III tempora floruerunt. 38 38*. Parisiis: unpublished.

Migne, J. P. 1886. *Patrologiæ cursus completus, seu bibliotheca universalis, integra, uniformis, commoda, oeconomica, omnium SS. Patrum, doctorum scriptorumque ecclesiasticorum, qui ab ævo apostolico ad usque Innocenti III (anno 1216) pro latinis et ad Concilii Florentini tempora (ann. 1439) pro græcis tempora floruerunt: recusio chronologica omnium quæ exstitere monumentorum catholicæ traditionis per quindecim priora ecclesiæ sæecula ...in qua prodeunt patres, doctores scriptoresque ecclesiæ græcæ A S. Barnaba ad Bessarionem]*. Parisiis: apud Garnier Fratres, editores et J. P. Migne successores.

Mundell Mango, M. 2001. 'Polychrome Tiles Found at Istanbul: Typology, Chronology, and Function'. In *Lost Art Rediscovered: The Architectural Ceramics of Byzantium*, edited by S. E. J. Gerstel and J. A. Lauffenburger, 13–43. Baltimore: Walters Art Museum; University Park: Pennsylvania State University Press.

Nenna, M. D. 1995. 'Les Éléments d'Incrustation: Une Industrie Égyptienne du Verre'. In *Alessandria e il Mondo Ellenistico-Romano, II Congresso Internationale Italo-Egiziano, Alessandria 1992*, edited by Nicola Bonacasa and Antonino Di Vita, 377–84. Rome: L'Erma di Bretschneider.

Papangelos, I. A. 1989–90. 'To horion tu Solinos stin Kassandra'. *Makedonika* 27: 171–82.

Papangelos, I. A. 1995. 'Anaskafikes erevnes sti Halkidiki kata to 1995'. Unpublished, oral presentation at the 9th Conference Arheologiko Ergo sti Makedonia kai Thraki.

Papangelos, I. and Doukas, K. 2008. 'The Early Christian Basilica of Ierissos'. Unpublished, oral presentation at the 21st Conference Arheologiko Ergo sti Makedonia kai Thraki 2008 (in Greek).

Papangelos, I. and Doukas, K. 2011. 'The Early Christian Basilica of Ierissos'. *Kyttaro Ierissou, politismiko periodiko entypo* 6: 14–1 (in Greek).

Pittarakis, B. 2007. 'L'orfèvre et l'architecte: autour d'un groupe d'édifices constantinopolitains du VIe siècle'. In *The Material and the Ideal: Essays in Medieval Art and Archaeology in Honour of Jean-Michel Spieser – The Medieval Mediterranean*, edited by A. Papaconstantinou and A. Cutler, 63–74. Leiden and Boston: Brill.

Sdrolia, S. 2013. *The Castle of Melivoia, Velika Agia*. Larissa: Hellenic Ministry of Culture/7th Ephorate of Byzantine Antiquities.

Stern, E. M. and Schlick-Nolte, B. 1994. *Early Glass of the Ancient World*. Ostfildern: Verlag G. Hatje.

Thomas, E. B. 1973. 'Der Helm von Budapest'. In *Spätrömische Gardehelme*, edited by Hans Klumbach, 39–50. München: Beck.

Weitzmann, K. (ed.) 1977. *Age of Spirituality: Late Antique and early Christian Art, Third to Seventh Century*. Catalogue of the exhibition at The Metropolitan Museum of Art, 19 November 1977–12 February 1978. New York: Metropolitan Museum of Art.

Whitehouse, D. 1997. *Roman Glass in the Corning Museum of Glass, Volume 1*. Corning, NY: Corning Museum of Glass.

2
Gold-glasses: From their origin to Late Antiquity in the Mediterranean

Giulia Cesarin

Abstract

The chapter introduces the preliminary stage of a wide-ranging research into gold-glasses, the aim of which is to investigate different techniques combining gold and glass in Greek and Roman times. The objects considered start from the fourth century BCE and include the various productions of Late Antiquity. The most relevant objects found in the Mediterranean and the adjacent areas will be examined, combining the close study of the glass artefacts and their typological and stylistic classification, with research on their distribution and chronological patterns.

The high value and rarity of these glasses enable not only the analysis of the technological details of such complex techniques, which are still not fully understood, but also the investigation of the socio-economical dynamics, related to the diffusion of these luxury items.

The objective of the research is to find an eventual common thread, connecting productions so far considered separately, but probably resulting from a process of transmission of products, trends, techniques and possibly migration of artisans in the Mediterranean, during the early centuries of the first millennium CE.

Introduction

The research is progressing through several stages. The current PhD project on gold-band glass (from late Hellenistic to early Roman luxury glass production: a systematic analysis on gold-band glass), conducted at the University of Cologne (Professor Ortisi), in conjunction with the University of Padua (Professor Bonetto), represents the next step after my master's thesis in Classical Archaeology at the University of Padua. The study focused on Hellenistic sandwich gold-glass vessels (late third to early second centuries BCE), but revealed a great variety of gold-glass techniques, before and after this particular limited production (Cesarin 2012). The investigation on gold-glass begins with the earliest objects that used glass to cover a gold-foil or gold-leaf decoration (finger-rings, inlays and shallow lidded bowls, dating from the fourth to third centuries BCE) and includes different products, spread around the Mediterranean basin in the following centuries. The distinction between foil and leaf is based on the thickness of the gold, respectively >10 μm and <10 μm (Darque-Ceretti et al. 2011, 541), but concerning glass with gilded decoration, this distinction is mostly very vague in the literature.

Although gold-glasses have attracted remarkable interest in scholarly literature, essentially because of the rarity and luxury of the objects, the current state of the art lacks an up-to-date and global approach. Generally, most of the publications offer a mere iconographic analysis, especially concerning the Late Antique *fondi d'oro*, bases of vessels decorated with sandwiched gold-leaf decoration (the Italian name is used in the text to avoid misunderstandings with the other gold-glass groups). Furthermore, these groups are mostly examined separately. Only a few authors have considered collectively different gold-glass techniques: either as a prelude to the most famous Hellenistic sandwich gold-glass (Barag 1990, 19–25), or as different gilding techniques in Roman times (Whitehouse 1996, 4–12); Goldstein skipped from Hellenistic sandwich gold-glass to Islamic gold-glass vessels (Goldstein 1989, 115–9).

Some products have not been analysed properly as a class and would benefit from inclusion in a catalogue. The principal issues needing clarification concern technological aspects, the location of the workshops and the chronology of each single group. A technological connection can be distinguished between gold-glass objects up to Late Antiquity and will be further investigated. Particular attention will be dedicated to the process of transmission of products, trends, techniques and possibly migration of artisans from the eastern Mediterranean to Italy and the western provinces, likely to have occurred between the middle of the first century BCE and the first century CE.

Object of the study

This chapter considers several gold-glass techniques, dating from the fourth century BCE to the fifth centuries CE, offering an overview of the technological development that occurred during this millennium.

Unfortunately, chronology has been often misunderstood by scholars, because of the longevity of some items, in some cases buried decades or even centuries after they were made, and also because of the lack of knowledge of each single gold-glass technique.

From a preliminary analysis, it is possible to divide the objects into two main groups, separating them on the basis of a simple technological division:

- Sandwich techniques, with the gold-foil or gold-leaf covered by a glass layer, allowing a practical use of the object and ensuring a better preservation of the decoration. These gold-glasses are generally documented in jewellery (rings, beads and gems), furniture or architectural decorations (inlays and plaques), lavish table services (sandwich gold-glass bowls; mosaic glass plates and bowls with gold-glass tesserae; gold-band glass bowls; *fondi d'oro*; vessels with gilded-thread inscription, sandwiched on the base; Nuppengläser (decorated with gold-leaf roundels, etc.) and cosmetic containers (gold-band glass alabastra, pyxides, unguentaria).
- Techniques employing superficial gilding (sometimes combined with cold-paint decoration): the objects, both vessels and plaques, were not covered by a glass layer. Some of them were probably purposely created as funerary goods or ritual objects (Schlangenfadengläser gilded plates, bowls, ewers, etc.), since the practical use would have increased the chances of damage and the loss of the decoration.

An intermediate point between these groups is represented by the shallow lidded bowls identified as exaleiptra (Stern 1999, 34–5). The decoration is superficial, yet partially protected through the superimposition of the two parts. The decoration occurs on the inner surface of the bowl, and on the lower surface of the outsplayed rim of the lid.

Each class must be considered as exceptionally rare and the prerogative of an extremely restricted élite. In total, just over 500 objects of gold-glass from Late Antiquity are currently reported to exist (see Howells 2015, 7). Although an accurate count of the objects with superficial gilding is not possible, because the decoration is easily lost, it may be stated that the *fondi d'oro* represent the only extensive gold-glass production.

Late Classical period

The earliest classes considered date to the fourth to third centuriesBCE: finger-rings (Figure 2.1), inlays and shallow lidded bowls (exaleiptra). These groups are reasonably recognised as the prelude to the Hellenistic sandwich gold-glass vessels.

Scholars suggested that the first use in Greece of colourless glass to cover the gold occurred in Olympia, thanks to the genius of the master Phidias (Schiering 1991, 14–16; Stern 1999, 39; 2002, 354). Pottery moulds and colourless glass inlays were recovered in a dump connected to the master's workshop. Larger moulds in the shape of sections of the garments were employed for sagging large sections of glass (Letsch et al. 1983, 96–105). Some even earlier inlays using glass covers were created in the ninth to eighth centuries BCE (Barag 1990, 19–25), but I will not concentrate on these products, since the connection between them and

Figure 2.1 Glass ring with gold-leaf, representing a winged figure, probably a Nike. Corning (New York), Corning Museum of Glass, 71.1.15. Fragmentary, glass hoop broken off. Finger-rings, with inlays and exaleiptra, represent the earlier products with colourless glass covering a gold decoration (fourth–third century bce). They could be interpreted as the prelude to the more elaborated sandwich gold-glass technique of Hellenistic times.
Source: © Corning Museum of Glass

the Greek tradition, starting with Phidias a few centuries later, is hardly verifiable.

A similar use of colourless glass is attested at the Macedonian court and evidenced by the findings in royal Macedonian tombs. Funerary couches, thrones and other precious grave goods (i.e. the shield found in the tomb of Philip II) were adorned with ivory, gold and glass (Andronikos 1984, 34–5, 122–37; Ignatiadou 2001, 4–7; Kottaridou 2011, 70–90).

Iconography connects Macedonian inlays with the gold-glass rings (winged figures, gods, goddesses or mythological figures, hippocamps and sea monsters, kalathiskos dancers). Both groups were presumably produced in northern Greece or Macedonia starting from the early fourth century BCE (Ignatiadou 2001, 7). A precise chronology is difficult, since in very few cases the archaeological contexts are known. Gold-glass rings and gems may be divided into three types:

- Rings completely cast in colourless glass, both the main part, consisting of hoop and bezel, and the upper cover. The cut and embossed gold-foil is sandwiched between them. The parts are assembled by partial fusion (e.g. British Museum; Metropolitan Museum; Corning Museum of Glass; for all objects locations see Appendix A). Such rings probably represent the latest of the three groups.
- Gems composed of two layers (the upper one always in colourless glass), sandwiching the cut and embossed gold-foil. The gem is mounted in a metal setting and hoop (e.g. Musée du Louvre; Hermitage; furthermore, some gems that were probably mounted in rings are held in private collections).
- Gems composed of three layers (the two external covers in colourless glass), sandwiching a cut and embossed gold-foil on both sides. The gem is mounted on a metal setting and is pierced, allowing it to rotate on a pivot connected to the hoop (e.g. Hermitage – Homolion, hoop missing; Antikensammlung, Berlin – hoop and setting casket missing; J. P. Getty Museum; Museo Archeologico di Taranto).

Recently, Ignatiadou hypothesised a slightly earlier production for the gold-glass gems than the Macedonian inlays, based on the use of gold-silver alloy in the latter (Ignatiadou 2002, 306, 327), except for the inlays recovered from the tomb of Philip II, which are made of pure gold (Ignatiadou 2017).

A similar provenance and a slightly later chronology may be supposed for the exaleiptra, shallow lidded bowls (diameter 12–19 cm), which served for mixing and dispensing scented oils and salves. Ceramic exaleiptra already existed in previous centuries, although the profile is not strictly similar to the glass exaleiptra. Stern suggested this definition essentially based on their function (Stern 1999, 33–5; 2002, 355). This shape is not common in glass (11 specimens counted by Stern 1999, 46–9) and seems to be enduring. A very few specimens yielded traces of gold-leaf decoration, mostly combined with cold painting (e.g. Archaeological Museum of Thessaloniki; Museo Archeologico di Taranto; Hermitage; Musée du Louvre). The specimen from Pydna was found in a tomb dated 290 BCE (Ignatiadou 2000, 35–8), providing probably the first example of the use of gold-leaf on glass.

Hellenistic period

The use of thinner gold-leaves is attested in different products of the Hellenistic age.

Sandwich gold-glass represents an extremely rare production, commonly attributed to Alexandria (Harden 1968, 21–47), included in the so-called Canosa Group (Grose 1989, 185–8). Less famous are other contemporary classes (late third to second centuries BCE), also belonging to the Canosa Group, such as mosaic glass bowls or plates containing gold-glass tesserae, and some rare plates with gilded and eventually painted decoration. The latter, related to the exaleiptra because of the decoration, remain unfortunately poorly examined (Rostovcev 1963, 151–79).

Sandwich gold-glass vessels (Figure 2.2) have been found in southern Italy, Rhodes, Anatolia, Syria-Palestine, Egypt, Mesopotamia, Black Sea and the Caucasus. So far, 22 specimens are known (20 are reported in Cesarin 2012, two further are not described). The technique consists of the assembly of two vessels of transparent colourless glass, between which cut gold-leaf triangles and stripes, assembled to form different motifs, are sandwiched. In order to fit together, the inner and outer bowls had to be fashioned to an exact and predetermined shape and size, refined through grinding and polishing. The gold decoration was applied to the outer wall of the inner bowl, maybe using an adhesive. The two layers were partially fused together.

The bowls take hemispherical, parabolic or shallow forms (a unique example is the skyphos in the Metropolitan Museum) and are decorated using different arrangements, which employ geometrical and/or vegetal motifs; rarely figurative scenes are represented. It was possible to recognise several shapes and types, with different rim morphologies. The

Figure 2.2 Sandwich gold-glass bowl from Canosa (Apulia). London, British Museum, GR 1871,0518.2. Within the end of the third and the second century BCE different types of bowls in the sandwich gold-glass technique were produced. The gold-leaf was applied onto the exterior surface of the inner bowl, then covered with the external bowl. The two vessels were cast separately, grinded in order to fit perfectly, assembled and fixed through partial fusion.
Source: © Trustees of the British Museum

comparative analysis of morphology and decoration revealed a correlation among shapes, technical details and subdivision of the decorated surface.

The hemispherical bowls show either an outsplayed or a straight rim. The hemispherical type with outsplayed rim has an undecorated band below the rim, since the outer bowl is shorter and does not cover the decoration up to the lip. They are decorated with a calyx of alternating acanthus and nymphaea leaves, enclosing imbrication and floral filler details. This complex decoration is delimited by a horizontal double band of waves just below the undecorated part (e.g. two twin bowls in the British Museum; another two twin bowls in the Musée d'Arts et d'Histoire in Geneva; a small fragment with the same decoration was found in Olbia, Black Sea, probably belonging to the same shape).

Hemispherical bowls with a straight rim show decoration on several registers up to the lip (e.g. Museum of Art and Archaeology of Columbia; World of Glass, St Helens; Museo Archeologico Nazionale di Taranto).

The same organisation of the decorated space is recognisable on the parabolic bowls (e.g. Corning Museum of Glass; Hermitage).

Only two specimens of the 22 known so far, both shallow bowls, stand out because of the decorative design with a figurative scene (Cesarin 2016): an entire bowl found in Tresilico (Museo Archeologico Nazionale di Reggio Calabria) and a fragment coming from Egypt (Pushkin State Museum of Fine Arts, Moscow).

The recognition of the workshops' location on an archaeological basis remains difficult. Nevertheless, the presence of very few highly specialised workshops in the eastern Mediterranean (Alexandria, Aegean, Syria-Palestine) seems the most probable (Cesarin 2012).

A new experimental study conducted by a Japanese team (Fujii and Namiki 2017) reproduced the hemispheric bowl in the British Museum with Kirikane, Japanese decorative technique, which applies lines, diamonds and triangles cut in metal leaf. The aim of the work is to shed light on sandwich gold-glass techniques, considering not only the cutting and application of the gold-leaf (a probable forerunner of Kirikane), but also on the fusing process of the glass layers.

Another notable Hellenistic production was mosaic glass with sections of preformed canes and tesserae (Figure 2.3). The canes were generally composed of translucent dark-coloured glass (mostly blue) and opaque white or yellow, creating a star or spiral pattern. The tesserae were usually in solid or layered monochrome colours; very few vessels show gold-glass tesserae.

Characteristic are plates (diameter *c.*30 cm) with outsplayed sides and rims, flat or slightly convex bottoms, bands of cut-grooves (e.g. Corning Museum of Glass; British Museum); parabolic bowls (e.g. Metropolitan Museum, British Museum); and hemispherical bowls (e.g. Metropolitan Museum, Toledo Museum of Art). A unique example is the amphoriskos of the Corning Museum of Glass (Harden 1968, 25–7; Oliver 1968, 49–51; Goldstein 1979, 176, pl. 21, 23.460).

The plate shape was contemporarily produced in monochrome glass. In very few specimens some traces of gold-leaf decoration have survived (e.g. British Museum).

Late Hellenistic and early Roman period

The late Hellenistic period yielded gold-band glass (Oliver 1967, 13–33), a new class combining coloured glass and gold-leaf.

Gold-band glass objects were fashioned using different working methods, structured in a sequence of phases. First, variously coloured

Figure 2.3 Mosaic glass plate containing gold-glass tesserae from Canosa (Apulia). London, British Museum, GR 1871,0518.3. Less common than sandwich gold-glass, and also belonging to the Canosa Group (third–second century BCE), mosaic glass vessels are mostly composed by blue tesserae with opaque white spirals or stars, interspersed with segments of yellow and white glass and gold-glass tesserae. The most common shapes are plates and hemispherical bowls.
Source: © Trustees of the British Museum

glass bands were created (often layering translucent coloured glass with opaque white or yellow glass). A strip of gold-leaf was sandwiched between two colourless glass layers. Then, after being placed side by side, the bands were reheated and manipulated in different ways, in order to create small vessels or jewellery.

According to the chronology and the distribution pattern, gold-band glass objects belong to two main groups:

- Late Hellenistic alabastra (Figure 2.4) and bowls, with few beads and gems, probably dating between the second and the first centuries BCE, distributed across the eastern Mediterranean, with a western limit in southern and central Italy.
- Roman unguentaria, pyxides and bowls, the chronology of which may be restricted to a limited period, between 50 BCE and 50 CE, found mostly in Italy and the western provinces.

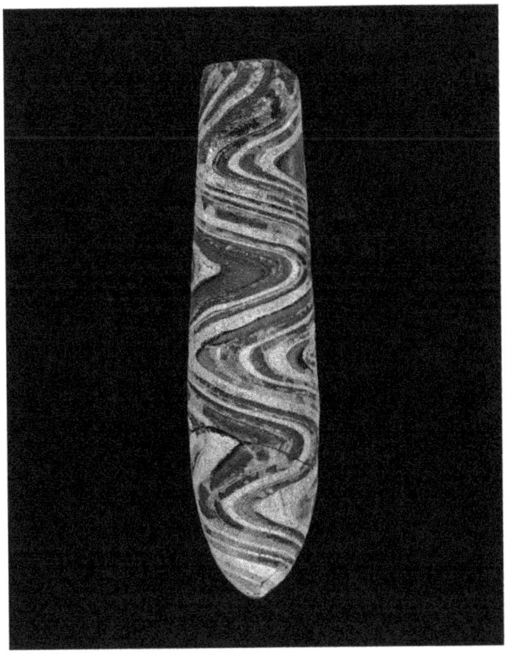

Figure 2.4 Gold-band glass alabastron. Corning (New York), Corning Museum of Glass, 55.1.9. Hellenistic gold-band glass (alabastra, bowls, beads and gems) combined coloured bands with colourless glass covering a gold-leaf, obtaining a wavy pattern through hot manipulation. These objects were spread across the eastern Mediterranean, with a western limit in southern and central Italy, and date probably between the second and the first century BCE.
Source: © Corning Museum of Glass

During the Hellenistic period four different types of alabastra are known. They are differentiated based on profile, technological details and pattern (e.g. British Museum; Victoria and Albert Museum; Metropolitan Museum; Corning Museum of Glass; Antikensammlung, Berlin; Musée du Louvre). Very few bowls are known (e.g. Museo Archeologico Nazionale delle Marche) and beads and gems are also very rare (e.g. Miho Museum; Rijskmuseum Leiden).

The Romans produced: carinated (Figure 2.5) and globular unguentaria (e.g. Hermitage; British Museum; Metropolitan Museum; Corning Museum of Glass; Römisch-Germanisches Museum of Cologne; Musée du Louvre; Museo Civico Archeologico di Bologna), pyxides (e.g. Hermitage;

Figure 2.5 Gold-band glass unguentarium. Corning (New York), Corning Museum of Glass, 59.1.87. Roman gold-band glass vessels (unguentaria, pyxides and bowls) have been found mostly in Italy and western Provinces, and date probably between 50 BCE and 50 CE. Although the Roman group seems to be inspired by the Hellenistic one, new shapes with new colours, new arrangements and new patterns can be observed. The working methods also changed and improved.
Source: © Corning Museum of Glass

British Museum; Metropolitan Museum; Corning Museum of Glass; Antikensammlung, Berlin; Musée du Louvre; Museo Archeologico Nazionale di Aquileia; Museo Archeologico Nazionale di Napoli) and shallow, hemispherical and carinated bowls (e.g. Museo Archeologico Nazionale di Aquileia; Römisch-Germanisches Museum of Cologne).

Although the Roman group seems to be inspired by the Hellenistic one, new shapes with new colours, arrangements and patterns can be observed. The working methods also changed and improved, but they are, for both periods, still not clearly explained and require further investigation (Cummings 1980, 40–1; Lierke 2009, 42, 45, 49). A preliminary analysis suggests that both the Hellenistic and the Roman gold-band glass includes a major group of cosmetic and perfume containers and a secondary group of bowls and jewellery (more than 250 objects are catalogued so far).

Contemporary with the Roman gold-band glass but, at the current state of knowledge, restricted to the city of Pompeii are rare examples of gilded plaques decorating walls of private houses, for example, the famous Domus degli Amorini Dorati (Sogliano 1908, 34–6; Seiler 1992, 50, fig. 312–15; Beretta and Di Pasquale 2004, 219, no. 1.57).

Late Roman period

The second century and the beginning of the third century CE provide only sporadic evidence, mostly poorly preserved, and not clearly understood. Some gold-glasses, both vessels and plaques with superficial gilding, are known, for example, in France (Foy and Nenna 2001, 92, 219) and in Egypt (Cooney 1976, 69–71).

From the beginning of the third century CE, we may observe a great variation of techniques, shapes and styles, leading to the prolific production of the so-called *fondi d'oro* (Figure 2.6).

The two main decorative innovations of the third century CE are the use of gilded threads and the application of coloured glass blobs in order to cover gold-leaf roundels (Nuppengläser, known also as medallions when the single blob survived). Both represent developments of long-standing decorative techniques. Both threads and blobs appear in different areas of the Roman empire, but seem to be combined with the gold-leaf decoration only in the Rhineland (Schlangenfadengläser in the East: von Saldern 2004, 327–31; western Schlangenfadengläser: von Saldern 2004, 331–7; eastern origin of the Nuppengläser: von Saldern 2004, 347–9). Gilded threads were used both superficially (Schlangenfadengläser) and sandwiched between the bottom of the vessel and the base with its foot-ring, creating an inscription (Figure 2.7).

Schlangenfadengläser commonly employed colourless, red and blue threads. In very few cases these were combined with some colourless threads covered by gold-leaf, shaped mostly into spirals and leaves (the most famous is the Masterpiece, Römisch-Germanisches Museum

Figure 2.6 *Fondo d'oro*. Corning (New York), Corning Museum of Glass, 66.1.37. Base of a vessel decorated with gold-leaf representing shepherd and flock. The figures are surrounded by the inscription DICNITAS AMICORUM PIE ZESES VIVAS.

Fondi d'oro were mostly obtained from bases of bowls or dishes and inserted as signacula near the graves in the Catacombs of Rome. Source: © Corning Museum of Glass

of Cologne: Harden 1987, 124–6). The same kinds of threads were fashioned in various decorative motives on Schlangenfadengläser and as inscriptions and frames on the vessels with an inscription on the bottom. While the first group seems to be peculiar to the Rhineland and adjacent areas, and worked in this region (Harden 1987, 104, 107–8), the second group is widely spread throughout the western provinces. Both classes are very restricted.

About 20 specimens, belonging to the second group, are known (Alarcão 1968, 71–9; Filippini 1996, 113–28; Howells 2015, 29–30, 3). We cannot state their shapes for certain, since usually only the base has survived, although we may hypothesise that they were fashioned according to the trend of the period: free-blowing. The inscriptions, often surrounded by a cartouche, represent salutations of antique convivial tradition (e.g.

Figure 2.7 Bottom of cup, with gilded inscription. Corning (New York), Corning Museum of Glass, 66.1.31. Base of vessel sandwiching the gilded-thread inscription, in Greek, EPHESI/ZE-S[]IS, in two lines, surrounded by gilded-threads, with pediment flanked by ivy branches on the upper side. Small part of sides remain.
Source: © Corning Museum of Glass

ANNI BONI, VITA TIBI, A ME BIBE). Both cartouche and inscription are made of glass threads, gilded, variously coloured (white, blue, red) or colourless (e.g. Musée de la Société Anonyme Belge des Mines, Aljustrel; British Museum; Museo Archeologico Nazionale di Aquileia; Römisch-Germanisches Museum of Cologne; Corning Museum of Glass; Aquincumi Muzeum Budapest; Musée du Petit Palais, Paris; Pokrajinski Muzej, Ptuj).

Another group widely recorded in the western regions, the so-called Nuppengläser, provides some examples with gilded decoration. This category, named after the glass blobs (in German Nuppen) applied to the walls of the vessel, has a long tradition and many varieties (Harden 1987, 101–3; von Saldern 2004, 347–51). Some vessels were characterised by gold-leaf roundels, applied externally onto the vessel, and covered by blue or green blobs. The common shapes are difficult to recognise, since mostly only single blobs are preserved (Whitehouse 1996). The only vessel known so far, although fragmentary, was found in Cologne (St Severin bowl: Figure 2.8). Six fragments from this bowl are kept in the British Museum. The open vessels decorated with blobs were blown and likely utilised for drinking and eating or serving, the decoration is in fact

Figure 2.8 Fragmentary Nuppenglas bowl from St Severin (Cologne). London, British Museum, 1881,0624.1. Fragmentary bowl (six fragments survived) in colourless glass. The outer surface is decorated with 21 gold-leaf roundels (figures of the Holy Scripture and flowers), covered by green and blue glass blobs.
Source: © Trustees of the British Museum

visible from the inside. Since the iconographies are very similar to the *fondi d'oro*, it is possible that the manufacturing centers were the same.

Vessels with superficial gilding are relatively rare, mostly poorly preserved. Some unique specimens show gold-leaf decoration combined with engraving or painting. The chronology and workshops are difficult to identify, since the products are very different in shape and style (von Saldern 2004, 352–61). Whitehouse hypothesised three production areas, active between the third and the fourth centuries CE, in the Roman empire: the eastern Mediterranean, Italy and the Rhineland. A notable concentration of glass objects with gilded decoration is recorded in Cologne (Fremersdorf 1967). Whitehouse suggested an earlier chronology (first to second centuries CE) for the blue glass ewer with gilded decoration held in the Corning Museum of Glass, generally dated third to fourth centuries CE (Figure 2.9). He also considered two of the best preserved specimens, the Daphne Ewer and the bottle representing the myth of Apollo and Marsyas, eastern Mediterranean products, dated to the third to fourth centuries CE,

Figure 2.9 Blue glass ewer with gilded decoration. Corning (New York), Corning Museum of Glass, 70.1.3. The superficial gilding is almost lost, but it is still possible to recognise a heterogeneous decoration disposed on a sequence of horizontal bands. In the Roman period a great variety of gold-glass techniques existed; many are the products not covered by a second glass-layer. The main areas, where these glasses were spread, and probably also produced, are Syria-Palestine, Italy, and the Rhineland.
Source: © Corning Museum of Glass

while considering the Rhineland as the most probable area of origin for the Disch Cantharus (Whitehouse 1996, 4–12).

A limited and very skilful production is characterised by a brushed technique employing powdered gold-leaf enriched with painting in order to represent portraits (Howells 2015, 28–9, 2). These were sandwiched in gold-glass medallions with a blue base. Although often considered together with the *fondi d'oro*, they seem to be from an earlier period. They are dated to the late second to third centuries CE and were probably produced in Italy by Alexandrian workers, according to the Greek dialect of some inscriptions (Whitehouse 1996, 10). This group also stands out from the other gold-glass objects based on chemical composition (Meek 2013, 126).

As mentioned above, the *fondi d'oro* are the most numerous gold-glass class (the well-known catalogue by Morey counts several hundreds, although lacking many specimens). They were the first gold-glasses ever discovered, thanks to the numerous explorations of the Roman catacombs from the seventeenth century onwards. They were mostly found set in plaster as *signacula* of the *loculi* in the catacombs, which is still the most prolific find spot. Although some early studies revealed the real nature of these objects, as bases of vessels (Vopel 1899, 80), they were commonly thought to be medallions produced for the purpose of decorating the graves (Haevernick 1962, 58–9). The technique is simpler than that of the small group of medallions and the decoration varies from mythological, Christian or Jewish representations to portraits, landscapes or depictions of animals.

Numerous publications on the *fondi d'oro* are essentially catalogues, which sometimes also include other contemporary, or slightly earlier, gold-glass objects (Morey 1959; Zanchi Roppo 1969; Faedo 1978, 1025–70; Pillinger 1984). Until recently, the *fondi d'oro* were merely studied from an iconographical perspective (von Saldern 2004, 363–74). The first in-depth analysis of the technological process, supported by experimental replicas, was published by Howells (Howells 2013, 112–20; 2015). Recent chemical characterisation on a selection of gold-glasses preserved in the British Museum revealed the existence of three compositional groups, partially coincident with grouping based on technical and decorative details (Meek 2013).

Methodology for further work

Although many studies on gold-glass techniques exist, they are mostly outdated publications, rarely providing safe hypotheses on the technological processes, the location of workshops, or the chronology. To date, catalogues are incomplete (e.g. Oliver 1967 on gold-band glass; Morey 1959 on *fondi d'oro* and other Roman gold-glass objects) and most of the techniques have not been convincingly explained. A comprehensive analysis, combining different approaches, could significantly improve the understanding of gold-glass, moving beyond the mere typological study and developing the high scientific potential of this research theme.

The wide-ranging literature collected so far and the direct observation of 165 objects, preserved in many European museums (e.g. British Museum; Victoria and Albert Museum; Fishbourne Roman Palace; Antikensammlung, Berlin; Landesmuseum Württemberg, Stuttgart; Römisch-Germanisches Museum, Cologne; Musée du Louvre; Rijskmuseum Leiden; Gemeentemuseum den Haag; Museo Archeologico Nazionale delle Marche; Museo Civico Archeologico di Bologna; Museo Archeologico Nazionale di Aquileia; Museo Archeologico Nazionale di Napoli; Museo Archeologico Nazionale di Altino) has allowed the understanding of the complexity of the topic and enabled the identification of several open questions that require an appropriate investigation. Because of the extent and the complexity of the subject, it was decided to focus sequentially on the various classes.

Beside the analytical macroscopic examination, taking measurements and photographs, some of the objects were also examined by optical microscope.

The first aim of this research is the creation of a catalogue, organised by production methods and periods, to obtain a clear and reliable classification of the shapes and the technical details. The comparative analysis of decorative motifs and technological details, together with the research on distribution of the finds, will be fundamental in supplying more data for the chronology and hopefully will allow us to hypothesise about the location of the workshops.

Preliminary results

From a preliminary analysis, we can state that several different areas were involved in the production of gold-glasses, including both the eastern Mediterranean regions, Italy, and the western provinces.

The earliest classes (finger-rings, inlays and exaleiptra) appear to be produced in Macedonia and northern Greece, between the fourth and the third centuries BCE. A wider area could be suggested for the Hellenistic productions belonging to the Canosa Group (sandwich gold-glass, mosaic plates and bowls with gold-glass tesserae, plates with gilded and painted decoration) and, slightly later, for the Hellenistic group of gold-band glass. The distribution patterns of these classes, the chronological delimitation of which will be better defined, are similar, and extended eastwards from central and southern Italy. This allows us to hypothesise about diverse workshops, in an area comprising the Aegean, the Syrian-Palestinian coast and Egypt.

In the early Imperial age, Roman gold-band glasses were probably produced in Rome and Venetia, according to both distribution patterns, a comparison with other mosaic techniques and the small amount of evidence of glass-working. This production acquires great significance for the hypothesis of a migration of artisans from the eastern Mediterranean to Italy, between the end of the first century BCE and the early first century CE.

Contemporary with these are rare examples of gilded plaques from Pompeian houses. The extraordinary preservation of the architecture and furniture of the Campanian sites does not allow us to consider these plaques a peculiarity of Campania for this early period.

The second and the third centuries CE provide scarce and scattered evidence, generally consisting of glass with superficial gilding, the poor state of conservation of which does not enable us to locate the workshops and to state a precise chronology.

The various and numerous products (i.e. *fondi d'oro*, Schlangenfadengläser, Nuppengläser, vessels with superficial gilding, etc.) spread from the eastern Mediterranean to the western provinces, from the third to the fifth centuries CE and were probably made in different workshops, either located in the eastern Mediterranean, Rome or the Rhineland.

At the current state of knowledge, all of these regions lack archaeological indicators of glass-working specifically related to gold-glass production, beside the third century BCE context, documented at Rhodes (Triantafyllidis 2002, 30–2).

Conclusion

The main aim of this project is to investigate three principal issues: the location of the workshops, the chronology and the working process of each production.

The accurate collection of data, organised in a reasoned, exhaustive and updated catalogue, will yield an improved typological classification, and will allow a systematic mapping. This step will be crucial for advancing reliable hypotheses on the questions above mentioned.

Moreover, the particular lavishness and rarity of these glasses enable us to investigate the socio-economical dynamics related to the diffusion of these luxury items, which were doubtless manufactured in a small number of specialised workshops, and their meaning as status symbols,

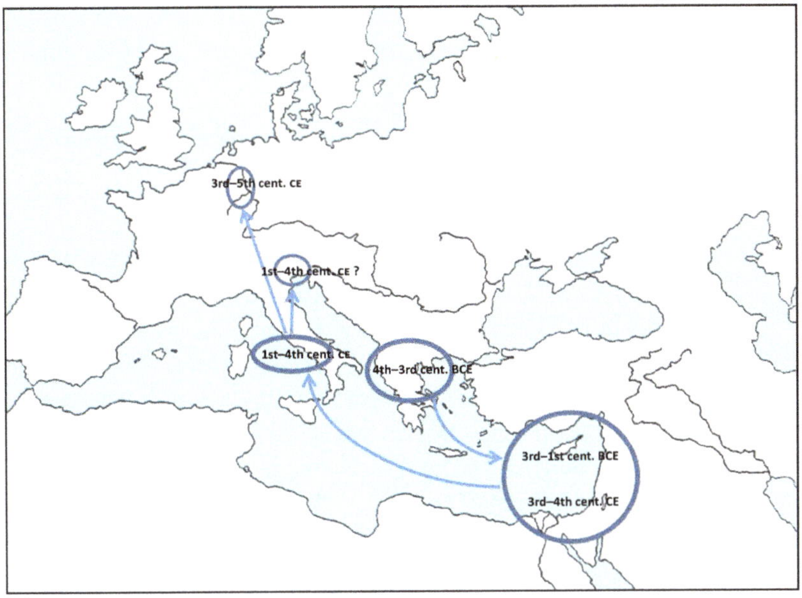

Figure 2.10 Mediterranean basin. The different areas probably involved in gold-glass production through centuries.

intended for an extremely restricted élite. This consideration leads to a completely different approach, if compared to glassware in everyday use, which was mostly created locally, extremely standardised in the whole Roman empire, and distributed on a small regional scale.

The newly assembled data will provide a significant contribution in the validation or rejection of the current hypothesis of connection and continuity among the gold-glass productions (Figure 2.10), offering a new perspective on contacts and circulation of products, ideas and artisans throughout the Mediterranean, during the early centuries of the first millennium CE.

Appendix A

The following list provides the location of a selection of representative objects mentioned above:

- Rings: British Museum, no. 1872,0604.291; Metropolitan Museum, no. 17.194.2537; Corning Museum of Glass, no. 71.1.15; Musée du Louvre, no. Bj 1279; Hermitage, no. 2495/70, no. Пab.4; Volos,

Archaeological Museum, no. M 58; Berlin Antikensammlung, no. 1966.8; J. P. Getty Museum, no. 88.AN.106; Museo Archeologico di Taranto, no. 12.292.

- Exaleiptra: Archaeological Museum of Thessaloniki, no. Py 6435, no. Py 6436; Museo Archeologico di Taranto, no. 40.072, no. 40.073; Hermitage, no. E 805; Musée du Louvre, no. S 2584, no. S 2585, no. CP 9194, no. N III 3169.
- Sandwich gold-glass: Metropolitan Museum, no. 23.160.76; British Museum, no. 1871,0518.1, no. 1871,0518.2, no. 1885,0101.296; Musée d'Arts et d'Histoire in Geneva, no. MF 3634; Museum of Art and Archaeology of Columbia, no. 77.198; Museo Archeologico Nazionale di Taranto, no. 40.058, no. 40.059; Corning Museum of Glass, no. 71.1.5; Hermitage, no. Kz 5323/5636, no. Ol.1903.222; Museo Archeologico Nazionale di Reggio Calabria, no. 6171; Pushkin State Museum of Fine Arts, Moscow, no. 116.1.
- Mosaic plates and bowls with gold-glass tesserae: Corning Museum of Glass, no. 66.1.35; British Museum, no. 1871,0518.3, no. 1871,0518.4, no. 1868,0501.86; Metropolitan Museum, no. 17.194.281, no. 17.194.266.
- Gold-band glass: Metropolitan Museum, no. 17.194.284, no. 17.194.285, no. 17.194.286, no. 15.130.11, no. 91.1.2053, no. 30.115.16, no. 81.10.328, no. 29.100.88, no. 17.194.259, no. 06.1035.2; British Museum, no. 1868,0501.75, no. 1868,0501.76, 1895,0602.1, no. 1856,1226.1132, no. 1871,0518.3; Victoria and Albert Museum, no. 1868–1023; Corning Museum of Glass, no. 76.1.46, no. 55.1.9, no. 76.1.24, no. 76.1.25, no. 55.1.3, no. 59.1.87; Berlin, Antikensammlung, no. 451x, no. 1961.5; Musée du Louvre, no. MNE 94, no. MNE 93, no. S 2383, S 2288; Rijskmuseum Leiden, no. 511/a–b, no. R.O.II,161, no. B 1952/10.17; Hermitage, no. П1883.6, no. E698, no. E1044; Ljubljana, Narodni muzej Slovenije, NMS R 2095.
- *fondi d'oro*: Metropolitan Museum, no. 18.145.1a–b, no. 28.57.24, no. 16.174.1, no. 18.145.2, no. 11.91.4, no. 16.174.2; Corning Museum of Glass, no. 54.1.83; British Museum, no. 1898,0719.1, no. 1898,0719.1, no. 1863,0727.12, no. 1870,0606.12, no. 1863,0727.6, no. 1893,0426.183, no. 1859,0618.2, no. 1859,0618.1, no 1863,0727.10; Bonn, Rheinisches Landesmuseum, no. 17293.
- Brushed Medallions: Metropolitan Museum, no. 26.258, no. 17.190.109a; Corning Museum of Glass, no. 90.1.3.
- Vessels with gilded inscription: British Museum, OA.858; Corning Museum of Glass, no. 66.1.31, no. 66.1.147; Paris, Musée du

Petit Palais, no. A.DUT.244, no. A.DUT.254; Aquileia, Museo Archeologico, no. 12897; Cologne, Römisch-Germanisches Museum, no. 40.551.

- Nuppengläser: British Museum, no. 1881,0624.1, no. 1854,0722.17, no. 1863,0727.17, no. OA.4308, no. OA.857, no. OA.4309; Metropolitan Museum, no. 18.145.8.
- Vessels with superficial gilded decoration: Corning Museum of Glass, no. 70.1.3, no. 66.1.267, no. 55.1.86, no. 78.1.1; Marseille, Musée d'Histoire, no. 99.2.34; Bonn, Rheinisches Landesmuseum, no. LXVIII.

References

Alarcão, J. de. 1968. 'Une coupe à fond d'or découverte à Farrobo, Portugal'. *Journal of Glass Studies* 10: 71–9.

Andronikos, M. 1984. *Vergina. The Royal Tombs and the Ancient City*. Athens: Ekdotike Athenon.

Barag, D. 1990. 'The Prelude to Hellenistic Gold-Glasses'. *Annales du 11e Congrès de l'Association internationale pour l'histoire du verre (Bâle, 1988)*, 19–25.

Beretta, M. and Di Pasquale, G. 2004. *Vitrum. Il vetro fra arte e scienza nel mondo romano*. Firenze: Giunti.

Cesarin, G. 2012. 'I vetri ellenistici realizzati nella tecnica del sandwich gold-glass: nuove proposte interpretative alla luce dei dati editi'. Unpublished thesis, Università degli Studi di Padova.

Cesarin, G. 2016. 'Hunters on Horseback: New Version of the Macedonian Iconography in Ptolemaic Egypt'. In *Alexander the Great and the East: History, Art, Tradition*, edited by Krzysztof Nawotka and Agnieszka Wojciechowska, 41–50. Harrassowitz: Verlag.

Cooney, J. D. 1976. *Glass: Catalogue of Egyptian Antiquities in the British Museum*. London: Trustees of the British Museum.

Cummings, K. 1980. *The Technique of Glass Forming*. London: Batsford.

Darque-Ceretti, E., Felder, E. and Aucouturier, M. 2011. 'Foil and Leaf Gilding on Cultural Artifacts: Forming and Adhesion'. *Revista Matéria* 16 (1): 540–99.

Faedo, L. 1978. 'Per una classificazione preliminare dei vetri dorati tardoromani'. *Annali della Scuola Normale Superiore di Pisa, Classe di Lettere e Filosofia* 8 (3): 1025–70.

Filippini, P. 1996. 'Blown Gold-Sandwich Glasses with Gilt Glass-Trail Inscriptions'. *Annales du 13e Congrès de l'Association Internationale pour l'Histoire du Verre (Pays Bas, 1995)*, 113–28.

Foy, D. and Nenna, M. D. 2001. *Tout feu tout sable mille ans de verre antique dans le Midi de la France*. Catalogued exposition, Musée d'histoire de Marseille. Marseille, Aix-en-Povence: Edisud Musées de Marseille.

Fremersdorf, F. 1967. *Die römischen Gläser mit Schliff, Bemalung und Goldauflagen aus Köln. Die Denkmäler des römischen Köln 8, 1*. Köln: Auftr. der Archäologischen Gesellschaft und dem Römisch-Germanischen Museum Köln.

Fujii, Y. and Namiki, H. 2017. 'A Study of the Cut Gold Leaf Decoration Techniques on Ancient Gold-Sandwich-Glass, with emphasis on the Hellenistic "Kirikane" technique'. *Annals of the 20th Congress of the International Association for the History of Glass (Fribourg – Romont, 2016)*, 68–72.

Goldstein, S. M. 1979. *Pre-Roman and Early Roman Glass in the Corning Museum of Glass*. Corning, NY: The Museum.

Goldstein, S. M. 1989. 'Old Glass, New Glass, Gold Glass: Some Thoughts on Ancient Casting Technology'. *Kölner Jahrbuch für Vor- und Frühgeschichte* 22: 115–9.

Grose, D. F. 1989. *Early Ancient Glass: Core-Formed, Rod-Formed, and Cast Vessels and Objects from the Late Bronze Age to the Early Roman Empire, 1600 BC to AD 50*. New York: Hudson Hills Press in association with the Toledo Museum of Art.

Haevernick, T. E. 1962. 'Beiträge zur Geschichte des antiken Glases VIII. Zu den Goldgläsern'. *Jahrbuch des Römisch-Germanischen Zentralmuseums Mainz* 9: 58–61.

Harden, D. B. 1968. 'The Canosa Group of Hellenistic Glasses in the British Museum'. *Journal of Glass Studies* 10: 21–47.

Harden, D. B. 1987. *Glass of the Caesars*. Milano: Olivetti.

Howells, D. T. 2013. 'Making Late Antique Gold Glass'. In *New Light on Old Glass: Recent Research on Byzantine Mosaics and Glass*, edited by C. Entwistle, 112–20. London: British Museum.

Howells, D. T. 2015. *A Catalogue of the Late Antique Gold Glass in the British Museum*. London: British Museum.

Ignatiadou, D. 2000. 'Three Cast-Glass Vessels from a Macedonian Tomb in Pydna'. *Annales du 14e Congrès de l'Association internationale pour l'histoire du verre (Italia, Venezia – Milano, 1998)*, 35–8.

Ignatiadou, D. 2001. 'Glass and Gold on Macedonian Funerary Couches'. *Annales du 15e Congrés de l'Association internationale pour l'histoire du verre (New York/Corning, 2001)*, 4–7.

Ignatiadou, D. 2002. 'Macedonian Glass-Working in the 4th Century BC'. In *Hyalos, Vitrum, Glass: History, Technology and Conservation of Glass and Vitreous Materials in the Hellenic World*, edited by G. Kordas, 63–70. Athens: Glasnet.

Ignatiadou, D. 2017. 'Gold in Glass'. *Annals of the 20th Congress of the International Association for the History of Glass (Fribourg – Romont, 2016)*, 61–7.

Kottaridou, A. 2011. *Macedonian Treasures: A Tour Through the Museum of the Royal Tombs of Aigai*. Athens: Kapon Editions.

Lierke, R. 2009. *Die nicht-geblasenen antiken Glasgefässe: ihre Herstellung von den Anfängen bis zu den Luxusgläsern der Römer*. Offenbach/Main: Deutsche Glastechnische Gesellschaft.

Letsch, J., Noll, W. and Schiering, W. 1983. 'Glasformgehung in Tonmatrizen: Eine meistterliche Technologie der Werkstatt des Phidias in Olympia'. *Glastechnische Berichte* 56 (4): 96–105.

Meek, A. 2013. 'Gold Glass in Late Antiquity: Scientific Analysis of the British Museum Collection'. In *New Light on Old Glass: Recent Research on Byzantine Mosaics and Glass*, edited by C. Entwistle, 121–30. London: British Museum.

Morey, C. R. 1959. *The Gold-Glass Collection of the Vatican Library: With Additional Catalogues of Other Gold-Glass Collections*. Città del Vaticano: Biblioteca apostolica vaticana.

Oliver, A. 1967. 'Late Hellenistic Glass in the Metropolitan Museum'. *Journal of Glass Studies* 9: 13–33.

Oliver, A. 1968. 'Millefiori Glass in Classical Antiquity'. *Journal of Glass Studies* 10: 48–69.

Pillinger, R. 1984. *Studien zu römischen Zwischengoldgläsern*. Wien: Verlag der Österreichischen Akademie der Wissenschaften.

Rostovcev, M. I. 1963. 'Vasi di vetro dipinto del periodo tardo-ellenistico e la storia della pittura decorativa'. *Archeologia Classica* 15: 151–79 (Italian translation from the original Russian 'Stekljannyia raspisnyia vazy pozdne-ellenisticeskago vremeni i istoria dekorativnoj zivopisi'. *Izvestija Imperatorskoi Arkheologicheskoi Komissii*, 50, 1914).

Schiering, W. 1991. *Die Werkstatt des Pheidias in Olympia*. Berlin: De Gruyter.

Seiler, F. 1992. *Casa degli Amorini dorati (VI 16,7.38)*. Häuser in Pompeji. Deutsches Archäologisches Institut. München: Hirmer.

Sogliano, A. 1908. 'Domus degli Amorini Dorati'. *Notizie degli Scavi di Antichità: comunicate alla R. Accademia del Lincei per ordine di S. E. il ministro della pubblica Istruzione* 5: 34–6.

Stern, E. M. 1999. 'Ancient Glass in Athenian Temple Treasures'. *Journal of Glass Studies* 41: 19–50.

Stern, E. M. 2002. 'Glass for the Gods'. In *Hyalos, Vitrum, Glass: History, Technology and Conservation of Glass and Vitreous Materials in the Hellenic World*, edited by G. Kordas, 353–65. Athens: Glasnet.

Triantafyllidis, P. 2002. 'The Art and Craft of Glass in South-East Aegean'. In *Hyalos, Vitrum, Glass: History, Technology and Conservation of Glass and Vitreous Materials in the Hellenic World*, edited by G. Kordas, 30–2. Athens: Glasnet.

von Saldern, A. 2004. *Antikes Glas*. München: Beck.

Vopel, H. 1899. *Die altchristlichen Goldgläser: ein Beitrag zur altchristlichen Kunst- und Kulturgeschichte. Volume 5*. Heidelberg, Germany: JCB Mohr.

Whitehouse, D. 1996. 'Glass, Gold and Gold-Glasses'. *Expedition* 38 (2): 4–12.

Zanchi Roppo, F. 1969. *Vetri paleocristiani a figure d'oro conservati in Italia*. Bologna: Patron.

3

A Late Antique manganese-decolourised glass composition: Interpreting patterns and mechanisms of distribution

Anastasia Cholakova and Thilo Rehren

Abstract

The analytical study of Late Antique glass vessel assemblages from present-day Bulgaria identified a distinct compositional group, primarily dated to the fifth century CE. It is characterised by manganese decolouration and virtually absent antimony, and is recognised here as *série 3.2* of Foy et al. (2003). We discuss this specific glass group and its distribution as attested with materials found in contexts from the late fourth century CE through to the early sixth century CE, from the western Mediterranean, Italy and several sites in the Balkans, among others. These comparisons provide evidence about the overall chronology of *série 3.2* and suggest that its wide spatial circulation had various patterns and was governed by various socio-economic mechanisms, from an inter-regional through to various regional and local levels. We discuss the relationship of this predominantly fifth-century CE glass group with the later *série 2.1* of Foy et al. (2003), which gradually replaces the earlier glass group, possibly starting around the turn of the sixth century CE. We highlight specific differences in production technology of the two groups at the level of primary production while also emphasising the significance of reuse and recycling as another instance of spread of glass compositions.

Introduction

Almost 15 years ago D. Whitehouse summarised the essence of the raw glass production and distribution in the Roman and post-Roman world by associating them with the original 'Things That Traveled' articulation of M. McCormick (Whitehouse 2003; cf. McCormick 2001, 281). Although this short note of D. Whitehouse is addressed to a wider 'non-glass audience', it outlines quite aptly the meaning of the compositional provenancing of glass, and hints at the important differentiation between the movement of finished vessels and the circulation of raw glass (Whitehouse 2003, 301–2).

Nowadays, the advance in analytical studies on Roman and Late Antique glass allows us to discuss in great detail different primary glass production groups, their characteristics and geographical origins, the latter being either archaeologically well-attested through furnace sites, or at least supposed on the basis of indirect evidence (e.g. geochemical characteristics of the raw materials). In this way, a widely recognised potential of the research – to trace supply routes through provenancing glass finds found at various sites across the Mediterranean and beyond – provides the initial 'things that travelled' notion with a particular meaning, even if sometimes this meaning seems almost compulsory reduced to the geographical model 'Levant versus Egypt' regarding the departure points of these 'travels'. At the same time, another line of enquiry – exploring the socio-economic mechanisms that governed the distribution of glass during Roman and Late Antique periods – is also promising and can open wider research perspectives. Such an interpretative approach, related to the fields of economic theory and economic anthropology (cf. Laiou 2002; Morrisson 2012), would contribute to our more comprehensive understanding of those various strands, besides the mere spatial movement, which brought into being the 'things that travelled' phenomenon.

The present note is an attempt to examine the patterns and mechanisms of distribution of glass – both as raw material and as finished vessels – using the example of a particular primary compositional group produced in Late Antiquity that features manganese-based decolourising. The analysed finds come from the Balkans (Bulgaria) and primarily date to the fifth century CE. Their preliminary partial interpretation in terms of vessel morphotypology and analytical results is given in Cholakova 2009, Rehren and Cholakova 2014 and Cholakova et al. 2016;

full data presentation and detailed discussion are beyond the scope of this short contribution and will be published elsewhere. The purpose of the following concise paragraphs is to place the data in the context of similar materials from the region and farther afield, and in regard to the various levels of spatial distribution (Cholakova 2014). Furthermore, we aim to elaborate on the complexities of compositional grouping of Late Antique glass, initially outlined in the research on the sixth-century CE glass from the same region (Cholakova et al. 2016), and to hypothesise another form of spread of this compositional group through recycling.

Materials

The Mn-decolourised vessel fragments and unworked glass chunks considered here were found during excavations at three sites in present-day Bulgaria – Dichin (Bulgarian-excavated Area F of the site), Serdica and Odartsi – which provided the materials for an integrated study of the Late Antique vessel glass in the Lower Danube region (Cholakova 2014; Cholakova 2016). The present subset of finds from this research project is in general immediately preceding, in terms of chronology, the sixth-century CE glass from the three sites (see Cholakova et al. 2016 for details about the sites, archaeological contexts of the finds, analytical methods and data processing applied in the project).

In total, 44 samples of this predominantly fifth-century CE Mn-decolourised composition were analysed (Table 3.1). The analytical set comprises four glass chunks and fragments from at least 34 individual vessels. Apparently, in several instances from the Dichin assemblage one and the same production event (batch) is represented by two or more fragments, which may come from one and the same or from more than one individual vessel. The appearance of the finds varies from almost clean colourless glass, often with very faint yellowish or purplish tint, to bluish glass and even darker greenish glass of the bigger chunks (Figure 3.1). Nevertheless, colourless or nearly colourless fragments prevail and this indicates that the vessels were likely produced with the intention of attaining a particular visual quality of the material.

Table 3.1 Chemical compositions of the samples from Dichin (abbreviation 'G'), Serdica (abbreviation 'SER') and Odartsi (abbreviation 'ODR'), with concise object descriptions and dates of the context of discovery (combined EPMA and LA-ICP-MS data; cf. Cholakova et al. 2016, Appendix B(1)). Likely groups of samples belonging to one and the same vessel or production batch are highlighted in grey

Sample code	*Object*	*Illustration*	*Date of context of discovery*
Main group			
G 43	rim fragment of a bowl (Isings 96a, plain, cracked-off	Rehren and Cholakova 2014; fig. 11.8.9.	*c.*410–470 CE
G 44	rim fragment of a bowl (Isings 96a, plain, cracked-off, same vessel/batch as G 43		*c.*410–470 CE
G 82	neck fragment of a jug/flask, self-coloured trailed decoration in relief	Fig. 1.	*c.*410–470 CE
G 83	rim fragment of a jug/flask, self-coloured trailed decoration in relief	Rehren and Cholakova 2014; fig. 11.8.7	*c.*470–490 CE
G 85	rim and wall fragment of a cup, fine self-coloured trailed decoration	Rehren and Cholakova 2014; fig. 11.8.6.	*c.*410–470 CE
G 86	wall fragment, self-coloured trailed decoration in relief, same batch as G 85	Fig. 1.	*c.*470–490 CE
G 54	rim and wall fragment of a cup, blue trailed decoration	Rehren and Cholakova 2014; fig. 11.8.10.	*c.*410–470 CE

(continued)

Table 3.1 (cont.)

Sample code	*Object*	*Illustration*	*Date of context of discovery*
G 57	rim fragment of a bowl, blue trailed decoration		*c.*410–470 CE
G 58	rim fragment, blue trailed decoration		disturbed context
G 59	rim fragment of a cup/beaker, blue trailed decoration		*c.*470–490 CE
G 18	wall fragment of a bowl, engraved decoration	Rehren and Cholakova 2014; fig. 11.8.4.	*c.*470–490 CE
G 19	wall fragment of a bowl, engraved decoration, same vessel/batch as G 18	Fig. 1.; Rehren and Cholakova 2014; fig. 11.8.5.	disturbed context
G 20	wall fragment of a bowl, engraved decoration	Rehren and Cholakova 2014; fig. 11.8.3.	*c.*410–470 CE
G 45	bowl with fire-rounded rim, rounded base with pontil mark, abraded decoration	Rehren and Cholakova 2014; fig. 11.8.1.	*c.*410–470 CE
G 46	same vessel as sample G 45	same vessel as sample G 45	*c.*410–470 CE
G 47	same vessel as sample G 45	same vessel as sample G 45	*c.*410–470 CE
G 48	rim fragment, plain, fire-rounded, same vessel/batch as G 45–G 47?		*c.*410–470 CE
G 22	base and wall fragment, plain, rounded, same vessel/batch as G 45–G 47?		*c.*410–470 CE
G 21	base fragment of a bowl?, plain		disturbed context
G 23	base fragment of a bowl? single abraded line		disturbed context

G 65	base fragment of a bowl? plain, slightly concave, with massive pontil mark	Fig. 1.	*c.*410–470 CE
G 66	base fragment of a bowl? plain		disturbed context
G 81	base fragment of an oil lamp, ball-shaped end, with pontil scar		*c.*410–470 CE
SER 49	rim fragment of a beaker/lamp, blue trailed decoration	Fig. 1.	late 4th–5th c.
SER 50	rim fragment of a bowl, blue trailed decoration		possibly 6th c.
SER 51	rim and wall fragment of a beaker/lamp, blue trailed decoration	Fig. 1.	late 4th–5th c.
SER 54	base fragment of a cup? applied ring of light blue glass	Fig. 1.	late 4th–early 5th c.
SER 56	rim fragment of a bowl/lamp, blue trailed decoration	Fig. 1.	5th c.
SER 57	base fragment of a cup? applied ring of blue glass	Fig. 1.	disturbed context
SER 10	unworked chunk	Fig. 1.	late 4th–early 5th c.

(continued)

Table 3.1 (cont.)

Sample code	*Object*	*Illustration*	*Date of context of discovery*
SER 2	unworked chunk	Fig. 1.	possibly 6th c.
SER 9	unworked chunk	Fig. 1.	2nd–3rd quarter of the 4th c.
High Sr sub-group			
SER 41	base fragment of a stemmed goblet Isings 111		late 4th–5th c.
SER 42	base fragment of a stemmed goblet Isings 111		possibly 6th c.
SER 3	unworked chunk	Fig. 1.	possibly 6th c.
ODR 36	rim fragment, blue trailed decoration	Fig. 1.	terminus ante quem *c.*610 CE
ODR 1	base fragment of a stemmed goblet Isings 111		terminus ante quem *c.*610 CE
G 55	rim and wall fragment of a beaker/oil lamp, blue trailed decoration	Rehren and Cholakova 2014; fig. 11.9.1–2.	*c.*470–490 CE
G 56	rim fragment, blue trailed decoration		disturbed context
G 49	rim fragment of a bowl, plain, fire-rounded		disturbed context
G 80	base fragment of an oil lamp, pointed drop-shaped end, with pontil scar	Rehren and Cholakova 2014; fig. 11.8.8.	disturbed context
G 24	wall fragment, straight, single abraded line		*c.*470–490 CE
Outliers			
SER 55	base fragment of a cup? applied ring of blue glass		late 4th–early 5th c.
SER 31	wall fragment of a beaker? blue blobs decoration		late 4th–5th c

	wt%												ppm							
	SiO_2	Na_2O	Al_2O_3	CaO	K_2O	MgO	Fe_2O_3	P_2O_5	Cl	SO_3	TiO_2	MnO	ZrO_2	Y_2O_3	CeO_2	BaO	SrO	Sb_2O_3	CuO	PbO
Main group																				
G 43	69.7	19.4	1.71	5.82	0.40	0.50	0.41	338	1.24	0.04	0.08	0.57	57	6	12	199	537	0	13	12
G 44	69.7	19.2	1.71	5.89	0.42	0.51	0.40	350	1.24	0.05	0.08	0.58	60	7	12	198	542	0	8	5
G 82	69.4	18.5	1.85	6.37	0.40	0.49	0.64		1.05	0.07	0.09	0.53								
G 83	69.2	18.4	1.98	5.97	0.44	0.55	0.66	300	0.94	0.18	0.11	0.80								
G 85	70.7	18.2	1.76	5.78	0.35	0.35	0.40	349	1.00	0.06	0.06	0.75	56	7	16	251	511	0	26	2
G 86	70.4	18.4	1.70	5.74	0.36	0.34	0.37	100	1.05	0.18	0.04	0.72								
G 54	70.8	18.4	1.83	6.24	0.34	0.46	0.42	375	1.02	0.26	0.08	0.58	64	7	12	174	506	0	8	21
G 57	68.1	19.3	1.83	6.48	0.34	0.48	0.65	300	1.43	0.30	0.09	0.77								
G 58	66.3	19.9	2.08	6.50	0.37	0.59	0.79	300	1.48	0.28	0.11	0.81								
G 59	69.7	18.6	1.68	6.18	0.42	0.36	0.55	300	1.35	0.26	0.07	0.64								
G 18	68.6	19.3	1.99	5.70	0.45	0.48	0.52	300	1.49	0.27	0.08	0.83								
G 19	68.7	19.3	1.99	5.73	0.46	0.47	0.52	300	1.51	0.26	0.08	0.82								
G 20	69.8	18.8	1.81	6.03	0.49	0.31	0.54	400	1.39	0.25	0.08	0.62								
G 45	69.4	17.5	1.74	6.88	0.37	0.41	0.54	300	1.54	0.22	0.08	0.75								
G 46	69.3	17.3	1.74	6.92	0.36	0.41	0.55	300	1.57	0.22	0.08	0.93								

(continued)

Table 3.1 (cont.)

	wt%												ppm							
	SiO_2	Na_2O	Al_2O_3	CaO	K_2O	MgO	Fe_2O_3	P_2O_5	Cl	SO_3	TiO_2	MnO	ZrO_2	Y_2O_3	CeO_2	BaO	SrO	Sb_2O_3	CuO	PbO
G 47	69.4	17.4	1.76	6.96	0.37	0.42	0.50	300	1.55	0.21	0.09	0.73								
G 48	70.5	17.8	1.79	6.77	0.38	0.46	0.50	428	1.16	0.16	0.09	0.74	75	8	13	200	569	0	17	14
G 22	69.7	17.4	1.74	6.76	0.36	0.45	0.53	200	1.19	0.14	0.09	1.03								
G 21	69.6	17.0	2.06	7.10	0.47	0.56	0.69	200	1.03	0.10	0.11	1.05								
G 23	70.7	18.2	1.80	5.33	0.30	0.52	0.51		1.00	0.11	0.07	1.05								
G 65	70.2	18.5	1.83	6.15	0.39	0.45	0.48	462	1.04	0.20	0.09	0.99	71	8	14	247	565	1	16	11
G 66	69.8	19.7	1.73	5.31	0.39	0.45	0.40	362	1.16	0.16	0.08	0.77	63	7	11	230	481	8	7	52
G 81	70.2	18.6	1.58	5.89	0.44	0.37	0.51		0.97	0.07	0.06	0.81								
SER 49	68.0	19.8	1.90	5.89	0.33	0.53	0.66	300	1.09	0.28	0.08	0.92								
SER 50	67.0	18.5	2.00	7.73	0.47	0.68	0.59	400	0.95	0.32	0.10	0.85								
SER 51	67.1	19.4	1.95	7.02	0.35	0.57	0.65	400	1.16	0.21	0.11	0.62								
SER 54	66.8	20.7	1.88	6.02	0.34	0.58	0.51	200	1.30	0.29	0.07	0.62								
SER 56	67.2	19.5	2.09	6.50	0.41	0.52	0.62	400	1.03	0.32	0.09	0.99								
SER 57	68.7	19.8	1.79	5.64	0.32	0.48	0.37	200	1.22	0.26	0.07	0.66								
SER 10	66.2	21.0	1.99	5.91	0.40	0.54	0.70	487	1.15		0.09	1.02	67	8	13	301	551	0	30	14
SER 2	66.1	20.7	2.01	5.68	0.41	0.83	0.75	366	1.14		0.12	1.26	72	7	14	520	558	5	72	25
SER 9	66.9	21.0	1.94	5.27	0.30	0.80	0.61	341	1.40		0.09	0.84	62	7	13	218	504	2	17	0

	wt%												*ppm*							
	SiO_2	Na_2O	Al_2O_3	CaO	K_2O	MgO	Fe_2O_3	P_2O_5	Cl	SO_3	TiO_2	MnO	ZrO_2	Y_2O_3	CeO_2	BaO	SrO	Sb_2O_3	CuO	PbO
High Sr sub-group																				
SER 3	65.7	19.3	2.09	7.21	0.43	0.64	0.64	758	0.95	0.40	0.11	1.51	68	7	13	290	700	0	30	9
SER 41	63.9	21.1	2.51	8.04	0.52	0.74	0.83	635	1.07		0.13	0.86	111	9	17	309	712	2	32	27
SER 42	66.8	19.6	1.98	7.43	0.53	0.95	0.73	935	0.71		0.11	0.86	87	8	14	294	717	81	119	71
ODR 1	66.6	19.1	1.93	7.86	0.47	0.80	0.68	783	0.95		0.11	1.23	81	8	13	289	774	64	50	32
ODR 36	67.3	19.3	2.15	7.30	0.39	0.61	0.77	590	0.99		0.10	0.91	87	9	13	251	655	3	43	142
G 55	65.9	18.8	2.30	8.81	0.57	0.84	0.84	773	1.00	0.29	0.12	0.81	84	8	15	244	835	0	17	92
G 56	65.8	19.5	2.30	8.19	0.45	0.70	0.86	579	0.96	0.30	0.11	0.94	80	7	13	278	631	0	15	19
G 49	65.9	19.3	2.38	7.96	0.60	0.73	0.77	634	1.00	0.16	0.13	0.80	104	8	16	295	837	2	32	26
G 80	65.3	18.7	1.91	7.40	0.50	0.72	0.77	787	1.05	0.21	0.10	0.87	82	8	13	252	679	1	20	72
G 24	65.3	19.3	2.33	8.28	0.58	0.69	0.73	768	1.38	0.33	0.11	0.91	87	7	15	304	814	0	35	130
outliers																				
SER 55	66.6	19.9	2.19	5.26	0.29	0.74	0.84	400	1.29	0.21	0.24	1.55								
SER 31	66.4	20.6	2.37	5.80	0.32	0.67	1.22	614	1.37		0.13	0.89	88	10	14	187	471	5	43	13

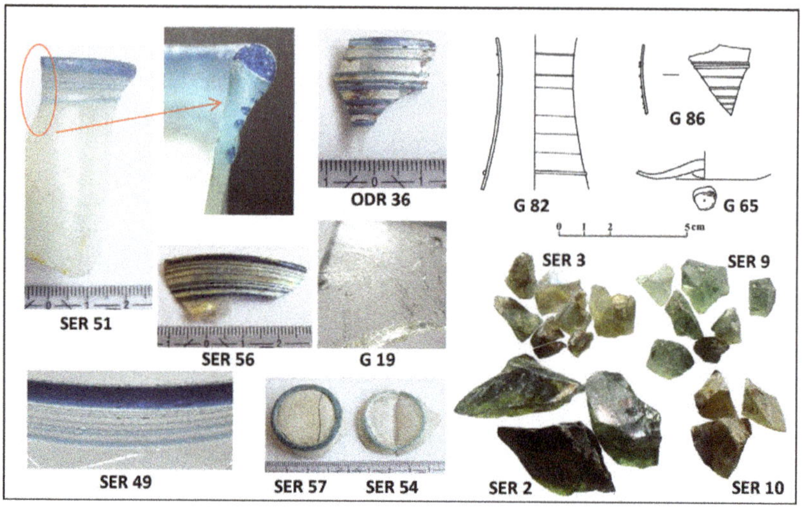

Figure 3.1 Examples of unworked glass chunks and vessel fragments, various shapes and techniques of manufacture and decoration, characteristic of the Mn-decolourised composition in Dichin, Serdica and Odartsi assemblages (after Cholakova 2009 and unpublished); indicated sample numbers correspond to the data in Table 3.1. The four sampled unworked chunks were selected among others on the basis of a preliminary grouping of the pieces according to their findspots and visual characteristics, as illustrated here. Note the distinctive technique of blue trailed decoration marvered flush with the vessel wall, as seen in the detail of the rim section of SER 51. The overall fashion of such a decoration is likely influenced by the east Mediterranean tradition but the particular craft style and its numerous examples from the eastern Balkans suggest their regional popularity and manufacture.

Remarkably, the range of vessel shapes, finishing techniques and decoration is quite diverse (cf. Rehren and Cholakova 2014), and includes bowls, cups, oil lamps, jugs/flasks and stemmed goblets. The majority of them have fire-rounded rims and pontil marks, and in only two instances cracked-off rims are preserved. A few fragments have cold-worked engraved or abraded decoration, in some cases very skilfully performed. Hot-worked ornamentation of self-coloured trails in relief and blue trailed decoration marvered flush with the vessel wall surface are very characteristic of the group overall (Figure 3.1). Such diversity strongly suggests that the vessels came from multiple secondary glass workshops, working in different craft traditions and at different artistic levels. According to their contexts of discovery, the finds are dated to the timespan beginning from the late fourth century CE and possibly continuing up into the (early?) sixth century CE (Table 3.1). The fragments found in well-dated contexts of Dichin (Area F) belong all to the fifth-century CE occupation period of the settlement (cf. Rehren and Cholakova 2014 about the periodisation of the site).

Characteristics of the chemical glass composition

The chemical makeup of the studied finds is characterised by two main traits: (1) relatively low levels of mineral-derived impurities in the glass (such as alumina and lime), as a result of using cleaner glass-making sands; and (2) intentionally added manganese acting as glass decolouriser (Table 3.2, top row). Our preliminary earlier study of the Dichin assemblage linked this group to a somewhat more generic definition of 'Roman blue-green glass' (Rehren and Cholakova 2014). Later on, more detailed research on the analytical data obtained on samples from all three sites unequivocally confirmed that they are identical with a chemical composition defined for the first time among the Late Antique glass finds from Southern France and labelled as '*série 3.2*' (Foy et al. 2003; Cholakova et al. 2016). The low levels of alumina and to a certain extent lime separate this glass group from other known Mn-decolourised compositions (e.g. Jackson and Paynter 2016 High-Mn and Low-Mn; Silvestri et al. 2008, CL2), while at the same time they strongly resemble the makeup of antimony decolourised glass popular during the earlier Roman period (Groupe 4 in Foy et al. 2004) but also used in Late Antiquity as well (Type 1 in Meek 2013). The initial interpretation of *série 3.2* by Foy et al. 2003 associated this composition with the Syro-Palestinian primary glass production. However, the similarity between Sb-decolourised glass on the one hand, and *série 3.2* on the other, was recently pointed out, and their common, probably Egyptian origin was suggested, including on the basis of isotopic evidence (Maltoni et al. 2016; cf. Schibille et al. 2017 based on a compositionally less consistent dataset).

The opportunity to study a bigger and relatively well-dated group of *série 3.2* samples enables us for the first time to identify an internal compositional trend of gradual increase of almost all sand-deriving minor and trace oxides within this group. The present study suggests the separation of a sub-group of 10 samples, which differ most evidently in their higher levels of lime, phosphate and strontium oxide,

Table 3.2 Average concentrations of major, minor and selected trace oxides in the samples of Mn-decolourised composition *série 3.2* from Dichin, Serdica and Odartsi (the two outliers are omitted from the averaging; full data in Table 3.1). The data are presented as general average of the group as a whole for comparison with the published compositions from elsewhere (listed in the lower part of the table), and also separately for the main group and for the strontium-rich sub-group

	wt%												*ppm*		
	SiO_2	Na_2O	Al_2O_3	CaO	K_2O	MgO	Fe_2O_3	P_2O_5	Cl	SO_3	TiO_2	MnO	ZrO_2	SrO	Sb_2O_3
Dichin, Serdica, Odartsi	**68.2**	**19.0**	**1.93**	**6.59**	**0.42**	**0.56**	**0.60**	**0.04**	**1.16**	**0.21**	**0.09**	**0.84**	**76**	**634**	**8**
(n = 42; for trace oxides n = 20)	*1.9*	*1.0*	*0.21*	*0.91*	*0.07*	*0.15*	*0.14*	*0.02*	*0.21*	*0.09*	*0.02*	*0.20*	*15*	*118*	*22*
Main group	**68.9**	**18.9**	**1.85**	**6.19**	**0.39**	**0.50**	**0.55**	**0.03**	**1.21**	**0.20**	**0.08**	**0.80**	**65**	**532**	**2**
(n = 32; for trace oxides n = 10)	*1.5*	*1.1*	*0.13*	*0.59*	*0.05*	*0.12*	*0.11*	*0.01*	*0.20*	*0.09*	*0.02*	*0.17*	*6*	*30*	*3*
High Sr sub-group	**65.9**	**19.4**	**2.19**	**7.85**	**0.50**	**0.74**	**0.76**	**0.07**	**1.01**	**0.28**	**0.11**	**0.97**	**87**	**735**	**15**
(n = 10)	*0.9*	*0.7*	*0.21*	*0.51*	*0.07*	*0.10*	*0.07*	*0.01*	*0.16*	*0.09*	*0.01*	*0.23*	*12*	*75*	*30*
Barnsley Park, Britain Foster and Jackson 2010,		**18.5**	**1.81**	**5.77**	**0.29**	**0.67**	**0.48**	**0.03**			**0.09**	**1.14**	**62**	**523**	**720**
Colourless 2a (n = 5)	**n.r.**	*0.5*	*0.26*	*0.41*	*0.04*	*0.11*	*0.05*	*0.01*	**n.r.**	**n.r.**	*0.01*	*0.16*	*5*	*39*	*360*
Stojnik, Serbia Marić-Stojanović et al. 2015,	**69.0**	**18.4**	**1.97**	**6.32**	**0.45**	**0.67**	**0.57**		**1.16**	**0.40**	**0.09**	**0.92**	**75**	**405**	**200**
K1 (n = 13)	*2.3*	*2.8*	*0.18*	*0.45*	*0.03*	*0.24*	*0.04*	**n.r.**	*0.13*	*0.06*	*0.01*	*0.07*	*20*	*63*	*800*

	wt%												*ppm*		
	SiO_2	Na_2O	Al_2O_3	CaO	K_2O	MgO	Fe_2O_3	P_2O_5	Cl	SO_3	TiO_2	MnO	ZrO_2	SrO	Sb_2O_3
Classe, Italy	**68.3**	**19.0**	**1.93**	**6.70**	**0.57**	**0.66**	**0.76**	**0.04**	**1.30**	**0.28**	**0.13**	**0.66**	**94**	**553**	<400
Maltoni et al. 2015, CL3 (n= 25)	*1.4*	*1.1*	*0.21*	*0.92*	*0.25*	*0.17*	*0.39*	*0.02*	*0.19*	*0.08*	*0.05*	*0.26*	*30*	*96*	
Aquileia, Italy	**68.2**	**19.2**	**1.77**	**6.62**	**0.38**	**0.56**	**0.70**	**0.04**	**1.26**	**0.34**	**0.11**	**0.87**	**83**	**538**	<400
Maltoni et al. 2016, FC/3 (n = 7)	*1.2*	*1.1*	*0.21*	*0.50*	*0.09*	*0.10*	*0.37*	*0.02*	*0.14*	*0.06*	*0.01*	*0.20*	*27*	*51*	
Aquileia, Italy	**68.4**	**19.2**	**1.95**	**6.19**	**0.41**	**0.64**	**0.79**	**0.05**	**1.56**	**0.28**	**0.12**	**0.98**	**85**	**526**	<400
Gallo et al. 2014, A0/3 (n = 9)	*2.0*	*1.3*	*0.10*	*0.52*	*0.04*	*0.10*	*0.21*	*0.01*	*0.18*	*0.08*	*0.02*	*0.25*	*15*	*46*	
Southern France	**68.1**	**18.8**	**1.92**	**6.99**	**0.44**	**0.65**	**0.70**	**0.08**	**n.r.**	**n.r.**	**0.09**	**0.95**	**77**	**634**	**22**
Foy et al. 2003, *série 3.2* (n = 17)	*1.5*	*0.9*	*0.15*	*0.74*	*0.08*	*0.16*	*0.15*	*0.03*			*0.02*	*0.34*	*15*	*125*	*41*
Padova, Italy Silvestri et al. 2011, MSG1c (n = 20)	**69.0**	**18.3**	**2.21**	**6.50**	**0.45**	**0.72**	**0.69**	**0.06**	**1.35**	**0.23**	**0.10**	**1.10**	**80**	**517**	**195**
	1.2	*1.1*	*0.22*	*0.50*	*0.11*	*0.12*	*0.19*	*0.03*	*0.21*	*0.05*	*0.02*	*0.20*	*54*	*28*	*166*

Note: only one of the samples from Stojnik has detectable antimony oxide level, while antimony in all the other samples in the Stojnik assemblage is lower than the stated limit of detection of 200 ppm Sb (Marić-Stojanović et al. 2015, table 1). Standard deviation is given in *italics*; n.r. = not reported.

when compared to the main group of *série 3.2* (Table 3.2, second and third row). The increase of SrO is the most striking (but not the only) peculiarity of this sub-group, with an average SrO to CaO ratio of approximately 0.0094 (compared to a ratio of 0.0086 for the main group), since it resembles the elevated SrO values in sixth-century CE glasses consistent with *série 2.1* (Cholakova et al. 2016). The increased levels of other minor oxides in the Sr-rich sub-group (such as alumina, magnesia, iron oxide and titania), compared to the main group, are also evident. However, this increase appears gradual and indicative of common group affiliation, while the difference of SrO to CaO ratio identifies the Sr-rich samples as a clearly outlined sub-group within the overall set. Further analytical research is necessary to better understand the relationship of the sub-group to the main group; published data of the Mn-decolourised composition shows that the Sr-rich sub-group occurs more widely in the archaeological record (e.g. Foy et al. 2003, 85, Annexe 3).

Although no tight dating of the Sr-rich sub-group is possible, it is important to note that the three examples of stemmed goblets in our *série 3.2* set belong to this sub-group, all of them produced in the so-called 'stem-cum-foot' technique, which became popular not earlier than in the very late fifth century CE (Fünfschilling and Laflı 2013).

In addition, two samples in the current set are defined as outliers within the overall *série 3.2* group because of a higher titania level (SER 55) and a higher iron oxide concentration (SER 31), which may have resulted from compositional alterations/mixing at the level of secondary glass-working.

The presence of *série 3.2* in the Lower Danube region during the fifth century CE is expectedly further confirmed by the recently published analytical results from the glass in the UK-excavated areas of the Dichin site (Smith et al. 2016). Despite the inconsistent labels used (alternating between HIMT 2 and HIMT G1), numerous samples from this part of the Dichin assemblage have a composition identical to our own analyses, including the low alumina levels (*c.*1.80–2.30 wt% Al_2O_3) and the same Mn-based decolourising as seen in the present compositional group recognised here as *série 3.2* (cf. Figure 3.2).

Chronology, patterns and mechanisms of distribution

The Mn-decolourised composition identified in the samples from Dichin, Serdica and Odartsi is attested in other regions of the Late

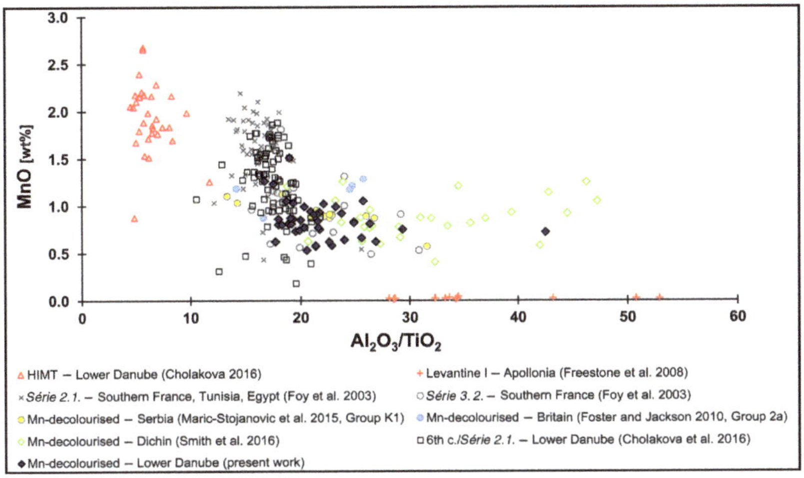

Figure 3.2 Alumina to titania ratio versus values of manganese oxide in the samples in the present study compared to respective data from the Balkans, Southern France and Britain, and to some well-recognised compositional groups of Late Antiquity (i.e. Levantine I, HIMT, *série 2.1*). This juxtaposition of characteristics of the glass-making sands determined by geological factors (Al_2O_3/TiO_2 ratio – cf. Schibille et al. 2017, fig. 9) and a recipe-related anthropogenic feature of the glass compositions (levels of added MnO) suggests that the Mn-decolourised glass (= *série 3.2*) is closely related to but still different from *série 2.1*. The high Al_2O_3/TiO_2 ratios in some of the analyses from Smith et al. (2016) are probably due to generally too low titania levels in their analyses.

Antique world, too (Table 3.2), even though the group does not seem to be always recognised as being the one first defined by Foy et al. in 2003. Five vessel fragments from a fourth-century CE context in Britain are probably among the earliest examples of *série 3.2* (Foster and Jackson 2010, Group 2a; the same chemical makeup is denoted as 'Rom-Mn low Ca' in Schibille et al. 2017). Interestingly, they also demonstrate some of the lowest published alumina and lime values of this compositional group, supporting the suspected gradual increase in sand-deriving impurities over time. A small set of window pane samples from the region to the South of the Danube in present-day central Serbia belongs to the same compositional group, tentatively dated to the fourth century CE (Marić-Stojanović et al. 2015, Group K1; the earlier dates for some of the finds suggested in the publication should be considered with caution since they are not based on site stratigraphy. Active habitation of the site is dated to the second half of the fourth century CE and there is no evidence of fifth-century CE occupation – M. Glumac pers. comm.). Three sites from north-eastern Italy – Aquileia, Classe and Padova, provide evidence that *série 3.2* glass composition was in circulation in this region during the fifth and the sixth century CE, used as vessels, mosaic tesserae and also in local secondary glass-working (Silvestri et al. 2011, MSG1c; Gallo et al. 2014, AQ/3; Maltoni et al. 2015, CL3; Maltoni et al. 2016, FC/3). The dated samples from Southern France (Marseilles) belong to the very end of the fifth century CE to the beginning of the sixth century CE, and both glass chunks and finished vessels are attested there (Foy et al. 2003, *série 3.2*).

Several more instances of Late Antique Mn-decolourised glass with low levels of alumina may be tentatively assigned to *série 3.2* (e.g. from Buthrotum (Butrint) on the Adriatic Balkan coast – Conte et al. 2014, sample BT17). Unworked glass chunks of similar chemical makeup from Iustiniana Prima in the central Balkans are of particular interest since they would possibly confirm the production of this composition well into the sixth century CE (530s CE are the earliest probable terminus post quem for Iustiniana Prima glass – Drauschke and Greiff 2010, cf. sample 261). Furthermore, closer inspection of the compositional data on early Byzantine glass weights may also help to recognise well-dated sixth-century CE examples of *série 3.2* (e.g. Schibille et al. 2016, cf. BM 1987,0703.4).

This summarised overview of the distribution of the Late Antique Mn-decolourised glass demonstrated that for well over a century this primary group had a fairly wide circulation across the empire, even if the analysed finds are not always being labelled in a consistent way in the literature (e.g. finds from Carthage in Siu et al. 2017, Group 1 are defined as 'weak' HIMT or HIMT 2). The unworked chunks and production debris of *série 3.2* found as far afield as Southern France, north-eastern Italy and in the Balkans suggest that the main mode of distribution of this primary glass was the inter-regional trade of raw material for the secondary glass workshops located in different parts of the empire. At the regional and local level, various glass vessel producers were then using these supplies to satisfy their markets and consumers' needs of ordinary plain glassware for common usage (e.g. Isings 96a cups with cracked-off rims – Rehren and Cholakova 2014, fig. 11.8.9.; Isings 106c beakers – Maltoni et al. 2015, table 1, D52). Like the window panes, these mass produced and probably locally made utilitarian vessels usually show little or negligible regional specifics of morphology or techniques of manufacture. At the same time, certain more elaborate vessel groups demonstrate clear distinctions between various traditions of secondary glass-working at regional level. In this way, we are able to recognise that the same composition of *série 3.2* was fed into the regional production of blue trailed vessels found to be typical for the Balkan assemblages in the fifth–early sixth century CE (Figure 3.1; Rehren and Cholakova 2014, fig. 11.9.1–2; cf. Adam-Veleni 2010, 350, no. 376), and also into the broadly contemporaneous production of vessels with mould-blown decoration of Christian symbols distributed in western Europe (Foy et al. 2003, fig. 22; 2010). Furthermore the 'travel' of *série 3.2* can also be traced in the movement of certain examples of finished vessels that, because of their higher quality and aesthetic appeal (cf. fragments with engraved and abraded decoration in Rehren and Cholakova 2014, fig. 11.8.4, 5), became objects of commercialised trade and/or, quite possibly, represent particular occasions of non-commercial long-distance movement of luxurious items as signs for social status and links. Here is not the space to explore how these different travel modes related to each other and whether all of them (trade in raw chunks; local/regional trade in finished objects; interregional transport of exceptional or prestige items) were active in all regions where glass of the composition of *série 3.2* was found. However, these summarised examples of different patterns and mechanisms of glass distribution clearly represent different economic and social situations, and emphasise the importance of a more holistic research approach in the studies of primary production glass groups in order to reveal the social meaning behind their spatial movements.

Mn-decolourised Late Antique composition and *Série 2.1*

Foy et al. (2003, 61–2) have distinguished their *Groupe 3* from the *Groupe 2* glasses on the basis of lower levels of iron, magnesium, titanium and zirconium in the former, and its suspected origin from workshops using sand of Belus river type in Palestine. The recently suggested association of the Mn-decolourised glass *série 3.2* with the generally later glass group known as *série 2.1* on the basis of the similarities in their geochemical characteristics (Cholakova et al. 2016) lead to the formulation of a composite heading 'Foy 2', which seems to encompass variable chemical makeups (Schibille et al. 2016; Schibille et al. 2017), even though such an overarching label does not appear in the original publication of these glass groups (Foy et al. 2003). Such a generalisation would certainly help to overcome the ambiguities of compositional interpretation, since clear and straightforward differentiation between both glasses *série 3.2* and *série 2.1* is not always possible. Nevertheless, there are various other aspects, besides provenancing, which would remain unconsidered if one were to follow such an approach of overall discounting of the distinctions between the two compositions. For example, the chronological distribution of both groups, taken together, covers a period of more than three centuries which are also the most crucial centuries for the socio-cultural transformations towards the early Middle Ages. Understanding the character of the transformations within the primary glass industry in this period is certainly an important task of present-day analytical glass studies. Furthermore, the available information so far does not allow us to definitely reconstruct a simple linear transition from the Mn-decolourised composition of *série 3.2* with its high-Sr sub-group leading to *série 2.1*, since there is evidence for a certain chronological overlap and co-existence of both groups (see, e.g. Rosenow and Rehren 2017). While the geochemical similarity of the glass-making sands used for both primary productions is relatively well recognised, probably even forming a compositional continuum, recipe changes seen in the amount of added manganese (Figure 3.2) and its geological source (cf. Cholakova et al. 2016, fig. 8) suggest that more complex factors played a role in the dynamics of early Byzantine glass production.

Indeed, the internal variability of *série 3.2* and *série 2.1* and their somewhat blurred boundary are challenging when trying to establish well-defined compositional groupings. Probably more evidence from well-dated archaeological contexts is necessary to better understand some of these features of the primary glass groups, but the hypothesis of just a gradually deteriorating quality of the sand source used by a single large-scale producer over approximately three centuries may seem too schematic.

Here, we argue that a possible key for the interpretation of the relationship between *série 3.2* and *série 2.1* should be sought in the recycling practices of Late Antiquity. The samples of the predominantly fifth-century CE composition *série 3.2* from the Lower Danube region show little evidence of recycling (especially with the virtual absence of Sb_2O_3), similarly to the type material from Southern France (Foy et al. 2003, 85, Annexe 3) and the finds from Aquileia (Maltoni et al. 2016, 12). Significantly, the only two examples of elevated Sb_2O_3 in the current dataset belong to the Sr-rich sub-group – both stemmed goblets, contextually and typologically dated to the end of the fifth–sixth century CE (Table 3.1, samples SER 42 and ODR 1). A comparison of the trace oxides related to glass recycling in the *série 3.2* and *série 2.1* samples from Dichin, Serdica and Odartsi demonstrates much higher levels in the latter composition, including the unworked chunks, and a particularly sharp difference in antimony oxide concentrations (Figure 3.3; cf. Cholakova et al. 2016, table 1). The current short chapter is not the place for a comprehensive discussion of the natural background levels of transition metals in the glass-making sands. Suffice it to say that antimony oxide is naturally present only in negligible quantities in glass-making sands (Sb<1.4 ppm – Brems and Degryse 2014, 79), and any elevated levels are due to some additives. The low, but still elevated concentrations as seen here in the samples of *série 2.1* composition, ranging from 20 to almost 800 ppm Sb_2O_3 in the individual samples (cf. Cholakova et al. 2016, table 1) can result not from deliberate addition but are certainly contamination due to re-melting of mixed batches containing small amounts of pre-existing Sb-rich glass. However, a hypothetical recycling of Sb-decolourised vessel cullet in the sixth century CE (as suggested in Schibille et al. 2017; Schibille et al. 2016) seems highly unlikely, taking into account the decline and eventual halt of production of Sb-decolourised glass by the (early) fifth century CE at the latest. Therefore, instead of Sb-decolourised vessel cullet, re-melting of Sb-opacified mosaic glass tesserae is a more probable source of antimony oxide which re-appeared in *série 2.1*, after being virtually absent in *série 3.2* (Figure 3.3). The data from the sixth-century CE glass from the Lower Danube region is consistent with the observation of Foy and co-authors that even unworked chunks of *série 2.1* contain elevated Sb_2O_3. Accordingly, our results reinforce their hypothesis that the incorporation of pre-existing glass took place at the stage of primary glass-making, as a technological recipe element intended to improve the efficiency of production (Foy et al. 2003, 46; see also Vichy et al. 2007, 57). Nevertheless, simple mathematical estimations based on generalised Sb_2O_3 levels of *c.*1 or 2 wt% in the tesserae glass suggest that such an addition of tesserae could not exceed just a few per cent of the overall volume of the primary batch, if the resulting glass has about 200 ppm Sb_2O_3. It is unlikely that the addition of such a small amount could have had a real impact on the melting process, and neither would it have increased substantially the final output of production.

Therefore, we argue that as far as there are no reasons for preferential and selective re-melting of tesserae only, the elevated antimony oxide

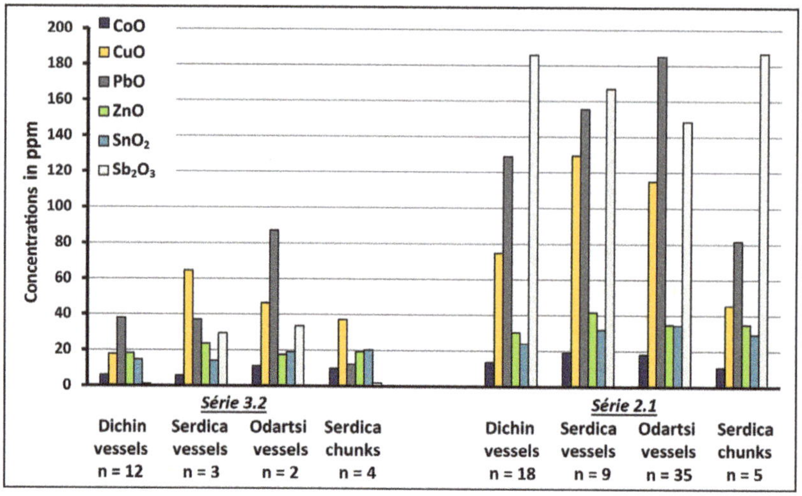

Figure 3.3 Average concentrations of trace oxides indicative of glass recycling in the samples of Mn-decolourised composition *série 3.2* and *série 2.1* from Dichin, Serdica and Odartsi site assemblages (LA-ICP-MS data from Cholakova et al. 2016, unpublished and from the present work). Note that the elevated Sb_2O_3, CuO and PbO concentrations in the *série 3.2* vessel fragments from Serdica and Odartsi are due to two individual examples of stemmed goblets from the Sr-rich sub-group (cf. Table 3.1). The further increase of copper and lead oxides in the finished vessels in *série 2.1*, compared to the unworked chunks, may well be a result of additional rounds of recycling at the stage of local secondary glass-working.

concentrations in *série 2.1* represent just the analytically detectable 'tip of the iceberg'. This reflects a much larger scale of indiscriminate recycling of mixed cullet likely comprising vessel fragments, as well as window panes, tesserae, etc. as part of the primary production technology of this compositional group (cf. Foy et al. 2003, *série 2.2*). Other commonly acknowledged evidence of the reuse of pre-existing glass can be found in the levels of minor oxides related to fuel vapour and ash contamination (Paynter 2008; Rehren and Brüggler 2015, 176; Cholakova et al. 2016, table 1; Jackson and Paynter 2016, 78–9; Schibille et al. 2017, fig. 8). No quantification of this recycling practice as part of the primary glass production at the end of Late Antiquity is possible since we are facing here the phenomenon of 'invisible recycling' and 'like being mixed with like' as quite reasonably described by Jackson and Paynter (2016, 83). This suspected recycling technology in *série 2.1* glass-making certainly relied on the available contemporaneous glass in circulation (instead on glass produced one or two centuries earlier, e.g. Sb-decolourised), and *série 3.2* glass must have formed a considerable part of this potential cullet reservoir prior to the mid-sixth century CE. Accordingly, complex and probably iterated large-scale processes of blending between both groups in the late fifth to the first half of the sixth century CE lead to an overall blurring of the compositional differences between the two glasses, as observed in numerous analytical datasets.

In contrast to this, such a technology of extensive cullet reuse at the level of primary production probably was not involved in the making of pristine low alumina Mn-decolourised composition *série 3.2* in the late fourth to the fifth century CE. However, the production of the predominantly sixth- to seventh-century CE glass *série 2.1* seems to have absorbed a certain volume of the Mn-decolourised glass, providing it with another kind of its spread, in the form of compositional diffusion. The emerging picture of significant technological transformations in primary glass-making, which tentatively took place at the turn of the sixth century CE is far from being clearly outlined yet. However, this picture includes elements of gradual change of raw material quality (seen in sand geochemistry), as well as anthropogenic changes in the production formula (Figure 3.2), sourcing of the ingredients (e.g. change in the Mn-bearing additive: Cholakova et al. 2016, 630) and a distinct approach in primary batch compilation with systematic cullet addition, possibly on a large scale.

Future research, preferably on diagnostic glass assemblages from stratified sites with tight absolute dates, is necessary to shed light on these dynamics of the glass industry and what they can tell us about their socio-cultural milieu in Late Antiquity. The characterisation and proper recognition of different compositional glass groups in particular site contexts is important as a means to identify their various 'travels' through space (in terms of geographical distribution of raw material, circulation of finished vessel groups, and even distinct personal possessions) and though time (in terms of reuse and recycling), and how these 'travels' relate to the general processes of economy and technology.

Acknowledgements

This research formed part of the PhD project of AC at the UCL Institute of Archaeology, as early stage researcher within the NARNIA (New

Archaeological Research Network for Integrating Approaches to ancient material studies) ITN funded by the FP7 (Grant agreement no.: 265010) and coordinated by V. Kassianidou, University of Cyprus. The support of the National Institute of Archaeology with Museum – Bulgarian Academy of Sciences and personally of V. Dinchev, M. Ivanov and L. Doncheva-Petkova is gratefully acknowledged. The sample export permit was granted by the Ministry of Culture, Republic of Bulgaria and analyses were possible thanks to the work and kind support of K. Reeves and P. Connolly (UCL), J. Lankton and B. Gratuze (IRAMAT). We are indebted to I. Freestone for helpful discussions, to S. Stamenković for the comments regarding the chronology of the Serbian sites, and to the editors of this volume for their patience. This publication was partly made possible by NPRP grant 7-776-6-024 from the Qatar National Research Fund (a member of Qatar Foundation). The statements made herein are solely the responsibility of the authors.

References

Adam-Veleni, P. 2010. *Glass Cosmos: Catalogue*. Thessaloniki: Archaeological Museum of Thessaloniki.

Brems, D. and Degryse, P. 2014. 'Western Mediterranean Sands for Ancient Glass Making'. In *Glass-Making in the Greco-Roman World: Results of the ARCHGLASS Project* (Studies in Archaeological Sciences 4), edited by P. Degryse, 27–49. Leuven: Leuven University Press.

Cholakova, A. 2009. 'Part VI: Glass Vessels from Gradishteto'. In *Bulgarian–British Archaeological Excavations of Gradishteto Near the Village of Dichin, Veliko Tarnovo Region, 1996–2003: The Results of the Bulgarian Team* (Excavations and Research 39), edited by V. Dinchev, 257–307. Sofia: National Institute of Archaeology – Bulgarian Academy of Sciences (in Bulgarian).

Cholakova, A. 2014. 'Networks of Distribution at the Margins of the Empire: Late Antique Glass Vessels from the Lower Danube Region'. In *The NARNIA Project: Integrating Approaches to Ancient Material Studies*, edited by V. Kassianidou and M. Dikomitou-Eliadou, 94–104. Nicosia: The NARNIA Project and the Archaeological Research Unit, University of Cyprus.

Cholakova, A. 2016. 'Networks of Distribution at the Margins of the Empire: Late Antique Glass Vessels from the Lower Danube Region'. Unpublished PhD thesis, UCL.

Cholakova, A., Rehren, Th. and Freestone, I. 2016. 'Compositional Identification of 6th c. AD Glass from the Lower Danube'. *Journal of Archaeological Science: Reports* 7: 625–32.

Conte, S., Chinni, T., Arletti, R. and Vandini, M. 2014. 'Butrint (Albania) Between Eastern and Western Mediterranean Glass Production: EPMA and LA-ICP-MS of Late Antique and Early Medieval Finds'. *Journal of Archaeological Science* 49: 6–20.

Drauschke, J. and Greiff, S. 2010. 'Chemical Aspects of Byzantine Glass from Caričin Grad/Iustiniana Prima (Serbia)'. In *Glass in Byzantium – Production, Usage, Analyses* (RGZM – Tagungen 8), edited by J. Drauschke and D. Keller, 25–46. Mainz: Römisch-Germanisches Zentralmuseum.

Foster, H. and Jackson, C. 2010. 'The Composition of Late Romano-British Colourless Glass: Glass Production and Consumption'. *Journal of Archaeological Science* 37: 3068–80.

Foy, D., Picon, M., Vichy, M. and Thirion-Merle, V. 2003. 'Caractérisation des verres de l'Antiquité tardive en Méditerranée occidentale: l'émergence de nouveaux courants commerciaux'. In *Échanges et Commerce du Verre dans le Monde Antique. Actes du colloque de l'Association Française pour l'Archéologie du Verre, 2001* (Monographies Instrumentum 24), edited by D. Foy and M.-D. Nenna, 41–78. Montagnac, Monique Mergoil.

Foy, D., Thirion-Merle, V. and Vichy, M. 2004. 'Contribution à l'étude des verres antiques décolorés à l'antimoine'. *Revue d'Archéométrie* 28: 169–77.

Foy, D., Vrielynck, O., Van Wersch, L. and Cabart, H. 2010. 'Les coupelles à décor chrétien soufflées dans un moule (seconde moitié V^e-première moitié VIe siècle. État de la documentation'. In *D'Ennion au Val Saint-Lambert. Le Verre Soufflé-Moulé. Actes des 23e Rencontres de l'Association Française pour l'Archéologie du Verre* (Scientia Artis 5), edited by C. Fontaine-Hodiamont, 267–313. Bruxelles: Institut Royal du Patrimoine Artistique.

Freestone, I., Jackson-Tal, R. and Tal, O. 2008. 'Raw Glass and the Production of Glass Vessels at Late Byzantine Apollonia – Arsuf, Israel'. *Journal of Glass Studies* 50: 67–80.

Fünfschilling, S. and Laflı, E. 2013. *Hadrianopolis II: Glasfunde des 6. und 7. Jahrhunderts aus Hadrianopolis, Paphlagonien (Türkei)* (Internationale Archäologie 123). Rahden, Westf.: Verlag Marie Leidorf.

Gallo, F., Marcante, A., Silvestri, A. and Molin, G. 2014. 'The Glass of the "Casa delle Bestie Ferite": A First Systematic Archaeometric Study on Late Roman Vessels from Aquileia. *Journal of Archaeological Science* 41: 7–20.

Jackson, C. and Paynter, S. 2016. 'A Great Big Melting Pot: Exploring Patterns of Glass Supply, Consumption and Recycling in Roman Coppergate, York'. *Archaeometry* 58: 68–95.

Laiou, A. 2002. 'Economic and Noneconomic Exchange'. In *The Economic History of Byzantium from the Seventh through the Fifteenth Century* (Dumbarton Oaks Studies 39), edited by A. Laiou, 681–96. Washington, DC: Dumbarton Oaks Research Library and Collection.

McCormick, M. 2011. *Origins of the European Economy. Communications and Commerce A.D. 300–900*. Cambridge and New York: Cambridge University Press.

Maltoni, S., Chinni, T., Vandini, M., Cirelli, E., Silvestri, A. and Molin, G. 2015. 'Archaeological and Archaeometric Study of the Glass Finds from the Ancient Harbour of Classe (Ravenna – Italy): New Evidence'. *Heritage Science* 3:13. doi: 10.1186/s40494-015-0034-5.

Maltoni, S., Silvestri, A., Marcante, A. and Molin, G. 2016. 'The Transition from Roman to Late Antique Glass: New Insights from the Domus of Tito Macro in Aquileia (Italy)'. *Journal of Archaeological Science* 73: 1–16.

Marić-Stojanović, M., Šmit, Ž., Glumac. M. and Mutić, J. 2015. 'PIXE–PIGE Investigation of Roman Imperial Vessels and Window Glass from Mt. Kosmaj, Serbia (Moesia Superior)'. *Journal of Archaeological Science: Reports* 1: 53–63.

Meek, A. 2013. 'Gold Glass in Late Antiquity: Scientific Analysis of the British Museum Collection'. In *New Light on Old Glass: Recent Research on Byzantine Glass and Mosaics* (British Museum Research Publication 179), edited by C. Entwistle and L. James, 121–30. London: British Museum.

Morrisson, C. 2012. 'Introduction'. In *Trade and Markets in Byzantium*, edited by C. Morrisson, 1–9. Washington, DC: Dumbarton Oaks Research Library and Collection.

Paynter, S. 2008. 'Experiments in the Reconstruction of Roman Wood-Fired Glass-Working Furnaces: Waste Products and Their Formation Processes'. *Journal of Glass Studies* 50: 271–90.

Rehren, Th. and Brüggler, M. 2015. 'Composition and Production of Late Antique Glass Bowls Type Helle'. *Journal of Archaeological Science: Reports* 3: 171–80.

Rehren, Th., and Cholakova, A. 2014. 'Glass Supply and Consumption in the Late Roman and Early Byzantine Site *Dichin*, Northern Bulgaria'. In *Neighbours and Successors of Rome: Traditions of Glass Production and use in Europe and the Middle East in the Later 1st Millennium AD*, edited by D. Keller, J. Price and C. Jackson, 83–94. Oxford: Oxbow Books.

Schibille, N., Meek, A., Tobias, B., Entwistle, C., Avisseau-Broustet, M., DaMota, H. and Gratuze, B. 2016. 'Comprehensive Chemical Characterisation of Byzantine Glass Weights', *PLoS ONE* 11 (12): e0168289. doi: 10.1371/journal.pone.0168289.

Schibille, N., Sterrett-Krause, A. and Freestone, I. C. 2017. 'Glass Groups, Glass Supply and Recycling in Late Roman Carthage'. *Archaeological and Anthropological Sciences* 9: 1223–41.

Silvestri, A., Molin, G. and Salviulo, G. 2008. 'The Colourless Glass of *Iulia Felix*'. *Journal of Archaeological Science* 35: 331–41.

Silvestri, A., Tonietto, S. and Molin, G. 2011. 'The Palaeo-Christian Glass Mosaic of St Prosdocimus (Padova, Italy): Archaeometric Characterisation of "gold" Tesserae'. *Journal of Archaeological Science* 38: 3402–14.

Siu, I., Henderson, J. and Faber, E. 2017. 'The Production and Circulation of Carthagian Glass Under the Rule of the Romans and the Vandals (Fourth to Sixth Century AD): A Chemical Investigation'. *Archaeometry* 59: 255–73.

Smith, T., Henderson, J. and Faber, E. 2016. 'Early Byzantine Glass Supply and Consumption: The Case of Dichin, Bulgaria'. In *Recent Advances in the*

Scientific Research on Ancient Glass and Glaze (Series on Archaeology and History of Science in China 2), edited by F. Gan, Q. Li and J. Henderson, 207–31. New Jersey: World Scientific/World Century.

Vichy, M., Thirion-Merle, V. and Picon, M. 2007. 'Note sur le recyclage du verre dans l'antiquité et sur les groupes de recyclage'. *Bulletin de l'Association Française pour l'Archéologie du Verre*, 55–7.

Whitehouse, D. 2003. '"Things That Travelled": The Surprising Case of Raw Glass'. *Early Medieval Europe* 12: 301–5.

4

Glass production and consumption in Cyprus in Late Antiquity (fourth–seventh century CE)

Peter Cosyns and Andrea Ceglia

Abstract

At the economic crossroad of the eastern Mediterranean, Cyprus provides an ideal case study for the investigation of changing trade networks in the eastern Mediterranean during Late Antiquity. This chapter presents the preliminary results from ongoing research on Late Antique glass vessels from Cypriot early Christian basilicas. A combination of archaeological data with chemical and optical spectroscopic measurements allows the characterisation of specific vessel production groups that can be associated with either imported or locally produced glassware.

The ongoing research focuses on the glass vessels from ecclesiastical contexts from the fourth to seventh century CE, which formed a significant component within the church design as lighting devices. A uniform distribution pattern of specific glass vessels within ecclesiastical buildings not only enables a comparison of ecclesiastical contexts within Cyprus during Late Antiquity in the first place but allows also a wider investigation on the material from similar contexts throughout the entire eastern Mediterranean.

Introduction

Defining specific groups of vessel production related to imported or locally produced glassware falls within material culture studies, which increasingly focus on the better understanding of economic and cultural networks (Wellman 1983; Rutherford 2007; Riedel 2013). The application of network theory to material culture has already proven to be useful for the understanding of diachronic socio-cultural processes that occurred within a large-scale area (Brughmans 2010). However, for the Mediterranean world these models have hitherto been based solely on pottery studies, which could lead to biased conclusions. Moreover, the current insights concerning the eastern Mediterranean in Antiquity are predominantly based on pottery evidence from Hellenistic and early Roman times (Peacock 1982; Peacock and Williams 1986; Lund 1999, 2006; Lund et al. 2006; Fenn and Römer-Strehl 2013), and, generally, the resulting model(s) of regional idiosyncrasies and inter-regional trade relations are extrapolated from these earlier periods to the Late Antique period. However, since the socio-economic and political situation in the late Roman empire differed significantly from the previous period, it is unlikely that these extrapolations fully reflect the socio-economic situation in Late Antiquity. Therefore, it is essential to examine different types of consumer goods from Late Antiquity itself in order to test the validity of the prevailing models. As a result, a more complete and balanced overview of the connectivity patterns and interrelated diversity in the eastern Mediterranean during Late Antiquity can be acquired.

Although Bonifay's study (2004) has already shown that pottery is a good medium for the study of inter-regional networks in the western Mediterranean during Late Antiquity, it appears that for the eastern Mediterranean world, glass would also be a most appropriate medium with which to evaluate economical models of connectivity. Indeed, glass appears abundantly in the archaeological record of the late Roman period. In particular, ecclesiastical contexts of the fourth to mid-seventh century CE are relevant in examining evidence for commercial activity during Late Antiquity, because glass vessels were a significant component within the church design, as lighting devices: after all, from the Constantinian period onwards the erection of a monolithic church building programme resulted in intensive building activities based on a common design plan including the lighting, i.e. lamps and window sheets (Theis 2001; James 2006).

In previous research we discovered that in eastern Mediterranean ecclesiastical contexts specific lamp types were intended for the same specific spots within the building (Cosyns and Ceglia forthcoming). The fact that they are always found at precise locations within the early Christian basilicas and in association with other specific material emphasises the specific use of particular types of Late Antique glass vessels. This uniform distribution pattern of similar glass vessels within ecclesiastical buildings enables the comparison of ecclesiastical contexts within the entire eastern Mediterranean, and, consequently, the investigation of patterns of local versus a so-called 'globalised' empire wide production and consumption.

Cyprus is an appropriate case study because the island was an important player on the east to west and south to north trade routes in Late Antiquity (Mitchell 2007; Lawall and Lund 2013). It was, for instance, the main hub for food supply from Egypt to Constantinople. Driven by a continuous economic growth, this prosperous Roman province displayed an increasing building programme of Christian basilicas between the fourth and mid-seventh century CE. Due to its central geographical position in the eastern Mediterranean and the prevailing sea currents, Cyprus acted as the crossroad of the three major economic actors in the eastern Mediterranean during Late Antiquity: Constantinople, Antioch and Alexandria. The Levant and Egypt were major glass production centres and Cyprus not only consumed raw glass from both centres (Freestone et al. 2002) but also imported finished glass objects from both. However, the exact diachronic distribution patterns have yet to be investigated, although these data for Late Antique Cyprus could be valuable for the exploration of the complexity of the glass consumption in the eastern Mediterranean during Late Antiquity. Therefore the intrinsic advantages of studying Cypriot Late Antique glass material have not yet been exploited and research on Cypriot Late Antique glass has remained restricted to the material study of glass in site excavation reports (Manning 2002; McClellan 2003), or to chemical analyses of a very restricted amount of samples from a single site (Freestone et al. 2002). Finally, the study of Late Antique glass from Cyprus would represent a significant addition to the ongoing research on production, distribution and consumption of late Roman and early Byzantine glass (e.g., Laflı 2009; Drauschke and Keller 2010; Fünfschilling and Laflı 2013; Keller et al. 2014).

The present chapter provides an introductory typological overview of the archaeological glass finds from the early Christian basilica of Yeroskipou-Ayioi Pente, and the archaeometric study of the glass from this site as well as from two other sites on the Cypriot south coast: Maroni-Petrera and Kalavasos-Kopetra (Ceglia et al. 2015, 2016). This research will be extended to a number of other sites, e.g. Alassa-Ayia Mavri, Katalymmata ton Plakoton and Ayios Kononas (Figure 4.1) in order to verify the possible regional differences between the Cypriot

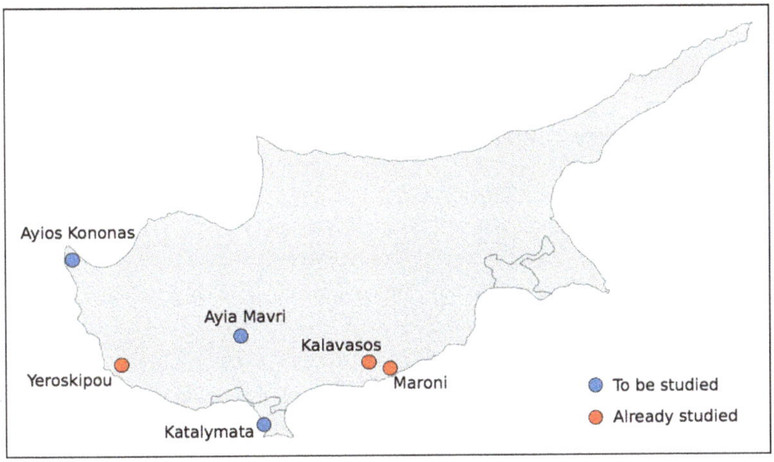

Figure 4.1 Map of Cyprus with all the relevant sites.

coastline and the more inland sites, and to refine our general knowledge of glass distribution in Late Antique Cyprus.

Impact of sea currents and wind-driven circulations on the distribution of glass in (Late) Antiquity

The distribution of consumer goods such as glass vessels, is in some way a reflection of the economic evolution of the various regions, resulting from the connectivity between the different regions. It is clear from the sea currents and wind-driven circulations within the eastern Mediterranean that Cyprus acted as a perfect hub within the trade network between the metropolitan cities Constantinople, Antioch and Alexandria (Morton 2001). An additional but key concern to this issue is the island's adjacency to both major centres of raw glass production and consequently Cyprus cannot simply be considered a consumer of the ubiquitous glass commodities but also a dispatcher of both Levantine and Egyptian raw glasses towards the West, though large amounts of glass were recycled. The early Christian basilicas in Cyprus provide ample but very consistent material, as vessel glass is almost limited to lamps. It would be very useful to extend the research with a comparative study on the lighting devices in glass from contemporaneous ecclesiastical buildings in Anatolia, Cyrene, Egypt, Greece and the Levant so to define regional idiosyncrasies as well as widespread commodities. The distribution of glass resulted from a long-distance sea trade on a large scale (e.g. Nenna 2008), and it is essential to take into consideration the wind-driven and sea currents to better understand the distribution pattern of the Levantine and Egyptian raw glass and finished products. Until now, the circulation arrows on the maps have represented practical visualisations of the trade routes between the supplier and receiver of raw materials or consumer goods to make clear the interaction between two overseas areas. However, Knappett et al. (2008, 1009–10) have pointed out that commonly, site interactions 'are simply drawn as lines, without weight or direction', while the main interest of examining inter-site networks is to define the impact of each site within the interchange and how this could have taken place. Outlining the character of the mutual connectivity between two settlements advances understanding of those aspects that are under-represented in historical sources, such as the interregional economical organisation. The investigation of settlement patterning in Antiquity has always been strongly influenced by an oversimplified theoretical approach based on the actual distance between sites. It is not enough to calculate travel distances that people can afford over land by walking or by using a chariot or over water by boat via rivers, along the coastline by cabotage or through the open sea. Such assessment needs to be verified in view of natural influences like, for instance, the prevailing natural navigation conditions. For example, the location of the Milesian settlement of Sinope, halfway along the northern Anatolian coastline, was not coincidental as from there they could easily make use of the prevailing surface sea current heading north to the Crimea where Miletus again founded various colonies at the northern Black Sea coast, e.g. Panticapaeum (Kerch) at the eastern side of the Crimean Peninsula along the Kerch Strait (Gates 2011, 304–5) (Figure 4.2). From there, ships could take advantage of a current heading west towards Romania and back to the Bosporus to return to the Mediterranean Sea, or heading eastward to the Caucasus. As there were no power-driven ships in Antiquity, seafarers were at the mercy of currents and winds, so that it would have been frequently necessary to take a detour to reach a desired destination.

The Strait of Gibraltar was important as the source of all surface currents and tides (Morton 2001; Bergamasco and Malanotte-Rizzoli 2010). Dividing at the western coast of Sicily, the surface currents, on the one hand, head south towards the North African Gulf of Sirte or directing further eastwards towards the Levantine Sea and, on the other hand, turn north to head along the Italian coast. From there they either curl counter clockwise back southwards along the Sardinian east coast

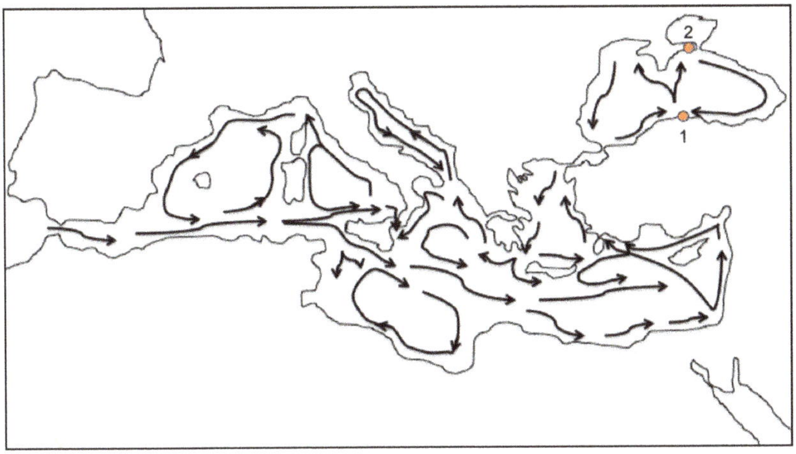

Figure 4.2 Prevailing summer surface currents and tides in the Mediterranean and Black Sea (based on Morton 2001, fig. 21) with indication of (1) Sinope (Sinop) and (2) Panticapaeum (Kertch).

within the Tyrrhenian Sea, or head further north into the Ligurian Sea along the French coastline and back south along the Spanish coast in the Balearic Sea (Figure 4.2). The sea currents in the Levantine Sea head north along the Levantine coast and turn counter clockwise around Cyprus towards Rhodes and Crete, making both islands logical passage stops or final destinations. In particular, Rhodes has been demonstrated to have played an important strategic role in trade as pivot for the Aegean to (re)distribute raw materials and finished products north to the Black Sea along the Anatolian west coast or towards Crete and the southern Greek mainland (Gabrielsen 1997; Coullié and Filimonos-Tsopotou 2014; Deligiannakis 2016).

In addition to sea currents and tides it is important to have help from the winds in order to increase speed and ease navigation when sailing or sail upstream. The knowledge of seasonal variations in strength and directions of the prevalent winds indicates that trade experienced cyclical undertakings concentrated from April to October as the summer winds (i.e. the Etesians) are more steady than the winter winds (i.e. Bora and Sirocco) (Morton 2001). Another factor to be considered is that ancient seafarers were not restricted to secure coastline routes, i.e. cabotage. Merchant ships also appreciated short cuts through the deep open sea when heading towards specific destinations (Morton 2001).

Considering Cyprus, two routes from Egypt turn alongside the Sinai. A first route heads towards the Levantine coast and up to Anatolia supplying the island at Salamis and Kition via a minor sea current that links east Cyprus with the Syrian coast. A second route goes into the open sea towards the west end of Cyprus where Nea Paphos is situated. Technological innovations in shipbuilding and sailing conditions possibly influenced the relocation of the former capital of Palaepaphos in the late Classical period, which until then must have been supplied through cabotage coming from the northern Levant. This element requires a detailed evaluation as it tackles the issue of the impact of a single destination trade between Egypt and Cyprus importing exclusively Egyptian material, as opposed to itinerant merchant ships sailing along the Levantine coast to enter Cyprus from the East, then sailing clockwise around the island with an assortment of Egyptian and Levantine commodities.

Objectives

The main objective of the research is to better understand Cyprus' economic role in the eastern Mediterranean during Late Antiquity by means of research into glass from archaeological contexts. A first concern in the assessment of the glass production and consumption in Cyprus is to determine the impact of the two major glass-producing regions, i.e. the Levant and Egypt. Despite the fact that this allows the calculation of the ratio of imported glass of both production centres, it does not show whether the glass was imported as raw glass chunks or as finished artefacts or whether Cyprus was supplied with both categories of material. To detect a possible local production of finished artefacts in secondary glass workshops, a techno-typological study is required, because technological, formal and decorative idiosyncrasies can be markers of specific workshops. In order to differentiate local Cypriot production from imported artefacts, it is necessary to compare vessel types found in Cyprus with those from published sites in the Levant and Egypt. The resulting typology will enable a distribution pattern of imported and locally produced glass vessels. In this way, possible intra-regional differences will be recognised.

In addition, Late Antique Cypriot glass will be evaluated on (1) an intra-site level to better understand its use and function within early Christian basilicas and on (2) an inter-site level to identify the Cypriot consumption pattern. Finally, the Cypriot production and consumption patterns will be compared to those of the surrounding areas in the eastern Mediterranean. In this way, the project can add valuable information to the study of the trans-regional trade and connectivity during Late Antiquity.

The research questions fall under two headings – glass production and glass consumption. The aims concerning glass production are:

- to identify the compositional groups of raw glass in order to define the provenance of the imported glasses, and thus the origin of the glass types present in ecclesiastical contexts in Cyprus – i.e., Egypt and Levant;
- to establish the ratio of imported glass from the two main primary glass production centres so as to elucidate the varying impact of both glass-supplying centres per ecclesiastical context;
- to distinguish possible Cypriot vessel types (shapes, decoration, technological features, and glass colours) from published Late Antique glass vessels from fourth- to seventh-century CE ecclesiastical contexts and secondary workshops in other eastern Mediterranean regions;
- to determine which glass types were used to produce the Cypriot vessel types (matching glass types and Cypriot vessel types);
- to assess in which glass types the imported finished products were produced (matching glass types and imported vessel types).

The research goals regarding the glass consumption are:

- to characterise the glass vessel distribution pattern on Cyprus to identify possible regional differences;
- to consider whether different regions on Cyprus had privileged trade connections with either the Levant or Egypt (by inter-site evaluation);
- to assess the specific use in the ecclesiastical contexts of the identified glass vessels (by intra-site evaluation);
- to evaluate the prevailing economic model based on historical research and on pottery studies and propose an alternative one with the glass data integrated;
- to assess the interaction and connectivity between the various regions in the eastern Mediterranean during the Late Antique period.

First results from study of the material

The glass from the early Christian basilicas Ayioi Pente at Yeroskipou (Cosyns and Ceglia forthcoming), Maroni-Petrera (Manning 2002) and Kalavasos-Kopetra (Rautman 2003) shows very clearly that the vessels form the largest part of the material retrieved. Despite the fact that windowpanes, tesserae and jewellery made in glass are also frequently attested, these categories remain rather minor groups within the glass assemblages (Figure 4.3). Although the results of the glass research of the more remote early Christian basilica of Katalymmata ton Plakoton on the Akrotiri peninsula remains very preliminary and cannot be included in detail, we noticed an unexpected large quantity of windowpanes there. Further investigation will indicate whether the glass tesserae are also still present in abundance. The first idea is that the sites of Yeroskipou, Maroni and Kalavasos were quarried soon after their destruction in the mid-seventh century CE whereas the quite isolated early Christian basilica of Katalymmata must have remained concealed and protected from looting. This Akrotiri site will form a major section in the analysis and assessment of the glass assemblages from the early Christian basilicas in Cyprus.

A great number of the fragments remain non-diagnostic and are consequently not attributable to a specific vessel type; however, lamps and goblets form the largest proportions of determined vessel shapes (Figure 4.4; Table 4.1). So far no beakers, cups, dishes, plates or jars have been identified in the early Christian basilica of Yeroskipou and with the exception of the lamps and stemmed goblets (most likely also used as

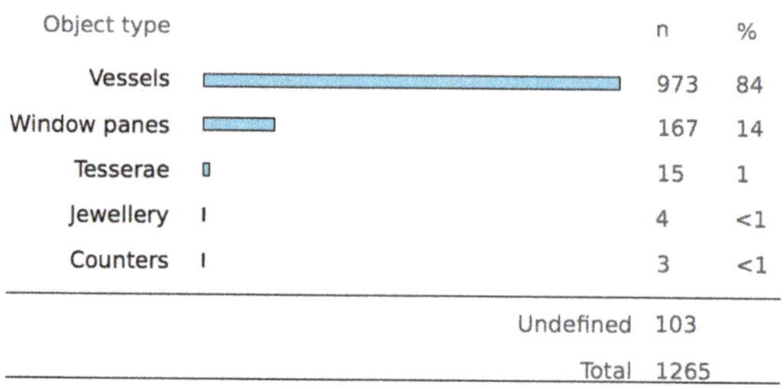

Figure 4.3 The different functional types of glass material from the early Christian basilica of Yeroskipou-Ayioi Pente.

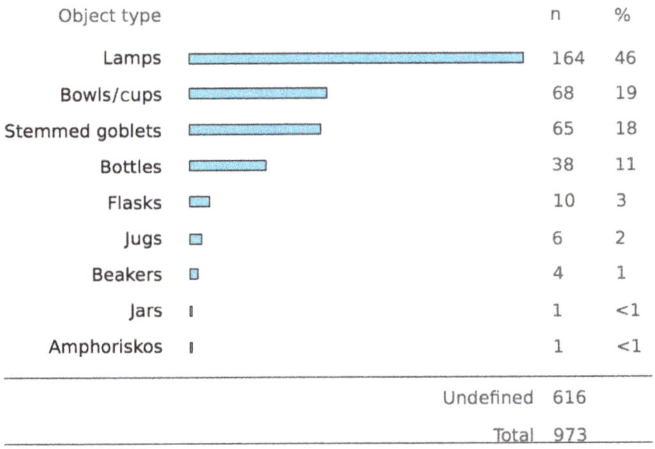

Figure 4.4 The various glass vessel shapes from the early Christian basilica from Yeroskipou-Ayioi Pente.

lamps) all other catalogued vessel shapes – i.e. flasks, bowls, bottles and jugs – remain minor categories.

The glass lamps form the largest part of the glass vessels. When also considering the stemmed goblets or so-called wine-cups as lamps, lighting vessels covers 85 per cent of all identified vessels (Figure 4.4). This assessment is likely to be a consequence of lamps and goblets being the easier forms to define, and in particular because only very few types occur. More than a quarter of the material remains indefinite, but most likely these undiagnostic fragments were derived from very thin-walled vessel shapes.

The high numbers of lamp fragments retrieved from the basilica Yeroskipou-Ayioi Pente are limited to five specific shapes – the hemispherical bowl-lamp (Figure 4.5a); the shallow conical bowl-lamp with handles (Figure 4.5b-c); the hollow-stemmed lamp (Figure 4.5d); the knobbed-base tall conical lamp (Figure 4.5e); and the stemmed goblets (Figure 4.5f). Despite the fact that three types – hemispherical and conical bowl-lamps and stemmed goblets – can stand on their bases, all five were almost certainly used as hanging oil lamps with a burning internal wick.

Most of the 297 lamps defined so far are stemmed goblets and hollow-stemmed hanging lamps (Figure 4.4). It is significant that undecorated hollow-stemmed lamps with rounded end account for almost all the fragments recorded at the sites of Yeroskipou-Ayioi Pente,

Table 4.1 Lamp shapes from the early Christian basilica of Yeroskipou

	Hemispherical bowl-lamp	*Shallow conical bowl-lamp*	*Stemmed lamp for polykandela*[1]	*Knobbed-base conical lamp*	*Stemmed goblets*
Features	- decorated and undecorated - everted rim with cut edge - no handles - mould-blown honeycomb pattern or plain free-blown - normally without foot but can also occur with a stemmed foot	- undecorated - rounded or vertically folded rim - three vertical handles - kicked-in base - no foot - sometimes with a cylindrical tube inside	- undecorated - rounded rim - hemispherical body - funnel-shaped bottom - hollow stem - no foot	- undecorated - everted rim with cut edge - tall conical shaped body - large globular hollow knobbed base	- undecorated - rounded rim - cylindrical body - hollow or solid stem - discoid foot can be flat, slightly conical and strongly conical; rim tubular or rounded
Correlations	The honeycomb decorated bowls described as a ritual/ liturgic objects (Stern 1985, 39); Considered a Syro-Palestinian product. Shape reminiscent of Sassanian facetted bowls in rock-crystal and in thick decolourised glass	Crowfoot and Harden 1931 type C (4th–7th c. CE); Isings 1957 form 134 (4th–5th c. CE); Uboldi 1995 type I.1 (4th–8th c. CE); Hadad 1998 type 1; Gill 2002 type 1–5 A variant of the so-called handled bowl-lamps includes a glass tube at the centre of the inner base that functioned as a wick holder[2] (see Hadad 1998 type 7)	Crowfoot and Harden 1931 type B2b; Uboldi 1995 type IV.2; Hadad 1998 type 4 (5th–early 8th c. CE); Gill 2002 type 6	Comparisons are known from Jerusalem, dated 7th–9th century CE, and Corinth (Davidson 1952, 121, pl. 60: 802) but the example from Thessaloniki is dated late 4th–5th century CE (Crowfoot and Harden 1931, 202, pls. xxviii, 11–12)	Isings 1957 form 111 (Crowfoot and Harden 1931; Stern 1985; Olcay 2001) This type of lamp is dated late 4th–6th century CE

	Hemispherical bowl-lamp	*Shallow conical bowl-lamp*	*Stemmed lamp for polykandela*[1]	*Knobbed-base conical lamp*	*Stemmed goblets*
Illustrations	Figure 4.5a	Figures 4.5b–c	Figure 4.5d	Figure 4.5e	Figure 4.5f
quantity	2 ex.	11 ex.	81 ex.	2 ex.	50 ex.
percentage	1.2%	6.7%	49.0%	1.2%	30.3%

1 A good example of a Byzantine *polykandelon* for the suspension of 7 stemmed lamps – 6 in a circle and 1 central in the Maltese cross – has been excavated in Corinth, Greece (Davidson 1952, 128, pl. 63: 859).

2 Due to the degree of fragmentation it cannot excluded that the preserved rim and handle fragments of type 1 are of the variant with wick-tube. Only base fragments allow this identification, which may result in a much lower number of the handled bowl-lamps with wick-tube.

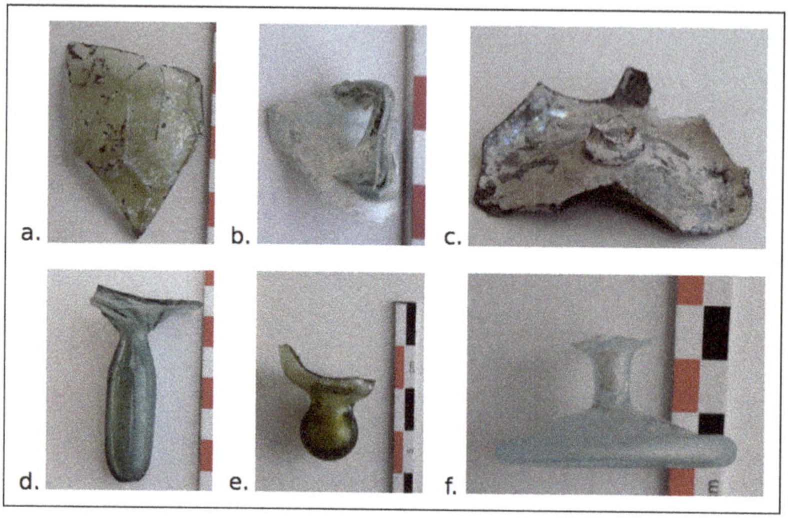

Figure 4.5 (a) honeycomb decorated hemispherical bowl (ID no. 1); (b) handled bowl-lamp (ID no. 65); (c) handled bowl-lamp with wick-tube (ID no. 634); (d) undecorated hollow-stemmed lamp with rounded end (ID no. 103); (e) conical lamp with knobbed base (ID no. 569); (f) stemmed goblet or so-called wineglass (ID no. 16).

Maroni-Petrera and Kalavasos-Kopetra. Lamps with solid stem – plain or knobbed – and hollow-stemmed lamps with pointed end are represented only by single pieces. Sometimes sets of the hollow-stemmed hanging lamp were found together, making the use of polykandela almost certain in specific areas of the basilica. The large quantities of hollow-stemmed hanging lamps in transparent pale blue-green, pale blue, pale yellow-green or green glass from the early Christian basilica at Yeroskipou demonstrate that different glasses were contemporaneously in use. The very few hemispherical and conical bowl-lamps (Figure 4.5a–c) and the conical lamps with knobbed base (Figure 4.5e) are to be seen as special lamps, which were used individually on specific places in the basilica. For instance the mould-blown hemispherical bowl-lamp with honeycomb pattern (Figure 4.5a) is said to have functioned as a lamp hanging on a prominent place reminiscent of the piece in deep blue glass from Anemurium, Turkey (Stern 1985, 39).

First results through archaeometric study

In a recent paper we discussed the glass consumption patterns from Yeroskipou-Ayioi Pente, Kalavasos-Kopetra and Maroni-Petrera from a material sciences perspective (Ceglia et al. 2016). Large sets of samples were chemically and optically analysed. Chemical analysis was used as standard approach to study ancient glass because it is a good method to categorise glass fragments. With the development of a methodological approach with optical spectroscopy we were able to increase significantly the quantity of examined material on their composition by discussing the relations between colour and chemical composition.

First we have carried out an *in situ* campaign with UV–vis–NIR spectroscopy. This method allowed us to obtain the transmission spectra on 416 'naturally' coloured glass fragments, 206 from the early Christian basilica of Yeroskipou-Ayioi Pente, 144 from the site of Maroni-Petrera and 67 from Kalavasos-Kopetra (Ceglia et al. 2016).

In addition, we have analysed a selected set of 179 glass fragments from those three sites by using wavelength dispersive electron probe microanalysis (EPMA) to characterise their composition in terms of major and minor elements. A part of these samples were selected on the basis of the results from the *in situ* optical analysis, while the remaining glasses were selected among the material that could not be analysed optically due to the specific shape, e.g. tubular stems of the hollow-stemmed lamps (Figure 4.5d)(Ceglia et al. 2015).

On the basis of the archaeometric work we have distinguished six glass types on the basis of the chemical composition: Levantine 1, HLIMT, two types of HIMT (named HIMTa and HIMTb), Egypt 1 and HIT. Apart from Levantine 1 glass, which certainly has a Syro-Palestinian origin, all the other recognised glass types are most likely to have been produced in Egypt. The analysis of the chemical composition of the Late Antique glass samples from Cypriot settlements contributes to an improved interpretation of the HIMT families. We have, for instance, proposed that HLIMT glass is almost certainly a separate Egyptian primary production that started to be manufactured during the sixth century CE onwards (Ceglia et al. 2015; Cholakova et al. 2015).

At the current stage of our research we can state that the island was supplied with raw glass and/or finished objects by both Egyptian and Syro-Palestinian primary producers. The majority of glasses belong to three groups: Levantine, HIMT and HLIMT. Two other types, HIT and Egypt 1 are represented in minor quantities, suggesting that objects made of this type of glass very likely have been imported as finished objects – either as consumer goods or as gifts (Ceglia et al. 2015).

In Yeroskipou-Ayioi Pente there are similar quantities of Levantine and Egyptian materials, while Egyptian glass is limited in Maroni-Petrera and nearly absent in Kalavasos-Kopetra. Such glass consumption pattern leads to two possible interpretations. On the one hand, it may reflect the trade networks as determined by the prevailing sea currents, indicating that east Cyprus is connected to the Syro-Palestinian coast, while west Cyprus is more oriented towards the Aegean areas and Egypt.

Alternatively, data may reflect a chronological evolution of glass imports, as the production of HIMT dominated the market during the fifth century CE, declined by the end of that century and definitely stopped by the mid-sixth century CE. The consequence of such a chronological interpretation of the HIMT-presence in the three basilicas implies that: (1) Ayioi Pente in Yeroskipou must have received large quantities of glass vessels during the fifth century CE that were discarded after the destruction of the first basilica phase, and accordingly should be linked to the pre-Justinian building phase (Cosyns and Ceglia forthcoming); (2) that the glass assemblage of the early Christian basilica of Maroni-Petrera is to be dated at the end of the fifth century CE; and (3) that the excavated structures of the different early Christian buildings at Kalavasos-Kopetra do not precede the mid-sixth century CE. In this case, the HLIMT glass should then be linked to the Justinian building phase of the considered sites because HLIMT glass was a new Egyptian production of the sixth century CE, that briefly took a large share of the market from the eastern Mediterranean to the western provinces. No tangible chronological implication can be ascribed to the Levantine material because this glass type was regularly produced and supplied to Cyprus through the period under consideration with no major changes in chemical composition.

The latter hypothesis concurs with recent research on the Late Antique glass from three Bulgarian sites (Cholakova et al. 2015). Based on very well-dated material they noticed a similar evolution showing the use of HIMT, HIT and Levantine glass during the fifth century CE, whereas the dominant glass type from their sixth-century CE contexts corresponds with our HLIMT glass.

Single melting event

Among the material from Maroni-Petrera, some objects had an analytically identical composition, meaning that they belong to the same melting event. The most striking example consists of five samples coming from the same batch (Figure 4.6, Table 4.2). Four samples were from the stems of hollow-stemmed lamps and an additional one was from a wall fragment. The minimum number of individual objects (MNI) is four objects and they are of a Levantine 1 composition.

The benefit of assessing archaeological glass assemblages with recognised batches is the possibility to connect specific typological features of the objects with the manufacturing process of a distinct workshop in a single moment and perhaps even by the same artisan. Moreover, from an historical point of view, it can be an indication that objects were commissioned by the church on a particular moment (Freestone et al., 2009).

Figure 4.6 Hollow-stemmed lamps of a single batch from the early Christian basilica of Maroni-Petrera.

Table 4.2 Chemical composition by EPMA of the five hollow-stemmed lamps from the early Christian basilica of Maroni-Petrera demonstrating they are from a single batch event (Ceglia et al. 2015)

	SF41	*SF83*	*SF84*	*SF77*	*SF36*
SiO_2	67.4	67.7	67.9	67.9	67.1
Al_2O_3	3.18	3.18	3.20	3.13	3.19
Fe_2O_3	0.61	0.61	0.61	0.62	0.63
TiO_2	0.09	0.09	0.09	0.09	0.09
MnO	0.06	0.06	0.05	0.06	0.07
Na_2O	16.3	16.4	16.2	16.2	16.1
K_2O	0.61	0.62	0.62	0.60	0.63
CaO	11.0	11.0	11.1	10.9	11.2
MgO	0.75	0.75	0.75	0.74	0.76
Cl	0.78	0.77	0.74	0.77	0.72
SO_3	0.13	0.11	0.11	0.11	0.11
P_2O_5	0.08	0.09	0.09	0.08	0.09

Conclusion

This chapter highlights the benefits of an integrated approach to the study of glass consumption in Cyprus in Late Antiquity and its contribution to a better understanding of intra-regional and the interregional circulation and trade.

Besides a regional differentiation in the glass distribution there seems from the three sites considered that there is a strong chronological influence on the distribution of glass types.

The study has also made an important contribution in terms of analytical methodology. *In situ* optical spectroscopy can be applied on large numbers of glass pieces, allowing a better screening of the entire glass assemblage resulting in a valuable selection for sampling targeted glass groups. An important ongoing step of the research is the addition of a trace element study, which will provide the chemical fingerprint of the glass fragments. With this extra information we may be able to refine our understanding of the provenance of the glass groups identified up to now on the island.

At this stage, it is premature to ponder conclusions on the use of glass at an intra-site level as well as on an inter-site level. In order to refine these conclusions more material from (well-)dated contexts needs to be studied. At some point it is planned to undertake a more in-depth contextual analysis, along with more optical and chemical analysis from other Cypriot sites in order to cover the whole accessible coastline.

At the time of writing we have received the possibility of working on the material from the basilicas of Ayios Kononas, on the Akamas peninsula, Katalymmata ton Plakoton on the Akrotiri peninsula and Ayia Mavri at Alassa.

References

Bergamasco, A. and Malanotte-Rizzoli, P. 2010. 'The Circulation of the Mediterranean Sea: A Historical Review of Experimental Investigations'. *Advances in Oceanography and Limnology* 1 (1): 11–28.

Bonifay, M. 2004. *Etudes sur la céramique romaine tardive d'Afrique* (BAR Series 1301). Oxford: Archaeopress.

Brughmans, T. 2010. 'Connecting the Dots: Towards Archaeological Network Analysis'. *Oxford Journal of Archaeology* 29 (3): 277–300.

Ceglia, A., Cosyns, P., Nys, K., Terryn, H., Thienpont, H. and Meulebroeck, W. 2015. 'Late Antique Glass Distribution and Consumption in Cyprus: A Chemical Study'. *Journal of Archaeological Science* 61: 213–22.

Ceglia, A., Cosyns, P., Nys, K., Terryn, H., Thienpont, H. and Meulebroeck, W. 2016. 'Light Through Glass: The Spectrum of Late Antique Glass from Cyprus'. *Journal of Archaeological Science: Reports* 7: 614–24.

Cholakova, A., Rehren, Th., and Freestone, I. C. 2015. 'Compositional Identification of 6th c. AD Glass from the Lower Danube'. *Journal of Archaeological Science: Reports* 7: 625–32.

Cosyns, P. and Ceglia, A. Forthcoming. 'The Glass'. In *The Early Christian Basilica of Agioi Pente at Yeroskipou*, edited by D. Michaelides.

Coullié, A. and Filimonos-Tsopotou, M. (eds) 2014. *Rhodes: Une île grecque aux portes de l'Orient – XVe-Ve siècle avant J.-C.* Paris: musée du Louvre/Somogy éditions d'Art.

Crowfoot, G. M. and Harden, D. B. 1931. 'Early Byzantine and Later Glass Lamps'. *The Journal of Egyptian Archaeology* 17 (3/4): 196–208.

Davidson, G. R. 1952. *Corinth XII: The Minor Objects*. Princeton: The American School of Classical Studies at Athens (ASCSA).

Deligiannakis, G. 2016. *The Dodecanese and the Eastern Aegean Islands in Late Antiquity, AD 300–700* (Oxford Monographs on Classical Archaeology). Oxford: Oxford University Press.

Drauschke, J. and Keller, D. (eds) 2010. *Glass in Byzantium – Production, Usage, Analyses* (International Workshop Organised by the Byzantine Archaeology Mainz, 17–18 January 2008), Römisch-Germanisches Zentralmuseum (RGZM). Mainz: Verlag des Römisch-Germanischen Zentralmuseums.

Fenn, N. and Römer-Strehl, C. (eds) 2013. *Networks in the Hellenistic World: According to the Pottery in the Eastern Mediterranean and Beyond* (BAR International Series 2539). Oxford: Archaeopress.

Freestone, I., Ponting, M. and Hughes, M. J. 2002. 'Origins of Byzantine Glass from Maroni Petrera, Cyprus'. *Archaeometry* 44: 257–72.

Freestone, I., Price, J. and Cartwright, C. 2009. 'The Batch: Its Recognition and Significance'. In *Annales du 17e Congrès de l'Association pour l'Histoire du Verre*, edited by K. Janssens, P. Degryse, P. Cosyns, J. Caen, and L. Van't dack, 130–5. Antwerp: University Press Antwerp (UPA).

Fünfschilling, S. and Laflı, E. 2013. *Hadrianopolis II: Glasfunde des 6. und 7. Jhs. aus Hadrianopolis, Paphlagonien [Türkei]* (Internationale Archäologie 123). Rahden/Westfalen: Verlag Marie Leidorf.

Gabrielsen, V. 1997. *The Naval Aristocracy of Hellenistic Rhodes* (Studies in Hellenistic Civilization 6). Aarhus: Aarhus University Press.

Gates, C. 2011. *Ancient Cities: The Archaeology of Urban Life in the Ancient Near East and Egypt, Greece and Rome*. 2nd edition. London/New York: Routledge.

Gill, M. A. V. 2002. *Amorium Reports, Finds I: The Glass (1987–1997)*. (BAR International Series 1070). Oxford: Archaeopress.

Hadad, S. 1998. 'Glass Lamps from the Byzantine through Mamluk Periods at Bet Shean, Israel'. *Journal of Glass Studies* 40: 63–76.

Isings, C. 1957. *Roman Glass from Dated Finds* (Archaeologica Traiectina 2). Groningen-Djakarta: J. B. Wolters.

James, L. 2006. 'Byzantine Glass Mosaic Tesserae: Some Material Considerations'. *Byzantine and Modern Greek Studies* 30 (1): 29–47.

Keller, D., Price, J. and Jackson, C. (eds) 2014. *Neighbours and Successors of Rome: Traditions of Glass Production and use in Europe and the Middle East in the Later 1st Millennium AD*. Oxford: Oxbow Books.

Knappett, C., Evans, T. and Rivers, R. 2008. 'Modelling Maritime Interaction in the Aegean Bronze Age'. *Antiquity* 82: 1009–24.

Laflı, E. (ed.) 2009. *Late Antique/Early Byzantine Glass in the Eastern Mediterranean (Colloquia Anatolica et Aegaea Acta: Congressus Communis Omnium Gentium Smyrnae II)*. Izmir: Hürriyet Matbaası.

Lawall, M. L. and Lund, J. (eds) 2013. *The Transport Amphora and Trade of Cyprus*. Aarhus: Aarhus University Press.

Lund, J. 1999. 'Trade Patterns in the Levant from ca. 100 BC to AD 200 – as Reflected by the Distribution of Ceramic Fine Wares in Cyprus'. *Münsterische Beiträge zur antiken Handelsgeschichte* 18 (1): 1–22.

Lund, J. 2006. 'On the Circulation of Goods in Hellenistic and Early Roman Cyprus'. In *Panayia Ematousa I. A Rural Site in South-Eastern Cyprus (Monographs of the Danish Institute at Athens 6, 2)*, edited by L. Sørensen W. and Winther Jacobson, K., 31–49. Athens: Aarhus University Press.

Lund, J., Malfitana, D. and Poblome, J. 2006. 'Rhosica vasa mandavi (Cic. Att.6.1.13): Towards the Identification of a Major Ceramic Tableware

Industry of the Eastern Mediterranean: Eastern Sigillata A. *Archaeologia Classica* 57: 491–507.

McClellan, M. 2003. '6. Glass'. In 'A Cypriot Village of Late Antiquity: Kalavasos-Kopetra in the Vasilikos Valley' (*Journal of Roman Archaeology* supplementary series no. 52, edited by M. Rautman). *Portsmouth-Rhode Island: Journal of Roman Archaeology*, 217–34.

Manning, S. W. 2002. *The Late Roman Church at Maroni Petrera. Survey and Salvage Excavations 1990–1997, and Other Traces of Roman Remains in the Lower Maroni Valley, Cyprus*. London: A. G. Leventis Foundation.

Mitchell, S. 2007. *A History of the Later Roman Empire, AD 284–641: The Transformation of the Ancient World* (Blackwell History of the Ancient World). Oxford: Blackwell.

Morton, J. 2001. *The Role of the Physical Environment in Ancient Greek Seafaring* (Mnemosyne supplementum 213). Leiden/Boston/Cologne: Brill.

Nenna, M. D. 2008. 'Production et commerce du verre à l'époque impériale: nouvelles découvertes et problématiques'. *Facta* 1: 125–47.

Olcay, B. Y. 2001. 'Lighting Methods in the Byzantine Period and Findings of Glass Lamps in Anatolia'. *Journal of Glass Studies* 43: 77–87.

Peacock, D. P. S. 1982. *Pottery in the Roman World: An Ethnoarchaeological Approach*. London/New York: Longman.

Peacock, D. P. S. and Williams, D. F. 1986. *Amphorae and the Roman Economy*. London: Longman.

Rautman, M. (ed.) 2003. 'A Cypriot Village of Late Antiquity. Kalavasos-Kopetra in the Vasilikos Valley'. *Journal of Roman Archaeology Supplementary Series No. 52*. Portsmouth-Rhode Island: Journal of Roman Archaeology.

Riedel, S. 2013. 'Hellenistic Pottery in a Wider Perspective: On the Use and Misuse of the Application of Network Theory to Material Culture'. In N. Fenn and C. Römer-Strehl (eds), *Networks in the Hellenistic World: According to the Pottery in the Eastern Mediterranean and Beyond* (BAR International Series 2539), 371–6. Oxford: Archaeopress.

Rutherford, I. 2007. 'Network Theory and Theoretic Networks'. *Mediterranean Historical Review* 22 (1): 23–37.

Stern, E. M. 1985. 'Ancient and Medieval Glass from the Necropolis Church at Anemurium'. In *Annales du 9e Congrès de l'Association Internationale pour l'Histoire du Verre (Nancy, France 22–28 mai 1983)*. Liège: AIHV, 35–64.

Theis, L. 2001. 'Lampen, Leuchten, Licht'. In *Byzanz. Das Licht aus dem Osten. Kult und Alltag im Byzantinischen Reich vom 4. bis zum 15. Jahrhundert* (Exhibition Catalogue in the Archbishopric Diözesenmuseum Paderborn), edited by C. Stiegemann, 53–64. Mainz: Christoph Stiegemann.

Uboldi, M. 1995. 'Diffusione delle lampade vitree in età tardoantica e altomedievale e spunti per una tipologia'. *Archeologia Medievale*, XXII: 93–145.

Wellman, B. 1983. 'Network Analysis: Some Basic Principles'. *Social Theory* 1: 155–200.

5

Things that travelled: Precious things for special people?

Sally Cottam and Caroline Jackson

Abstract

Over the last 20 years, considerable progress has been made in identifying the origins of the materials used to produce Roman glass and the location of the primary furnaces where raw glass was made. Testimony to the movement of unworked glass around the Mediterranean is known from shipwreck cargoes and the final links in the production chain, the secondary vessel-forming furnaces, are also increasingly well documented.

But exactly how these glass journeys were structured and the networks of trade and exchange in raw glass in the Roman period remain unclear. The contemporary literary references on the subject are sketchy and the archaeological evidence is tantalising and open to wide-ranging interpretations.

Within the early Imperial glass vessel repertoire, emerald green vessels form an unusual compositional and typological group. Unlike most of the glass of the late Hellenistic and Roman period, emerald green glass was produced with the addition of plant ashes. Examination of the range of forms produced in this relatively short-lived colour also reveals distinct trends and surprising omissions. This chapter illustrates how the focused examination of this single glass colour and of the specific vessel types it was used to produce can begin to clarify some of the essential questions concerning the organisation of the early Imperial glass industry.

Introduction

This chapter explores certain anomalies that have become evident during a programme of research into a particular group of first-century CE vessels, those produced in dark, emerald green glass. This study has produced an extensive database of compositional profiles of emerald green glass concentrating on vessels of known form and provenance. An understanding of the typological characteristics of these vessels is regarded as an essential element of the research strategy. This combination of approaches has allowed us to explore how this colour was produced and how it was exploited, in turn throwing light on the currently limited understanding of industrial organisation of the early glass industry in the Roman world.

Two main themes have arisen from this research that illustrate why emerald green glass is a distinctively interesting colour to investigate. The analytical results show that the overwhelming majority of vessels in this colour had elevated concentrations of elements, which would indicate the introduction of plant ash to the glass recipe, setting them apart from most other early Roman glass (Jackson and Cottam 2015). On the typological side of the study it appears that while some vessel forms were often produced in emerald green glass, other common forms were never or very rarely produced in the colour, even at the height of its popularity in the middle of the first century CE. To understand why these peculiarities occur we are re-examining the entire pathway of emerald green production, from the primary phase of raw glass manufacture to the final processes of vessel finishing, interrogating and challenging some established assumptions along the way. This chapter explores two parts of this complex story, presenting new thoughts on colour formation and exploring some ideas concerning its place in the extended process of glass production. The discussion brings together evidence from secondary furnace sites where emerald green glass is known to have been worked to see whether this idiosyncratic colour can provide clues to the relationship between the production of distinct vessel forms and workshop organisation in the early Imperial period.

Emerald green glass and primary production

The origin of the glass used to make emerald green vessels is most likely to have been the eastern Mediterranean. There is some indication that the sands used for the production of emerald green glass have a source

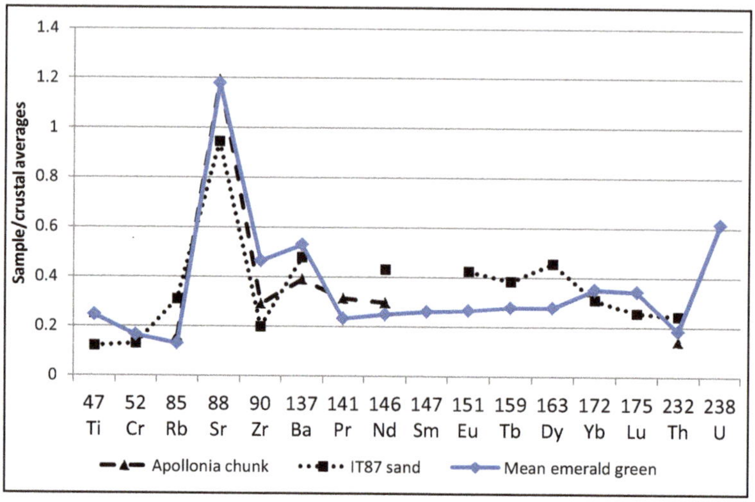

Figure 5.1 Mean trace element signature of emerald green glasses from Barzan and Ribnica (10 samples) normalised to the crustal average (Wedepohl 1995) compared to primary glass from Apollonia (Freestone et al. 2000) and IT87 sand from Italy (Brems and Degryse 2014).

common with other Roman glasses (Jackson and Cottam 2015). Raw glass extracted from primary furnaces at Apollonia, for example, has a very distinctive trace element pattern with a high peak at strontium (Figure 5.1 – Sr peak). A mean of the trace elements for emerald green glass shows a similar though not identical pattern, and while the emerald green vessels are earlier in date, the similarity suggests that the sands used might come from the same general region, with any slight differences perhaps contributed by the addition of other raw materials, such as plant ashes, to the batch.

Wherever the site of the primary glass production (and other locations, even perhaps further west, cannot be ruled out (Brems and Degryse 2014, IT87 sand fig. 1)) it seems most likely that primary production of the glass for emerald green vessels took place in the same general area that was home to the large natron-based glass production industry. On the basis of this assumption we are now exploring whether the production of emerald green glass represents a distinct industry, or can be related to natron-glass traditions.

To answer this, two fundamental points need to be addressed. First, did the plant ash alkali found almost exclusively in emerald green glass enter the mix as the basic, perhaps sole, flux to assist the melting process, or alternatively was it added to a natron-based glass during colouring, either to facilitate the production of the emerald green colour or as a by-product of other colouring components?

What flux was used for emerald green glass?

Emerald green glass has two main colourants, copper and iron, but these alone do not produce the intense green hue observed. It has been noted that magnesia-containing glasses may provide the most suitable base for green transmission (Weyl 1951) and that the addition of plant ash, higher in magnesium, calcium and potassium than natron, and containing small amounts of charcoal, would also favour the formation of the green colour (see Jackson and Cottam 2015 145, for a discussion of this process). This would point to plant ash as an ideal component in the recipe for emerald green glass, but does not necessarily indicate that plant ashes fulfilled the role of the flux in this recipe as proposed in some discussions of these compositional traits (Lemke 1998; Jackson et al. 2009; Gallo et al. 2013).

To identify whether plant ash was added to a natron glass we need to try to assess whether mineral soda is present in the samples of emerald green glass that we have studied. Roman natron glasses typically contain concentrations of potash and magnesia below 1wt% and at or above 1.5wt% in a soda-ash glass. The levels of potassium and magnesium in the emerald green glasses are at the lower end of what might be expected of a glass using only a high-soda plant ash as the flux and they are variable. Some glasses show only slightly raised concentrations of potassium or magnesium above those seen in glasses produced with a natron flux (Table 5.1). Phosphorus is higher than has been previously observed in plant ash glasses. Moreover there is no correlation between these different elements. This points to the use of a flux that is predominantly composed of soda and on present evidence, this is most likely to be natron. The presence of higher concentrations of these other elements must derive from the addition of plant ash, but not necessarily for the purpose of fluxing the glass. These compositional traits can be seen occasionally in other published analyses of emerald green fragments such as Avenches, Switzerland (Amrein 2001, 130, fig. 97 and Table 5.1). Very rarely, emerald green glass appears to have been created without the addition of any plant ash. The published analysis of a dark green chip of what appears to be raw glass from the workshop of La Montée de la Butte in Lyon does not have elevated levels of potassium or magnesium but has levels of sodium that correspond with a natron

Table 5.1 Range of compositions seen in the analysed dataset (Jackson and Cottam 2015; Barzan, Ribnica, Fréjus; blue-green unpublished data) and other published data from raw glass chips from Avenches (Amrein 2001, 130 fig. 97) and unpublished data from Montée de la Butte, Lyon (Robin 2012a)

	Sample	Na_2O	MgO	Al_2O_3	SiO_2	P_2O_5	SO_3	*Cl*	K_2O	*CaO*	TiO_2	*MnO*	*FeO*	*CuO*	SnO_2	Sb_2O_5
1st c. blue-green natron glass	US1158n.d.5	16.45	0.64	2.65	67.78	0.19	0.17	1.02	0.71	7.92	0.05	0.42	0.42	0.04	<LLD	0.09
Frejus	158	17.57	0.83	2.43	65.39	0.27	0.16	0.86	1.01	7.15	0.13	0.59	0.73	2.11	0.19	0.34
Ribnica	5757	16.17	0.99	2.95	67.23	0.15	0.19	1.03	0.72	4.83	0.20	0.97	1.19	2.03	0.05	0.04
Barzan	BRZ34	17.06	1.44	2.90	62.53	0.48	0.30	0.91	1.44	6.69	0.20	0.60	1.12	2.32	<LLD	0.57
Ribnica	51299	20.00	2.37	3.44	60.09	0.42	0.44	0.87	1.18	6.10	0.36	0.55	1.40	2.90	<LLD	0.08
Ribnica	51168	15.18	3.47	2.17	62.44	1.09	0.16	0.96	1.94	6.83	0.15	0.53	1.23	2.32	<LLD	0.13
Avenches raw glass	8253–9	15.0*	1.8	2.3	65.4	nm	0.39	0.69	2.7	6.7	0.25	0.56	1.45	1.88	0.20	0.32
Avenches raw glass	8253.9	15.0*	1.3	1.7	61.9	nm	0.17	0.53	2.5	5.9	0.23	0.52	1.35	5.35	0.24	0.39
Avenches raw glass	8268–371	15.0*	1.9	3.8	64.3	nm	0.09	0.42	0.9	6.2	0.38	0.32	1.97	3.77	0.36	0.02
Avenches raw glass	9268–371	15.0*	2.2	3.7	64.3	nm	0.44	0.53	0.8	6.1	0.38	0.31	1.92	3.28	0.31	0.03
Montée de la Butte	VRR787	16.58	0.53	2.60	65.26	0.09	nm	nm	0.51	8.42	0.06	0.11	0.40	4.3	0.60	0.04

Note: <LLD, below detection; nm, not measured, *sodium oxide is given as 15 wt% for all samples in Amrein 2001.

glass (Robin 2012a, 50, fig. 27, Annexe 1, VRR787). There are other contemporary emerald green glasses found in beads, which also seem to be a standard natron glass composition with perhaps slightly raised potash concentrations (Bertini et al. 2011). These non-plant ash emerald glasses are, however, very exceptional.

The results of other analytical programmes are also providing clues that the relationship between glasses that contain plant ash and the natron-glass industry might be close. The analyses of samples from the primary furnace sites of Bir Hooker and Zakik in the Wadi Natrun indicate that at some point at least, from the third century BCE into the first two centuries CE, glasses containing plant ash were being produced alongside a much larger natron-based glass industry (Picon et al. 2008). This is based on four samples, however, and it is not clear from the report what colour they are.

When and where was emerald green glass coloured?

These considerations are closely connected to a second fundamental question concerning the chain of production in the early Imperial glass industry – the point at which colourants are added to glass. The importance of this question to the study of emerald green glass and other coloured glasses of the mid-first century CE is profound, as it is closely linked to the complex typological considerations that we have highlighted concerning this colour and that are also germane to other colour groups, in particular colourless glass.

Emerald green is a Roman glass colour appearing in the first decades of the first century CE and going out of general use by the last quarter of that century. During this period, emerald green is one of the more common of the strong colours – often on a parity with dark blue and more common than purple and the opaque colours such as red, pale blue and white (Cottam forthcoming).

However, while being widely used in glass production, it is ignored in the manufacture of some of the most common first-century vessel forms. This anomaly was pointed out by David Grose in his research on early imperial cast/non-blown vessels (Grose 1991, 2–11). He noted (with one possible rare exception) that emerald green was not used to make the hugely popular and widespread monochrome non-blown ribbed bowls (Isings form 3). The list of common forms not produced in emerald green can be expanded to include Augustan 'linear-cut' bowls and blown ribbed bowls (Isings form 17) and it is also a very unusual colour in the production of jugs, amphorisks and jars.

To understand how colour selection relates to final vessel form, the production sequence must be examined in more detail. It has often been assumed that any deliberate colouration of glass was undertaken in the primary furnace, as it is easier to add many colourants to the glass mix during initial fusion than to attempt to change the colour of glass during secondary working (Foy and Nenna 2001, 29). The fact that pre-coloured blocks of raw glass are known from shipwrecks at Les Sanguinaires A (dark blue) and Embiez-ouest 1 (colourless) (Foy and Nenna 2001, 102, 110–1; Foy and Fontaine 2007) implies that some glass at least was being coloured/decoloured at source, unless the less likely scenario of a further intermediary colouring stage between primary and secondary furnaces, where shaping takes place, is adopted. The discovery of chips of raw coloured glass at the mid-first-century secondary furnace sites at Avenches and Lyon provides further, albeit circumstantial, support for this hypothesis (Amrein 2001, 17–21; Robin 2012a, 48–50 fig. 27).

Contemporary references to glass production make occasional reference to the processes by which colour is introduced to the glass mix, but shed only limited light on the exact point at which colourants are added. Pliny the Elder, for example, describes the production of raw glass before continuing: 'After being reduced to lumps, the glass is again fused in the workshop and is tinted. Some of it is shaped by blowing, some machined on a lathe and some chased like silver' (Natural History XXXVI, 66).

In the context of our current understanding of glass production, it is unclear here whether Pliny's 'workshop' forms part of the initial industrial complex of raw glass production, or connects to the subsequent sentence, being more closely linked to the secondary, vessel formation, stage.

Whether Strabo's famous commentary on glass production in the Augustan period refers to primary or secondary production is also unclear, but it may imply that some colouration was taking place in a secondary phase of glass production: 'and at Rome, also, it is said that many discoveries are made both for producing the colours and for facility in manufacture, as, for example, in the case of glass-ware, where one can buy a glass beaker or drinking-cup for a copper' (Strabo, Geography Book XVI Chapter 2, 25, Loeb Classical Library edition).

Intriguing findings have also come from a recent analysis of a collection of second-century CE glass tesserae and two cakes of opaque glass from West Clacton in Essex. The authors suggest that 'all of the copper-coloured turquoise glass, including the turquoise cake and three turquoise tesserae were probably made using *recycled* (our italics) Sb-Mn glass as a base', which by implication means that the colouring of this glass did not take place at the primary manufacturing stage (Paynter et al

2015, 71). The samples of emerald green glass in this research project show no obvious signs of having been recycled, however, antimony, copper, tin and lead are present as additives and so cannot be used as markers for recycling and concentrations of cobalt are no higher than might be expected in the glass-making raw materials. Other indicators for recycling such as slightly raised concentrations of potassium, magnesium, calcium and phosphorus (Paynter 2008), are again masked by the intentional addition of plant ashes. One possible scenario is that glasses that do not require strict control of reduction or oxidation conditions in the furnace and are commonly used in vessel production, for example, cobalt blue, may have been coloured during primary production, while other more complex colours that required more skilled control of reduction and were less common, including opaque colours such as those observed by Paynter et al. (2015), may have been coloured later in the sequence.

Emerald green glass and secondary production

An approach that puts greater emphasis on the vessel forms produced in emerald green glass may furnish further clues about the addition of colour and the links between raw glass supply and vessel manufacture. A particular association has often been noted between the range of non-blown early- to mid-first-century CE tablewares known as 'ceramic forms' or 'fine wares' (including for example Isings forms 2 and 22) and the emerald green colour. In Donald Harden's report on the glass from Camulodunum (1947, 300) he noted that within monochrome wares of this class the predominant colour was emerald green, 'not only at Colchester but everywhere'. This sentiment is echoed in the more extensive survey of early glass from Colchester which incorporates Harden's earlier samples, where 59 per cent of the cast monochrome vessels were of this colour (Cool and Price 1995, 35). Laudine Robin's analysis of the forms imitating metal and ceramic vessels from Rue Bourgelat, Lyon, shows the same pattern (Robin 2012b, 12). David Grose too pointed out that non-blown cylindrical bowls (described by him as *pyxides*) were predominantly made in emerald green glass (Grose 1991, 8). The partiality for this colour for these forms is puzzling, but it does appear to link them as a group – a classification that has been traditionally followed by glass specialists since Donald Harden first brought them together under the title 'pressed and rotary-polished wares' in his report on the assemblage from Camulodunum. It would also suggest that for this group at least, a degree of workshop specialisation was occurring, as it is unlikely that multiple workshops would show a similar preference for an individual colour in the production of particular forms or groups of forms.

Workshop specialisation is very difficult to identify. Few early Imperial secondary production sites have been excavated and published. At sites that have been explored it is difficult to determine the types of vessel being produced as the vessel fragments found might potentially be items brought there for recycling.

One of the most extensively explored secondary workshops is at Avenches in Switzerland, active in the middle of the first century CE (Amrein 2001). The site was remarkable for the very large number of fragments of thin-walled unguentaria (including Isings forms 6, 8, 10, 11 and 28) found. The quantity in which this particular class of vessel occurred strongly implies that these were being produced there; in fact Amrein suggests the glass makers at Avenches may have specialised in the production of these unguentaria (Amrein 2001, 61–5, 95). However, there is no evidence as yet that colour was a factor in vessel specialisation at this particular site. All the major mid-first-century translucent colours are represented in the glass-working debris, and the chips of raw emerald green glass and the emerald green moils, drops and twists give a clear indication that this colour was being blown alongside other colours (Figure 5.2).

One other contemporary glass-making site may provide tentative evidence about the relationship between colour selection and form production within the workshop setting. At the furnace site of la Montée de la Butte in Lyon, emerald green raw glass chips as well as moils and other glass production waste were again found alongside other strong colours (Robin 2012a, 50, fig. 27, 54–5 fig. 29). A number of common forms both blown and non-blown (cast) have been identified as being made at this workshop, including tubular rimmed bowls (Isings form 44 and 45), convex wheel-cut cups (Isings form 12), convex ribbed blown bowls (Isings form 17) and non-blown ribbed bowls (Isings form 3). It is particularly interesting that monochrome non-blown ribbed bowls (Isings form 3) and blown ribbed bowls (Isings form 17), which are not made in emerald green, *were* identified as part of the repertoire of the workshop alongside forms frequently produced in the colour, such as shallow tubular rimmed bowls (Isings form 44) and convex wheel-cut cups (Isings form 12) (Robin 2012a, 61–72, fig. 38). The range of forms being made at la Montée de la Butte is very diverse, with both blown and non-blown tablewares in the repertoire, along with mould-blown bottles, unguentaria and twisted batons. Here at least, workshop specialisation in a particular range of forms does not appear to have been

Figure 5.2 Vessel and production waste and chips of raw glass from Avenches, Switzerland. © C. Jackson.

the case. The suggestion that forms not associated with emerald green were being produced at a workshop where the production of emerald green vessels was clearly taking place could mean that at this site at least, the colour was available, but for some reason not chosen to produce certain forms, placing the moment of colour/form selection at the secondary stage in the hands of the vessel producers. However, it is not possible to be certain that all these forms were in production simultaneously as establishing what constitutes exact contemporaneity at a glass production site is an almost impossible task. While glass-making debris of different colours may be deposited together, it is possible that consignments of raw glass in different colours were acquired at different points in the lifetime of the workshop, and correspond with phases in vessel output.

The apparent selection of individual colours to produce specific vessel types raises questions concerning the nature and extent of contact between vessel manufacturers and the sources of raw material. Recent work on glass in the context of maritime trade, points to a complex system where raw glass was often shipped as part of a larger mixed cargo, in ships that may have made multiple visits to different ports, loading and unloading goods along the route (Radić Rossi 2012; Wilson et al. 2012; Fontaine 2014; Fontaine and Cibecchini 2014). The apparent association of particular forms, and perhaps workshops, with select colours needs therefore to be set within the wider framework of maritime trade networks. While the existence of individual *negotiatores* dealing in glass is unknown in the early Imperial period, the considerable evidence for merchants in other commodities (see Rice 2016 for a review of merchant inscriptions) might lead us to envisage the existence of a network of specialised traders, with contacts across the primary and secondary industries, in a position to supply particular products, including coloured glasses, on request. Conversely, an argument could be made for a more random sporadic acquisition process, and that our associations of form and colour are the result of cargoes of coloured glasses being obtained by casual, serendipitous deals.

Discussion

The glass debris from Avenches and Montée de la Butte and its interpretation in conjunction with the particular characteristics of emerald green vessels contributes rare and important information to our understanding of the complex story of glass vessel production in the mid-first century CE, at a time of expanding markets and increased glass consumption. At these two workshops there is sufficient evidence to explore the use of different glass colours and to gain some insight into the relationship between colour and form. At Avenches there does seem to be some degree of form specialisation, but no evident preference for any of the main translucent colours, and the shapes made here are all ones that are known in emerald green as well as other colours. At Montée de la Butte the variety of vessel types noted in the assemblage and the use of both blown and non-blown techniques suggests that here there was no focus on a particular form or class of forms. However, there does appear to be colour selection, or more specifically non-selection in the case of emerald green for some of the types, as forms widely noted as never or rarely being produced in this colour *do* appear to be among the output of the workshop. Within the scope of our current state of knowledge, no workshop producing the forms that appear to be preferentially produced in emerald green (such as Isings form 2 and 22) has been identified. Despite this missing element in the jigsaw it is possible to speculate that individual workshops, specialising in certain forms had easier access to a supply of emerald green glass. There could be many reasons why this might happen, including the location of workshops, the chronology of emerald green production and the nature of long distance trading links (see Jackson and Cottam 2015 for a discussion of these factors).

It is also worth assessing the status of emerald green as a colour and with it the possibility that some form of embargo existed, perhaps related to cost, on its use for certain common forms, a proposition that might be supported by the evidence from Montée de la Butte. The general popularity of the colour and the relative frequency with which it is used for one of the most common types of mid-first-century cup (Isings form 12) would, however, argue against any elite status. Similarly, there is no evidence that emerald green glass was difficult to work into certain forms or types of decoration or that it required specialised skills in its manipulation.

The study of emerald green glass is providing clues to what is undoubtedly a complex system of long distance trade and the primary/secondary workshop relationship. The chemistry of the glass suggests that it is part of a natron-glass production system, possibly being made in the same general region, but exactly where is unclear. The introduction of plant ashes high in phosphorus, which may indicate wood ash or fuel ashes, seems to be related to colour production. From the limited evidence at the secondary production centres we have examined it appears that emerald green glass is reaching these sites at the same time as other colours, such as dark blue, purple, amber and blue-green and being used alongside them.

The evidence also suggests that at least one first-century CE workshop was producing a variety of different forms and was selecting colours preferentially for some vessel forms, but we are faced, however, with a very sparse dataset. Very few mid-first-century furnace sites are known, and even fewer have been thoroughly excavated and published. Until further work is published we certainly have not ruled out the possibility that some sort of workshop specialisation in certain vessel types did exist.

The anomalous case of emerald green glass provides a unique dataset with which to explore the organisation of the glass industry in the early Roman period. In this chapter we have used the data to explore fundamental questions concerning the organisation of the early Imperial glass industry, concentrating in particular on the point at which raw glass was coloured and whether the relationships between colour and form can be identified from the existing workshop evidence. The process of glass vessel production from raw ingredients to finished item has been increasingly divided into discrete segments with the development and adoption of a model separating raw glass production (with the evidence currently pointing predominantly to an eastern Mediterranean locus) from vessel production, which is a highly dispersed activity occurring throughout the empire. The special qualities of emerald green glass allow us to scrutinise these separate stages, to assess the extent to which these areas of production are interconnected and to start to see the glass industry as an organised operation driven by producers, glass traders and consumers alike. Pulling these themes together allows a greater insight into production and trade, and the role of different artisans in shaping the material culture of the early Roman world.

Acknowledgements

We would like to thank our colleagues in the Musée Archéologique at Fréjus, Irena Lazar for permission to sample the fragments from Ribnica and Trojane, and the Castle Museum at Colchester for access to the glass fragments for sampling. Our gratitude also goes to Mme Meylan Krause and Mme Chantal Martin Pruvot for permission to view the glass at the Museum at Avenches, and to Dr Laudine Robin for access to her thesis before publication. We thank NERC (NERC OSS/340/0207) for funding trace element analysis at the ICP-MS facility University of Kingston/ Imperial College London (Beniot Disch and Kym Jarvis) and EPSRC (through EP/F019750/1) for EPMA analysis (Eddy Faber).

References

Amrein, H. 2001. *L'atelier de verriers d'Avenches: L'artisanat du verre au milieu du 1er siècle après J.-C.* Lausanne: Cahiers d'Archéologie Romande 87, Aventicum XI.

Bertini, M., Shortland, A., Milek, K. and Krupp, E. M. 2011. 'Investigation of Iron Age North-Eastern Scottish Glass Beads Using Element Analysis with LA-ICP-MS'. *Journal of Archaeological Science* 38: 2497–872.

Brems, D. and Degryse, P. 2014. 'Trace Element Analyses in Provenancing Roman Glass-Making'. *Archaeometry* 56, 116–36. doi: 10.1111/arcm.12063.

Cool, H. E. M. and Price, J. 1995. *Roman Vessel Glass from Excavations in Colchester, 1971–85. Colchester Archaeological Report 8*. Colchester: Archaeological Trust.

Cottam, S. Forthcoming. Thesis, King's College London.

Fontaine, S. 2014. 'Maritime Roman Glass Trade: An Archaeological Case Study of Arles Harbour (France)'. *Journal of Glass Studies* 56: 357–64.

Fontaine, S. and Cibecchini, F. 2014. 'An Exceptional Example of Martime Glass Trade; The Deep Wreck Cap Corse 2 (France, Corsica)'. *Journal of Glass Studies* 56: 354–7.

Foy, D. and Fontaine S. 2007. 'L'épave Ouest-Embiez 1, Var; Le Commerce Maritime du Verre Brut et Manufacturé en Méditerranée Occidentale dans l'Antiquité'. *Revue Archéologique de Narbonnaise* 40: 235–68.

Foy, D. and Nenna, M.-D. 2001. *Tout Feu, Tout Sable: Mille Ans de Verre Antique dans le Midi de la France*. Marseille: Musée d'Histoire de Marseille, Musées de Marseille.

Freestone, I. C., Gorin-Rosen, Y. and Hughes, M. J. 2000. 'Primary Glass from Israel and the Production of Glass in the Late Antiquity and the Early Islamic period'. In *La route du verre: ateliers primaires et secondaires du second millénaire av. J.-C. au Moyen Âge*, edited by M.-D. Nenna, 65–84, Lyon: Travaux de la Maison de l'Orient Méditerranéen–Jean Pouilloux.

Gallo, F., Silvestri, A. and Molin, G. 2013. 'Glass from the Archaeological Museum of Adria (North-East Italy): New Insights into early Roman Production Technologies'. *Journal of Archaeological Science* 40: 2589–605.

Grose, D. 1991. 'Early Imperial Roman Cast Glass; the Translucent Coloured and Colourless Fine Wares'. In *Roman Glass: Two Centuries of Art and Invention*, edited by M. Newby and K. Painter, 1–18. London: Society of Antiquaries.

Harden, D. B. 1947. 'The Glass'. In *Camulodunum, First Report on the Excavations at Colchester 1930–1939. Research Reports of the Society of Antiquaries of London 14*, edited by C. F. C. Hawkes and M. R. Hull, 287–307. Oxford: Oxford University Press.

Isings, C. 1957. *Roman Glass from Dated Finds*. Groningen: J. B. Wolters Groningen.

Jackson, C. M. and Cottam, S. 2015. 'A Green Thought in a Green Shade: Compositional and Typological Observations Concerning the Production of Emerald Green Glass Vessels in the 1st Century A.D'. *Journal of Archaeological Science* 61: 139–48.

Jackson, C. M., Price, J. and Lemke, C. 2009. 'Glass Production in the 1st Century AD: Insights into Glass Technology'. In *Annales du 17e Congrès de l'Association Internationale pour l'Histoire du Verre*, edited by K. Janssens, P. Degryse, P. Cosyns, J. Caen and L. Van't dack 150–6. Anvers: Aspeditions.

Lemke, C. 1998. 'Reflections of the Roman Empire: The First Century Glass Industry as Seen Through Traditions of Manufacture'. In *The Prehistory and History of Glassmaking Technology* (Ceramics and Civilisation 8), edited by P. McCray and W. D. Kingery, 269–92. Westerville: The American Ceramic Society.

Paynter, S. 2008. 'Experiments in the Reconstruction of Roman Wood-Fired Glass-Working Furnaces: Waste Products and Their Formation Process'. *Journal of Glass Studies* 50: 271–90.

Paynter, S., Kearns, T., Cool, H. and Chenery, S. 2015. 'Roman Coloured Glass in the Western Provinces: The Glass Cakes and Tesserae from West Claction in England'. *Journal of Archaeological Science* 62: 66–81.

Picon, M., Thirion-Merle, V. and Vichy, M. 2008. 'Les Verres au Natron et les Verres aux Cendres du Wadi Natrun (Egypte)'. *Bulletin de l'Association Française pour l'Archéologie du Verre*, 36–41.

Radić Rossi, I. 2012. 'Shipwreck at Cape Glavat on the Island of Mljet'. In *Glass Odessy: Glass in the Ship's Equipment and Cargo*, edited by Radić Rossi, 17–24. Zadar: Muzej Antičkog Stakla.

Rice, C. 2016. 'Mercantile Specialization and Trading Communities'. In *Urban Craftsmen and Traders in the Roman World* (Oxford Studies on the Roman Economy), edited by A. Wilson and M. Flohr, 97–114. Oxford: Oxford University Press.

Robin, L. 2012a. *Le Verre à Lyon-Lugdunum durant le Haut-Empire, Production et Consommation*. Lyon: Editions Mergoil.

Robin, L. 2012b. 'Un Lot en Verre Remarquable daté du milieu du 1er siècle après J-C à Lyon-Lugdunum'. *Bulletin de l'Association Française pour l'Archéologie du Verre*, 11–16.

Wedepohl, H. 1995. 'The Composition of the Continental Crust'. *Geochimica et Cosmochimica Acta* 59 (7): 1217–32.

Weyl, W. A. 1951. *Coloured Glasses.* Sheffield: Society of Glass Technology.

Wilson, A. I., Schörle, K. and Rice, C. 2012. 'Roman Ports and Mediterranean Connectivity'. In *Rome, Portus and the Mediterranean* (Archaeological Monographs of the British School at Rome), edited by S. Keay, 367–91. London: Oxbow Books.

6
Trading North: Glass-working beyond the edge of the empire

Mary Davis and Ian C. Freestone

Abstract

An assemblage of glassy materials from Culduthel, an Iron Age site in north-east Scotland, mainly comprises fragments and beads of just a few millimetres in size and is unique in the region. The glasses were analysed by scanning electron microscopy-energy dispersive X-ray analysis. Opaque red glass comprises mainly droplets and fragments, is typical of the late Iron Age and may have been used to manufacture inlay in copper alloy metalwork recovered from the site. Compositional characteristics of the red suggest that it was derived from a single block or ingot. Opaque yellow occurs mainly as beads and antimony-opacified and lesser amounts of tin-opacified glass are present. Evidence for the melting of antimony-opacified yellow glass occurs in a composite fragment of opaque red, yellow and colourless glass and may reflect the manufacture of beads. Blue glass is less abundant and more variable in composition; it is likely to have been acquired over a longer period. The base glass for the majority of samples is the high-lime, high-alumina manganese-decolourised variety, typical of the Hellenistic and early Roman periods and originating in the Levant. The absence of low-lime, low-alumina antimony-decolourised Roman glass from the assemblage indicates an original date of manufacture before the middle of the first century CE.

Introduction

The majority of the chapters in the current volume are concerned with glass that was worked within the boundaries of the Roman empire and its successors (but see also Duckworth, Chapter 7). Evidence for glass production beyond this region is sparse, and in northern Europe particularly before the early medieval period. The present study concerns a rare occurrence where there is evidence for melting and shaping glass in north-eastern Britain, beyond Hadrian's Wall. The data provide evidence for the types of glass-working and the level of technology involved, and the very long distances over which the raw glass is likely to have travelled. The analysis also suggests a date for the material that is more or less consistent with the archaeological evidence for the site.

Culduthel is situated on a terrace overlooking modern Inverness in north-east Scotland (Figure 6.1); excavations prior to development of the land revealed a large and significant Iron Age industrial site. Within this settlement were found a total of 17 roundhouses (including 2 very large buildings); 8 metal-working furnaces, which between them produced over 250 kg of iron slag; and also over 170 iron objects, including tools for working wood, metal and leather, plus fragments of several weapons. There was also evidence for non-ferrous metal-working such as copper-working slag, crucibles and mould fragments. On the basis of radiocarbon dating and artefact typology the excavator suggests that the 'bulk of the industrial activity at Culduthel was in the late centuries BCE and just into the first century CE, and though there is evidence of contact with the Roman world the industrial technology is distinctly pre-Roman' (Murray 2007, 22).

Of interest to the present study was the discovery of evidence for glass-working; this included rods, lumps and molten waste, as well as a number of very small or broken beads. These artefacts were mostly found during wet-sieving, and came from the areas associated with non-ferrous metal-working. The overall amount of glass was small, as the surviving pieces were mostly tiny beads or waste fragments less than 4 mm in diameter, but the nature and quantity of the finds are significant to the understanding and importance of glass as a material in the Iron Age in north-east Scotland, and the assemblage is one of very few in Britain with secure evidence for glass-working.

The glass from Culduthel comprised many small beads, plus a number of 'blobs' and working off-cuts such as rods and flakes. The majority of the glass objects were yellow, red and blue, though

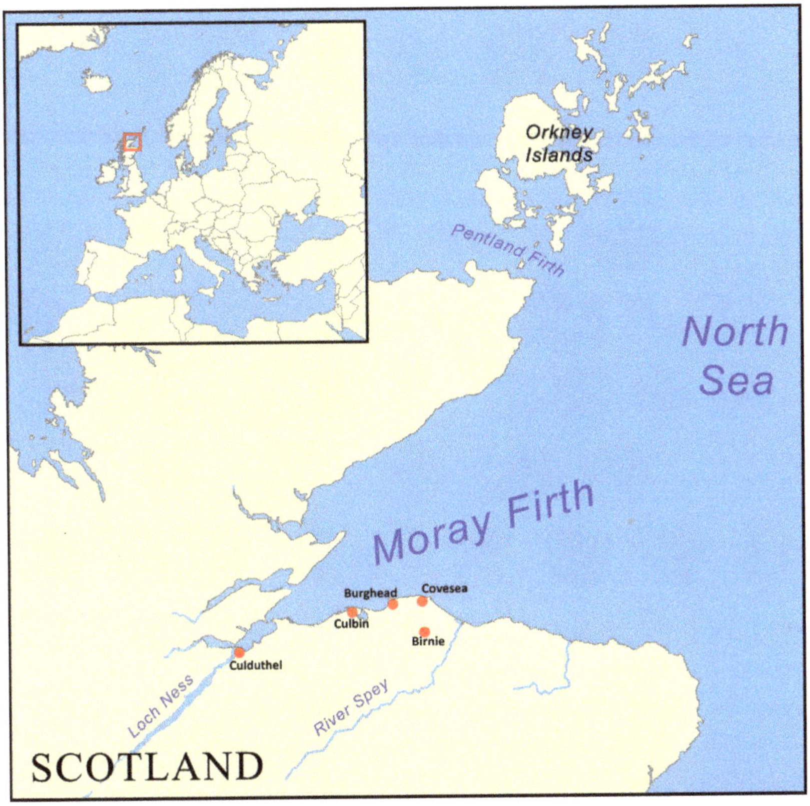

Figure 6.1 Map showing the location of Culduthel in north-east Scotland, plus other nearby sites where Iron Age glass objects have been found. Source: image derived from Map of the Moray Firth, © Wikipedia Commons

decorated clear glass and black and green beads were also present (Figure 6.2, Figure 6.3).

The evidence for glass-working occurs in the form of trails and irregular drops of red glass (Figure 6.4), a probable working piece in the form of a twisted spiral of blue and white glass, and a small composite thread of twisted yellow and colourless glass melted against a lump of opaque red. There are also a number of flakes of opaque red, which suggest that it was being crushed or fragments being broken on site; however, in itself this does not prove hot-working. Overall, these small fragments, typically a few millimetres across, are suggestive of bead-making and, as will be seen below, the manufacture of metalwork inlaid with soft glass ('enamel'). Although this is a picture that has had to be

Figure 6.2 Iron Age and Romano-British glass objects from Culduthel, plus slag and post-medieval intrusions (lowest line). Not to scale; however, the toggle (row 3 end) is the longest object at approx. 18 mm in length, and the yellow sphere (row 6 end) is approx. 2.5 mm in diameter.

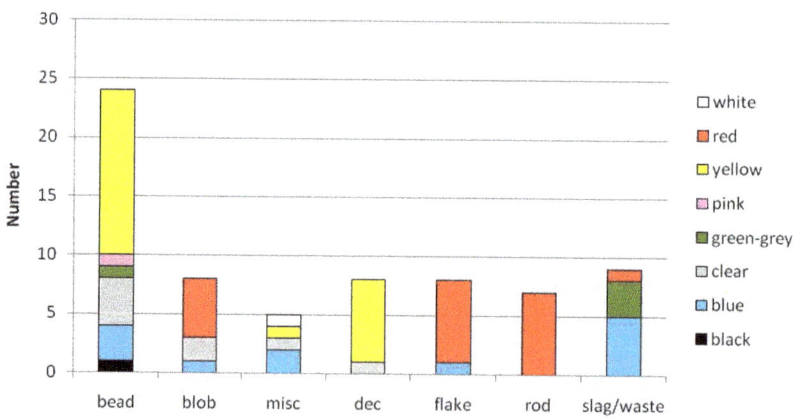

Figure 6.3 Colours and types of object present in the assemblage. Dec = decoration.

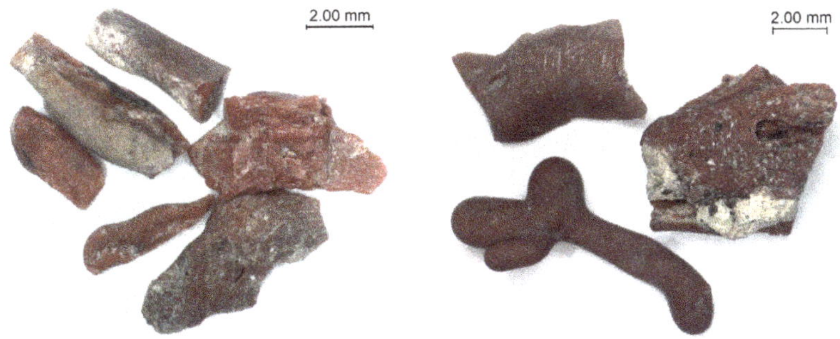

Figure 6.4 Various red glass fragments (CF 05 2454/1212 and 3022/1193).

constructed on the basis of a very small amount of recovered material, it is fully consistent with our understanding of the glass technology of the region and period.

Materials and analytical methods

The glass from the site was sent to the National Museums Wales and Cardiff University for analysis by the authors using scanning electron microscopy-energy dispersive X-ray analysis (SEM-EDS). Some 40 samples of glass were taken for analysis; most of the objects were sampled once, though where these were decorated, or consisted of more than one colour, further samples were taken (see Table 6.1 for results). A total of 11 out of the 20 red glass fragments were sampled (many of these fragments had the same context and arrived in the same bag).

The glass was analysed using a CamScan Maxim 2040 scanning electron microscope fitted with an Oxford Instruments energy dispersive X-ray detector and ISIS spectrometer. Operating conditions employed a 30° take-off angle, a 20 kV accelerating voltage, and the samples were detected for 100 live seconds using a count rate of *c*.4,000 counts per second when on a metallic cobalt standard.

The spectrometer was calibrated using pure elements, oxides and minerals; Sheffield glass standards were also used to improve the silica to lead oxide ratio in highly leaded glass. Corning and Sheffield glass standards were used further to assess the accuracy and precision of the analysis.

Many of the beads and fragments were so small that two methods of sampling were employed. The red glass was sampled in the conventional way: approximately 1 mm^2 pieces were removed and embedded

Table 6.1 Compositions of glass from Culduthel by SEM-EDXA

Form	*Colour*	*Context*	*Find*	Na_2O	MgO	Al_2O_3	SiO_2	P_2O_5	Cl	K_2O	CaO	TiO_2	MnO	FeO	CuO	SnO_2	Sb_2O_3	PbO
flake	red	2548	990E	11.18	0.51	1.57	41.56	0.37	0.64	0.65	4.71	0.12	0.46	0.51	10.63	<0.6	0.98	26.07
heated flake	red	2548	990A	11.54	0.56	1.69	42.37	0.34	0.65	0.84	5.13	0.08	0.43	0.46	8.65	<0.6	0.61	26.63
rod	red	2550	989	10.65	0.43	1.83	41.15	0.40	0.65	0.61	4.90	0.10	0.40	0.58	9.64	<0.6	0.85	27.81
rod	red	2548	1212B	10.16	0.39	1.66	42.03	0.34	0.65	0.58	4.70	0.03	0.47	0.53	11.03	<0.6	1.14	26.28
flake	red	2548	1212A	10.65	0.46	1.93	42.57	0.43	0.64	0.77	5.27	0.11	0.40	0.63	9.35	<0.6	0.83	25.90
heated frag.	red	3022	1193B	11.22	0.55	2.00	42.59	0.35	0.63	0.80	5.26	0.14	0.42	0.60	8.82	<0.6	0.79	25.73
yel, red, clr lump	red	3022	1193A	11.18	0.42	1.77	42.28	0.30	0.67	0.56	4.66	0.14	0.38	0.55	9.90	<0.6	1.01	26.16
rod	red	2100	355	10.97	0.33	1.44	43.82	0.41	0.76	0.46	4.54	0.08	0.29	0.32	6.67	<0.6	1.21	28.64
rod, 'squared'	red	2548	610	11.04	0.35	1.46	43.09	0.33	0.76	0.52	4.36	0.04	0.34	0.37	7.76	<0.6	1.09	28.45
rod, 'squared'	red	2548	610	11.21	0.44	1.71	42.27	0.34	0.62	0.58	4.70	0.08	0.36	0.50	10.56	<0.6	1.07	25.53
flake	red	2677	1037	11.13	0.40	1.59	42.68	0.34	0.69	0.55	4.53	0.06	0.35	0.44	9.16	<0.6	1.08	26.99
flake, burned	red	2677	1037	11.13	0.54	1.89	41.84	0.29	0.60	0.81	5.36	0.19	0.44	0.59	9.97	<0.6	0.87	25.45
flake	blue	3548	990	18.43	0.66	2.42	59.40	0.18	030	0.93	8.68	0.10	0.35	2.01	<0.5	<0.6	4.89	1.00
bead	blue	1779	574	22.14	0.56	1.55	63.51	0.11	1.12	0.49	7.38	0.15	0.05	1.13	<0.5	<0.6	0.51	0.78
yel/blue toggle	blue	4380	938	19.51	0.54	2.52	62.51	0.07	0.99	1.21	8.10	0.08	0.55	0.84	<0.5	<0.6	<0.5	0.80
blue spiral	blue	1075	1011	17.02	0.72	2.72	59.08	0.23	0.96	6.63	8.52	0.07	1.73	1.59	<0.5	<0.6	<0.5	<0.3
bead	blue	2471	963	15.78	1.11	0.89	67.35	0.40	1.10	5.16	6.73	0.05	0.18	0.47	<0.5	<0.6	<0.5	<0.3

bead	blue	2877	1138	25.40	1.27	1.78	54.57	0.14	1.29	1.39	4.90	0.12	6.67	0.93	<0.5	<0.6	<0.5	0.98
bead	yellow	1869	325	10.87	0.41	2.19	55.85	0.27	1.05	0.69	6.20	0.05	0.13	1.77	<0.5	<0.6	0.80	19.08
bead	yellow	3961	739	12.88	0.46	2.12	54.55	0.27	0.76	0.69	7.16	0.09	0.50	0.95	1.21	<0.6	1.41	16.83
ball	yellow	3402	1316	11.52	0.73	1.85	42.78	0.62	0.51	2.05	3.99	0.10	0.72	1.60	<0.5	<0.6	3.74	29.15
bead	yellow	2725	1228	16.18	0.47	2.00	46.48	0.31	0.70	0.49	5.39	0.07	0.08	1.37	1.41	<0.6	2.26	22.75
bead	yellow	3458	1331	15.86	0.50	2.27	53.89	0.29	0.77	1.20	6.15	0.04	0.52	0.77	1.30	<0.6	1.23	15.18
bead	yellow	3467	1469A	13.89	0.85	1.93	46.90	0.65	0.66	1.46	4.83	0.10	0.73	1.32	0.88	<0.6	2.42	23.27
bead	yellow	3467	1469B	10.45	0.84	1.64	42.55	0.62	0.54	1.17	3.93	0.08	0.44	1.34	1.20	<0.6	1.97	33.23
bead	yellow	1888	603	13.07	0.46	2.29	56.75	0.23	0.95	4.28	5.43	0.04	0.04	0.79	<0.5	<0.6	0.68	14.42
bead	yellow	2223	612	14.06	0.43	2.15	52.47	0.26	0.98	0.79	5.17	0.09	0.00	1.13	<0.5	<0.6	0.32	21.44
bead	yellow	2223	632	13.76	0.43	2.12	53.30	0.28	0.90	0.68	5.65	0.07	0.11	0.88	0.76	<0.6	0.79	20.23
bead	yellow	2285	782	14.04	0.49	2.13	51.23	0.35	0.81	1.25	6.25	0.06	0.55	0.86	<0.5	<0.6	0.93	19.93

Figure 6.5 Secondary (left) and back-scattered (right) SEM images of flakes from bead 2156 305. When viewed in tandem this allowed the selection of a flat, clean surface, not shadowed by other pieces (SEI image) with a consistent atomic number and lack of surface abnormalities or corrosion (BSE image).

in polyester resin that was then polished to a flat surface using silicon carbide and alumina polishing agents.

The other objects, mostly beads plus some fragments, were sampled using the method devised by Bronk and Freestone (2001), which employs a re-usable diamond-coated file, the edge of which is scored across a small section of the surface of the object to produce fine glass flakes. Following initial experiments carried out on Corning glass standards to determine the accuracy and practicality of the method, it was found that a number of flakes could be removed relatively easily from a small bead (*c.*3 mm in diameter) (Figure 6.5) by inserting a wooden cocktail stick into the hole of the bead to hold it steady, and running the file adjacent to this. All sampling was carried out under a low-powered optical microscope. The flakes were collected from the file itself, and also as loose pieces that fell and were collected onto polyester film sheet. These were picked up by pressing an adhesive carbon tab mounted on an SEM stub on to the fragments, while pressing down onto the polyester sheet to make the microscopic flakes lie as flat as possible. The stubs were then carbon coated.

The fragments could be examined thoroughly by a combination of both secondary (SE) and back-scattered electron (BSE) images in the SEM; the two images when viewed in tandem allowed the selection of a flat, clean surface, not shadowed by other pieces (SE image) and with a lack of surface abnormalities or corrosion (BSE image) (Figure 6.6).

The sizes of the flakes varied; Bronk and Freestone (2001) found that relatively small flakes (smaller than 100 μm or at a magnification greater than x4,000 in the SEM) produced poor reproducibility in terms

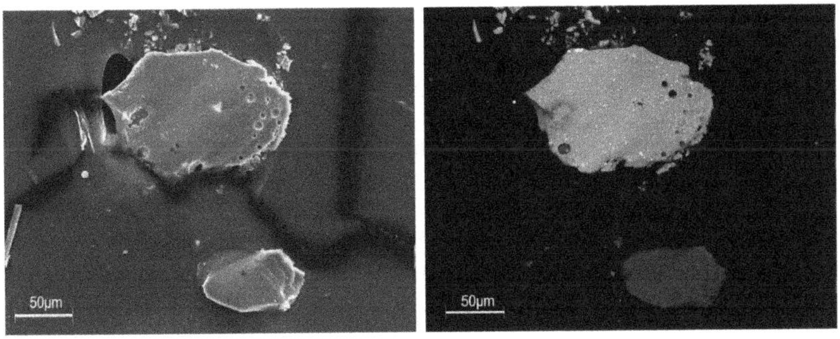

Figure 6.6 Secondary (left) and back-scattered (right) SEM images of flakes from a clear glass blob (Figure 6.15 bottom right hand corner) with opaque yellow glass at one end (CDF 05 3022/1219). For the SEI surface undulation in the flake can be seen; for the BSE fine particles of lead antimonate can be seen in the upper fragment (yellow glass), but not in the lower fragment (clear glass).

of analysis, with low overall totals. They concluded this was partly due to the thermal loss of sodium under the beam at this intensity. In practice, it was not always possible to analyse large flakes, as the analytical protocol required at least five measurements to be taken from each sample, where possible from different flakes or different areas on a flake and from as large an area free from contamination or corrosion as possible. Again, the protocol devised by Bronk and Freestone (2001) requires analyses to be as close to 100 per cent as achievable; in practice the majority of analyses fell within 90–110 per cent, but with some problematic samples having greater variation (very small flakes or flakes that were not lying flat).

The overall percentage totals varied due to surface irregularities and variation in orientation of the flakes towards the primary beam and the detector. Sometimes considerable time was needed to locate the most appropriate flakes, or areas within these to achieve the best analyses. All the totals were normalised to 100 per cent so they could be compared to one another and to other results. As with Bronk and Freestone's initial study, the standard deviation for the flakes was slightly greater than that for polished samples; but also as with the polished samples, the largest errors occurred in sodium, possibly due to its volatility, and lead, antimony and tin (plus copper in red glass), probably due to uneven dispersal of these metal compounds within the glass matrix, especially when used as colourants. While instrumental precision and accuracy as determined on the standard glasses was typical of the EDS technique (Freestone et al. 2000; Bronk and Freestone 2001), it is not possible to be more specific in the present case because the opaque glasses are heterogenous on a scale close to that of the size of some of the flakes.

Results and discussion

Results are given in Table 6.1 as the means of the individual analyses of the samples. Initial interpretation indicated that some of the pieces were later intrusions: this included several pieces of blue/grey slag (possibly from iron production), two pieces of green slag, a piece of mineralised bronze, and several pieces of coloured glass with clearly anachronistic compositions. These are excluded from further discussion.

All of the glasses have a soda-lime-silica base with varying amounts of transition metal colourants and opacifiers based upon copper, lead, antimony and tin. MgO contents are below 1.5 per cent, and typically less than 1 per cent, typical of the natron glass of the period. However, some of the samples analysed by the flake method have higher than anticipated K_2O, exceptionally ranging up to 5 or 6 per cent. Some colours, notably the colourless beads, show a correlation between K_2O and CaO, shown in Figure 6.7, and the high potash glasses tend to have higher P_2O_5, suggesting an ash-related contamination. As shown experimentally by Paynter

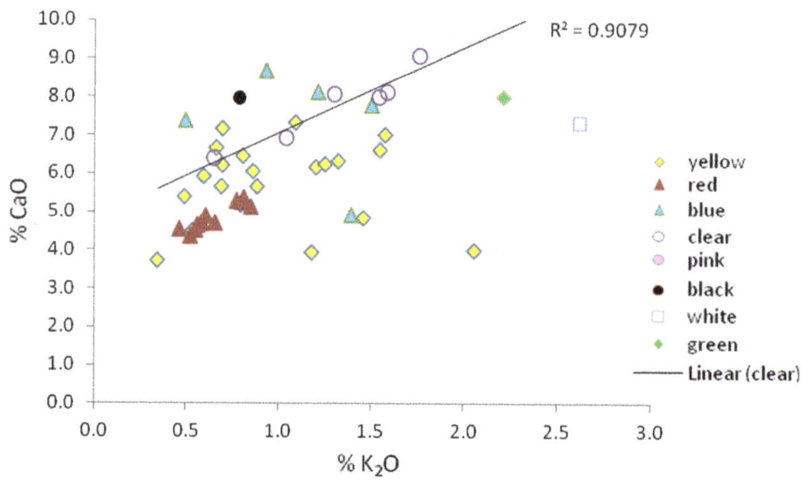

Figure 6.7 Scatter diagram of potash v lime showing a strong correlation; there are higher values for potash glass sampled by the 'flake' method (e.g. yellow, clear) rather than embedded polished samples (red).

(2008) and noted for example by Rehren et al. (2010) and Al-Bashaireh et al. (2016) for glass vessel assemblages, prolonged heating and reworking or recycling in the glass workshop can result in contamination of this type. While it is not impossible that some of the glasses in the present assemblage have indeed been extensively recycled, this seems unlikely in deeply coloured blue or yellow glasses where the colouration would be diluted or spoiled. We suggest the most likely origin for these characteristics lies in the sampling method, which results in the analysis of a thin sliver of glass from the surface of the bead. It is quite possible that the bead surfaces were sometimes contaminated due to prolonged flame working or annealing in hot ash. We therefore interpret all of the glasses as having been originally low-magnesia, low-potash natron-type glasses, sometimes contaminated by workshop practices.

It is now well understood that there were two main primary glass types in use in the period of interest. Manganese-decolourised glass, with higher lime and alumina, was produced from at least the Hellenistic period in the Levant, while a glass with lower lime and alumina, higher soda and decolourised by antimony was probably made in Egypt from the first century CE. Frequently, glass with both antimony and manganese is encountered, reflecting the mixing of the two end-members through recycling (e.g. Silvestri 2008; Silvestri et al. 2008; Freestone 2015; Jackson and Paynter 2016). Figure 6.8 shows these two major glass groupings, in terms of lime versus alumina. Data for Mn-decolourised and higher-CaO glass that was not decolourised are from fourth-century CE Jalame (Brill 1988), first-century BCE Jerusalem (unpublished data of Freestone and Israeli); first-century BCE–first-century CE mosaic glass (Freestone and Stapleton 2015), and Augusta Pretoria (Mirti et al. 1993). Those for Sb-decolourised glass are from first to third-century Roman Britain (Heyworth et al. 1990; Jackson 2005; Paynter 2006). For comparative purposes, colourants, decolourisers and opacifiers were excluded and the 'reduced' compositions re-cast to 100 per cent were used (Brill 1999).

It is observed (Figure 6.8) that the great majority of the glass from Culduthel occurs in the upper group in the diagram (higher alumina and lime; Mn-decolourised), and the great majority contain MnO at levels in excess of 0.1 per cent, indicative of deliberate addition (Table 6.1). Only one sample appears attributable to the low-lime,-low-alumina group associated with antimony-decolourisation. As shown below, this exception is a blue glass with a composition that does not correspond to Roman antimony-decolourised glass in a number of other respects. As the low-lime, low-alumina antimony-decolourised glass composition appears to have become widespread in the mid-to late first century CE, this is fully

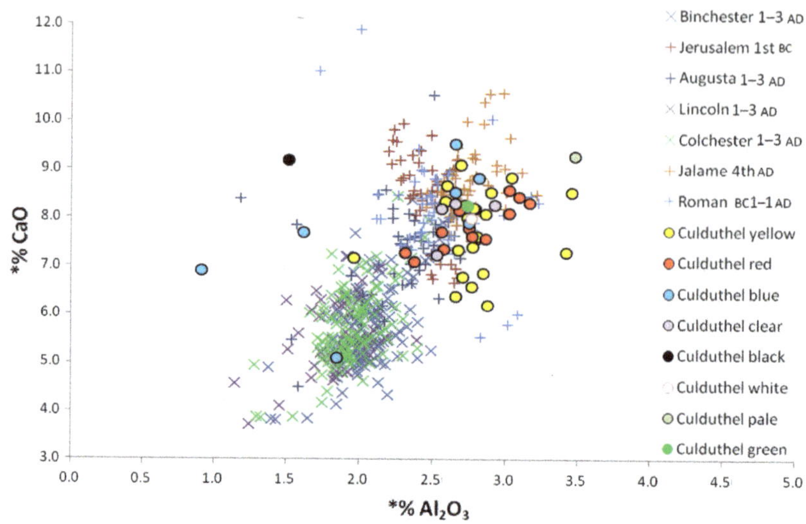

Figure 6.8 Scatter diagram of first- to third-century antimony-decolourised low-lime low-alumina glass from Britain and high-lime, high-alumina green-blue or Mn-decolourised glass from the Mediterranean of various dates, showing the majority of glass from Culduthel more closely matches the high-lime type rather than the later antimony-decolourised material. *indicates "reduced" compositions (see text). Data from Brill 1988; Heyworth et al. 1990; Mirti et al. 1993; Jackson 2005; Paynter 2006; Freestone and Stapleton 2015; unpublished data of Freestone and Israeli.

consistent with the early first-century date proposed for the assemblage; the Sb-decolourised low lime-composition would be expected to be present in any assemblage post-dating the middle of the century.

Opaque red glass

The red glass from Culduthel consists entirely of small pieces of working debris (Figure 6.2) in the form of offcuts and waste fragments; there are 20 of these, many show discolouring on the outer surface and signs of melting due to heating (Figure 6.4). 'Sealing wax' red glass of the type identified was used in the 'Celtic' European Iron Age to decorate prestigious metal items, and in the first century CE its use increased dramatically within Britain for the decoration of Late Insular La Tène artefacts, especially those related to horses and chariots. It is highly probable that the glass was used as an inlay into copper alloy objects such as the

Figure 6.9 Cruciform strap union with unfilled cells (for glass or enamel) and fantail brooch with inlaid red, yellow and blue glass; both from Culduthel. Not to scale.
Source: after Murray (2007: 25)

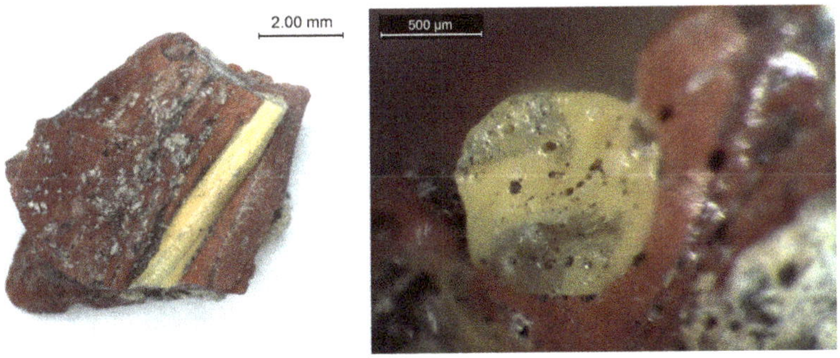

Figure 6.10 Red glass attached to a strand of spiralled clear and yellow glass – general view (left) and cross-section (right).

cruciform harness piece or the fantail brooch found at the site and shown in Figure 6.9. The glass would have been heat-softened and pressed into champlevé recesses in the metal object; the darker oxidised surface could then be polished down *in situ* (Bimson 1963, 1987). One further important aspect of the red glass from Culduthel is that it is found fused to both yellow and clear glass from the site, giving direct evidence for contemporaneous use of some of the coloured glasses, probably in bead manufacture (Figure 6.10).

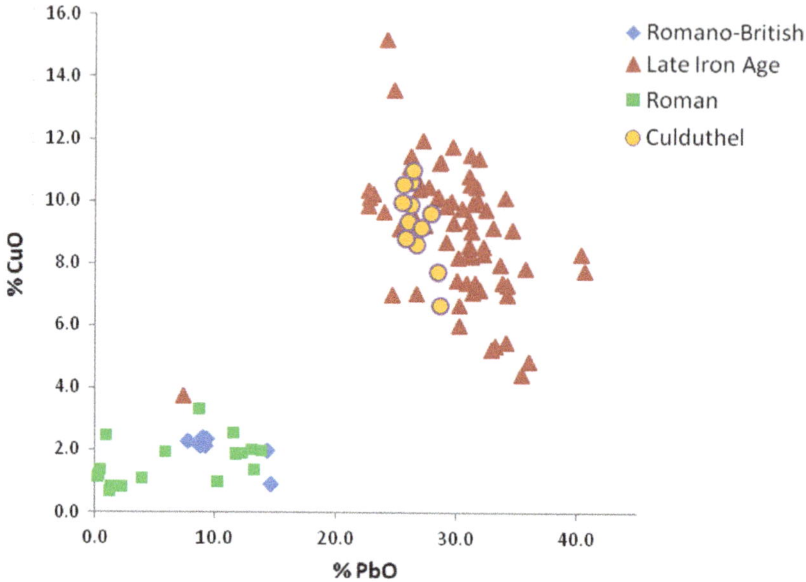

Figure 6.11 Scatter diagram showing the lead oxide and copper oxide content for Iron Age and Roman red glass. Comparative data: Bateson and Hedges 1975; Bayley 2001, 2005; Freestone et al. 2003; Davis 2014; Freestone and Stapleton 2015; unpublished data of Freestone.

The composition of the red glass fragments is similar to much late Iron Age 'sealing wax' glass from Britain. It is a soda-lime-silica glass with large quantities of lead and copper (Figure 6.11), plus a significant antimony content. The composition of this glass is slightly different to the earlier continental La Tène and middle Iron Age 'sealing wax' red glass, specifically in the use of antimony rather than iron as an internal reducing agent (Davis 2014). The copper is in the form of cuprite dendrites within the glass matrix, which gives it an intense colour and opacity (Figure 6.12). It is highly likely that this coloured glass was traded as ingots or blocks; several of these with similar compositions have been found, for instance, from Tara Hill in Ireland (Stapleton et al. 1999, 915) and Fish Street in London (Freestone et al. 2003).

Comparison of the base glass compositions of the Culduthel reds with the other coloured glasses from the site indicates that it is a fairly typical Levantine type (Figure 6.8), although some of the reds tend to have rather high alumina. In the context of a large number of opaque red late Iron Age glasses from Britain, this alumina enrichment is not extreme (Figure 6.13). However, there is a very strong correlation

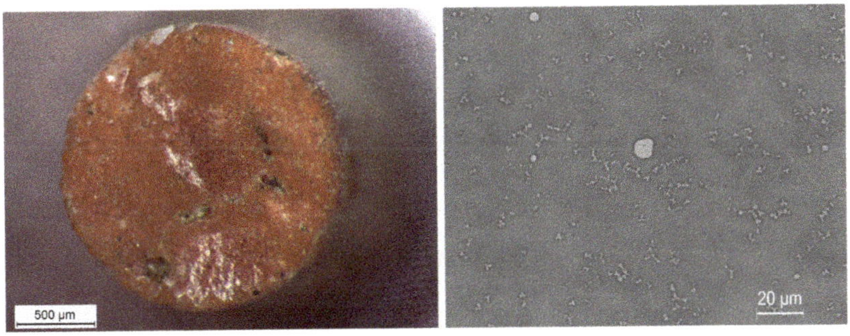

Figure 6.12 Photograph of fracture cross-section of opaque red rod CF 05 2548/990D and SEM BSE image of CF05 2550/989, showing cuprite dendrites in the glass matrix.

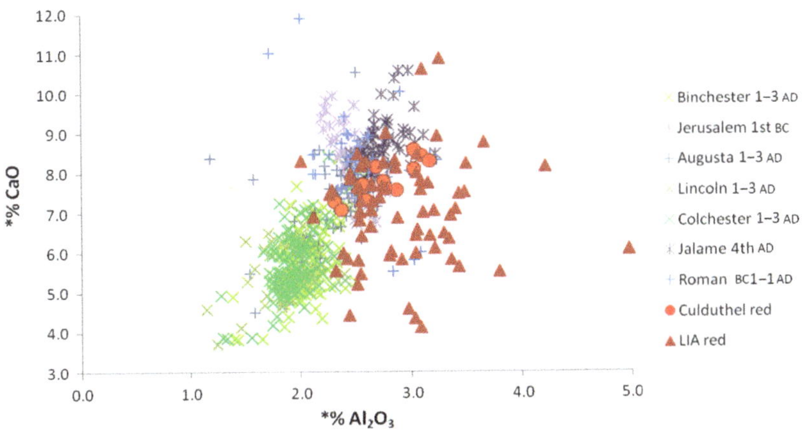

Figure 6.13 Scatter diagram showing Culduthel in relation to other red glass from Britain, and to colourless and weakly coloured Roman vessel glass (for sources of comparative data, see Figures 6.8 and 6.11).

between alumina and iron oxide levels in the fragments (Figure 6.14); the ratio Fe_2O_3: Al_2O_3 is about 4:10, which is close to the ratio of these components in alluvial clay (Kamber et al. 2005). It may therefore be inferred that this relationship is due to contamination by clay. Given the reactive character of lead-rich glass, it seems probable that this reflects a reaction with the crucible, when the glass was melted or possibly when it was coloured. This resulted in the absorption of varying amounts of alumina and iron oxide from the crucible. Evidence for a similar effect may be seen in many of the analysed Iron Age opaque red glass (Figures 6.13

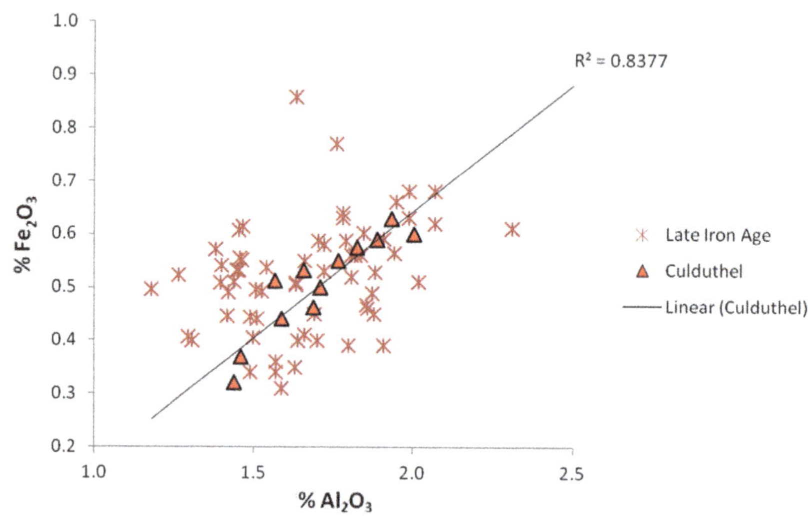

Figure 6.14 Scatter diagram showing the strong correlation between alumina and iron oxide in red glass in general, and in particular from Culduthel. Data taken from Freestone et al. 2003; Davis 2014; Freestone and Stapleton 2015; Freestone unpublished.

and 6.14), suggesting that trace and isotopic compositions of opaque red glasses from this period should be interpreted with caution as there may be significant contamination from clay-based ceramic.

The strong correlation of the Culduthel reds seen in Figure 6.14 suggests an origin as a single composition and that the red glass was produced in a single production event. It seems likely that they come from a single traded block or ingot of glass; this was used for a range of activities and they form a distinct group despite their varied morphology. This block would have been imported to Culduthel but its origin is unknown. The base glass is clearly eastern Mediterranean, but may have been coloured further west. Small numbers of similar high-lead red opaque glasses are encountered in the Mediterranean region but no colouring workshops have been reported.

Opaque yellow glass

The most numerous type of glass artefacts from the site are small, opaque, annular yellow beads, typically 3–4 mm diameter. There are 14 of these, plus one small yellow ball, which may have been made in preparation to be converted into a bead. Yellow glass was also used to decorate other objects;

Figure 6.15 Objects with yellow glass from Culduthel. Not to scale.

mainly larger colourless beads, but also a dark blue toggle of Iron Age type (Hunter forthcoming). There is one blob of colourless/pale green-blue glass (3022/1219) with a small amount of yellow on one side (Figure 6.15), plus the yellow, clear and red piece discussed above (Figure 6.10). Yellow-coloured glass was probably highly suitable for applied decoration, as the high lead content would have lowered its melting point.

Almost all the opaque yellow glass was coloured and opacified using lead antimonate, by far the most common colourant used in the Iron Age and Roman periods for the production of yellow glass. The reduced compositions fall in the same area of the lime-alumina plot as the other colours but a number of them have higher Al_2O_3 contents (Figure 8.6). This alumina-enrichment has also been observed in the opaque yellows in the approximately contemporary mosaic glass vessels, and is attributed to the two-stage manufacture of the colour, where lead and antimony are reacted in a preliminary stage in a ceramic crucible to form a lead antimonate pigment or 'anime' before mixing with the soda-lime-silica glass (Shortland 2002, Freestone and Stapleton 2015). Like the sealing wax red glass, the base glass was originally made in the Levant and is likely to have been distributed from one or more colouring workshop as yellow blocks or ingots (Tite et al. 2007). Although the lead antimonate coloured glasses from Culduthel are similar to one another, their composition is more variable than for the red fragments. For example, the lead and antimony distributions indicate

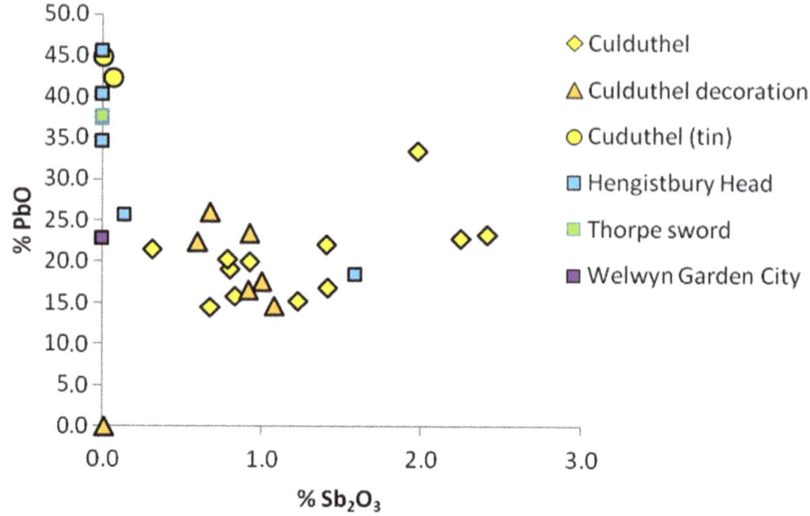

Figure 6.16 Iron Age yellow glass; the tin coloured glass is located on the Y-axis, and often contains slightly more lead than antimony coloured glass. For sources of comparative data, see text.

that much of the yellow glass used for decoration seems to fall into a distinct group with the majority of the beads; but there were possibly two or three different groups/ingots worked on the site (Figure 6.16). The similarity of the artefacts and decorative styles suggests that these were used within overlapping time frames.

Yellow glass is known to have been used as 'enamel' inlay in Iron Age copper alloy metalwork along with red, for example, in the armlets from Pitkelloney (British Museum P&E 1838,0714.3) and Castle Newe (1946,0402.1, 2), and the majority of such items appear to come from north-eastern Scotland. Indeed, there is an example of red and yellow (plus blue) glass inlaid into the copper alloy fantail brooch from Culduthel (Figure 6.9).

Two of the beads, 2223/583 and 3218/1268, virtually undistinguishable from the others visually (the top row of Figure 6.15, shows one antimony- and one tin-opacified annular bead), were coloured using lead stannate. This is a relatively rare colourant in the Iron Age, but Henderson and Warren (1982) analysed and noted a number of tin-opacified yellow artefacts (mainly beads) from Britain and Ireland ranging in date from the third century BCE to the third century CE. Tin-opacified yellow glass was also used for armlets from Hengistbury Head (Henderson 1987), on the gaming pieces from Welwyn Garden City (Werner and Bimson 1967) and on the hilt of a sword from Thorpe Hall, Yorkshire (unpublished data of Freestone) (Figure 6.16). Tite et al. (2007, 68) note that tin-based opacifiers were used in addition to antimony-based opacifiers in the production of glass beads found in Britain and France during the second to first centuries BCE.

Blue glass

The blue glass from Culduthel consists of three small, individually distinctive annular beads, one flake, one lump, a toggle decorated with yellow glass and a twisted spiral of blue and white glass (Figure 6.2, top row and end of row 3).

Three of the blue glass artefacts have compositions consistent with eastern Mediterranean glass: flake 3548/990 (Table 6.1), blue and white spiral 1075/1011 and dark blue toggle 4380/938. These could all have been associated with glass-working on the site, and show alumina and silica levels similar to the majority of the glass from Culduthel (Figure 6.17). The flake has relatively high antimony oxide at 4.89 per cent and the 1 per cent associated lead oxide is characteristic of a class of opaque blue glass found in Roman mosaic tesserae, for example. The toggle, decorated with yellow glass, is Iron Age in style rather than Roman or Romano-British (Hunter forthcoming).

The remaining three blue glasses have very diverse compositions. Bead 2877/1138 (Figure 6.2, fifth object, row 1) is very unusual with over 25 per cent Na_2O and 6.7 per cent MnO (Table 6.1). It does not compare closely to any ancient glass known to us, but the high chlorine content indicates that it is not modern. Beads 1779/574 (sixth object, row 1) and 2471/963 (third object, row 1) contain lower alumina than typical of the other colours and of Levantine primary glass (Figure 6.18). Low-alumina natron glass is more characteristic of the early to middle Iron Age (e.g. Conte et al. 2016). It should be noted that bead 2471/963 has an MgO content of 1.1 per cent, which is at the higher end of the range for natron glass. The high K_2O content of this sample, 5.16 per cent is attributed to fuel contamination in the workshop (see above) but an alternative alkali source for the base glass cannot be ruled out.

The variability of the blue objects compared to the other colours from Culduthel suggests a wider range of origins, possibly being supplied over a longer period of time. It seems likely that Iron Age blue glass objects were being made at Culduthel, as the toggle is distinctively native in style and colour, and decorated with yellow glass similar in composition to the majority of yellow glass from the site; furthermore, the twisted cane in

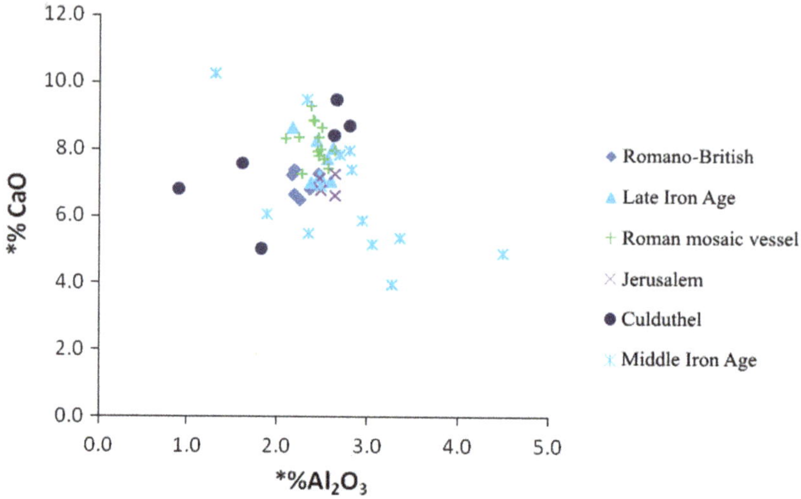

Figure 6.17 Base glass composition of Iron Age, Roman and Romano-British blue glass, showing the range of glass from Culduthel. Roman mosaic glass and Jerusalem data taken from Freestone and Stapleton 2015 and unpublished data of Freestone and Israeli. The remaining samples are sorted by date and taken from Bateson and Hedges 1975; Henderson 1981, 1987; 1989; Davis 2014; and unpublished data of Davis.

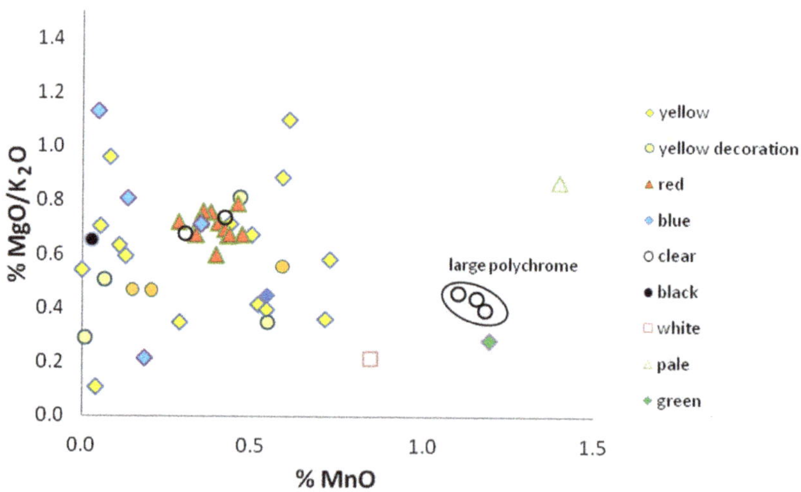

Figure 6.18 Scatter diagram showing similarity in composition of the three large polychrome beads relative to other colours from Culduthel.

blue and white appears to reflect local hot-working. However, there is no evidence the blue beads were made there. It seems the availability of blue glass was different to that of the red and yellow glasses.

Clear glass

The colourless glass at Culduthel consists of two very small fragments (only one analysed), one small blob with a minute amount of yellow glass (Figure 6.2 row 2 – tinged blue in the photograph) and three polychrome beads decorated with yellow glass (shown in Figure 6.2 row 3; two are broken); there is also a small thread twisted with yellow glass and attached to a red lump (Figure 6.10). All the pieces seem to originate from the eastern Mediterranean on the basis of their lime and alumina contents (Figure 6.8).

The colourless glass used for the polychrome beads has a very uniform composition (Table 6.1, Figure 6.19); they are characterised by over 1 per cent MnO, which is typical of the addition of this element as a decolouriser in colourless Hellenistic and early Roman glass (e.g. Reade and Privat 2016). Along with the use of added yellow decoration of consistent composition (Figure 6.16), the close similarity of these compositions implies that they were made in a single episode of glass-making, perhaps from a single batch. They are of a form parallel to other late Iron Age decorated beads from Scotland (Hunter forthcoming). The polychrome working fragment comprising a twisted yellow and colourless thread attached to a piece of opaque red implies that colourless glass was worked at Culduthel. If the colourless beads were made at the site, then the lack of colourless waste may reflect the ease with which this glass may be recycled; its colour would not have been compromised if no other colours were mixed.

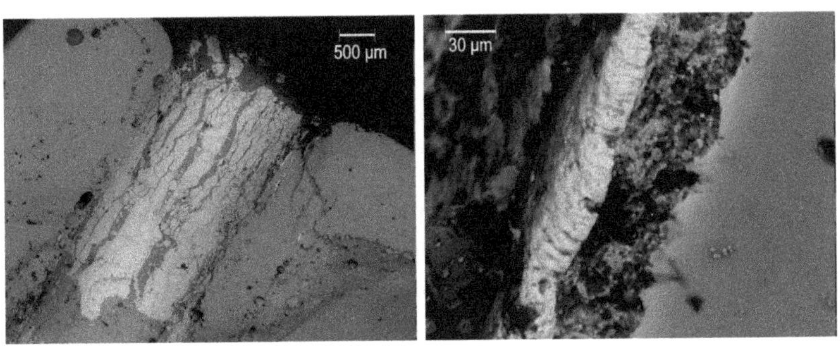

Figure 6.19 SEM BSE image of bead 2156 399, showing iron scale lining the inside of the hole (left), and a cross-section of the iron scale in the hole (right).

Other colours

There are a number of other coloured objects; a small greenish blue annular bead coloured by copper (Figure 6.2 end of row 2), and the opaque white of a blue and white spiral fragment (Figure 6.2 start of row 1) both have base glass compositions suggesting an eastern Mediterranean origin like much of the assemblage: there are no other objects or working debris in these colours. This could imply a pre-worked imported cane; although other spiral rods including the amber and yellow glass on bead 4342/846 (Figure 6.15, start of row 2), and the clear and yellow spiral in the red glass on fragment 3022/1193b (Figure 6.10) may imply that canes were manufactured on the site. The amber glass is a typical eastern Mediterranean type with no added MnO, a typical characteristic of amber glass of the period, which appears to be coloured due to reducing conditions in the primary glass furnace (Freestone and Stapleton 2015).

There is also a small black bead, coloured by a large quantity of iron (Figure 6.2, start of row 2). This bead has a composition consistent with Romano-British black glass (Bateson and Hedges 1975). Van der Linden et al's. study of 'black' Roman glass would suggest that a bead with high iron was probably manufactured after 150 CE (Van der Linden et al. 2009, 828, 837). However, the alumina content of 1.31 per cent is not consistent with Roman black glass and analyses of Iron Age black glass from France and Switzerland, dating into the second century BCE includes glass with similar iron oxide, alumina and potash levels (Gratuze 2009).

Bead fabrication

Many of the beads contain the residues of iron scale in their central piercings (Figure 6.19), suggesting they were worked on iron mandrels. It is likely that iron rods were pre-heated to develop a scale that would adhere to the heated glass and was removed as part of the bead (removing glass directly from iron rods without some form of release agent is very difficult). Beads can easily be rounded and trail decoration incorporated, by rotating heated glass on a mandrel.

Discussion and conclusions

The absence of low-lime, low-alumina antimony-decolourised Roman glass from the assemblage places it around or before the middle of the first century CE, as this type of glass became common in Britain at about that time. In addition, the use of antimony as a reductant in the red glass is typical of the late Iron Age, so that glass composition would appear to date workshop activity to late in the first century BCE. through to the second half of the first century CE.

The analyses suggest that a range of glass-working activities may have been occurring at Culduthel, including the production of hot inlay or 'enamel', and the manufacture of beads and other small objects. Glass was not made from its raw materials, nor was it coloured, but was imported. The base glass is overwhelmingly Hellenistic or early Roman in character, of the type associated with production on the Levantine coast, although several blue beads are of a composition that appears to be older, dating to the middle of the first millennium BCE. These could represent heirlooms from a period pre-dating the workshop activity.

The origin of the base glass in the eastern Mediterranean does not imply that the colours were made there and they are likely to have been produced in secondary workshops located elsewhere. Furthermore there is no reason to suppose that the red and yellow colours were made in the same location and the presence of both antimony- and tin-opacification practices in the assemblages suggests at least two original sources for opaque yellow. As tin-opacification is represented in only two beads, these are more likely to have been imported rather than fabricated on-site.

Although soda-lime-silica glass will melt at approximately 1100°C, so requires a relatively high level of pyrotechnic sophistication, it is possible to re-shape, decorate and anneal glass at much lower temperatures, above the glass transition temperature, when it has become ductile. Leaded glasses, in particular, readily soften at lower temperatures, which would have been the case for both the red and yellow glass from Culduthel. Extra heat would increase the glass flow, which could be varied depending on the needs of the glass worker. This level of technology would allow red glass to be softened enough to be pressed into metal recesses, allow cullet to be re-shaped into beads, and allow yellow glass to be shaped into artefacts or used for trailing decoration. While there is evidence for such relatively low-temperature activity at Culduthel, there is no evidence for the use of higher temperature activity needed to colour glass; and it is pertinent that no glass crucibles were recovered from the site.

The recovery of most of the glass finds from an area of the site associated with non-ferrous metal-working, along with metalwork with cells for inlay, strongly suggests that the main purpose of the red glass was to decorate metalwork. However, other waste is suggestive of hot-working on site, probably in the production of beads, and the occurrence of polychrome waste including red and yellow glass suggests that both colours were in use for this purpose. Compositional similarities between the yellow in the waste and some of the beads might reflect the fact that they were made at Culduthel. However, an alternative possibility is that the yellow beads were being imported to be worn and/or represent a raw material for forming a yellow inlay or 'enamel', although we have no evidence for its use in this way on the site. The compositions of the red glass fragments are consistent with derivation from a single consignment of glass, possibly a single ingot, so the active use of hot glass on the site is unlikely to have been a prolonged affair. There is no evidence for the melting of blue glass. Indeed, the fact that the compositions of the blue glass objects and fragments from the site are so variable could imply pieces were being acquired when and if the chance occurred, possibly via 'Roman' routes rather than more established 'Celtic' Iron Age trade links. No lumps or ingots of blue glass have been discovered in Britain from this period, though imported Roman tesserae are not uncommon in slightly later Roman contexts (Bayley 2015; Paynter et al. 2015).

In a more general sense, the compositional information for the opaque red and yellow glasses confirms that significant contamination from clay-based container materials is likely in these glass types, and the interpretation of detailed trace and isotopic analyses of these glass types should be undertaken with this in mind.

This analysis of a handful of very small items, mainly recovered by sieving, has produced surprisingly detailed information on the glass used at the site of Culduthel in the Iron Age and supports the important evidence for the manipulation of hot glass in the early first century BCE. It emphasises the value of combining modern methods of archaeological recovery with detailed scientific analysis.

Acknowledgements

The practical work was undertaken when MD was a member of staff of the National Museum of Wales and IF a member of the Department of Archaeology, Cardiff University. We thank Phil Parkes for his support for the SEM, and Fraser Hunter for making the material accessible, and for supplying background information on the site at Culduthel and on the Iron Age in north-east Scotland in general.

References

Al-Bashaireh, K., Al-Mustafa, S., Freestone, I. C. and Al-Housan, A.Q. 2016. 'Composition of Byzantine Glasses from Umm el-Jimal, Northeast Jordan: Insights into Glass Origins and Recycling'. *Journal of Cultural Heritage* 21: 809–18.

Bateson, J. D. and Hedges, R. E. M. 1975. 'The Scientific Analysis of a Group of Roman-Age Enamelled Brooches'. *Archaeometry* 17 (2): 177–90.

Bayley, J. 2001. *Evidence for Enamelling from Elms Farm, Heybridge, Essex. Centre for Archaeology Report 001/2002*. Portsmouth: English Heritage.

Bayley, J. 2005. 'Roman Enamel and Enamelling: New Finds from Castleford, Yorkshire'. *Annales du 16e Congrès de l'Association Internationale pour l'Histoire du Verre*, 72–4.

Bayley, J. 2015. 'Roman Enamels and Enamelling'. In *Glass of the Roman World*, edited by J. Bayley, C. Jackson and I. Freestone, 178–89. Oxford: Oxbow Books.

Bimson, M. 1963. 'Opaque Red Glass and Its Use as an "Enamel"'. British Museum unpublished report.

Bimson, M. 1987. 'Opaque Red Glass: A Review'. In *Early Vitreous Materials*, edited by M. Bimson and I. C. Freestone, Occasional Paper 56, 165–71. London: British Museum.

Brill, H. R. 1988. 'Scientific Investigations of the Jalame Glass and Related Finds'. In *Excavations at Jalame: Site of a Glass Factory in Late Roman Palestine*, edited by G. D. Weinberg, 257–93. Columbia: University of Missouri Press.

Brill, H. R. 1999. *Chemical Analyses of Early Glasses*. Vols I and II. New York: Corning Museum of Glass.

Bronk, H., Freestone, I.C. 2001. 'A Quasi Non-Destructive Microsampling Technique for the Analysis of Intact Glass Objects by SEM/EDXA'. *Archaeometry* 43 (4): 517–27.

Conte, S., Arletti, R., Mermati, F. and Gratuze, B. 2016. 'Unravelling the Iron Age Glass Trade in Southern Italy: the First Trace-Element Analyses'. *European Journal of Mineralogy* 25: 409–33.

Davis, M. 2014. 'Technology at the Transition: Relationships Between Culture, Style and Function in the Late Iron Age Determined Through the Analysis of Artefacts'. Appendix 4, 5 and 8. PhD Thesis, Cardiff University. http://orca.cf.ac.uk/73215/12/Updated%202015davismphd.pdf.

Freestone, I. C. 2015. 'The Recycling and Reuse of Roman Glass: Analytical Approaches'. *Journal of Glass Studies* 57: 29–40.

Freestone, I. C., Gorin-Rosen, Y. and Hughes, M. J. 2000. 'Composition of Primary Glass from Israel'. In *Ateliers primaires et secondaires de verriers du second millénaire av. J.-C. au Moyen-Âge*, edited by M.-D. Nenna, 65–84. Lyon: Travaux de la Maison de l'Orient Méditerranéen.

Freestone, I. C. and Stapleton, C. 2015. 'Composition, Technology and Production of Coloured Glasses from Roman Mosaic Vessels'. *Glass of the Roman*

World, edited by J. Bayley, C. Jackson and I. Freestone, 90–105. Oxford: Oxbow Books.

Freestone, C. Stapleton, C. and Rigby, V. 2003. 'The Production of Red Glass and Enamel in the Late Iron Age, Roman and Byzantine Periods'. In *Through a Glass Brightly Studies in Byzantine and Medieval Art and Archaeology Presented to David Buckton*, edited by C. Entwistle 142–54. Oxford: Oxbow Books.

Gratuze, B. (2009) 'Les Premiers Verres Au Natron Retrouvés En Europe Occidentale: Composition Chimique et Chrono-Typologie'. In *Annales du 17eme Congres de l Association Internationale pour l'Histoire du Verre*, edited by K. Janssens, P. Degryse, P. Cosyns, J. Caen and L. Van't dack, 8–14. Antwerp: Antwerp University Press.

Henderson, J. 1981. 'X-ray Fluorescence Analysis of Iron Age Glass: Beads from Meare and Glastonbury Lake Villages'. *Archaeometry* 23 (1): 83–94.

Henderson, J. 1987. 'Glass Analyses: Appendix 6:A10–11'. *Hengistbury Head Dorset, Volume 1: The Prehistoric and Roman Settlement 3500 BC–AD 500*. edited by B. Cunliffe, Monograph no.13, 160–3, 180–6. Oxford: Oxford University Committee for Archaeology.

Henderson, J. 1989. 'Analysis of Enamels and Glasses Used in the Decoration of Brooches from Prestatyn and its Archaeological Interpretation'. In *Prestatyn 1984–5: An Iron Age Farmstead and Romano-British Industrial Settlement in North Wales*, edited by K. Blockley, 181–3. Oxford: British Archaeological Reports (British Series 210).

Henderson, J. and Warren, S. E. 1982. 'Analysis of Prehistoric Lead Glass'. In *Proceedings of the 22nd Symposium on Archaeometry*, edited by A. Aspinall and S. E. Warren, 168–80. Bradford: University of Bradford.

Heyworth, M. P., Baxter, M. J. and Cool, H. 1990. *Compositional Analysis of Roman Glass from Colchester Essex. Ancient Monuments Laboratory Report 53/1990*. London: English Heritage.

Hunter, F. Forthcoming. 'The Glass Artefacts and Glass-Working Debris: Catalogue, Typology and Discussion'. In Murray forthcoming.

Jackson, C. M. 2005. 'Making Colourless Glass in the Roman Period'. *Archaeometry* 47 (4): 763–80.

Jackson, C. M. and Paynter, S. 2016. 'Great Big Melting Pot: Exploring Patterns of Glass Supply, Consumption and Recycling in Roman Coppergate, York'. *Archaeometry*, 58 (1): 68–95.

Kamber, B. S., Greig, A. and Collerson, K. D. 2005. 'A New Estimate for the Composition of Weathered Young Upper Continental Crust from Alluvial Sediments, Queensland, Australia'. *Geochimica et Cosmochimica Acta* 69: 1041–58.

Mirti, P., Casoli, A. and Appolonia, L. 1993. 'Scientific Analysis of Roman Glass from Augusta Praetorian'. *Archaeomentry* 35 (2): 225–40.

Murray, R. 2007. 'Iron-Masters of the Caledonians'. *Current Archaeology* 212. www.archaeology.co.uk/articles/features/iron-masters-of-the-caledonians.htm.

Murray, R. Forthcoming. *Excavations at Culduthel, Inverness*.

Paynter, S. 2006. 'Analyses of Colourless Roman Glass from Binchester, County Durham'. *Journal of Archaeological Science* 33: 1037–57.

Paynter, S. 2008. 'Experiments in the Reconstruction of Roman Wood-Fired Glass-Working Furnaces: Waste Products and Their Formation Processes'. *Journal of Glass Studies* 50: 271–90.

Paynter, S., Kearns, T., Cool, H. and Chenery, S. 2015. 'Roman Coloured Glass in the Western Provinces: The Glass Cakes and Tesserae from West Clacton in England'. *Journal of Archaeological Science* 62: 66–81.

Reade, W. J. and Privat, K. L. 2016. 'Chemical Characterisation of Archaeological Glasses from the Hellenistic site of Jebel Khalid, Syria by Electron Probe Microanalysis'. *Heritage Science* 4(1): 20.

Rehren, Th., Marii, F., Schibille, N., Stanford, L. and Swan, C. 2010. 'Glass Supply and Circulation in Early Byzantine Southern Jordan'. In *Glas in Byzanz: Produktion, Verwendung, Analysen,* Mainz, RGZM Tagungen Band 8, edited by J. Drauschke and D. Keller, 65–81. Mainz: Verlag des Römisch-Germanischen Zentralmuseums.

Shortland, A. J. 2002. 'The Use and Origin of Antimonate Colorants in Early Egyptian Glass'. *Archaeometry* 44 (4): 517–30.

Silvestri, A. 2008. 'The Coloured Glass of Iulia Felix'. *Journal of Archaeological Science* 35 (6): 1489–501.

Silvestri, A., Molin, G. and Salviulo, G. 2008. 'The Colourless Glass of Iulia Felix'. *Journal of Archaeological Science* 35 (2): 331–41.

Stapleton, C. P., Freestone, I. C. and Bowman, S. G. E. 1999. 'Composition and Origin of Early Mediaeval Opaque Red Enamel from Britain and Ireland'. *Journal of Archaeological Science* 26 (8): 913–22.

Tite, M. Pradell T. and Shortland A. 2007. 'Discovery, Production and Use of Tin-Based Opacifiers in Glasses, Enamels and Glazes from the Late Iron Age Onwards: A Reassessment'. *Archaeometry* 50 (1): 67–84.

Van der Linden, V., Cosyns, P., Schalm, O., Cagno, S., Nys, K., Janssens, K., Nowak, A., Wagner, B. and Bulska, E. 2009. 'Deeply Coloured and Black Glass in the Northern Provinces of the Roman Empire: Differences and Similarities in Chemical Composition Before and After AD 150'. *Archaeometry* 51 (5): 822–44.

Werner, A. E. and Bimson, M. 1967. 'Technical Report on the Glass Gaming Pieces'. In I. M. Stead, 'A La Tène III Burial at Welwyn Garden City', *Archaeologia* 101: 1–62

7

Into Africa: The biography of Roman vessel glass in the Sahara Desert

Chloë N. Duckworth and David J. Mattingly

Abstract

The role of Roman vessel glasses that were traded to the central Sahara is presented, and their various social, material and cultural transformations are analysed from chemical and archaeological perspectives. In particular, the temporality of these objects, and the enabling and constraining factors of the desert trade by which they were transported, are considered as central factors in their interpretation. Their twentieth- and twenty-first-century recovery, conservation and current range of meanings are also discussed.

Introduction

> Geography can be a marvellous explanatory tool, so long as we avoid loading it with elementary determinism. It clarifies questions and formulates them, but it cannot resolve them. Men and their history complicate the picture and confuse the issue.
>
> (Braudel 1998, 157)

When we were approached to write a chapter for this volume, we considered how we could engage the interest of those working in the Mediterranean with this somewhat removed case study – of Roman vessel glass being transported into the heartlands of the Garamantes in Fazzan, central Sahara, well beyond the *limes* (see Figure 7.1). It struck us that the key to Roman glass in Fazzan is transformation: in use, value, meaning and even physical and chemical transformation (of which more below). In the Sahara, the usual methodological constraints of archaeology – too few data points, the danger of constructing static pictures in representation of a dynamic past – are amplified by the vast geographical distances involved, making it a challenging testing ground for recently developed approaches to the dynamic past.

Key among the aforementioned approaches is object biography. Many of our most valuable means of interpreting the material record, including the use of chemical analysis as a tool for provenance, have the side effect of 'flattening out' the temporality of an object, by drawing a direct line between production and deposition. In order better to account for the temporal dimension of the objects, we take in this chapter a loosely framed biographical/prosopographical approach, attempting to reconnect as much as possible with the 'life story' of Roman glass in Fazzan, from its primary production to deposition, recovery and beyond. The biographical approach to material culture may be seen as one of a set of approaches in current archaeological thinking which consider the ways in which human and material interact and mutually transform one another (Gosden and Marshall 1999, 169–78). By focusing on a particular 'strand' of evidence – in this case, the glass objects themselves – it is also possible to incorporate many different analytical and methodological techniques into a single approach. A further level of appreciation may be gained by considering the ways in which objects' biographies were understood by those who encountered or used them in the past.

The glasses were recovered from urban sites and cemeteries in the Garamantian heartlands of Fazzan, south-west Libya (see Figure 7.2): first by an Italian team in the 1930s (Pace et al. 1951); then under the direction of Mohammed Ayoub, a Sudanese archaeologist, between 1961 and 1969; and finally by two British archaeologists, Charles M. Daniels from 1958–77, and David Mattingly with the Fazzan Project (1997–2001) and the Desert Migrations Project (2007–11) (Mattingly et al. 2007, 2010, 2013). The latter project was prematurely halted due to the outbreak of civil war in Libya. The vast majority of the excavated material remains in Fazzan, while the excavation records along with a small subset of the material – much of it from the work of Charles Daniels – are currently being stored in the Trans-SAHARA Project archives in Leicester.

The Garamantes are mentioned in Roman historical sources, in which they variously figure as nomadic raiders, providers of trade goods and a society whose main centre merited the apellation metropolis (see summary in Mattingly et al. 2003, 76–90). The archaeological traces of the Garamantes are far more telling, and they present the story of an ethnically and probably culturally diverse oasis-based civilisation, which made use of advanced irrigation technology (*foggaras*). The most extensive pre-Islamic evidence for urban concentration and broader connectivity in Fazzan dates to the Classic Garamantian period, *c.* 1–400 CE. Traces of Garamantian production activity, focused primarily on metal-working and bead-making, are evident at Saniat Jibril, a satellite village close to the capital of Garama (modern Jarma – see Figures 7.1 and 7.2), sited in the large oasis belt known as the Wadi al-Ajal (for details on this site, see Mattingly et al. 2010, 123–204). Local resources include carnelian, which was worked and certainly traded with the Romans (and perhaps also to the south), and mineral salts that could potentially have been used in, or traded for, glass- and soap-making (Devulder et al. 2014; Duckworth et al. forthcoming). A number of northern imports are present in Fazzan, including Roman ceramics (both tablewares and transport ceramics containing wine or other consumable goods), glass, metalwork and building materials.

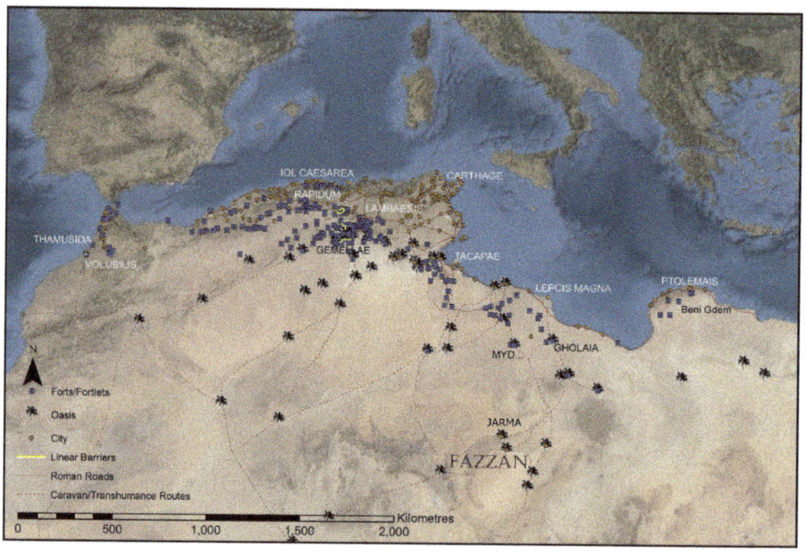

Figure 7.1 Map showing the cities of Roman North Africa, the line of forts that demarcates the *limes* and the most significant Saharan oasis sites. Map by Martin Sterry (originally published in Mattingly et al. 2013).

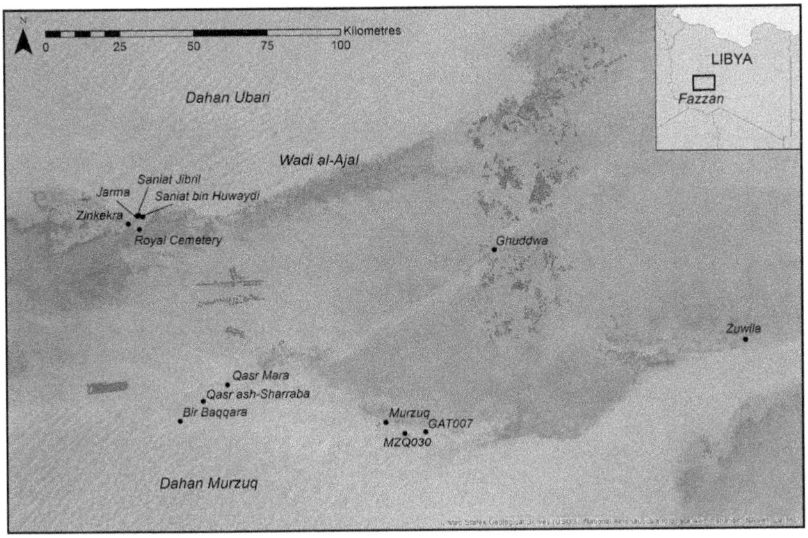

Figure 7.2 Map of Fazzan showing key Garamantian sites. Map by Martin Sterry.

There was almost certainly an equal or larger volume of less archaeologically visible commodities flowing into and out of Jarma, including textiles, dates, animals (the Romans may have procured wild beasts via the Garamantes) and human slaves. Remains of imports have been found in settlement contexts, notably Jarma itself, as well as at the manufacturing quarter of Saniat Jibril, but the majority (including all complete or near-complete glass vessels) were recovered from tombs, an example of which is shown in Figure 7.3.

The typology of the vessel glasses has been discussed extensively elsewhere, as have the first results of their chemical analysis, with further publications forthcoming (Duckworth forthcoming; Hoffman et al. 2010; Hoffmann 2013; Duckworth et al. 2016). We shall therefore limit ourselves to reporting some of the key facts here. Almost 2,000 fragments of vessel glass were found in Fazzan, the majority dating to between the first and fourth centuries CE, though vessel glass dating to as early as the first century BCE has been found. Table 7.1 summarises the locations in Fazzan from which Roman vessel glass has been recovered and the minimum numbers of vessels represented.

A range of typically Roman forms is encountered, including the so-called 'pillar-moulded' bowls of the first and early second centuries CE (see Figure 7.4), but relatively few glass storage vessels, and very

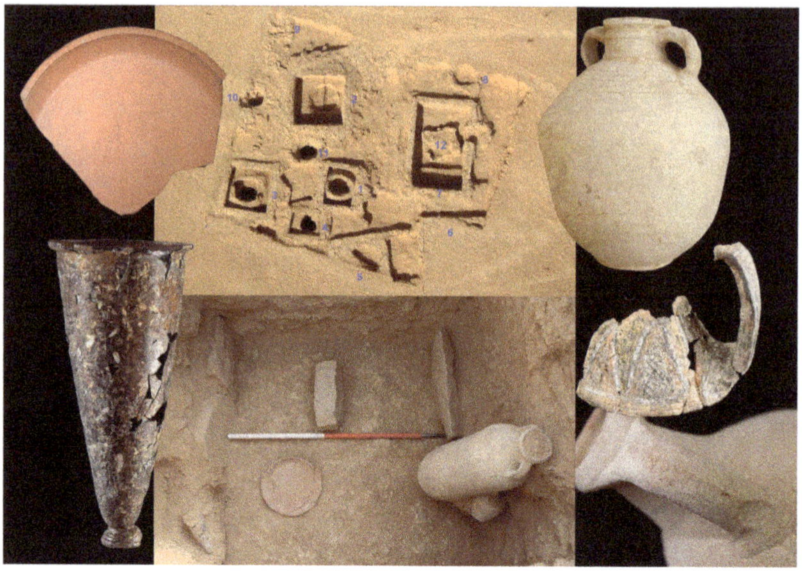

Figure 7.3 Garamantian burial at Taqallit cemetery 12, tomb 3 and selected grave goods including a glass rhyton (bottom left). Excavated as part of the Desert Migrations Project. The tomb contained both Roman and locally produced grave goods (such as the incense burner, centre right). Objects not to scale.
Source: composite image made by Chloë Duckworth using original photographs by Toby Savage, 2009

few perfume containers (making up 11.55 per cent and 2.22 per cent of the total assemblage, respectively). The compositional evidence for the vessel glass confirms that it was manufactured in the Roman world, using a mineral alkali such as natron. The glasses can be sub-divided into broad compositional groupings, which change in proportion over time: antimony-decoloured; manganese-decoloured; a group of glasses with both manganese and antimony; Roman blue-green glass; and HIMT (Duckworth et al. 2016, 635–8; Duckworth forthcoming).

Manufacture and provenance

Using a combination of typological assessment and compositional analysis, it is possible to make some propositions concerning the origin of the Roman glass from Fazzan, including changes over time. Birgitta

Table 7.1 Roman vessel glass in Fazzan, showing the minimum number of vessels of various types from the nine Fazzan sites with the most abundant archaeologically recorded glass remains

Name of site	*Type of site*	*1st century* BCE *to 2nd century* CE *cast*	*1st to 2nd century* CE *blown/mould-blown*	*Late 2nd to 5th century* CE	*Roman/Classic Garamantian, of uncertain date*
Jarma/Garama	Urban settlement (Garamantian capital)	>8 vessels	>3 vessels	>22 vessels	>80 vessels
Saniat Jibril	Urban settlement and manufacturing area	>7 vessels	>10 vessels	>21 vessels	>34 vessels
Saniat bin Huwaydi	Cemetery	>33 vessels	>8 vessels	>1 vessel	>4 vessels
'Royal Cemetery'	Cemetery	>5 vessels	>1 vessel	>43 vessels	>14 vessels
Zinkekra	Settlement and cemetery	>5 vessels	>4 vessels	None reported	>8 vessels
Watwat	Cemetery	>1 vessel	>3 vessels	>12 vessels	>4 vessels
Qasr bin Dughba	Settlement, *qasr* and cemetery	None reported	>1 vessel	>4 vessels	>4 vessels
Taqallit pyramid cemetery	Cemetery	None reported	None reported	>2 vessels	>2 vessels
Tinda	Settlement	>4 vessels	None reported	None reported	None reported

Figure 7.4 Highly corroded 'pillar-moulded' bowl in Jarma Museum. States of corrosion among the glass objects from Fazzan are highly variable, reflecting the different burial environments (from those close to irrigation systems, to those in arid zones) in the area.
Source: photograph by Birgitta Hoffmann

Hoffmann has made a thorough assessment of the glasses excavated by the Fazzan Project (Hoffmann 2013; Hoffmann et al. 2010), and we draw upon this work in our own discussion. The chemical analyses were conducted by Chloë Duckworth in 2014–15: further details of the methodology and results can be found in Duckworth (forthcoming).

Hoffmann notes that, among the pillar-moulded bowls from sites within the Jarma area, there is a very strong tendency towards a particular size, with diameters of 110–25 mm. She interprets this as, 'a conscious selection for carriage across the desert' (Hoffmann et al. 2010, 414). An alternative position is that the vessels were sourced from a relatively limited stock (e.g. from a single workshop and/or warehouse). We believe that the chemical evidence may support the latter interpretation, though we have regrettably few samples upon which to test this hypothesis. Three fragments of blue-green pillar-moulded bowls from the manufacturing area at Saniat Jibril were chemically analysed. As summarised in Table 7.2, they are remarkably close in composition, to the extent that they may well be from the same batch (they are sufficiently different in body and rim thickness to suggest they are not all three from the same vessel). Coupled with the aforementioned particularity in rim diameters, this may imply that the pillar-moulded bowls in Fazzan arrived in one or just a few shipments, perhaps from a single manufacturing centre. We are

Table 7.2 Analytical results for the three pillar-moulded bowl fragments from Saniat Jibril. Electron microprobe results are reported as oxides in weight percentage; laser-ablated, inductively coupled plasma mass spectrometry results are presented as elements, in parts per million

	Na_2O	MgO	Al_2O_3	SiO_2	P_2O_5	Cl	K_2O	CaO	TiO_2	MnO	Fe_2O_3	CuO
TSG082	15.5	0.64	2.37	69.9	0.14	1.36	0.60	8.97	0.05	0.34	0.34	0.00
TSG083	15.9	0.52	2.36	70.5	0.19	1.33	0.73	7.91	0.06	0.61	0.34	0.00
TSG084	16.5	0.47	2.43	71.1	0.13	1.52	0.54	7.38	0.05	0.51	0.31	0.00
	Li	**B**	**Ti**	**V**	**Cr**	**Co**	**Ni**	**Zn**	**As**	**Rb**	**Sr**	**Y**
TSG082	2.94	147	325	10.6	10.8	6.1	9.6	17.8	1.92	7.65	557	7.70
TSG083	3.68	106	351	13.4	9.7	18.3	10.7	21.7	2.09	7.99	492	7.33
TSG084	3.11	138	313	12.6	9.0	6.3	10.3	15.4	1.89	7.42	458	6.53
	Zr	**Nb**	**Mo**	**Sn**	**Sb**	**Cs**	**Ba**	**La**	**Ce**	**Pr**	**Nd**	**Sm**
TSG082	35.6	1.33	1.45	6.0	0.6	0.07	243	6.43	11.12	1.46	6.18	1.30
TSG083	37.0	1.41	2.34	12.6	92.9	0.08	255	6.23	10.97	1.40	5.97	1.33
TSG084	32.4	1.20	1.74	6.7	19.1	0.07	241	5.52	9.98	1.33	5.55	1.12
	Eu	**Gd**	**Tb**	**Dy**	**Ho**	**Er**	**Tm**	**Yb**	**Lu**	**Pb**	**Th**	**U**
TSG082	0.34	1.51	0.21	1.17	0.23	0.72	0.09	0.64	0.09	6.7	0.83	0.93
TSG083	0.36	1.19	0.19	1.21	0.24	0.59	0.10	0.62	0.07	50.9	0.84	0.88
TSG084	0.38	1.27	0.18	1.23	0.23	0.65	0.09	0.61	0.07	16.1	0.73	0.65

cautious in this interpretation, however, given the notable homogeneity of Roman glass composition, often particularly prominent in blue-green glass, and in this category of vessel (Brill and Stapleton 2013, 328). In order to test this, we are currently investigating the full set of trace element results in the hope of identifying any further potential batch twins that may be present in the material from Fazzan.

Other dimensional curiosities were noted by Hoffmann among the glass from Fazzan. Two *modioli* from tombs in Saniat bin Huwaydi are – at almost 200 mm high – among the largest known glasses of this type (so large, in fact, that Hoffmann notes they could not have been lifted by their tiny handles without risk of breaking them). From the same cemetery came six tubular rimmed bowls, also of an unusually large size. There are also several colourless and dark blue glass plates with very large diameters up to 340 mm (Mattingly et al. 2010, 414–16). An exceptionally large plate diameter of 480 mm was recorded by Pace et al. (1951, 313 fig. 106), but the whereabouts of this object are now unknown.

Given that much of the early (first- to second-century) glass assemblage is more characteristic of the western than the eastern Roman empire (Hoffmann 2013, 417), the question arises as to whether it was shipped directly from secondary glass workshops in Italy, from somewhere in North Africa, or produced near the northern end of the Saharan trade route in Tripolitania. Although it is not possible to be certain, we feel that the last option is more likely, largely because the added cost of oversea transport would seem an unnecessary additional risk and expense, but also because the assemblage – while not entirely 'typical' – does offer some hints of similarities with other North African material. For example, cast conical bowls lack a cut line under the outside rim, in common with fragments from Benghazi (northern Libya). In addition, it might be noted that the amphorae from Fazzan have been identified as Punic and then Roman Tripolitanian, while the majority of the ceramic finewares were identified as African Red Slip ware, also produced in Tunisia (Victoria Leitch, pers. comm.).

In any case, this picture is hardly static. As noted by Hoffmann (2013, 416–19), the later Roman assemblage from Fazzan is markedly different, and may well have arrived via different trade routes altogether. While the first- to second-century assemblage is dominated by plates and bowls, the majority of the late third- to seventh-century glasses are beakers, cups and lamps, a substantial shift in glass usage in Fazzan 'which only partly reflects general changes of glass usage in the Roman Empire' (Hoffmann 2013, 416–19). Methodological difficulties in dating third-century ceramics and glasses prevent us from closely tracing the transition between these two situations, but we may equally be seeing a hiatus in imports due to the political and economic situation in Rome. From the late third century onwards the glass assemblage is close in type and combination of vessel shapes to the western oases of Egypt, suggesting that by this period the usage of glass in Fazzan was more contemporary and 'Roman' than in the early phase. The compositional evidence supports this, with a significant proportion of the fourth- to fifth-century Roman vessel glasses falling into the so-called 'HIMT' (high iron, manganese and titanium) compositional group, which has been linked with production in Egypt (Freestone 1994; Freestone et al. 2005; Foster and Jackson 2009; Duckworth et al. forthcoming).

In addition, a greater proportion of luxury glassware is present in Fazzan in the later period, suggesting that the Garamantes were now tapping more directly into Roman valuation systems and possibly dining practices, perhaps via direct trade routes with the western oases of Egypt. In order to properly assess the value of the glassware, however, we must consider how it was received in Fazzan as well as its value while still in the Roman sphere of influence.

Trade and transport

We are discussing objects that moved between presumably very different cultural contexts, and that at some point passed between different systems of valuation. A key proposal made by Appadurai is that, 'the commodity situation in the social life of any "thing" be defined as the situation in which its exchangeability (past, present, or future) for some other thing is its socially relevant feature' (Appadurai 1986, 13). But what was the place of glass vessels in the two intersecting spheres of valuation, and at what point did they cross from one to the other?

In the Roman Mediterranean, it was common practice for a wide range of goods – and not just luxury items or foodstuffs – to be traded over long distances. This is true of glass, too, but only to an extent: it seems that, while large quantities of 'raw' glass, or broken glass cullet intended for recycling were traded across the Mediterranean (Fontaine and Foy 2007; Silvestri 2008, 1499), everyday glass objects were often made more locally, in secondary workshops throughout the empire.

The journey from the Mediterranean ports of Oea and Lepcis Magna to Jarma was *c.*1,000 km, a 30-day trek across difficult terrain. Glass must have been one of the most difficult materials to transport intact and this fact may have added extra value to the artefacts that survived the trip. Few of the objects found in Fazzan – particularly in the first- and second-century contexts – would have been counted among the most expensive glassware in the Roman world. The seemingly paradoxical selection of large vessels, despite their inherent fragility, surely reflects a Garamantian interest in exploiting the prestige value of this remarkable material, while for Mediterranean-based merchants, the preference for relatively cheap products that met the size criterion was a sensible investment in stock that would have had a high breakage rate in transit. The commercial value of the intact vessel glass that reached Fazzan was presumably inflated well above its cost at Mediterranean ports. This is also echoed to some extent in the ceramic evidence: as discussed by Victoria Leitch (Leitch et al. in press), mass-produced and quite large, open ceramic bowls were much more common than easier to transport cups. The merchants again sought to offset the difficult transport of larger forms by including some stock that show signs of being 'seconds', and this tendency was equally clear in the second condition of some of the first- and second-century amphorae, evidently selected purposefully for the hazardous cross-desert trip. Perhaps the best conclusion we can draw from these strands of evidence is that the consumer tastes of the Garamantes – in both form and size of vessels – were an important factor in the nature of vessels transported to their capital, but that merchants had strategies for maximising their profits in such exchanges. It is also apparent that the sources of Roman goods in Fazzan were relatively limited, perhaps the output of just a few manufacturers, or the stock of a small number of merchants, at any given time.

From a Garamantian perspective, it is fairly safe to assume that the mechanism by which glass reached Fazzan would have had a significant impact upon its perception, value and meaning. Indeed, the issue of transportation must lie at the centre of our analysis of these objects, because the Sahara has variously been seen as an inhospitable barrier between north and south, and a desert 'sea' linking the regions on its shores (Lecocq 2015, 23–4; Lydon 2015, 3–4). More rarely, the geographical and cultural variability and dynamics of the Sahara itself have been considered (Scheele 2012; Mattingly et al. in press).

The enduring image of Saharan trade is that of the camel as pack animal (see Figure 7.5). Camels were present in North Africa from at least the later first millennium BC, and were present in the Sahara by the early first millennium AD, with some of the earliest known Saharan camel bones (*terminus ante quem* second century AD) excavated in Jarma itself (Fothergill et al. forthcoming). Prior to the use of the camel, the only pack animals capable of transporting goods across the Sahara would have been donkeys and mules or hinnies. These animals continued in use alongside

Figure 7.5 Terracotta figurine of a camel carrying transport amphorae. Late second to early third century CE. Egyptian. Height 11.8 cm. Source: OASC image courtesy of The Metropolitan Museum of Art (www.metmuseum.org), gift of Mrs Lucy W. Drexel, 1889, accession number 89.2.2093

camels until recently. Horses were also used in the Sahara, and are depicted pulling chariots in rock art from Fazzan (Barnett and Mattingly 2003), and may have been suitable in raiding activity due to their speed, but would have made rather expensive and demanding pack animals.

Camel-breeding imposes a pastoral lifestyle, and Bulliet argues that the camel could only become an efficient means of transport in the Middle East once nomadic camel breeders had been successfully integrated with settled society and economy (Bulliet 1975, 90–1). Traders and camel-driving pastoralists were not necessarily one and the same people, and the need for local guides in an inhospitable environment means that changing of pack animals several times during a journey may well have been a necessity.

The regional level of organisation this implies has been highlighted in recent interpretations of Saharan trade. Andrew Wilson suggests that Saharan, or trans-Saharan trade should be viewed in terms of a network of independent sub-systems *within* the Sahara; of short-, medium- and long-distance exchange (Wilson 2012). Anthropological work on nineteenth- and twentieth-century Saharan trade similarly highlights the importance of the regional exchange of locally produced goods, and the significance of pastoral routes, dictated by the dietary needs of camels, over direct 'trade routes' in the movement of goods from one location to another (Scheele 2010, 298).

It might therefore be argued that the use of pack animals imposes additional degrees of separation between the Garamantes and the Roman world to the north. Local guides would have been needed at every stage in order to traverse the difficult Saharan terrain from the *limes* to Jarma, a journey that would have been divided into stints of a maximum of 10 days each between major wells or water sources, by most reckonings (Mattingly forthcoming). Water sources may have provided more or less permanent staging posts, but the need for pack animals to graze would also have affected trade routes, which may have varied from season to season (Scheele forthcoming). In short, while it is possible to argue for permanent stopping points at various oases, which may have formed long-term nodes on the map of trans-Saharan trade, it is not possible to delineate static trade routes between these: the dotted lines on Figure 7.6 represent hypothetical means between an ever-changing range of routeways.

Despite this, the exceptionality of the Garamantes' trade with Rome is demonstrated by the virtual absence of Roman vessel glass at other Saharan sites (with the notable exception of the tomb of Tin Hinan, see below). This suggests that Roman goods were traded directly to Fazzan,

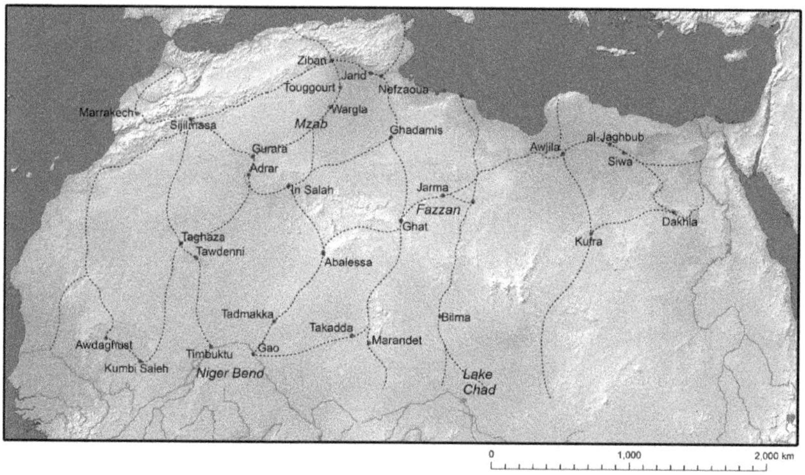

Figure 7.6 Key sites of relevance to trans-Saharan trade, with hypothetical trade routes in dotted lines. It should be noted that this static image cannot capture the dynamic and multiple systems in operation at any given time, and that the 'routes' themselves would be neither direct nor fixed. Map by Martin Sterry.

rather than arriving in a 'down the line' manner; further evidence that the Garamantes had a strong hand in the selection of the material culture that made it to Fazzan. Packs may well have been put together in a Roman harbour town such as Lepcis Magna and not dismantled until they reached Jarma: one of us (David Mattingly) has suggested that glass and ceramic finewares may have been wrapped in bales of textiles, which were also a key commodity of trans-Saharan trade, certainly in the Islamic period, and quite possibly before this time (Mattingly and Cole forthcoming). While trade goods and even traders themselves may have travelled the whole route, their guides and pack animals may well have changed several times. In order to ensure safe passage, traders would thus have required either highly stable mutually beneficial trade agreements, or a fair degree of military might.

Did this risky and presumably expensive method of transport render the Fazzan glass of exceptionally high status? It was certainly of limited distribution, even within the Garamantian heartlands. As shown in Figure 7.7, excavated vessel glass was preferentially located around Jarma, the Garamantian capital, and in some of the higher status tombs. Due to a combination of factors, but most significantly, looting in antiquity, and the small percentage of tombs excavated to date, we cannot push very far the significance of the recorded glass finds in terms of burial site or tomb type. We can note that glass had a similar, but more restricted distribution in Fazzan to that of Roman pottery, shown in Figure 7.8. The political centralisation of the glass

Figure 7.7 Roman glass vessel finds in Fazzan with (inset) detail of the Jarma area. Map by Martin Sterry.

Figure 7.8 Roman pottery finds in Fazzan with (inset) detail of the Jarma area. Map by Martin Sterry.

distribution patterns could imply that it was redistributed as a gift within Fazzan itself.

Roman glass vessels are not generally encountered far south from Fazzan, at least not in their original form (the matter of recycling into glass beads is considered below). No vessel glass has been found in Fewet, the closest region south of the Garamantian heartlands, although glass beads were encountered and have been analysed (Verità 2013). Roman glass is found in Sudan but would almost certainly have arrived there via the Nile or Red Sea trade routes. West African sites have yielded some evidence for glass beads and vessel glass, but any vessels post-date the Roman/Classic Garamantian periods, so we cannot find any significant evidence that Roman glass vessels were traded on from Fazzan. Central Saharan consumption of Roman vessel glass appears – at least on the present (and admittedly rather slim) evidence – to have been a Garamantian phenomenon and exceptional finds, as at Tin Hinan, are just that and could have been the product of rare gift exchange between the Garamantes and leading individuals in neighbouring groups. The same pattern also holds for Roman ceramics, as shown by the work of Victoria Leitch (Leitch et al. in press; see also Figure 7.8).

Despite all this, glass vessels were clearly not among the most restricted luxuries in Garamantian society. The sheer volume of glassware uncovered in the small number of excavations to date (by comparison with other materials in Fazzan and with other non-Roman sites in

Africa), and its finding in both tombs and urban contexts, suggests that large quantities of it were imported into Fazzan. At least some of this may have been earmarked for re-use, as evidenced by its presence in the manufacturing quarter of Saniat Jibril.

Use and re-use

> Following objects beyond the point of manufacture, purchase or gift also shows that traces of former property relations remain … ritualised attempts to sever previous relations and recast the objects and exchange relations anew indicate the labour needed to exorcise previous lives of things. It is not, *contra* Appadurai (1986), simply a matter of objects moving between gift and commodity relations. Things hang in limbo, are stored in warehouses, are dismantled, bear vestiges of earlier incarnations.
>
> (Alexander and Reno 2012, 22–3)

Depending on what we are trying to reconstruct, there may be problems with focusing on a single category based on the material from which it was made. Roman tablewares, for example, are best interpreted as a set regardless of whether they are made from ceramics, glass or metal. On the other hand, material constraints are highly significant when considering the context of production, and this is certainly true of glass, which required extremely specialist facilities and technical knowledge to produce. A key point to recognise here is that for recyclable materials such as glass, production – that is, making – can occur at several stages, as glass objects are broken, re-melted, and transformed.

Of course, we cannot assess the volume of vessel glass that may or may not have been recycled in Fazzan without more data on the composition of glass from Saharan and sub-Saharan sites. But we can look for clues as to whether it was being recycled or not. The most prominent among these is the presence of glass fragments at the manufacturing site of Saniat Jibril, and of glass production waste or glass bead wasters at several sites (Jarma, Saniat Jibril, Zinkekra and Zuwila), examples of which are shown in Figure 7.9. The glass bead wasters were found at the surface, in Zuwila, which is some distance from Jarma, and are probably the product of later activities than those considered here (see Duckworth et al. 2015, 8–10).

One of the key activities at Saniat Jibril (occupied from the first to the early fifth century AD) was the production of beads of various

Figure 7.9 Examples of vitreous production remains from sites in Fazzan. Clockwise from top left: chunk of vitreous production waste adhering to buff-coloured calcareous material, from Jarma (context dated to late first century CE); 'raw glass' chunk from Saniat Jibril (first to fourth century CE); glass drip or spill from Zinkekra (probably late first century CE); traces of blue glass adhering to sherds of local ceramics from (late second to fourth century CE); mis-shapen beads and bead-forming tube found during surface collection survey at Zuwila.

materials (including carnelian and ostrich eggshell). A number of bead-grinders – stone or ceramic used as an abrasive surface against which to work a bead to shape – were also found. Is it possible that the glass fragments from Saniat Jibril were being ground or even re-melted into beads at the site? At present it is difficult to say. Some 820 partial or complete glass beads have been recovered in Fazzan to date. Of these, 444 are from dateable contexts of the Classic Garamantian (1–400 CE) or late Garamantian (post-400 CE) periods. All come from tombs, and 375 of them come from just 10 tombs. Because most of them were excavated as part of the Desert Migrations Project, which was interrupted in 2011 with the onset of civil war in Libya, we have very little data on their forms, although the onsite specialist did identify among them one Indo-Pacific and 10 Indian red beads (Franca Cole, pers. comm.).

The chemical evidence, however, does shed some light on the matter. The majority of the beads available for quantitative analysis were gathered by Charles Daniels during surface collection survey. They include eye beads and plain, wound beads and based on find location and typology, date to between the last few centuries BCE (e.g. eye beads from Zinkekra) and the first to fourth centuries CE. Most are in various shades of blue or green; while the eye beads also feature applied decoration in opaque white, blue and yellow. There are also several beads that are almost certainly later European and Indian imports, and the analysed fragments of these have compositions consistent with the use of plant ashes as a flux.

As shown in Figure 7.10, even among the mineral fluxed 'Roman' glasses, many of the analysed beads – along with the vitreous production waste from Jarma (which may have been waste from glass production – see Duckworth et al. 2016, 637), and an imported glass stirrer – do not contain antimony or manganese in appreciable quantities. As comparison with the Roman vessel glass illustrates, this indicates that these particular objects are not the result of recycling Roman vessel glass.

Other samples shown in Figure 7.10, however, are potentially compatible with recycling of the sorts of Roman vessel glasses found at the site, for example with 1.09–1.65 per cent antimony pentoxide (Sb_2O_5) in three samples of differently coloured glass taken from a single bead. Another bead has elevated amounts of both antimony (0.59 per cent Sb_2O_5) and manganese (0.88 per cent MnO). Perhaps most interestingly, the chunk of 'raw' glass from Saniat Jibril also features slightly elevated manganese and antimony (0.14 per cent MnO and 0.74 per cent Sb_2O_5), the most likely explanation for which is the melting together of

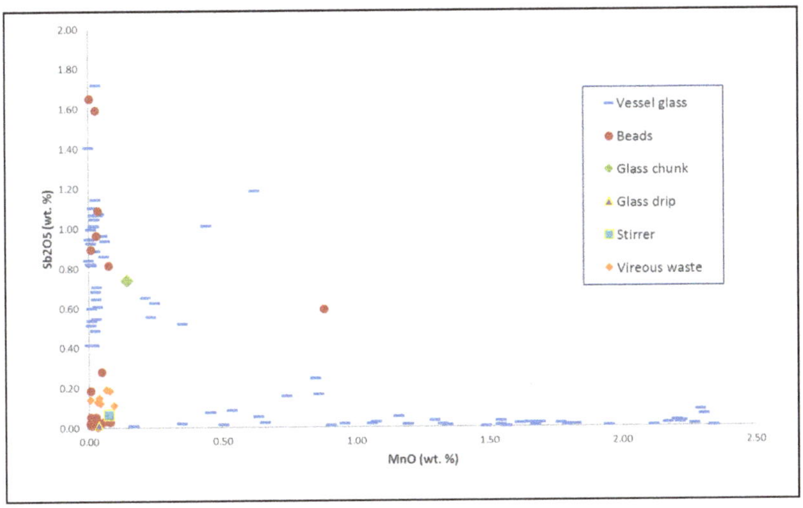

Figure 7.10 Manganese (Mn) plotted against antimony (Sb) for vessels and beads from Fazzan, given in parts per million (ppm).

antimony-decoloured and manganese-decoloured Roman vessel glasses. Some of the glass vessels themselves also feature this hybrid manganese-antimony composition, and it is not clear whether the chunk was the product of recycling elsewhere, with chunks of glass being traded into Fazzan, or whether it was the result of locally mixing vessel glass cullet like that found at Saniat Jibril. Either way, the presence of a chunk of raw glass in Fazzan is a very strong indication that some form of glass-working activity was taking place in the area.

To what extent does a physically recycled object retain traces of its former 'life'? Certainly the Garamantes – or some element(s) of their society – were aware that glass could be melted and reworked in a hot state, which must surely have affected its perception and value. How far this awareness of the provenance of the material extended beyond Fazzan is unclear. We do know that beads of a very wide range of provenances turn up at West African sites in increasing numbers throughout the first millennium CE (though there is almost no evidence for the first to fourth centuries CE); the extent to which the exoticism of the beads was valued as distinct from their material properties remains, however, unclear.

Curation, fetishism and discard

What then, of the transformation in meaning and value of glass objects over time? The possibility of curation must be considered as a potential source of discrepancy between dates of production and discard, but also as a factor in the treatment of objects after excavation. The term 'fetishism' is itself somewhat problematic, originally rooted in racist, colonialist discourse and later extended in various directions by a number of influential thinkers (Pietz 1985, 5; 1987, 23–4). We use the term here to refer to the perceived endowment of an object or class of objects with powers external to it. In particular, we are interested in the ascription of intrinsic value to objects based on their history.

It is in fact remarkably difficult to assess the degree of curation of glass vessels in Fazzan in the first millennium AD, though our best chance to do so certainly lies with the cemetery evidence. Some of the glass plates with large diameters were initially thought to indicate curation (Hoffmann et al. 2010, 414), but – as pointed out by Jennifer Price (pers. comm.) – examples of very large plates have been found in later (fourth- to early fifth-century contexts) elsewhere (see, for example, Nenna 2003, 94). There are hints of curation elsewhere, but none of these can be verified at present. A mould-blown glass beaker from Saniat bin Huwaydi is thought to date to the first century AD, but the tomb in which it was found was dated by Ayoub to the later third century AD. On the other hand, recent AMS dates for several of the glass-bearing tombs excavated as part of the Desert Migrations Project accord well with the dates assigned to the glass on the basis of typological comparison with various parts of the Roman world, suggesting that lengthy curation may not have been practised.

Of course, the life history of these objects did not end when they were deposited in the ground. The very act of deposition may have served to demarcate ownership. There is a notable association between cemeteries and the location of the complex, high labour-investment *foggara* irrigation systems and glass vessels are preferentially distributed – along with other Roman imports – in some of the richest cemeteries, though glass vessels are not a ubiquitous feature of the richest burials. Nor were the locations of tombs – which were often highly visible – forgotten by subsequent generations: looting may have taken place in several periods, as illustrated by the recently obtained AMS radiocarbon dates, that seem to indicate robbing of tombs in late medieval and early modern times. This is not unprecedented. In Algeria, the fourth-century burial of a woman known as Tin Hinan, near Abalessa, has long had legendary associations among the Tuareg. Among the richly furnished grave goods was a glass goblet, presumably Roman in origin (Thiry 1995, 451).

Once 'out of the ground', these long-curated objects entered a new phase. The majority of the individuals who have been involved in archaeological research in Fazzan have had backgrounds in Roman archaeology, so the presence there of Roman-made objects has had a direct impact upon its interpretation and perception. It is interesting that the very first archaeological work to put Fazzan on the international map was done by Italians during the Colonial Period (1911–51), when the pottery and glass were simplistically presented as evidence of the 'Romanisation' of the Garamantes. Ayoub, too, was a foreigner in Fazzan, albeit one with a different geographical bias (he came from Sudan). His interpretation of Jarma ties it very closely to the Roman world, to the extent that he believed it was uninhabited prior to the first century CE (see Mattingly et al. 2013, 20–1).

Today, the glass is arguably more valuable and symbolically endowed than ever. Its physical fragility coupled with chemical durability are emblematic of the partiality of the material record. In the age of chemical analysis, even the tiniest fragments of a material take on a new significance – indeed, this may be seen as the ultimate fetishism, with the object and sample standing for much more than their present form. On the one hand, the principles of conservation imply that the removal of even a small portion of an object for analysis is a destructive, rather than constructive act. A common argument against sampling references the future potential of the object (for example, the possibility of developing better non-destructive analytical techniques in years to come). Reference to the future, which is understood as infinite, endows the object with potentially limitless power to inform us about the past. On the other hand, when destructive analysis is permitted and conducted, the removed fragment itself is imbued with a potent representative meaning in its own right. The use of the term 'sampling' to refer not only to the removal of part of an object, but to the selection of objects as representative of a category or assemblage, further extends this. Archaeological objects, and the data derived from them, become points on a map, their significance magnified by the reduced dimensions of cartographic representation, including its timelessness.

Jean Baudrillard argues that the antique in the modern world is symbolic of time itself, of 'history simultaneously invoked and denied' (Baudrillard 1996, 78, fn 2). In the context of the museum, we might argue that the curation of the material record stands for control; over nature, humanity, even time. Without wishing to extend the parallels too far, it is worth noting that the majority of the Garamantian grave goods – many from cemeteries associated with particular irrigation systems and quite possibly demarcating ownership over land and water resources as argued above – are now under serious threat of destruction in Jarma Museum. The museum was a recent target of Tuareg attacks as they attempt to assert their own new political authority in a valley that has been the preserve of sedentary oasis cultivators for three millennia.

Conclusion

The approaches advanced here – namely, the application of object biography and prosopography – generate as many questions as they do answers in the study of these fluid objects and the material – glass – of which they are made. But they at least have the merit of bringing the issue of temporality to the fore, and preventing the material record from appearing static and unchanging. They also highlight just how many gaps there are in our knowledge, in spite of the excellence of archaeological science.

Perhaps the most important point to raise is just how vulnerable archaeological remains become once they have been excavated;

vulnerable not only to physical deterioration, loss or destruction, but to misinterpretation, de-contextualisation or mis-use. Needless to say, our own discourse stems from Western, Eurocentric prioritisations and can be questioned on many fronts. The vessel glass from Fazzan has lasted a long time and has retained a remarkable degree of its Roman identity throughout. It has travelled far through both space and time, but we should not forget that it is travelling still.

Acknowledgements

This chapter is an output of the European Research Council-funded Trans-Sahara Project (Grant Agreement No. 269418-TRANS-SAHARA), on which the first author was the Research Associate responsible for glass analysis under the direction of the second author (project PI). Thanks to Professor Jennifer Price for sharing with us her expertise on Roman glass forms in North Africa. We would also like to thank Dr Martin Sterry for his useful insights and expert map-making.

References

Alexander, C. and Reno, J. 2012. 'Introduction'. In *Economies of Recycling: The Global Transformation of Materials, Values and Social Relations*, edited by C. Alexander and J. Reno. London and New York: Zed Books.

Appadurai, A. 1986. 'Introduction: Commodities and the Politics Of Value'. In *The Social Life of Things: Commodities in Cultural Perspective*, edited by A. Appadurai, 3–63. Cambridge: Cambridge University Press.

Barnett, T. F. and Mattingly, D. J. 2003. 'The Engraved Heritage: Rock Art and Inscriptions'. In *The Archaeology of Fazzan*, edited by D. J. Mattingly, C. M. Daniels, J. N. Dore, D. Edwards and J. Hawthorne, vol. 1, 279–326. London: Society for Libyan Studies.

Baudrillard, J. 1996. *The System of Objects*. London: Verso.

Braudel, F. 1998. *The Mediterranean in the Ancient World*. London: Penguin Books.

Brill, R. H. and Stapleton, C. P. 2013. *Chemical Analyses of Early Glasses, Volume 3*. New York: The Corning Museum of Glass.

Bulliet, R. W. 1975. *The Camel and the Wheel*. Cambridge, MA: Harvard University Press.

Devulder, V., Vanhaecke, F., Shortland, A., Mattingly, D. J., Jackson, C. M. and Degryse, P. 2014. 'Boron Isotopic Composition as a Provenance Indicator for the Flux Raw Material in Roman Natron Glass'. *Journal of Archaeological Science* 46: 107–13.

Duckworth, C. N. Forthcoming. ‘Shattering Illusions: Using Analytical Evidence to Establish Clearer Pictures of Glass Production and Trade Within Africa’. In *Mobile Technologies*, edited by A. Cuénod, C. N. Duckworth and D. J. Mattingly, Trans-Saharan Archaeology, 3. Cambridge: Cambridge University Press and The Society for Libyan Studies.

Duckworth, C. N., Cuénod, A. and Mattingly, D. J. 2015. ‘Non-Destructive μXRF Analysis of Glass and Metal Objects From Sites in the Libyan Pre-Desert and Fazzan’. *Libyan Studies* 46: 14–34.

Duckworth, C. N., Mattingly, D. J. and Smith, V. C. 2016. ‘From the Mediterranean to the Libyan Sahara. Chemical analyses of Garamantian glass’. *Journal of Archaeological Science: Reports* 7: 633–9.

Fontaine, S. D. and Foy, D. 2007. ‘L’épave Ouest-Embiez 1, Var: le commerce maritime du verre brut et manufacturé en Méditerranée occidentale dans l’Antiquité’. *Revue archéologique de Narbonnaise* 40: 235–65.

Foster, H. E. and Jackson, C. M. 2009. ‘The Composition of “Naturally Coloured” Late Roman Vessel Glass from Britain and the Implications for Models of Glass Production and Supply’. *Journal of Archaeological Science* 36: 189–204.

Fothergill, B. T., Linseele, V. and Valenzuela Lamas, S. Forthcoming. ‘Movement and Management of Animals in the North and West of Africa from 1000 BC to AD 1000’. In *Mobile Technologies*, edited by A. Cuenod, C. N. Duckworth and D. J. Mattingly, Trans-Saharan Archaeology, 3. Cambridge: Cambridge University Press and The Society for Libyan Studies.

Freestone, I. C. 1994. ‘Appendix: Chemical Analyses of “Raw” Glass Fragments’. In *Excavations at Carthage: The British Mission*, edited by H. R. Hurst, 1–32. Oxford: Oxford University Press.

Freestone, I. C., Wolf, S. and Thirwall, M. 2005. ‘The Producion of HIMT Glass: Elemental and Isotopic Evidence’. *Annales du 16e Congrès de l’Association Internationale pour l’Histoire du Verre*, edited by H. E. M. Cool and M. D. Nenna, 153–7. Nottingham: Association Internationale Pour l’Histoire du Verre.

Gosden, C. and Marshall, Y. 1999. ‘The Cultural Biography of Objects’. *World Archaeology* 31 (2): 169–78.

Hoffmann, B. 2013. ‘Discussion of the Glass from Old Jarma’. In *The Archaeology of Fazzan Volume 4: Survey and Excavations at Old Jarma (Ancient Garama)*, edited by D. J. Mattingly, 409–19. London: Society for Libyan Studies.

Hoffmann, B., Mattingly, D. J., Tagart, C., Cole, F. and Wild, J. P. 2010. ‘Non-Ceramic Finds from CMD’s Excavations and the Work of M. S. Ayoub’. In *The Archaeology of Fazzan*, edited by D. J. Mattingly, 411–88. London: The Society of Libyan Studies.

Lecocq, B. 2015. ‘Distant Shores: A Historiographic View on Trans-Saharan Space’. *The Journal of African History* 56 (1): 23–36.

Leitch, V., Duckworth, C. N., Cuenod, A., Mattingly, D. J., Sterry, M. and Cole, F. In press. ‘Early Saharan Trade: The Inorganic Evidence’. In *Trade in the Ancient Sahara and Beyond*, edited by D. J. Mattingly, V. Leitch, C. N. Duckworth, A. Cuenod, M. Sterry and F. Cole, Trans-Saharan Archaeology, 1. Cambridge: Cambridge University Press and The Society for Libyan Studies.

Lydon, G. 2015. 'Saharan Oceans and Bridges, Barriers and Divides in Africa's Historiographical Landscape'. *The Journal of African History* 56 (1): 3–22.

Mattingly, D. J. Forthcoming. 'The Garamantes and the Origins of Saharan trade: State of the Field and Future Agendas'. In *Trade in the Ancient Sahara and Beyond*, edited by D. J. Mattingly, V. Leitch, C. N. Duckworth, A. Cuenod, M. Sterry and F. Cole, Trans-Saharan Archaeology, 1. Cambridge: Cambridge University Press and The Society for Libyan Studies.

Mattingly, D. J. and Cole, F. Forthcoming. 'Visible and Invisible Commodities of Trade: The Significance of Organic Materials in Saharan Trade'. In *Trade in the Ancient Sahara and Beyond*, edited by D. J. Mattingly, V. Leitch, C. N. Duckworth, A. Cuenod, M. Sterry and F. Cole, Trans-Saharan Archaeology, 1. Cambridge: Cambridge University Press and The Society for Libyan Studies.

Mattingly, D. J., Daniels, C. M., Dore, J. N., Edwards, D. and Hawthorne, J. 2003. *The Archaeology of Fazzan, Volume 1, Synthesis*. London: Society for Libyan Studies.

Mattingly, D. J., Daniels, C. M., Dore, J. N., Edwards, D. and Hawthorne, J. (eds) 2007. *The Archaeology of Fazzan Volume 2: Site Gazetteer, Pottery and Other Survey Finds*. London: Society for Libyan Studies.

Mattingly, D. J., Daniels, C. M., Dore, J. N., Edwards, D. and Hawthorne, J. (eds) 2010. *The Archaeology of Fazzan Volume 3: Excavations of C. M. Daniels*. London: Society for Libyan Studies.

Mattingly, D. J., Daniels, C. M., Dore, J. N., Edwards, D., Leone, A. and Thomas, D. C. (eds) 2013. *The Archaeology of Fazzan Volume 4: Survey and Excavations at Old Jarma (Ancient Garama) Carried out by C. M. Daniels (1962–69) and the Fazzan Project (1997–2001)*. London: Society for Libyan Studies.

Mattingly, D. J., Leitch, V., Duckworth, C. N. Cuenod, A., Sterry, M. and Cole, F. (eds) In press. *Trade in the Ancient Sahara and Beyond: Trans-Saharan Archaeology, Volume 1*. Cambridge: Cambridge University Press and Society for Libyan Studies.

Nenna, M. D. 2003. 'Verreries de luxe de l'Antiquite Tardive decouvertes a Douch, Oasis de Kharga, Egypte'. *Annales du 15me Congres de l'Association Internationale pour l'Histoire du Verre*, 93–7.

Pace, B., Sergi, S. and Caputo, G. 1951. 'Scavi sahariani'. *Monumenti Antichi* 41: 150–9.

Pietz, W. 1985. 'The Problem of the Fetish, I'. *Anthropology and Aesthetics* 9: 5–17.

Pietz, W. 1987. 'The Problem of the Fetish, II: The Origin of the Fetish'. *Anthropology and Aesthetics* 13: 23–45.

Scheele, J. 2010. 'Traders, Saints and Irrigation: Reflections on Saharan Connectivity'. *Journal of African History* 51: 281–300.

Scheele, J. 2012. *Smugglers and Saints of the Sahara: Regional Connectivity in the Twentieth Century*. Cambridge: Cambridge University Press.

Scheele, J. Forthcoming. 'The Need for Nomads: Camel-Herding, Raiding and Saharan Trade and Settlement'. In *Trade in the Ancient Sahara and Beyond*, edited by D. J. Mattingly, V. Leitch, C. N. Duckworth, A. Cuenod, M. Sterry and F. Cole, Trans-Saharan Archaeology, 1. Cambridge: Cambridge University Press and The Society for Libyan Studies.

Silvestri, A. 2008. 'The Coloured Glass of Iulia Felix'. *Journal of Archaeological Science* 35 (6): 1489–501.

Thiry, J. 1995. 'Le Sahara Libyen dans l'Afrique du Nord Medievale'. *Orientalia Lovaniensia Analecta* 72.

Verità, M. 2013. 'Vitreous Beads: A Scientific Investigation by SEM Microscopy and X-Ray Microanalysis'. In *Life and Death of a Rural Village in Garamantian Times: Archaeological Investigations of Fewet (Libyan Sahara)*, edited by L. Mori, 169–76. Arid Zone Archaeological Monographs 6. Borgo San Lorenzo: All'Insegna del Giglio.

Wilson, A. 2012. 'Saharan Trade in the Roman Period: Short-, Medium- and Long-Distance Trade Networks'. *Azania* 47(4): 409–49.

8

HIMT, glass composition and commodity branding in the primary glass industry

Ian C. Freestone, Patrick Degryse, James Lankton, Bernard Gratuze and J. Schneider

Abstract

New elemental data confirm the proposal by Ceglia et al. (2015) of two sub-groups of high iron, manganese and titanium glass, HIMTa and HIMTb, differing in their ratios Fe_2O_3/TiO_2 and Fe_2O_3/Al_2O_3. Neodymium and strontium isotopes are consistent with south-eastern Mediterranean coastal sand for both groups, allowing for an identifiable strontium contribution from the added manganese. Trace elements are consistent with an Egyptian origin, although a marked Eu anomaly in HIMTa is correlated with Ba, again added with manganese. Strong within-group correlations between manganese and iron oxides are not easily explained either as deliberate additions of manganese decolouriser or as a characteristic of the glass-making sand. Instead, HIMT glass is considered to have been deliberately tinted yellow-green by the primary glass makers to distinguish it from the green-blue glass of the Levant. The colour branding of the raw glass allowed glass workers to distinguish sodium-rich Egyptian HIMT glass from the more viscous, high working temperature Levantine glass, thereby offering savings in marginal costs, such as those relating to fuel.

Introduction

HIMT glass is a well-recognised and widespread glass compositional group, dating to the fourth–fifth centuries CE (Freestone et al. 2002a, 2002b, 2005; Foy et al. 2003; Foster and Jackson 2009; Nenna 2014 and work cited therein). From around the mid-fourth century CE, it became the major glass type in Western provinces such as Britain (Foster and Jackson 2009), and is found in high abundance across the Roman empire. A low-magnesia natron-type glass, it was originally named by Freestone (1994) on account of its concentrations of iron, manganese and titanium, which are high relative to other types of Roman glass. The history of research on HIMT, its chronology and distribution have been comprehensively reviewed by Nenna (2014) who concludes that HIMT and its close relatives were in use from the middle of the fourth century until the seventh century. However, some of the groups included in this broad grouping can be shown to have distinctive characteristics and specific chronological ranges and, even in the short time since Nenna's review, consensus as to what should and should not be included in this group has moved on, as outlined below.

HIMT differs in appearance from most Roman glass of the first to third centuries, and also from the later primary products of the furnaces of the Levantine coastal plain, in that it typically has yellow-greenish tint, as opposed to the blue-green of Levantine glass. Even so, the colour is variable and Nenna (2014) emphasises that HIMT can range from a deep yellow-green to a relatively pale tint.

Neodymium isotopic evidence bearing on the origins of HIMT was conducted in around 2005, but although the manuscript (Freestone et al. n.d.) has been formally and informally cited (e.g. Pollard and Heron 2008), it was withdrawn from publication because it was recognised that the meaning of the data was not fully understood. The present chapter formally presents these data, and takes the opportunity to re-consider the compositional character of this extremely widespread glass type in the light of recently published work, along with newly acquired trace element data. A new interpretation of the raw material characteristics of HIMT glass is offered, which leads to a new understanding of the reasons for the adoption of this compositional type.

Before introducing the new data, it is necessary to consider the nature of the HIMT group itself, as it is now clear that in some of the early work (e.g. Freestone 1994; Freestone et al 2002a, 2002b; as well as studies by other authors) more than one primary glass group is likely to have been included under the HIMT umbrella, and this has led to considerable confusion.

HIMT – compositional characteristics

Statistical approaches to the separation of HIMT from other glass compositional groups have been undertaken by Foy et al. (2003) and Foster and Jackson (2009). *Groupe 1* of Foy et al. (2003) and *HIMT 1* of Foster and Jackson share a number of characteristics, notably high TiO_2 (>0.2 per cent), Fe_2O_3 (>0.9 per cent), MgO (>0.8 per cent) and MnO (variable), as well as high Na_2O and low CaO relative to other primary glass groups of the first millennium. This combination of characteristics is generally sufficient to distinguish HIMT without recourse to any trace element data. There are correlations between MgO, Fe_2O_3, TiO_2 and also Al_2O_3, which on first analysis may reflect a clay-rich and/or heavy mineral component in the glass-making sand. The compositional situation of HIMT relative to other accepted primary glass groups is shown in Figure 8.1 in terms of the ratios of TiO_2, Al_2O_3 and SiO_2, which represent essentially the heavy mineral, feldspar and quartz contents of the

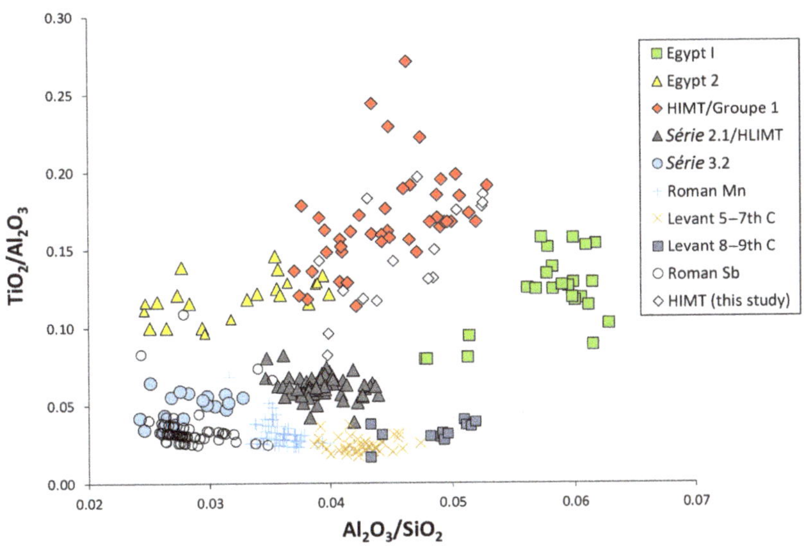

Figure 8.1 Major primary glass groups from the first millennium CE, in terms of the oxides of titanium, aluminium and silicon. The glasses analysed in the present study are also shown. Based upon Freestone (in press). Data sources: Foy et al. (2003: HIMT, *série 2.1*, *série 3.2*, Levant 5–7th c.); Silvestri (2008: Roman Sb, Roman Mn); Silvestri et al. (2008: Roman Mn); Gratuze and Barrandon (1990: Egypt 1, Egypt 2); (Freestone et al. 2015: Levant 8–9th c).

sands. In these terms HIMT is close to the *Egypt 2* group of Gratuze and Barrandon (1990) and its compositional characteristics are generally taken to indicate an Egyptian origin (Foy et al. 2003; Freestone et al. 2005; Nenna 2014).

A second group that has frequently been conflated with HIMT in the past is *série 2.1* of Foy et al (2003), also termed HLIMT by Ceglia et al. (2015). This group is widely found in western Europe in Frankish/Merovingian/Anglo-Saxon contexts and seems to be firmly situated in the sixth century, according to Cholakova et al. (2016). Figure 8.1 illustrates that the TiO_2 content of this group is substantially below that of HIMT *sensu stricto*, and the existence of two distinct groups, as originally indicated by Foy et al. (2003) is now well understood. Groupings of related material, with more iron than typical Roman glass but less titanium than HIMT, sometimes referred to as 'weak HIMT' frequently fall into this group. As noted by Ceglia et al. (2015), the high CaO content, frequently in the 7–9 per cent range, as opposed to the 4–7 per cent of HIMT, is a distinguishing characteristic; while CaO is not as reliable as a discriminant as the TiO_2/Al_2O_3 ratio (Figure 8.1), recourse to the CaO content is sometimes necessary when evaluating published data as the required precision in Ti and Al depends upon the analytical method and is not always attained.

Foster and Jackson (2009), in their comprehensive study of fourth- to fifth-century glass from Britain, identified sub-groups HIMT 1 and HIMT 2. While HIMT 1 is clearly similar to the HIMT recognised in other studies, HIMT 2 has lower titanium, iron and manganese oxides. Furthermore, as pointed out by Ceglia et al. (2015) HIMT 2 also differs from HLIMT/Foy *série 2.1*, in that it has a relatively low CaO content. On the basis of its TiO_2/Al_2O_3 and Al_2O_3/SiO_2 ratios (mean 0.053 and 0.033 respectively), HIMT 2 is close to the group recognised by Foy et al. (2003) as *série 3.2* (Figure 8.1), a fifth-century type, which is also reported from Italy by Maltoni et al. (2015, 2016) and from Bulgaria by Cholakova and Rehren (Chapter 3, this volume). As noted elsewhere (Maltoni et al. 2016; Schibille et al. 2017; Cholakova and Rehren Chapter 3, this volume) the similarity of this group to Roman antimony-decolourised glass suggests an Egyptian origin. Trace and minor levels of Sb frequently detected in the British HIMT 2 (typically *c.*0.1 per cent; Foster and Jackson 2009), as well as some compositional scatter, reflect the relatively high level of recycling of earlier Roman glass to be anticipated in the region, which by this time was administratively as well as geographically remote from the primary glass sources of the eastern Mediterranean.

Table 8.1 Composition of glass from Billingsgate Bath House by SEM-EDS (wt%)

Sample	*Form*	*Na_2O*	*MgO*	*Al_2O_3*	*SiO_2*	*P_2O_5*	*SO_3*	*Cl*	*K_2O*	*CaO*	*MnO*	*TiO_2*	*Fe_2O_3*	*BaO*	*Total*
6919–2	vessel	18.46	0.90	2.51	66.53	0.10	0.48	0.92	0.44	5.78	2.17	0.45	1.25	0.30	100.29
6919–3	bottle	18.49	1.08	2.44	65.40	0.12	1.28	1.01	0.52	5.67	2.41	0.40	1.33	<0.2	100.15
6919–4	bottle	17.71	0.94	2.76	66.02	<0.1	0.67	0.88	0.64	5.83	2.41	0.38	1.61	<0.2	99.85
6919–5	thin-walled vessel	18.20	0.92	2.55	66.37	<0.1	0.45	0.88	0.48	5.75	2.37	0.44	1.52	<0.2	99.93
6919–6	thin-walled vessel	18.69	0.91	2.59	66.09	<0.1	0.50	0.93	0.44	5.70	2.30	0.34	1.43	0.24	100.16
6919–7	thin-walled vessel	17.13	0.96	2.78	67.08	<0.1	0.44	0.96	0.51	5.42	2.36	0.51	1.89	<0.2	100.04
6919–8	conical beaker	19.18	0.92	2.44	65.68	<0.1	0.46	0.97	0.58	6.13	1.78	0.28	1.25	<0.2	99.67
6919–9	window/sheet	19.41	0.74	2.05	67.56	0.13	0.46	1.19	0.54	6.17	1.11	0.14	0.61	<0.2	100.11
6919–10	window/sheet	18.40	0.96	2.56	66.10	0.17	0.41	0.47	0.64	6.65	1.86	0.35	1.41	0.27	100.25
6919–11	window/sheet	18.36	0.92	2.55	66.60	0.11	0.47	1.01	0.63	5.61	1.95	0.46	1.41	<0.2	100.08
6919–12	window/sheet	18.48	0.91	2.26	66.31	<0.1	0.43	1.01	0.72	6.13	1.66	0.25	1.06	<0.2	99.22
6919–13	window/sheet	18.79	0.90	2.54	66.50	0.16	0.44	1.00	0.62	6.33	1.63	0.34	1.17	<0.2	100.42
6919–15	window/sheet	19.69	0.78	2.17	66.25	<0.1	0.46	1.17	0.57	6.33	1.07	0.08	0.78	<0.2	99.35
6919–16	window/sheet	18.61	0.97	2.32	66.88	0.16	0.35	0.93	0.62	6.35	1.48	0.26	1.03	<0.2	99.96

The present chapter focuses upon HIMT *sensu stricto*, i.e. Groupe 1 of Foy et al. (2003) and HIMT 1 of Foster and Jackson (2009). Priority is given to Foy et al. (2003) in the use of *série 2.1* and *série 3.2* for the apparently 'related' groups. Other terms which are encountered from time to time such as 'weak HIMT' incorporate glass from *série 2.1* or *série 3.2* and are no longer required.

A final subdivision of HIMT has been proposed by Ceglia et al. (2015) who, in the assemblages they analysed from Cyprus, recognised a category *HIMTb*, which has significantly higher Fe_2O_3/TiO_2 and Fe_2O_3/Al_2O_3 than *HIMTa*. A scatter plot of TiO_2 vs Fe_2O_3 for HIMT data from a number of sources, shown in Figure 8.2, appears to confirm this subdivision with the majority of glass analysed lying on a fairly well defined high TiO_2/Fe_2O_3 or HIMTa trend, and a scatter of HIMTb with higher relative iron. The apparent relative abundances of HIMTa and HIMTb in Figure 8.2 may not be representative; in the graph HIMTa is heavily weighted to just two data-rich studies – that on British glass by Foster and Jackson (2009) and that on the fourth-century Helle bowls from Germany by Rehren and Brüggler (2015). The significance of this grouping is discussed below.

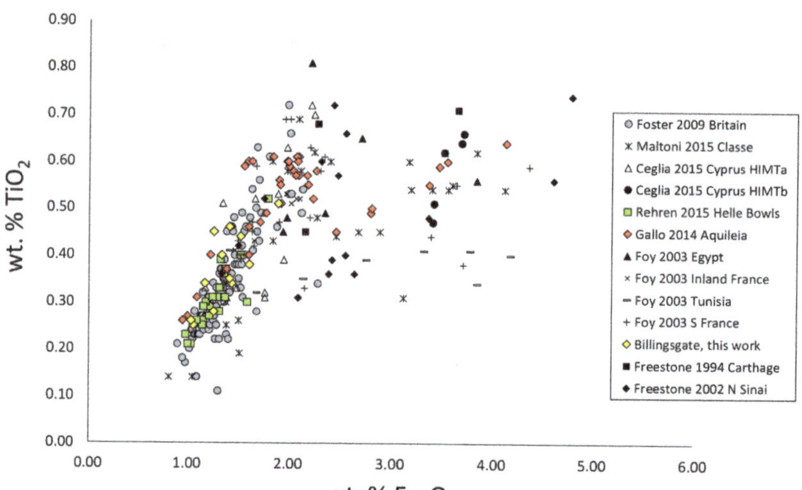

Figure 8.2 Selection of published data for HIMT, showing two apparent trends, higher and lower in iron, and corresponding to HIMTa and HIMTb of Ceglia et al. (2015). Data of Foy et al. (2003), Gallo et al. (2015), Maltoni et al. (2015), Foster and Jackson (2009), Freestone (1994), Freestone et al. (2002b), Rehren and Brüggler (2015), this work Table 8.1.

Materials and methods

The present chapter is based primarily around several previously unpublished sets of data for major and trace elements, and the isotopes of strontium and neodymium. Glass classed as HIMT has TiO_2 of c. 0.2 wt% or above, MgO above 0.9 wt% and CaO between 5.0 and 7.0 wt%. Examples of 'weak HIMT', Groupe 2 and *série 3.2* were excluded. The HIMT glass was selected on the basis of previous analyses to provide a more-or-less full range of Fe_2O_3 contents. Examples corresponding to both the HIMTa and HIMTb of Ceglia et al. (2015) were fortuitously included in the sample (the selection was made some years ago, before the work of Ceglia and co-workers).

The sample includes glass from contexts associated with the latest phase of Billingsgate Bath House, London (site code GM111), which was excavated by the Guildhall Museum and their successor, the Museum of London, between 1968 and 1974 and comprises a bath house centrally positioned in a courtyard between the wings of a Roman house. John Shepherd kindly provided the information on the archaeological context. Too small to be a public establishment, it has been suggested that it was a privately owned *mansio* (hostel). The fragments came from four contemporary contexts, three from the bath house (1280, 1298 and 1308) and one from the south end of the east wing of the house (1317) from the very latest phase of use of the buildings. This phase is dated by a coin hoard found in the furnace of the east wing of the house, containing coins of Arcadius dated to 395–400 CE. These contexts had been sealed by the collapse of the roofs of both the house and the bath house. The analysed glass from Billingsgate comprises pale to deep yellow-green fragments of window, square bottles, thin-walled bowls and a conical beaker. Major element analyses for this assemblage, discussed but not fully reported in Freestone et al. (2005), are presented here as Table 8.1. A subset of eight glasses were analysed for trace elements and three for isotopes.

Raw glass chunks dating to the fourth–fifth centuries in the excavation of the north side of the harbour at Carthage were analysed for major elements by Freestone (1994) and here isotopic and trace elemental compositions have been determined for three of the Carthage samples. Glass vessel fragments of fourth- to fifth-century date were found during field survey of the North Sinai and major element data were reported by Freestone et al. (2002b). Three of the vessels have been analysed for their isotopic compositions and eight for trace elements.

As comparative material a group of glass from Levantine primary furnaces at Apollonia and Bet Eli'ezer (Freestone et al. 2000) and of Egyptian 2 glass from Tel el Ashmunein (Bimson and Freestone 1985) were also analysed for trace elements and the Levantine glasses for isotopes. Trace element compositions of the Apollonia and Bet Eli'ezer samples have been reported in the supplementary data of Phelps et al. (2016).

Major elements were determined on 2–3 millimetre-sized fragments of glass by energy dispersive X-ray analysis in a scanning electron microscope (SEM-EDS); details of the technique and the uncertainty levels are given by Freestone et al. (2000).

New elemental analyses were undertaken using LA-ICP-MS (Laser ablation inductively coupled plasma mass spectrometry) on fresh fracture surfaces of small glass fragments at the Ernest-Babelon laboratory, IRAMAT, Orleans, France. Samples were ablated for 70 s (including 20 s pre-ablation) using a VG UV-laser, generated by an Nd YAG pulsed beam and operating at 266nm wavelength, 3–4 mJ power and 7 Hz frequency. An argon stream (1.15–1.35 l/min) carried the ablated material to the plasma torch and elements were quantified using a Thermo Fisher Scientific Element XR, double focusing magnetic sector field mass spectrometer equipped with a dual mode Secondary Electron Multiplier associated with a Faraday detector. Two areas were analysed per sample to check for heterogeneity. Calibration was performed using five reference standards; NIST610, Corning B, C and D, and APL1, which were run periodically to correct for drift. The standards are used to calculate the response coefficient (k) of each element (Gratuze 2016). The calculated values were normalised against ^{29}Si, the internal standard, to produce a final percentage. Corning A and NIST612 were analysed independently of calibration to provide comparative data.

For isotope analysis, samples of several hundred milligrams were dissolved in a 3:1 mixture of 22 N HF and 14 N HNO_3, dried and redissolved in aqua regia. Aliquots of these solutions were spiked with a highly enriched ^{84}Sr and ^{150}Nd tracer for separate concentration analyses by isotope dilution, whereas unspiked aliquots were used for determination of isotope ratios. Strontium and neodymium were separated and purified by anion exchange methods. Measurements were performed on a six-collector FINNIGAN MAT 261 thermal ionisation mass spectrometer (TIMS) running in static multi-collection mode. Repeated static measurements of the NBS 987 standard over the duration of the study yielded an average ^{87}Sr/^{86}Sr ratio of 0.71025 ± 4 (2σ, n = 22). Repeated measurements of the La Jolla Nd standard yielded ^{143}Nd/^{144}Nd = 0.511848 ± 9 (2σ, n=8).

Results

Major elements are presented in Table 8.1, traces in Table 8.2, and Sr and Nd isotopes in Table 8.3. Major element analyses show the typical values for HIMT glass, as discussed above. The majority of the glasses analysed plot clearly within the region of Foy et al. (2003) Groupe 1, when considered in a plot of TiO_2/Al_2O_3 vs Al_2O_3/SiO_2 (Figure 8.1). Two of the included samples, however, have lower TiO_2/Al_2O_3 and lie below Groupe 1, towards *série 2.1* and earlier Roman glasses. However, HIMT1 of Foster and Jackson (2009) also contains glass in this region and the absolute TiO_2 contents of these samples are over 0.2 per cent. Furthermore, these are from the Billingsgate group, and contain over 200 ppm antimony, which may suggest a significant content of recycled material, explaining their compositional divergence. They are therefore retained in the present sample. Three of the 16 samples have a distinctively low TiO_2/Fe_2O_3 ratio, and are classified as HIMTb, the remaining 13 as HIMTa (Figure 8.3a).

A correlation matrix for HIMTa shows that interelement correlations are high ($R>0.6$, typically >0.8) between Fe_2O_3, TiO_2, MnO, MgO and Al_2O_3 as well as a range of trace elements, including the lanthanide rare earths (REE), transition metals such as Cr, Ni, Co, V, As, W and high field strength elements such as Zr, Hf, Nb, Ga, Th and U (Figure 8.4). In particular Zr and Ti are very strongly correlated as was observed by Aerts et al. (2003). While HIMTa and HIMTb lie on the same correlation line for TiO_2 and Zr, they show distinctly different correlations between TiO_2 and Fe_2O_3 (Figure 8.3a). The association between these elements is usually related to heavy minerals, not only iron-titanium oxides and zircon, but in the context of the Nile sediment load and the eastern Mediterranean coast, pyroxenes and amphiboles (see Freestone et al. 2009; Brems and Degryse 2014). Another group of components showing a strong positive inter-correlation includes K_2O, P_2O_5, Sb, Pb, Cu, Ag, Sn, Zn; as noted by Al-Bashaireh et al. (2016) when correlated these elements, which are derived from contamination from fuel (K, P) and admixture of old coloured glass (transition metals), strongly indicate a contribution from recycled material.

The relatively high concentrations of Ti and Zr in HIMT glass are reflected in their ratios to other trace elements such as Th and La. These separate HIMT from many of the other categories of glass, including Groupe 2 (Figure 8.5). The relatively constrained field of the present samples in this diagram appears to justify the inclusion of those samples with low TiO_2/Al_2O_3 (above, Figure 8.1) in this group. The close similarity of HIMT and Egypt 2 is presumably a reflection of similar regions of origin.

Table 8.2 LA-ICP-MS analyses of HIMT samples (wt% oxide, ppm element, except chlorine in wt%)

Type	*site*	*sample*	SiO_2	Na_2O	*CaO*	K_2O	*MgO*	Al_2O_3	Fe_2O_3	$Ti\ O_2$	*MnO*	P_2O_5
HIMTa	Sinai north	6830 23	67.48	15.38	5.52	0.42	1.32	3.19	2.34	0.63	2.50	0.06
HIMTa	Sinai north	6830 21	64.09	18.37	5.45	0.35	1.15	3.37	2.41	0.61	2.84	0.06
HIMTa	Sinai north	6831 81 P	66.39	17.64	6.51	0.37	0.94	2.86	1.72	0.52	1.69	0.05
HIMTa	Sinai north	6830 27	67.73	17.09	5.58	0.42	1.05	2.65	1.38	0.38	2.37	0.07
HIMTa	Carthage	33027	65.81	17.03	5.40	0.42	1.28	3.32	2.19	0.58	2.52	0.07
HIMTa	Billingsgate	6919 6 P	65.10	18.50	6.40	0.41	0.95	3.16	1.45	0.42	2.26	0.05
HIMTa	Billingsgate	6919 5 M	65.29	18.21	6.32	0.44	0.98	3.14	1.50	0.41	2.34	0.05
HIMTa	Billingsgate	6919 7 R	65.81	17.65	5.95	0.51	0.97	3.20	1.83	0.48	2.26	0.07
HIMTa	Billingsgate	6919 11 X	64.68	20.54	5.82	0.57	0.91	2.66	1.34	0.33	1.72	0.08
HIMTa	Billingsgate	6919 8 W	65.52	19.08	6.37	0.53	0.93	2.80	1.34	0.33	1.68	0.09
HIMTa	Billingsgate	6919 12 K	64.98	20.24	6.29	0.57	0.94	2.59	1.11	0.25	1.60	0.08
HIMTa	Billingsgate	6919 10 T	64.80	19.71	6.36	0.62	0.94	2.84	1.39	0.33	1.67	0.07
HIMTa	Billingsgate	6919 16 W	66.27	18.99	6.55	0.62	0.91	2.64	0.99	0.22	1.39	0.09
HIMTb	Sinai north	6831 66 R	65.68	15.76	5.40	0.37	1.17	3.45	4.40	0.64	1.75	0.16
HIMTb	Sinai north	6830 28	67.68	16.45	6.27	0.49	0.94	3.06	2.41	0.44	1.08	0.12
HIMTb	Carthage	32832V	65.07	17.73	5.00	0.43	1.24	3.41	3.58	0.61	1.52	0.13

	Cl%	*B*	*Li*	*Ba*	*Sr*	*Rb*	*Cr*	*Zr*	*Hf*	*Y*	*Ga*	*Nb*	*Th*	*U*
6830 23	0.90	171	6.6	484	476	7.7	83	317	7.2	11.1	7.6	6.8	2.7	1.7
6830 21	1.04	158	7.7	597	431	7.3	81	297	6.8	11.5	7.8	6.6	2.4	1.6
6831 81 P	0.99	163	2.6	887	516	7.5	65	289	6.6	11.3	6.4	5.9	2.5	1.7
6830 27	1.05	202	4.2	317	487	8.4	48	202	4.5	9.5	6.4	4.4	1.8	1.2
33027	1.05	212	5.3	813	526	19.0	81	291	6.4	11.8	7.7	6.4	2.4	1.2
6919 6 P	0.93	205	12.4	1438	487	10.8	55	191	4.1	8.7	6.3	4.1	1.5	1.4
6919 5 M	0.91	214	11.8	1432	503	8.7	55	186	4.1	9.0	6.5	4.2	1.6	1.4
6919 7 R	0.96	142	13.2	882	443	8.5	66	206	4.5	9.1	6.6	4.6	1.5	1.0
6919 11 X	1.02	200	15.0	1177	410	8.6	50	137	3.1	6.6	5.5	3.3	1.1	1.0
6919 8 W	1.01	184	19.6	810	476	10.3	50	144	3.3	7.3	5.6	3.3	1.2	1.1
6919 12 K	1.09	199	11.0	361	455	7.6	36	111	2.5	6.7	5.3	2.8	1.1	1.0
6919 10 T	0.96	182	15.4	760	446	8.4	51	145	3.3	7.2	5.7	3.5	1.3	1.0
6919 16 W	1.05	197	18.5	316	450	8.7	32	96	2.2	6.2	5.1	2.4	0.9	0.9
6831 66 R	0.96	199	3.2	221	407	8.4	72	337	7.8	17.6	7.8	7.0	2.9	2.0
6830 28	0.83	143	4.5	249	503	6.8	55	222	5.0	11.6	6.4	5.1	2.1	1.7
32832	1.03	215	5.6	232	376	12.1	84	287	6.5	13.4	7.9	6.5	2.5	1.4

(*continued*)

Table 8.2 (cont.)

	V	*Sb*	*As*	*Pb*	*Cu*	*Ag*	*Co*	*Sn*	*Zn*	*Ni*	*Mo*	*W*	*Se*
6830 23	55	0	9	8	91	0.2	19	20	40	19	4.7	1.8	17
6830 21	63	1	11	10	79	0.2	20	21	41	21	4.8	2.0	5
6831 81 P	55	1	5	12	36	0.2	12	23	29	14	5.7	0.5	0
6830 27	46	7	5	52	65	0.3	11	28	34	18	6.9	0.6	14
33027	112	1	7	16	33	0.2	22	19	37	29	4.6	0.8	16
6919 6 P	53	4	4	61	68	0.4	11	25	28	16	3.7	0.6	128
6919 5 M	53	8	4	92	87	0.5	13	32	35	17	4.8	0.5	182
6919 7 R	57	45	5	38	75	0.4	14	26	62	19	5.3	0.5	115
6919 11 X	44	82	4	88	91	0.5	10	30	48	15	3.8	0.5	44
6919 8 W	40	95	4	92	92	0.6	11	37	44	15	4.3	0.4	154
6919 12 K	31	109	5	101	124	0.5	11	43	46	13	4.6	0.3	167
6919 10 T	43	115	4	120	81	0.4	10	68	39	16	3.9	0.4	115
6919 16 W	27	205	7	217	100	0.6	10	46	58	12	4.0	0.4	195
6831 66 R	102	1	23	22	93	0.2	14	21	52	51	5.9	0.5	5
6830 28	70	7	12	94	64	0.3	16	25	32	22	2.6	0.3	2
32832	88	1	16	32	84	0.2	12	24	52	36	2.9	0.4	5

	La	*Ce*	*Pr*	*Nd*	*Sm*	*Eu*	*Gd*	*Tb*	*Dy*	*Ho*	*Er*	*Tm*	*Yb*	*Lu*
6830 23	11.7	22.2	2.71	11.2	2.27	0.61	2.05	0.34	1.98	0.44	1.22	0.18	1.34	0.20
6830 21	11.4	21.0	2.63	11.1	2.29	0.65	2.12	0.35	2.09	0.44	1.28	0.19	1.38	0.21
6831 81 P	11.5	22.0	2.65	10.9	2.23	0.61	1.96	0.34	1.96	0.41	1.19	0.17	1.29	0.20
6830 27	10.2	17.1	2.22	9.6	1.80	0.51	1.69	0.30	1.63	0.35	1.04	0.15	1.06	0.16
33027	12.8	21.0	2.87	12.0	2.44	0.70	2.26	0.39	2.07	0.45	1.30	0.19	1.33	0.20
6919 6 P	7.1	13.9	1.69	7.3	1.65	0.75	2.22	0.28	1.43	0.31	0.93	0.14	1.01	0.14
6919 5 M	7.6	14.7	1.77	7.8	1.75	0.74	2.29	0.28	1.41	0.32	0.95	0.12	1.06	0.15
6919 7 R	8.0	14.8	1.84	8.1	1.71	0.68	2.50	0.30	1.52	0.34	0.99	0.14	1.04	0.15
6919 11 X	5.9	12.0	1.39	6.1	1.40	0.72	2.06	0.23	1.09	0.22	0.72	0.10	0.78	0.10
6919 8 W	6.4	12.7	1.57	6.8	1.41	0.62	2.15	0.25	1.22	0.27	0.77	0.11	0.89	0.12
6919 12 K	6.2	12.0	1.43	6.2	1.30	0.43	1.77	0.22	1.13	0.22	0.70	0.09	0.70	0.10
6919 10 T	6.5	13.0	1.54	6.5	1.38	0.64	2.20	0.25	1.19	0.26	0.80	0.10	0.85	0.11
6919 16 W	5.8	11.0	1.31	5.7	1.24	0.41	1.84	0.22	1.05	0.20	0.69	0.09	0.71	0.09
6831 66 R	20.1	23.7	4.54	18.9	3.95	1.02	3.42	0.61	3.40	0.72	1.97	0.28	1.95	0.28
6830 28	13.1	19.4	2.90	12.1	2.38	0.63	2.11	0.36	2.11	0.43	1.24	0.17	1.21	0.18
32832	15.0	22.1	3.48	14.2	2.93	0.77	2.60	0.43	2.52	0.53	1.49	0.21	1.53	0.22

Table 8.3 Isotopic data by TIMS

Sample	*Site*	*Type*	$^{87}Sr/^{86}Sr$	*Nd ppm*	$^{143}Nd/^{144}Nd$	ε_{Nd}
6831–1	Bet Eli'ezer	Levantine	0.70904	7.47	0.512352	-5.6
6831–2	Bet Eli'ezer	Levantine	0.70903	7.76	0.512344	-5.7
6831–3	Bet Eli'ezer	Levantine	0.70902	6.35	0.512331	-6.0
6831–10	Apollonia	Levantine	0.70911	n.a.	n.a.	n.a.
6831–11	Apollonia	Levantine	0.70905	6.89	0.512378	-5.1
6919–2	Billingsgate	HIMTa	0.70855	9.44	0.512374	-5.1
6919–11	Billingsgate	HIMTa	0.70860	8.44	0.512365	-5.3
6919–4	Billingsgate	HIMTa	0.70859	8.46	0.512358	-5.5
6831–20	North Sinai	HIMTb	0.70880	5.95	0.512351	-5.6
6831–27	North Sinai	HIMTa	0.70854	8.81	0.512366	-5.3
6831–28	North Sinai	HIMTa	0.70828	11.04	0.512377	-5.1
33027	Carthage	HIMTa	0.70810	11.95	0.512349	-5.6
32832	Carthage	HIMTb	0.70818	13.76	0.512339	-5.8
32833	Carthage	HIMTb	0.70864	10.87	0.512364	-5.3

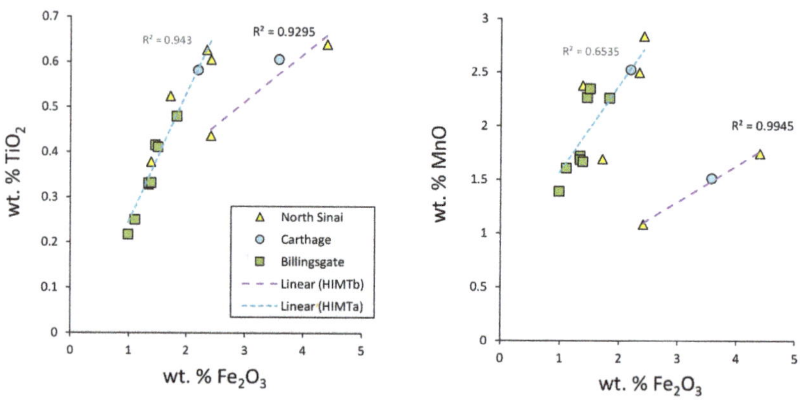

Figure 8.3 HIMTa and HIMTb glasses from the present study; left (a) titanium versus iron oxide and right (b) manganese versus iron oxide.

BaO is notably high in many HIMTa glasses. Whereas in most other glass groups it occurs at levels between 100–300 ppm, in HIMTa, values in excess of 300 ppm and up to 1,500 ppm are typical, rising exceptionally to over 3,000 ppm (Table 8.2; see also Wedepohl and Baumann 2000; Foy et al. 2003; Foster and Jackson 2009). There is a strong correlation between Ba and Eu (R = 0.86), but no correlation between Ba and the other lanthanide rare earth elements (REEs); Eu is the only REE that frequently occurs in the divalent state and it appears that in one of the raw materials of the glass, Ba^{2+} and Eu^{2+} occupied similar structural positions. Barium is not strongly correlated with any of the other measured components, although there is a weak correlation with Al_2O_3, possibly suggesting a feldspar component (Figure 8.4). Eu has a weak correlation with the other REEs, particularly the heavy REE such as Yb (Figure 8.4).

Rare earth elements were normalised to the MUQ average for the weathered continental crust (Kamber et al. 2005). Figure 8.6 shows that HIMTa frequently has a strong positive Eu anomaly, while HIMTb has a positive Eu anomaly and a very strong negative Ce anomaly. As noted above, in HIMTa the Eu is strongly correlated with Ba, and unsurprisingly there is a strong correlation between Ba in the samples and the magnitude of the Eu anomaly (Figure 8.7), so that the Ba content of the glasses has a very strong influence upon the appearance of the REE profile.

The isotopic results are presented in Table 8.3 and Figure 8.8. ε_{Nd} is in the range –5.1 to –6.0 for all samples, including the reference tank furnace samples from the Levant. There is no apparent difference in neodymium between HIMTa, HIMTb and the Levantine reference samples. As is well understood (Freestone et al. 2003; Degryse and Schneider 2008), the Levantine glasses have $^{87}Sr/^{86}Sr$ close to Holocene seawater (*c.*0.7092), implying the use of beach sand as raw material. There is a strong correlation of the Nd and Sr isotope ratios of the Levantine furnace glasses (Figure 8.8), clearly suggesting the contribution of a terrigenous component other than calcium carbonate to the strontium isotope composition, associated with the silicate fraction. However, this effect is relatively minor. As previously observed (Freestone et al. 2005), HIMT has $^{87}Sr/^{86}Sr$ significantly lower than the glasses from the Levantine coast. Furthermore, there appears no clear difference between the strontium isotope ratios of the HIMTa and HIMTb glasses. Recently it has been recognised that manganese added to glass as a decolourant may add an old strontium component, which can decrease $^{87}Sr/^{86}Sr$ (Ganio et al. 2012b; Gallo et al. 2015). Sr

	MnO	MgO	Al2O3	Fe2O3	TiO2	Co	Cr	Zr	Nb	La	Ce	Eu	Yb	Th	Ba	Sr
MnO	1.00															
MgO	0.74	1.00														
Al2O3	0.82	0.64	1.00													
Fe2O3	0.81	0.84	0.85	1.00												
TiO2	0.80	0.79	0.83	0.97	1.00											
Co	0.78	0.91	0.81	0.93	0.87	1.00										
Cr	0.78	0.81	0.86	0.99	0.98	0.90	1.00									
Zr	0.74	0.78	0.73	0.93	0.98	0.83	0.94	1.00								
Nb	0.77	0.82	0.76	0.95	0.98	0.87	0.95	1.00	1.00							
La	0.70	0.81	0.59	0.84	0.89	0.81	0.83	0.95	0.95	1.00						
Ce	0.66	0.77	0.61	0.87	0.92	0.79	0.86	0.98	0.97	0.98	1.00					
Eu	0.47	0.15	0.65	0.44	0.49	0.29	0.54	0.37	0.37	0.17	0.21	1.00				
Yb	0.79	0.76	0.78	0.92	0.97	0.82	0.92	0.99	0.98	0.94	0.96	0.40	1.00			
Th	0.68	0.79	0.64	0.88	0.93	0.80	0.88	0.98	0.98	0.97	1.00	0.25	0.97	1.00		
Ba	0.12	-0.25	0.35	0.01	0.11	-0.11	0.13	0.01	-0.01	-0.19	-0.13	0.86	0.06	-0.09	1.00	
Sr	0.22	0.32	0.26	0.18	0.34	0.25	0.26	0.43	0.39	0.52	0.48	0.13	0.47	0.49	0.17	1.00

Figure 8.4 Correlation matrix for selected components in HIMTa.

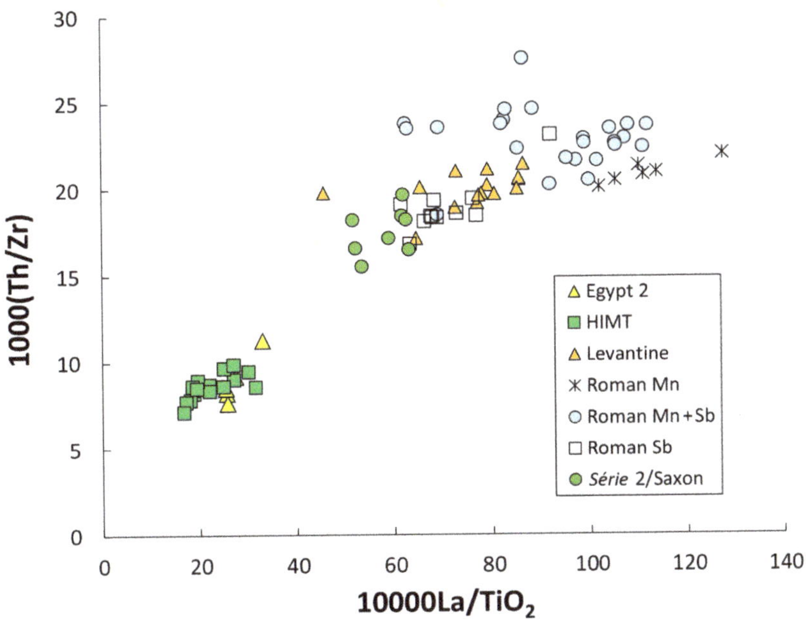

Figure 8.5 Separation of HIMT from other glass groups in terms of ratios of Th and La to Zr (in ppm) and TiO_2 (wt%). Note the similarity of HIMT and Egypt 2. HIMT data, this work; others, unpublished data of the authors for various sites including London, Apollonia, Bet Eli'ezer, Tel el Ashmunein.

and MnO are weakly correlated in HIMTa (Figure 8.4) but more significantly there is a relatively strong correlation between MnO and the ratio of strontium to calcium, shown in Figure 8.9 and indicating that addition of manganese added strontium over that present in shell. The trendline through the HIMTa samples extrapolates back through the Sr/CaO ratios of low-Mn Levantine glass, which presumably approximate to the values of eastern Mediterranean beach sand. The isotopic data are therefore fully consistent with the manufacture of HIMT using a sand from the eastern Mediterranean coastal region.

Discussion

Glass composition and the addition of manganese

The present results confirm the general features of HIMT glass as previously understood (Foy et al. 2003; Freestone et al. 2005; Foster and

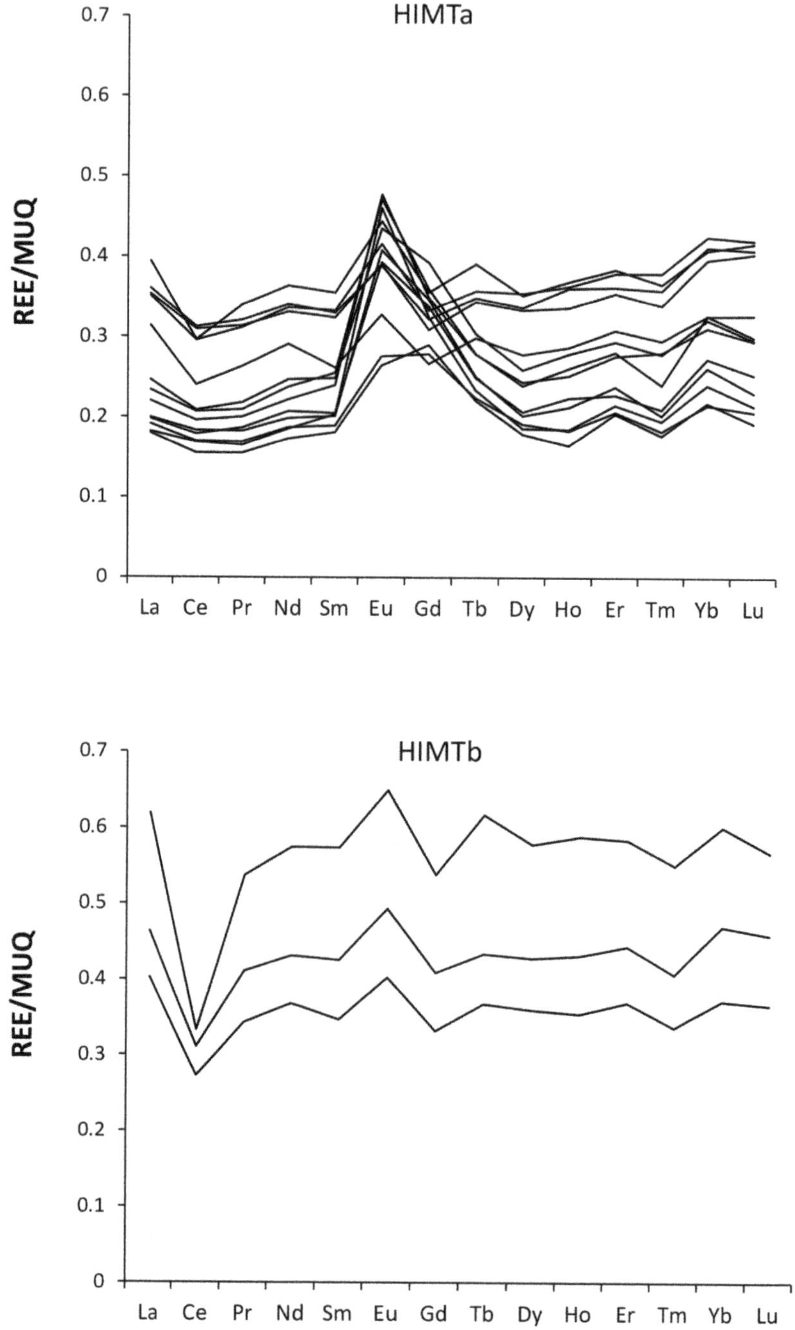

Figure 8.6 Rare earth elements in HIMTa and b, normalised to the weathered continental crust (MUQ).

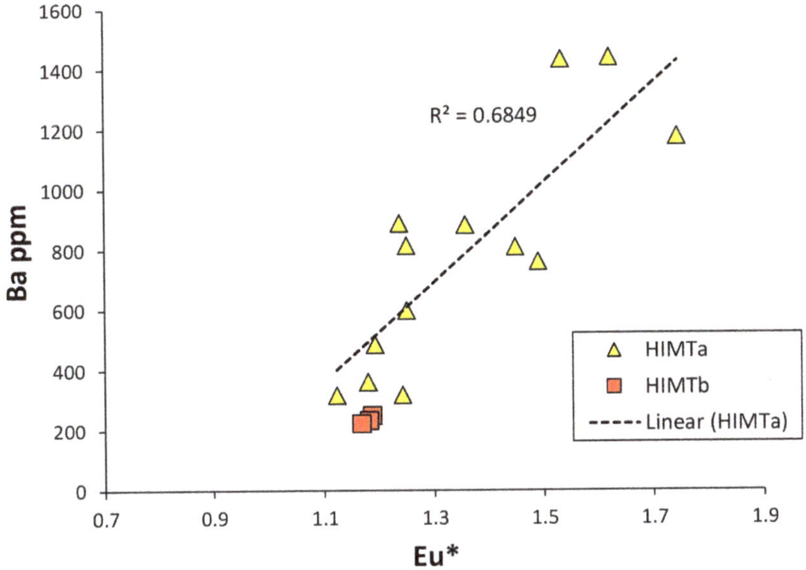

Figure 8.7 Correlation of barium concentration and europium anomaly (2Eu/(Sm + Gd), MUQ-normalised data) for HIMT samples analysed.

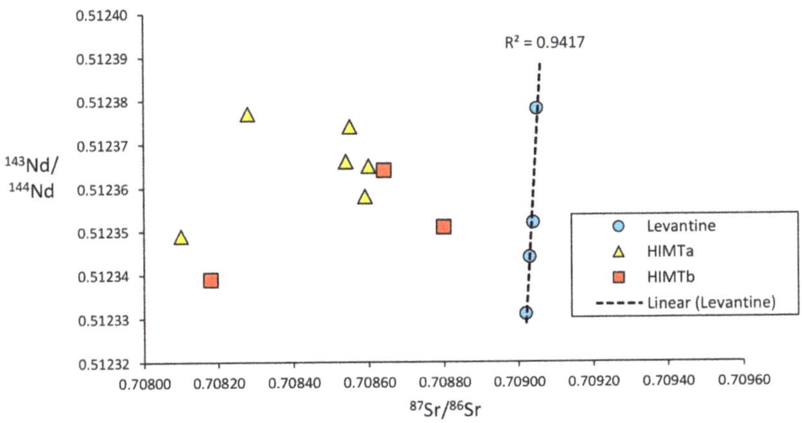

Figure 8.8 Neodymium and strontium isotope ratios for HIMTa and HIMTb glasses, compared with glass from Levantine tank furnaces.

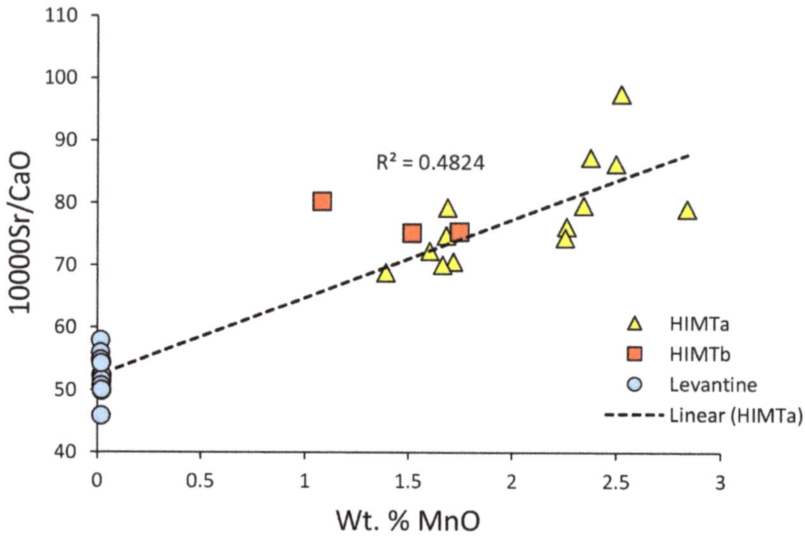

Figure 8.9 Correlation between manganese and ratio of strontium to calcium oxide in HIMTa glass, note the extension of the trendline through the centre of the Levantine compositions.

Jackson 2009; Nenna 2014). Its key characteristics include high Na_2O, TiO_2, Fe_2O_3, MnO, MgO but low CaO relative to most other glass groups of the period. There are strong inter-element correlations of titanium, iron, magnesium, many of the transition metals and the REE. The ε_{Nd} range of –5 to –6 corresponds to that of glass from eastern Mediterranean tank furnaces, suggesting an origin in the region. However, $^{87}Sr/^{86}Sr$ departs from the values expected of a beach sand, and is related to the addition of Sr-bearing manganese oxide. In a previous attempt to explain the chemistry of HIMT, Freestone et al. (2005) emphasised the variability of the strontium isotopes and suggested that they reflected the mixing of two sediment sources in the sand used as a raw material. In the light of the present results, that suggestion can no longer be considered viable. The isotopic results, however, strongly suggest an origin in the eastern Mediterranean, and the high TiO_2 and ZrO_2 contents support the origin in Egypt that has previously been suggested.

In addition to these previously understood characteristics it has been possible to confirm the sub-division of HIMT in to two groups, HIMTa and HIMTb, as proposed by Ceglia et al. (2015). As previously suggested these two categories may be differentiated principally in terms of their Fe_2O_3/TiO_2 and Fe_2O_3/Al_2O_3 ratios. The present analysis also suggests a major difference in MnO/Fe_2O_3, where HIMTb has relatively higher Fe_2O_3. The strong correlations between MnO and Fe_2O_3 that emerge when HIMT is considered as two groups (Figure 8.3b) pose a problem around the origin of the MnO, which is a component considered characteristic of the glass.

MnO has been considered a deliberate additive to natron glass and to HIMT in particular by virtually all authors who have considered the subject in recent years. It is generally held that the manganese was added as MnO_2, to oxidise the glass, thereby acting as a decolouriser by converting Fe^{2+}, which imparts a strong blue colouration, to Fe^{3+}, which imparts a weak yellow (Sayre 1963). As much HIMT is not fully decolourised, but is a fairly strong translucent green, Freestone et al. (2005) suggested that manganese was added not to fully decolourise but to oxidise the glass from a highly reduced state, where the colour would have been amber or even black. However, more recent studies using X-ray absorption spectroscopy and optical spectroscopy indicate that the iron in HIMT glass is largely oxidised, so the Fe^{3+}/Fe^{2+} ratio in the glass was shifted well beyond the condition required to remove the ferri-sulphide chromophore (de Ferri et al. 2011; Arletti et al. 2013; Ceglia et al. 2016), so that the hypothesis of Freestone et al. (2005) seems less likely. Even so, Rehren and Cholakova (2010) have pointed out that the existence of an HIMT-related glass without added manganese, termed by them HIT, is strong evidence supporting the deliberate addition of MnO_2.

If manganese was added as a decolouriser, the strength of the correlation between manganese and iron seen here is surprising. A rather broad but clearly identifiable positive correlation occurs between MnO and Fe_2O_3 in the colourless glass of Renaissance Venice, but as explained by Verità and Zecchin (2009) this was achieved by carefully balancing the glass colour at the secondary production (fabrication) stage – manganese oxide was carefully added to the glass until the colour was minimised and a similar proposal was made by Wedepohl et al. (2003) for glass now recognised as HIMT. However, the precision implied by the very strong correlation observed for HIMT would be unlikely to be achieved in such a way. Much HIMT glass has a variable weak to strong green tint, so that a uniform reduction of colour does not appear to have been attained and the putative titration of FeO in the glass with MnO_2 would not have had a constant end point.

The foregoing considerations argue against an addition of MnO_2 to HIMT glass to decolourise a pre-existing colour due to iron. Additionally it is recalled that the (assumed) primary glass chunks from Carthage lie on the correlations observed, implying that the addition of manganese was a primary glass-making practice rather than carried out in secondary workshops. The fact that glass from locations as far apart as North Sinai, Carthage and London lies upon a single correlation trend indicates that this was not a practice carried out in different secondary workshops, using different fuels, different furnaces and different practices, as they would have required different ratios of MnO_2 to Fe_2O_3 to achieve a full oxidation. The inevitable conclusion is that iron and manganese were added together to the glass batch at the primary stage in a single material that typically had a fairly constant Mn/Fe ratio.

If manganese and iron were added as a single component to the glass batch, they are likely to have been either components of the glass-making sand or of a decolourant or colourant added to the glass. Sands with high MnO/Fe_2O_3 ratios are uncommon, due to the relative solubilities of Mn- and Fe-oxides. The MnO/Fe_2O_3 ratio of the surface of the earth is less than 0.1 (e.g. Kamber et al., 2005) and to enhance the Mn content would require a substantial enrichment, such as that which occurs in an ore body. Such potential sand raw materials were not identified by Brems et al. (2012), in their survey of western Mediterranean sands, nor do they occur in the Nilotic sands analysed by Picon and co-workers, which are discussed by Nenna (2014). A sand source for the high MnO therefore seems unlikely. By elimination, it appears that the manganese 'decolouriser' added to HIMT glass at the primary melting stage also contained substantial amounts of Fe_2O_3. Although correlations between MnO and the REE, Zr, Ti, Cr and so on are not as strong as with Fe_2O_3 (Figure 8.4), they are high and the implication is that the 'manganese' additive also contained substantial amounts of these components.

Strong correlations between MnO and Fe_2O_3 are also present in the data of Foster and Jackson (2009; $R^2=0.44$ for HIMT 1, calculated for this study), Rehren and Brüggler (2015; $R^2=0.63$ for HIMTa, the one apparent HIMTb sample neglected) and has also been reported for glass from Hambach Forest, Germany (Wedepohl et al. 2003). Although HIMTb has been analysed less frequently than HIMTa, the three samples reported in the present study appear to show a strong correlation between MnO and Fe_2O_3 and samples of Ceglia et al. (2015) and Foy et al. (2003) cluster around the respective trendlines. The conclusion that manganese and iron were added together in a fairly constant ratio is therefore generally applicable to both HIMTa and HIMTb glass, although the ratio differed for each glass group.

Accepting that MnO_2 and Fe_2O_3 in HIMT represent a single additive, then it would appear that the base glass of HIMT contained somewhat less than 1.0 per cent Fe_2O_3 and 0.2 per cent TiO_2 (e.g. Figure 8.2). This would have been a relatively pale glass that, on the basis of comparison with groups such as Foy *séries 2.1* and *3.2*, could have been further decolourised by additions of MnO_2. Indeed, Mn-decolourised glass with a base composition that has similar soda and lime contents to HIMT is known from the fourth century, in the form of Group 2 of Foster and Jackson (2010). That HIMT was not decolourised leads to the conclusion that it was intentionally tinted by a Mn-Fe additive. The intention of the glass makers was to colour their product yellow-green rather than the green-blue that was the typical colour of primary glass to which no decolourant had been added, due to the relatively high concentration of reduced iron (Arletti et al. 2013).

There is a parallel here with the recent conclusions of Huisman et al. (2017), whose article became available online as the present chapter was being completed. On the basis of the analysis of a large number of La Tène (late Iron Age) beads, Huisman et al. conclude that a range of colours were generated by adding to the glass manganese ores with varying amounts of other components such as cobalt and copper. While we do not necessarily agree fully with the conclusions of these authors on Iron Age glass, a similar phenomenon to that which they envisage seems to occur in HIMT: different manganese oxides with constant ratios of MnO_2 to Fe_2O_3 were added to the glass to produce colours, which differentiated it from the glass of the Levant. According to this model, HIMTa and HIMTb were made by adding material from different manganiferous deposits, or different parts of the same deposit, to essentially the same base glass.

It is suggested below that the purpose of the HIMT colour modification is likely to have been for product recognition or commodity branding, a signal to the consumer that they could trust that this yellow-green glass had certain properties that differentiated it from green-blue glass, and that in some respects made it more desirable.

Commodity branding in the primary glass industry

Isotopic studies have made it increasingly clear over the past few years that the majority of Roman and later natron glass was made in two regions: Egypt and the coastal plain of present-day Israel (Brems et al. 2012, 2013a, 2013b; Ganio et al. 2012a, 2012b; Degryse and Schneider 2008; Degryse 2014; Gallo et al. 2015). Advantage was taken of the proximity to the high quality glass-making sands, derived ultimately from the Nile, and the essential natron flux deposits of the Wadi Natrun and the Egyptian delta, so that the location is apparently consistent with economic theory that indicates that production is generally located where costs, in this case those associated with the transport of raw materials, can be kept to a minimum (Weber and Friedrich 1929). It has been argued that the antimony-decolourised glass of the first–fourth centuries CE was primarily an Egyptian product (e.g. Degryse 2014; Schibille et al. 2017) and it is generally accepted that the more abundant Mn-containing colourless to greenish-blue glass was made on the Levantine coast (Nenna et al. 1997).

While makers' names on the bases of mould-blown containers and on special products such as Ennion's mould-blown tablewares clearly indicate that branding was a familiar practice in the marketing of shaped glass products or their contents (Stern 1999: 456–7), the concept of product branding of primary or raw glass has not been widely discussed. Unlike the late Bronze Age, where the distinctive and standardised shape of Egyptian glass ingots (Nicholson et al. 1997; Rehren and Pusch 1999) may have served to signify their origin (unfortunately evidence from Mesopotamia is slight), the irregular chunks of the first millennium CE could not be distinguished by shape, so that colour would have been the only distinguishing characteristic, short of testing of the molten glass at the mouth of the furnace. The emperor Diocletian's Edict of Maximum Prices (301 CE) makes it clear that the distinction between colourless Alexandrian glass and green Judaean glass was recognised in the fourth century and indicates that to purchase a pound of raw Alexandrian glass would cost almost twice as much as a pound of Judaean glass (Stern 1999: 460–4). Commodity recognition through colour would therefore have been a familiar concept to the glass workers – the fabricators of vessels – who acquired the primary raw materials and who were the consumers of raw glass.

The detailed discussion by Bevan (2010) emphasises that commodity branding becomes particularly necessary when networks of exchange are long, complex and inter-regional. This is precisely the situation of primary glass that was produced in the south-eastern Mediterranean and distributed to large numbers of glass workshops that were located as far away as Britain and Germany. Consumers (in the present case glass-workers) and producers (primary glassmakers) were widely separated and unable to communicate directly with one another. The glass workers needed some way of understanding what they were acquiring and the primary producers some way of differentiating their product from others to bring it to the attention of the consumer. Branding allowed a trust in product quality to be established along the supply chain between the producer, the consumer and the merchants or middlemen who linked them.

While the value of colourless glass over tinted or self-coloured glass is widely accepted and has been a characteristic of the glass industry since the time of Pliny through to the modern period, it is not at first obvious why the glass worker should have preferred a yellow-green Egyptian glass over a green-blue Judaean one – both were weakly tinted and not fully transparent, so an overwhelming appeal to the domestic consumer of tablewares is not obvious. Indeed, according to Foster and Jackson (2009), although HIMT is the dominant glass type from the mid-fourth century in Britain, the vessels are made in easier to work forms and less care seems to have been exercised over the quality of the glass, for example, the glass frequently has a high content of seed (bubbles). The appeal of HIMT to the glass workers is therefore likely to have been due to its preferred working properties, rather than being able to charge a higher price for the finished product.

Viscosities of several glasses were calculated using the model of Fluegel (2007). The composition of HIMT lies outside the limits of most available models, because of the high MnO_2 and Fe_2O_3 beyond those of modern glasses, so an accurate calculation of viscosity is not possible, but for illustrative purposes Figure 8.10 predicts that the average HIMTa glass from Billingsgate has a significantly lower viscosity than the average fourth-century glass from Jalame, as might be expected from its higher Na_2O and lower SiO_2. There is a suggested advantage of around 40°C lower working temperatures for HIMT, which would have been

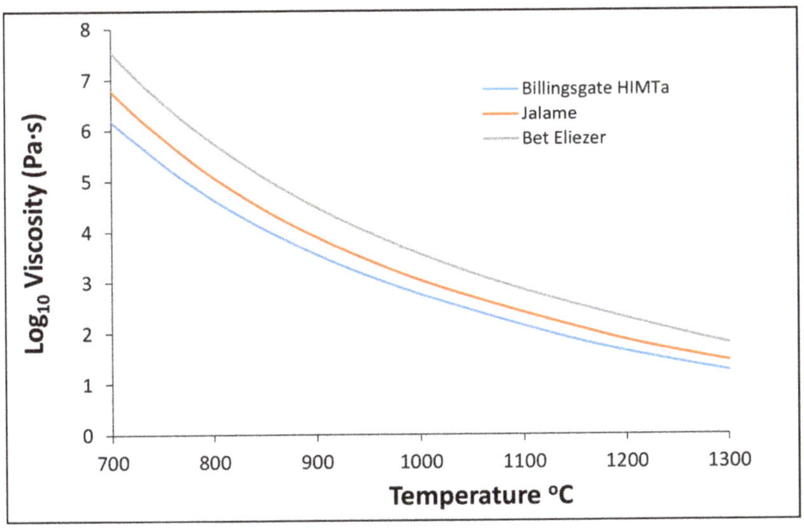

Figure 8.10 Viscosity-temperature relations for mean HIMTa from Billingsgate, London relative to mean Levantine glass. Data for Jalame from Brill (1988) and Bet Eli'ezer from Freestone et al. (2000). Model of Fluegel (2007).

advantageous in terms of fuel consumption and/or ease of working. A similar advantage would have occurred in the temperatures required to melt and refine the glass before working. It is suggested that HIMT glass offered significant advantages in ease and cost of working over glass from Levantine production centres such as Jalame, and was distinctively tinted by the glass makers to signify this.

The origins and distribution of HIMT

On the basis of an extensive study of glass from Britain, Foster and Jackson (2009) have concluded that HIMT was introduced in the mid-fourth century. At about the same time, the production of antimony-decolourised vessels ceased (Foster and Jackson 2010). Given that both HIMT and Sb-decolourised glass (Rom-Sb) of the first–fourth centuries have very similar major element base glass compositions in terms of relatively high Na_2O and low CaO, and both are likely to have been Egyptian products (see above), HIMT can be regarded as a continuation of the Rom-Sb tradition, possibly by the same Egyptian glass makers who no longer had access to a supply of antimony at an acceptable cost. A restriction in the availability of antimony also seems likely because it was also around the mid-fourth century that Sb-opacified glass appears to have been replaced by the tin-opacified equivalent in high-status objects such as wall mosaics and opus sectile (Turner and Rooksby 1959, 1961; Brill 1976; Brill and Whitehouse 1988; for a recent review see Tite et al. 2008).

It seems likely that in response to a restriction in the supply of antimony needed to decolourise their glass, Egyptian glass makers began to make their glass distinctive by giving it a yellowish tint, in contrast to the blue of Levantine glass. Once understood, glass with a yellowish tint would have been preferred by the glassworkers across the empire due to its more desirable working properties. This was apparently at least a partially successful strategy, as HIMT glass appears to have become dominant in western Europe (Foster and Jackson 2009). While the Egyptian glass makers were no longer producing a colourless glass that could be sold at a premium, they could still compete with and in some cases outsell Levantine glass due to the character of the glass itself.

Interestingly, in the Levant and adjacent regions such as Cyprus, the HIMT family of yellowish glasses does not seem to have dominated Levantine glass to the extent that it appears to have done in northwestern Europe, if at all (e.g. Ceglia et al. 2015). A recent study of glass from Carthage again suggests that Levantine glass was well represented (Schibille et al. 2017). These patterns are open to a number of interpretations that cannot be discussed in detail in the present chapter, but that clearly merit further investigation. One such issue is the response of the domestic consumer to the new yellowish glass. If there was resistance to the purchase of vessels in the new colour, and the traditional green-blue tint was preferred, then this would weigh against the advantages offered to the glass workers by the improved working properties and the concomitant marginal cost reduction. HIMT may then have been less competitive in regions where small cost differentials were less important in determining consumer choice, for example, in communities with higher proportions of relatively affluent individuals, such as in the eastern Mediterranean and large cities.

Conclusions

HIMT glass has neodymium and strontium isotopes characteristic of the beach sands of the south-eastern Mediterranean, particularly if allowance is made for the contribution of strontium by the manganese source. The high TiO_2/Al_2O_3 is characteristic of an Egyptian rather than a Levantine origin, and it appears to be readily distinguished from a range of other primary glass products that have lower TiO_2 or differ in Al_2O_3/SiO_2.

HIMT glass is proposed to have been intentionally coloured yellow-green rather than naturally coloured due to impurities in the sand. It was deliberately tinted to allow it to be recognised and differentiated from the green-blue glass of the Levant, which was competing in the marketplace but that had less favourable melting and working properties. HIMT represents a continuation of an Egyptian primary glass lineage in which its predecessor was Roman antimony-decolourised glass, which was also a high-soda, low-viscosity type. The glassworkers branded their product by inducing a yellow tint, so that it could be recognised by the consumers of primary glass, who were the craftsmen who blew the vessels. They would have seen the yellow-green glass as a material that they were able to melt and shape more economically, offsetting to some extent the loss of the advantage that they had previously possessed due to antimony decolourisation.

The material added to HIMT as a colourant is inferred to have been an impure manganese ore. In addition to MnO_2 and Fe_2O_3 a range of other impurities were added which complicate the trace element geochemistry of the glass. In particular barium, which is well known as an element associated with manganese deposits, is present to exceptionally high levels in some HIMT glass and has a dramatic effect on the appearance of the rare earth element pattern, due to its strong correlation with divalent europium. However, the lack of correlation between barium and the other rare earths suggests that there was a less significant modification of these elements and the data indicate that the Nile-derived neodymium isotope signature has not been greatly affected. At least two distinct types of manganese were added to colour HIMT, and these have higher and lower iron/manganese ratios, giving rise to the sub-groups HIMTa and HIMTb respectively, which were first recognised by Ceglia et al. (2015). A cursory examination suggests that other groups of high-manganese glass such as Foy *série 2.1* may prove to have been modified in a similar way to HIMT, but the complexities of the geochemistry may prove challenging. Similarly, the precise composition of the base glass of HIMT, before the addition of the manganese colourant is currently unclear.

Acknowledgements

We are grateful to Veronica Tatton-Brown, Yael Gorin-Rosen and John Shepherd, who generously provided samples for analysis. Matt Phelps kindly commented on the draft.

References

Aerts, A., Velde, B., Janssens, K. and Dijkman, W. 2003. 'Change in Silica Sources in Roman and Post-Roman Glass'. *Spectrochimica Acta Part B: Atomic Spectroscopy* 58: 659–67.

Al-Bashaireh, K., Al-Mustafa, S., Freestone, I. C. and Al-Housan, A.Q. 2016. 'Composition of Byzantine Glasses from Umm el-Jimal, Northeast Jordan: Insights into Glass Origins and Recycling'. *Journal of Cultural Heritage* 21: 809–18. http://dx.doi.org/10.1016/j.culher.2016.04.008

Arletti, R., Quartieri, S. and Freestone, I. C. 2013. 'A XANES Study of Chromophores in Archaeological Glass'. *Applied Physics A* 111: 99–108.

Bevan, A. 2010. 'Making and Marking Relationships'. In *Cultures of Commodity Branding,* edited by A. Bevan and D. Wengrove, 35–85. Walnut Creek: Left Coast Press.

Bimson, M. and Freestone, I.C. 1985. 'The Discovery of an Islamic Glass Making Site in Middle Egypt'. *Annales AIHV* 10: 237–43.

Brems, D. and Degryse, P. 2014. 'Trace Element Analysis in Provenancing Roman Glass-Making'. *Archaeometry* 56: 116–36.

Brems, D., Degryse, P., Hasendoncks, F., Gimeno, D., Silvestri, A., Vassilieva, E., Luypaers, S. and Honings, J. 2012. 'Western Mediterranean Sand Deposits as a Raw Material for Roman Glass Production'. *Journal of Archaeological Science* 39: 2897–907.

Brems, D., Ganio, M., Latruwe, K., Balcaen, L., Carremans, M., Gimeno, D., Silvestri, A., Vanhaecke, F., Muchez, P. and Degryse, P. 2013a. 'Isotopes on the Beach, Part 1: Strontium Isotope Ratios as a Provenance Indicator for Lime Raw Materials Used in Roman Glass-Making'. *Archaeometry* 55: 214–34.

Brems, D., Ganio, M., Latruwe, K., Balcaen, L., Carremans, M., Gimeno, D., Silvestri, A., Vanhaecke, F., Muchez, P. and Degryse, P. 2013b. 'Isotopes on the Beach, Part 2: Neodymium Isotopic Analysis for the Provenancing of Roman Glass-Making'. *Archaeometry* 55: 449–64.

Brill, R. H. 1976. 'Scientific Studies of the Panel Materials'. In *Kenchreai: Eastern Port of Corinth II. The Panels of Opus Sectile in Glass*, edited by L. Ibrahim, R. Scranton and R. Brill, 226–55. Leiden: Brill.

Brill, R. H. 1988. 'Scientific Investigations of the Jalame Glass and Related Finds'. In *Excavations at Jalame: Site of a Glass Factory in Late Roman Palestine*, edited by G. D. Weinberg, 257–91. Columbia: University of Missouri Press.

Brill, R. H. and Whitehouse, D. 1988. 'The Thomas Panel'. *Journal of Glass Studies* 30: 34–50.

Ceglia, A., Cosyns, P., Nys, K., Terryn, H., Thienpont, H. and Meulebroeck, W. 2015. 'Late Antique Glass Distribution and Consumption in Cyprus: A Chemical Study'. *Journal of Archaeological Science* 61: 213–22.

Ceglia, A., Cosyns, P., Nys, K., Terryn, H., Thienpont, H. and Meulebroeck, W. 2016. 'Light Through Glass: The Spectrum of Late Antique Glass from Cyprus'. *Journal of Archaeological Science: Reports* 7: 614–24.

Cholakova, A., Rehren, Th. and Freestone, I. C. 2016. 'Compositional Identification of 6th c. AD Glass from the Lower Danube'. *Journal of Archaeological Science: Reports* 7: 625–32.

De Ferri, L., Arletti, R., Ponterini, G. and Quartieri, S. 2011. 'XANES, UV-VIS and Luminescence Spectroscopic Study of Chromophores in Ancient HIMT Glass'. *European Journal of Mineralogy* 23: 969–80.

Degryse, P. 2014. *Glass Making in the Greco-Roman World: Results of the ARCHGLASS Project*. Leuven: Leuven University Press.

Degryse, P. and Schneider, J. 2008. 'Pliny the Elder and Sr–Nd Isotopes: Tracing the Provenance of Raw Materials for Roman Glass Production'. *Journal of Archaeological Science* 35: 1993–2000.

Fluegel, A. 2007. 'Glass Viscosity Calculation Based on a Global Statistical Modelling Approach'. *Glass Technology: European Journal of Glass Science and Technology Part A* 48: 13–30.

Foster, H. and Jackson, C. M. 2009. 'The Composition of "Naturally Coloured" Late Roman Vessel Glass from Britain and the Implications for Models of Glass Production and Supply'. *Journal of Archaeological Science* 36: 189–204.

Foster, H. E. and Jackson, C. M. 2010. 'The Composition of Late Romano-British Colourless Vessel Glass: Glass Production and Consumption'. *Journal of Archaeological Science* 37: 3068–80.

Foy, D., Picon, M., Vichy, M. and Thirion-Merle, V. 2003. 'Caractérisation des verres de la fin de l'Antiquitéen Méditerranée occidentale: l'emergence de nouveaux courants commerciaux'. In *Échanges et Commerce du Verre dans le MondeAntique*, edited by D. Foy and M. D. Nenna, 41–85. Montagnac: Éditions Monique Mergoil.

Freestone, I. C. 1994. 'Appendix: Chemical Analysis of "Raw" Glass Fragments'. In *Excavations at Carthage, Vol. II, 1. The Circular Harbour, North Side. The Site and Finds other than Pottery* (British Academy Monographs in Archaeology 4), edited by H. R. Hurst, 290. Oxford: Oxford University Press.

Freestone, I. C. In press. 'Glass Production in the First Millennium CE: A Compositional Perspective'. In *Glas und Glasproduktion in Ur und Frühgeschichtlicher Zeit*, edited by F. Klimscha, H. J. Karlsen, S. Hansen and J. Renn. Berlin: TOPOI.

Freestone, I. C., Degryse, P., Shepherd, J., Gorin-Rosen, Y. and Schneider, J. 'Neodymium and Strontium Isotopes Indicate a Near Eastern Origin for Late Roman Glass in London' (unpublished manuscript).

Freestone, I. C., Gorin-Rosen, Y. and Hughes, M. J. 2000. 'Composition of Primary Glass from Israel'. In *Ateliers primaires et secondaires de verriers du second millénaire av. J.-C. au Moyen-Âge*, edited by M. D. Nenna, 65–84. Lyon: Travaux de la Maison de l'Orient Méditerranéen 33.

Freestone, I. C., Greenwood, R. and Gorin-Rosen, Y. 2002b. 'Byzantine and Early Islamic Glassmaking in the Eastern Mediterranean: Production and Distribution of Primary Glass'. In *Hyalos – Vitrum – Glass. History Technology and Conservation of Glass and Vitreous Materials in the Hellenic World. 1st International conference Rhodes*, edited by G. Kordas, 167–74. Athens: Glasnet.

Freestone, I. C., Jackson-Tal R., Tal O. and Taxel, I. 2015. 'Glass Production at an Early Islamic Workshop in Tel Aviv'. *Journal of Archaeological Science* 62: 45–54.

Freestone, I. C., Leslie, K. A., Thirlwall, M. and Gorin-Rosen, Y. 2003. 'Strontium Isotopes in the Investigation of Early Glass Production: Byzantine and Early Islamic Glass from the Near East'. *Archaeometry* 45: 19–32.

Freestone, I. C., Ponting, M. and Hughes, M. J. 2002a. 'Origins of Byzantine Glass from Maroni Petrera, Cyprus'. *Archaeometry* 44: 257–72.

Freestone, I. C., Wolf, S. and Thirlwall, M. 2005. 'The Production of HIMT Glass: Elemental and Isotopic Evidence'. *Annales AIHV* 16: 153–7.

Freestone, I. C., Wolf, S. and Thirlwall, M. 2009. 'Isotopic Composition of Glass From The Levant and South-Eastern Mediterranean Region'. In *Isotopes in Vitreous Materials*, edited by P. Degryse, J. Henderson and G. Hodgins, 31–52. Leuven: Leuven University Press.

Gallo, F., Silvestri, A., Degryse, P., Ganio, M., Longinelli, A. and Molin, G. 2015. 'Roman and Late-Roman Glass from North-Eastern Italy: The Isotopic

Perspective to Provenance Its Raw Materials'. *Journal of Archaeological Science* 62: 55–65.

Ganio, M., Boyen, S., Brems, D., Scott, R., Foy, D., Latruwe, K., Molin, G., Silvestri, A., Vanhaecke, F. and Degryse, P. 2012b. 'Trade Routes Across the Mediterranean: A Sr/Nd Isotopic Investigation on Roman Colourless Glass'. *Glass Technology – European Journal of Glass Science and Technology Part A* 53: 217–24.

Ganio, M., Boyen, S., Fenn, T., Scott, R., Vanhoutte, S., Gimeno, D. and Degryse, P. 2012a. 'Roman Glass Across the Empire: An Elemental and Isotopic Characterization'. *Journal of Analytical Atomic Spectrometry* 27: 743–53.

Gratuze, B. 2016. 'Glass Characterization Using Laser Ablation-Inductively Coupled Plasma-Mass Spectrometry Methods'. In *Recent Advances in Laser Ablation ICP-MS for Archaeology*, edited by L. Dussubieux, M. Golitko and B. Gratuze, 179–96. Berlin/Heidelberg: Springer-Verlag.

Gratuze, B. and Barrandon, J. N. 1990. 'Islamic Glass Weights and Stamps: Analysis Using Nuclear Techniques'. *Archaeometry* 32: 155–62.

Huisman, D. J., van der Laan, J., Davies, G. R., van Os, B. J. H., Roymans, N., Fermin, B. and Karwowski, M. 2017. 'Purple Haze: Combined Geochemical and Pb-Sr Isotope Constraints on Colourants in Celtic Glass'. *Journal of Archaeological Science* 81: 59–78.

Kamber, B. S., Greig, A. and Collerson, K. D. 2005. 'A New Estimate for the Composition of Weathered Young Upper Continental Crust from Alluvial Sediments, Queensland, Australia'. *Geochimica et Cosmochimica Acta* 69: 1041–58.

Maltoni, S., Chinni, T., Vandini, M., Cirelli, E., Silvestri, A. and Molin, G. 2015. 'Archaeological and Archaeometric Study of the Glass Finds from the Ancient Harbour of Classe (Ravenna, Italy): New Evidence'. *Heritage Science* 3: 13.

Maltoni, S., Silvestri, A., Marcante, A. and Molin, G. 2016. 'The Transition from Roman to Late Antique Glass: New Insights from the Domus of Tito Macro in Aquileia (Italy)'. *Journal of Archaeological Science* 73: 1–16.

Nenna, M. D. 2014. 'Egyptian Glass Abroad: HIMT Glass and Its Market'. In *Neighbours and Successors of Rome*, edited by D. Keller, J. Price and C. Jackson, 177–93. Oxford: Oxbow Books.

Nenna, M. D., Vichy, M. and Picon, M. 1997. 'L'Atelier de verrier de Lyon, du 1er siècle après J.-C., et l'origine des verres "Romains"'. *Revue d'Archéométrie* 21: 81–7.

Nicholson, P. T., Jackson, C. M. and Trott, K. M. 1997. 'The Ulu Burun Glass Ingots, Cylindrical Vessels and Egyptian Glass'. *Journal of Egyptian Archaeology* 83: 143–53.

Phelps, M., Freestone, I. C., Gorin-Rosen, Y. and Gratuze, B. 2016. 'Natron Glass Production and Supply in the Late Antique and Early Medieval Near East: The Effect of the Byzantine-Islamic Transition'. *Journal of Archaeological Science* 75: 57–71.

Pollard, A. M. and Heron, C. 2008. *Archaeological Chemistry*. Cambridge: Royal Society of Chemistry.

Rehren, Th. and Brüggler, M. 2015. 'Composition and Production of Late Antique Glass Bowls Type Helle'. *Journal of Archaeological Science: Reports* 3: 171–80.

Rehren, Th. and Cholakova, A. 2010. 'The Early Byzantine HIMT Glass from Dichin, Northern Bulgaria/Ранновизантийско Стъкло тип HIMT от Градището При С. Дичин'. *Interdisciplinary Studies/Интердисциплинарни Изследвания* 22: 81–96.

Rehren, Th. and Pusch, E. B. 1999. 'Glass and Glass Making at Qantir-Piramesses and Beyond'. *Ägypten und Levante IX Jahrbuch des Romisch-Germanischen Zentral Museums Mainz* VIII: 171–9.

Sayre, E. V. 1963. 'The Intentional Use of Antimony and Manganese in Ancient Glasses'. In *Advances in Glass Technology, Part 2*, edited by F. R. Matson and G. E. Rindone, 263–82. New York: Plenum Press.

Schibille, N., Sterrett-Krause, A. and Freestone, I. C. 2017. 'Glass Groups, Glass Supply and Recycling in Late Roman Carthage'. *Archaeological and Anthropological Sciences* 9 (6): 1223–41.

Silvestri, A. 2008. 'The Coloured Glass of Iulia Felix'. *Journal of Archaeological Science* 35: 1489–501.

Silvestri, A., Molin, G. and Salviulo, G. 2008. 'The Colourless Glass of Iulia Felix'. *Journal of Archaeological Science* 35: 331–41.

Stern, E. M. 1999. 'Roman Glass-blowing in a Cultural Context'. *American Journal of Archaeology* 103: 441–84.

Tite, M., Pradell, T. and Shortland, A. 2008. 'Discovery, Production and Use of Tin-Based Opacifiers in Glasses, Enamels and Glazes From the Late Iron Age Onwards: A Reassessment'. *Archaeometry* 50: 67–84.

Turner, W. E. S. and Rooksby, H. P. 1959. 'A Study of the Opalising Agents in Ancient Glasses Throughout Three Thousand Four Hundred Years'. In *Glastechnische Berichte* VIII, 17–28. Sonderband: V Internationaler Glaskongress.

Turner, W. E. S. and Rooksby, H. P. 1961. 'Further Historical Studies Based on X-Ray Diffraction Methods of the Reagents Employed in Making Opal and Opaque Glasses'. *Jahrbuch des Romisch-Germanischen Zentral Museums Mainz*, 1–6.

Verità, M. and Zecchin, S. 2009. 'Thousand Years of Venetian Glass: The Evolution of Chemical Composition from the Origins to the 18th Century'. *Annales AIHV* 17: 602–13.

Weber, A. and Friedrich, C. J. 1929. *Alfred Weber's Theory of the Location of Industries*. Chicago: University of Chicago Press.

Wedepohl, K. H. and Baumann, A. 2000. 'The Use of Marine Molluskan Shells for Roman Glass and Local Raw Glass Production in the Eifel Area (Western Germany)'. *Naturwissenschaften* 87: 129–32.

Wedepohl, K. H., Gaitzsch, W. and Follmann-Schulz, A. B. 2003. 'Glassmaking and Glassworking in Six Roman Factories in the Hambach Forest, Germany'. *Annales AIHV* 15: 56–61.

9

Consumption, working and trade of Late Antique glass from north Adriatic Italy: An archaeometric perspective

Sarah Maltoni, Filomena Gallo, Alberta Silvestri,
Mariangela Vandini, Tania Chinni, Alessandra Marcante,
Gianmario Molin and Enrico Cirelli

Abstract

The present chapter aims to investigate the circulation of glass in north Adriatic Italy during Late Antiquity. The assemblages considered are composed of vessels and working waste (including chunks) and come from Aquileia (sites: 'Domus delle Bestie Ferite' and 'Domus of Tito Macro') and Classe (sites: 'Building 6' and 'US 4381', located in the productive area of the harbour), both Late Antique cities located on the north Adriatic coast and connected with the Levant and North Africa by means of commercial routes.

An integrated approach, which involves archaeological characterisation, geochemical study and statistical analysis, has been applied. In both cities glass of Late Antique compositional groups already established in the published literature – HIMT, *série 3.2* and Levantine 1 – were identified. The trade of raw glass and the secondary working activities of glass of the HIMT and *série 3.2* groups were attested in both locations while Levantine 1 glass, less represented in both cities, was probably worked only in Classe and no evidence of raw glass trade was identified.

The chemical and isotopic results allow us to hypothesise, for the two cities, similar trade routes and analogous supply of raw materials and raw glass from the eastern Mediterranean.

Introduction

The archaeometric study of Roman and Byzantine glass has been the subject of a large number of studies in the past decades (see for instance: Mirti et al. 1993; Freestone et al. 2000; Freestone et al. 2003; Silvestri et al. 2008; Silvestri 2008; Foster and Jackson 2009, 2010). The widespread presence of glass all around Europe and the Mediterranean basin proves that large-scale production took place in this chronological frame. The archaeological evidence suggests that the production of glass took place in two different steps: primary production, when the raw materials were fused together to produce raw glass, and secondary production, when the raw glass was shaped into objects. Secondary production (glass-working) could take place virtually anywhere a chunk of raw glass or cullet could be re-melted and shaped, while primary production (glass-making) was dependant on the proximity of the raw materials, which in the case of Roman and Byzantine glass, were mainly sand, natron and wood as a fuel. The availability of sand of suitable mineralogical composition markedly restricts the area of possible supply to a few locations around the Mediterranean basin; for this reason the identification of productive sites has become a theme of great interest and geochemical data have been widely employed in an attempt to trace the provenance of glass (see for instance: Freestone et al. 2003; Henderson et al. 2005; Degryse et al. 2008, 2009; Degryse and Shortland 2009; Ganio et al. 2012a).

Primary production of glass on the Levantine coast has been proven, at least for the Byzantine period (Brill 1988; Freestone et al. 2000, 2002), but in the case of early Roman glass a clear consensus is still lacking and two possible models of production have been hypothesised: a centralised model, according to which the primary production took place only in a limited number of locations along the Syro-Palestinian coast, and a dispersed model, that hypothesises the existence of primary glass factories also in the western empire. The Late Antique period, and in particular the fourth–fifth century CE, is a key point of the history of ancient glass-making, strongly influenced by the political and socio-economical revolutions that followed the fall of the Roman empire: alongside 'early' Roman glass, new compositions of glass start to circulate and new technological solutions are adopted for colouring and opacifying, probably to compensate for the scarcity of certain raw materials or the reduced accessibility of certain locations.

In this context, the north Adriatic area of Italy is located in a strategic position, and represented a meeting point between eastern and western Mediterranean; in addition, the area was connected to the Levant, northern Africa and the Transalpine area by means of terrestrial and maritime trade routes. The abundance of glass fragments brought to light during several decades of archaeological excavations, along with a few circumstantial evidence, encouraged the idea that primary glass production may have taken place in the area (Calvi 1968; Bertacchi 1987), while other scientists more prudently hypothesised the existence of secondary workshops (e.g. Buora et al. 2009). In any case the abundance of glass fragments, the presence of glass-working waste and chunks, the strategic position of the northern Adriatic area, paved the way to questions about the origin of the glass and in particular the provenance of the raw materials, and the existence of specific patterns of distribution.

Classe and Aquileia, both well-known harbours of the Late Antique period, are the subject of the present chapter, which aims to investigate whether the two harbours were characterised by similar patterns of glass distribution; in addition, the presence of glass-working wastes in Aquileia (including chunks) allows to investigate the presence of a glass-working activity in the city, so far only speculated. Clarifying the glass compositions that were traded, worked and used in the form of vessels, can provide valuable information about the role of the two cities and of the area in the Mediterranean glass trade network during the Late Antiquity.

Sites and materials

Sites

The cities of Aquileia and Classe represent two major sites of the Adriatic shore and hosted two of the largest Mediterranean harbours of the Antique and Late Antique times. Unlike Classe, which was founded as a city in the fifth century CE near Ravenna, as a consequence of the presence of the Imperial court in this city, Aquileia had a longer life, started in the early Roman times and continuing throughout the Late Antique period (Gallo et al. 2014 and references therein).

The assemblages from Aquileia here examined derive from two consumption sites. First, the Domus of Tito Macro (also known as Domus dei Fondi Ex Cossar), located along the via Annia not far away from the ancient harbour, and inhabited from first century BCE until the seventh century CE (Bonetto and Ghedini 2014). Second, the Domus delle Bestie Ferite, located in the forum area and inhabited between the first and the sixth century CE. The two Domus had a residential function, even though in the area of Tito Macro some small shops and traces of metal forging have also been identified. A more detailed description of Aquileia and of the two sites is reported in Gallo et al. (2014) and Maltoni et al. (2016) and references therein.

In ancient times the city of Classe, currently an inland village in the surroundings of Ravenna, was located close to the sea and connected to Ravenna and to the Adriatic Sea by a channel system. The harbour of Classe was of recognised importance in the Late Antique period and it supplied the imperial court and inland areas. Trade between the city and the Levant and North Africa are evidenced by the recovery of large quantity of amphorae (Cirelli 2007, 2014; Augenti and Cirelli 2010, 2012). The harbour area also contained some productive workshops, testified by the presence of residues of metal forging and various circular kilns. One of the kilns, found in a warehouse named Building n. 6, was surrounded by several kilograms of glass fragments. The fragments include cullet, glass-working debris, chunks and partly melted fragments and testify the existence of a secondary workshop in the area, probably active between the fifth and the early sixth century CE. Another glass assemblage was excavated in a small dump located in the same area, named US 4381, dated mainly to the sixth century CE.

Materials

Samples subjected to archaeometric analysis were selected in order to be representative of each assemblage and to maximise the possibility of comparisons among sites. The samples from the two Aquileian sites are composed of tableware dated to the late third–seventh century CE. In particular, the Tito Macro assemblage includes 41 samples, including two chunks and a single piece of glass-working waste, while the Bestie Ferite assemblage comprises 61 samples of tableware. To enhance the possibility of comparisons between the two Aquileia sites, the same systematic approach was applied, selecting the most represented types in all the available colours. In the present chapter, only transparent or translucent glass is considered; samples are mostly naturally coloured in various shades of yellow, green, pale blue; a few deep blue samples are also present in the analysed assemblage.

Due to the activity conducted in the glass-working workshop of Classe, the vessel fragments, probably cullet, are highly fragmented and include a large variety of forms, often non-identifiable. With the aim of collecting a representative selection, a wide range of glass-working debris, several chunks of different colour and a selection of samples from identifiable forms were chosen, alongside with some non-diagnostic fragments. A total of 74 samples, including 32 piece of glass-working waste and 5 chunks were selected. The largest group of the identified fragments are from drinking vessels, but other types, such as jugs, bottles, lamps and window panes, are also present. A larger number of beakers of the Isings 96, 106, 109 types and goblets of the Isings 111 type are represented in the excavated assemblage from this site and for this reason several samples of each type were selected for analysis. A summary of selected types, the relative abundance and dating are reported in Table 9.1.

Samples are classified after Isings classification (Isings 1957); when not eligible, references to other typological classification (Crowfoot and Harden 1931; Sternini 1995; Uboldi 1999; Foy 2000; Israeli, 2008) are reported. n.d.= not defined. The general dating of

Table 9.1 Analysed fragments from Aquileia-Tito Macro (AQ TM); Aquileia-Bestie Ferite (AQ BF) and Classe, subdivided by macro type and type (dating and number of fragments analysed for each site also reported)

Macro type	*Type*	*Dating (cent. CE)*	*Classe*	*Aq TM*	*Aq BF*
beaker	Isings 96	4th–5th	6	3(+2)	–
	Isings 109	4th–5th	4	1	–
	Intermediate form Isings 109b/111	1st half of the 5th	–	3	–
	Isings 96/106/109?	4th–5th?	2	–	–
	Isings 106/b	5th–6th	3	–	–
	Isings 106/c	4th–early 5th	1	5	21
	Isings 106 late	5th	2	6	–
	Isings 116	4th–early 5th	–	2	8
	Isings 117	4th–early 5th	–	6	5
goblet	Isings 111	2nd half of the 5th–8th	3	5	11
	Isings 111?	5th–8th	1	–	–
drinking vessel	undefined	n.d.	3	–	–

(*continued*)

Table 9.1 (cont.)

Macro type	*Type*	*Dating (cent. CE)*	*Classe*	*Aq TM*	*Aq BF*
bottle	Isings 132	late 3rd –early 5th	–	–	2
	Isings 104	4th–5th	–	4	6
	Isings 87/120	late 3rd –early 5th	–	–	7
	Isings 126	4th–6th	1	–	–
	Foy (2000), p. 281, fig. 29, n.13	5th–6th	1	–	–
	Sternini 1995, p. 279, fig. 11, n. 131	4th–6th	1	–	–
	n.i.	n.d.	1	–	–
dish	Isings 118	4th–early 5th	–	2	–
lamp	–	late 3rd–early 5th	–	–	1
	Israeli (2008)	5th–7th century	1	–	–
	Ubold (1999), p. 639, tay. 123, n.9	6th–7th	1	–	–
	Crowfoot and Harden (1931) – A	4th–early 5th	–	1	–
window pane	–	n.d	2	–	–
working debris	–	n.d.	32	1	–
	Chunks	n.d.	5	2	–
Total of analysed fragments			*74*	*41(+2)*	*61*

each form is here reported; for the specific dating of each fragment see Maltoni et al. (2015) for Classe and Gallo et al. (2014) for Aquileia-Bestie Ferite; in the case of Aquileia Tito Macro, in the absence of stratigraphic dating only the general dating of each form is assumed (see Maltoni et al. 2016).

Analytical methods

The chemical analysis of major, minor and trace elements was conducted by means of Wavelength Dispersive X-ray Fluorescence (WD–XRF) on all samples weighing ≥ 700 mg. These samples were prepared in fused discs. The measurement of Sn, Sb, Cl and S in all samples, and of the major, minor and some selected traces in samples with weight < 700 mg were performed by means of Electron Probe Micro Analysis (EPMA) on polished sections.

Isotopic analysis, Sr and Nd isotopic ratios were performed in cooperation with the Katholieke Universiteit Leuven, Belgium, by means of Multi Collector Inductively Coupled Plasma Mass Spectrometry. The sample preparation, instrumental parameters, analytical condition for XRF and EPMA analysis are fully reported in Silvestri et al. (2011a) and Silvestri and Marcante (2011). The detailed procedure for Sr and Nd isolation, quantification and definition of the isotopic ratios is reported in Ganio et al. (2012b).

Results and discussion

Compositional groups

The samples were chemically analysed in order to identify possible homogeneous compositional groups related to specific raw materials and/or production technologies. The XRF and EPMA analysis allowed all of the samples analysed to be classified as silica-soda-lime glass. The high soda content and the low concentration of magnesia, potash and phosphorus oxide are consistent with the use of natron as a flux, in accordance with the Roman and Byzantine glass-making tradition (Shortland et al. 2006). The complete analytical results on the samples from the Domus delle Bestie Ferite are published in Gallo et al. (2014), those from Classe in Maltoni et al. (2015) and those from Tito Macro in Maltoni et al. (2016). In the present work, the three assemblages are discussed in a comparative perspective.

On the basis of the content of the major and minor elements three compositional groups were identified: a first one, comparable to the reference group named HIMT (Freestone 1994); a second one that can be referred to the reference group Levantine 1 (Freestone et al. 2000), and a third one that is related to the so-called *série 3.2* group, reported by Foy and co-authors (Foy et al. 2003) (Figure 9.1). The same three compositions were identified in all the analysed assemblages, although with different internal

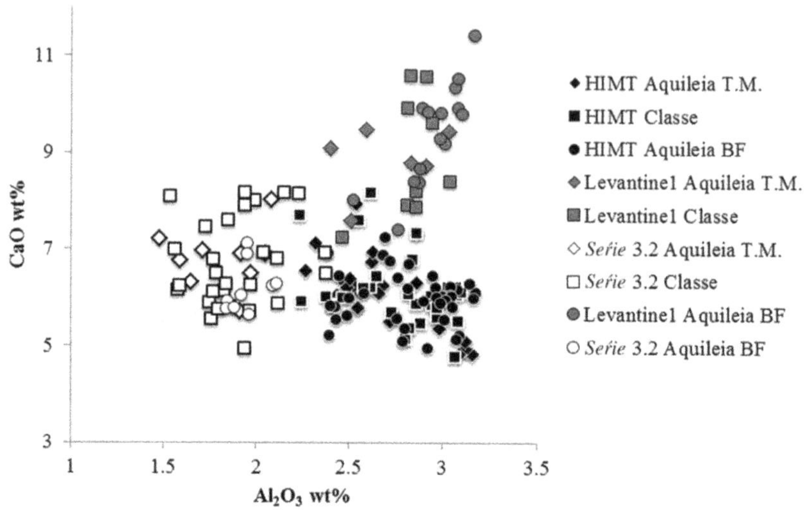

Figure 9.1 Binary diagram CaO vs Al_2O_3. Glass compositions are represented by colour: HIMT in black, Levantine 1 in grey, *série* 3.2 in white. The three sites are represented by different symbols: squares for Classe, diamonds for Aquileia Tito Macro and circles for Aquileia Bestie Ferite. Raw chemical data from Maltoni et al. 2015 for Classe; Maltoni et al. 2016 for Aquileia Tito Macro; Gallo et al. 2014 for Aquileia Bestie Ferite.

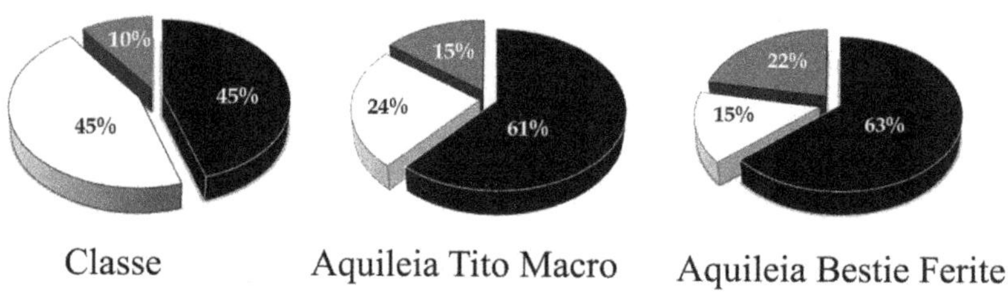

Figure 9.2 Pie-charts showing the relative distribution of the three glass compositions in the assemblages. Glass compositions are represented by colour: HIMT in black, Levantine 1 in grey, *série 3.2* in white.

distributions. The three assemblages are dominated by HIMT, while in the distribution of Levantine 1 and *série 3.2* a difference emerges: in Classe and Tito Macro the Levantine 1 glass is very scarce, conversely in the Bestie Ferite assemblage the proportion is inverted (Figure 9.2).

In the samples from Classe glass of HIMT and *série 3.2* compositions is equally distributed. The glass analysed at this site includes chunks and glass-working waste, which suggests that the two compositions were traded in the form of raw glass and locally worked. Similarly, at Tito Macro the presence (though scarce) of glass-working indicators of HIMT and *série 3.2* suggests that theses compositions were also traded and worked here.

A detailed description of each compositional group is reported in the following paragraphs, and the mean values and standard deviations are included in Table 9.2.

HIMT

The first compositional group to be discussed, corresponding to the literature group HIMT, includes the previously published groups FC/1 from Tito Macro (Maltoni et al. 2016), CL/1 from Classe (Maltoni et al. 2015) and AQ/1 from Bestie Ferite (Gallo et al. 2014). This composition is characterised by high soda, relatively low lime, very high iron, alumina, titanium, magnesium and manganese (Table 9.2), which suggests the use of a very impure sand, rich in accessory minerals, as that of the Egyptian coast between the Nile delta and North Sinai (Freestone et al. 2005; Freestone, et al. unpublished manuscript). This composition is well represented in archaeometric reports across the whole Mediterranean basin, in the northern provinces and the Balkans (e.g. Mirti et al. 1993; Freestone 1994; Foy et al. 2003; Foster and Jackson 2009; Conte et al. 2014; Nenna 2014; Rehren and Cholakova 2014; Ceglia et al. 2015).

Despite its widespread presence, HIMT glass does not represent a homogeneous and well-defined group and samples included in this group often show variable contents of the diagnostic elements, leading some scholars to subgroup in 'weaker' and 'stronger' HIMT depending on the content of their diagnostic elements (iron, manganese, titanium). The HIMT samples here investigated, differently, show an uncommon composition, characterised by extremely high contents of iron, titanium, manganese and alumina. Comparing the analysed samples with those reported in the archaeometric literature (Figure 9.3) all samples fall in the compositional range of the 'strong' reference groups. In particular, a relatively large group of samples with higher alumina and an iron content over 3.0 wt% Fe_2O_3, is evidenced. Such 'very strong' subgroup, characterised by an extremely high content of iron (even above 4 wt% Fe_2O_3) and titania, is well represented in the north Adriatic assemblages under investigation, while in the previously published assemblages it is

Table 9.2 Mean value and standard deviation (in italics) of the major oxides for the compositional groups HIMT, HIT, Levantine 1 and *série 3.2**

	n. samples	SiO_2	Na_2O	CaO	Al_2O_3	Fe_2O_3	MnO	TiO_2	MgO	K_2O	P_2O_5	SO_3	Cl
HIMT	94	65.34	18.29	6.08	2.79	2.24	1.88	0.50	1.16	0.49	0.08	0.25	1.24
		1.45	*1.33*	*0.70*	*0.27*	*0.89*	*0.40*	*0.14*	*0.24*	*0.15*	*0.04*	*0.08*	*0.20*
HIT (blue)	6	65.82	19.24	6.03	2.71	2.46	0.22	0.49	1.11	0.40	0.01	0.29	1.27
		1.70	*0.85*	*0.46*	*0.16*	*0.62*	*0.13*	*0.16*	*0.14*	*0.07*	*0.01*	*0.04*	*0.15*
Levantine 1	31	67.47	16.49	9.11	2.86	0.80	0.60	0.27	0.35	1.03	0.14	0.18	0.95
		1.89	*0.97*	*1.07*	*0.19*	*0.41*	*0.45*	*0.21*	*0.27*	*0.58*	*0.07*	*0.05*	*0.30*
Série 3.2	45	68.33	19.05	6.59	1.89	0.74	0.77	0.12	0.63	0.49	0.04	0.29	1.35
		1.57	*1.12*	*0.80*	*0.20*	*0.34*	*0.28*	*0.05*	*0.15*	*0.21*	*0.02*	*0.09*	*0.21*

* It should be stressed here that within HIMT group, a sub-group named HIT is identified and due to its particular chemical composition, is considered separately here. Further details on HIT glass are reported in the text.

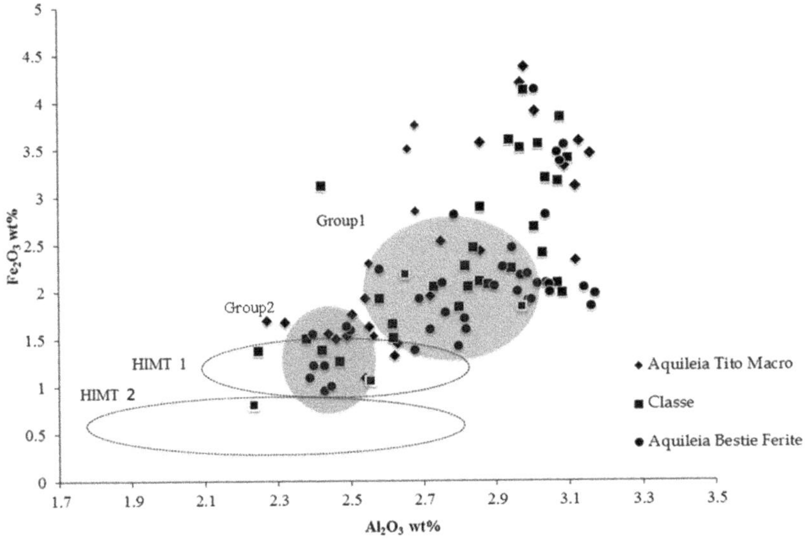

Figure 9.3 Binary diagram Fe_2O_3 vs Al_2O_3 of HIMT samples. Grey areas represent the compositional fields of Group 1 (strong) and Group 2 (weak) (Foy et al. 2003), dotted lines represent the compositional fields of groups HIMT 1 (strong) and HIMT 2 (weak) (Foster and Jackson 2009). Raw chemical data from Maltoni et al. 2015 for Classe; Maltoni et al. 2016 for Aquileia Tito Macro; Gallo et al. 2014 for Aquileia Bestie Ferite.

lacking or sporadically represented by isolated samples (Foy et al. 2003; Rosenow and Rehren 2014). The HIMT glass circulating in north Adriatic Italy seems to have a specific composition and it is possibly related to a specific primary production site that had a privileged commercial link with north Adriatic harbours.

Among the HIMT samples, eight samples (three from Classe and five from Aquileia Tito Macro) are intentionally coloured blue: five vessels (beakers and bottles), a chunk and two decorative drops applied on beakers. The decorative drops have a HIMT composition, and are coloured in one case by the addition of cobalt and copper (2737 ppm and 8242 ppm, respectively) and in the other case by copper only (49227 ppm) (Maltoni et al. 2016); the other six samples, including the chunk from Tito Macro, are coloured by cobalt (2204 ± 2190 ppm) and copper (2381 ± 927 ppm), show relatively high lead (2311 ± 2073 ppm), and have low (although not negligible) manganese, below 0.5 wt% MnO. Manganese is one of the distinctive elements of the HIMT glass, its presence being related to an intentional addition, probably aimed to contrast the colouring effect of iron that, in such high concentrations, would turn the glass black (Freestone et al. 2005). HIMT glass with no manganese (dubbed HIT by Rehren and Cholakova 2010) is very rare: naturally coloured samples are known in Bulgaria (Rehren and Cholakova 2014, 2010) and Cyprus (Ceglia et al. 2015), deep blue HIT glass was identified only in Albania (Conte et al. 2014) and North Sinai (see samples 77 and 85 of table 1 in Freestone et al. 2002), and in the current assemblages, all dated to the fifth–sixth century CE.

The presence of a chunk of blue HIT glass from Aquileia suggests that blue glass was traded in the form of raw glass, but the low manganese invites a question about its provenance. As manganese is one of the distinctive traits of HIMT glass, and as it was added at the primary stage of production to counteract the dark colour of the glass, it is possible that it was deliberately excluded from the batch when the glass makers aimed to colour the glass blue, as decolouring was not necessary and probably not fruitful. On the basis of this evidence, it is possible to hypothesise that HIT blue glass was a product of the same primary furnaces of HIMT, and that colouring could also take place at this stage of production. The occurrence of blue glass with HIMT composition, i.e. the decorations of two cups Isings 96, in the north Adriatic assemblage further suggests that glass-colouring took place in the secondary workshop where the vessel was shaped, in addition to the primary stage. Glass-colouring was therefore conducted as needed, as shown by the chemical similarity between the vessel body and the base glass of the respective blue decoration.

Levantine 1

The second composition to be discussed corresponds to the reference literature group Levantine 1 and includes groups FC/2 from Tito Macro (Maltoni et al. 2016), CL/2 from Classe (Maltoni et al. 2015) and AQ/2 from Bestie Ferite (Gallo et al. 2014). This composition is characterised by low soda and high lime, relatively high alumina, low iron, magnesium, titanium (Table 9.2) and trace elements (Gallo et al. 2014; Maltoni et al. 2015, 2016) that are indicative of the use of a relatively pure sand, poor in heavy and accessory minerals and rich in feldspars and carbonates, consistent with a Syro-Palestinian provenance (Freestone et al. 2000). This composition is well represented in the Mediterranean basin as in the northern provinces (Freestone et al. 2000; Gorin-Rosen 2000; Foy et al. 2003; Freestone et al. 2008; Foster and Jackson 2009; Conte et al. 2014; Rosenow and Rehren 2014; Ceglia et al. 2015). Levantine 1 samples from Aquileia and Classe are also characterised by high potash, on average above 1 wt% K_2O (Table 9.2), as already identified in some Levantine glasses (see, for instance, some of those excavated in the primary furnace of Dor (Freestone et al. 2000)). However, when evaluating the content of potash in natron glass, the possible vehicles of potash shall be taken into account: alongside with the potassium-bearing minerals of the sands, furnace ashes can also be responsible for the introduction of this element in the batch. The concentration of potash has been shown to increase with increasing time of permanence in the firing chamber (Paynter 2008). In the case of very high potash contents in natron glass, as in some samples from Classe (see also Maltoni et al. 2015), it is possible to relate this analytical evidence to the secondary working.

Another characteristic of glasses of the Levantine 1 composition is the variable content of MnO, which ranges from negligible to more than 1 wt% MnO. In particular, samples from Aquileia and Classe, split in two groups, a first with high manganese (around 1.30 wt% MnO) and a second with very low or negligible manganese; differently, samples from Classe have a more gradual distribution and a tendency to lower concentrations of this element, between 0.03 and 0.91 wt% MnO (Figure 9.4).

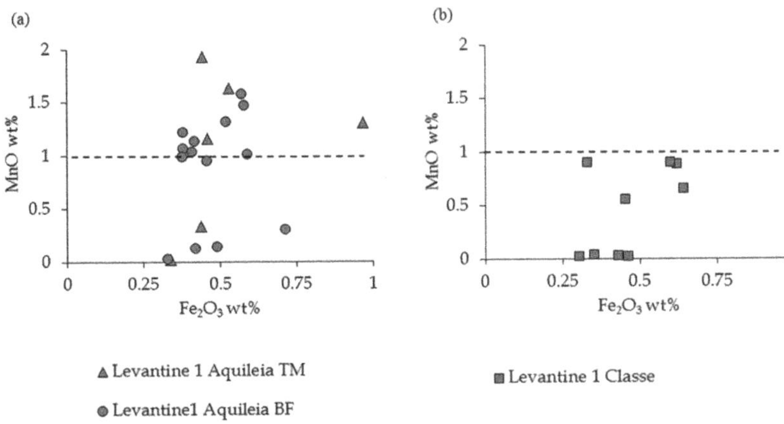

Figure 9.4 Binary diagram MnO vs Fe_2O_3 of Levantine 1 samples. (a) Glass from Aquileia; (b) glass from Classe. The broken line refers to the threshold of the intentional addition of manganese oxide according to Brems et al. (2012). Raw chemical data from Maltoni et al. 2015 for Classe; Maltoni et al. 2016 for Aquileia Tito Macro; Gallo et al. 2014 for Aquileia Bestie Ferite.

The existence of Levantine glass with or without manganese is testified also in primary production sites (see for instance Brill 1988) and the presence of this element in high concentration can be considered as deliberate productive choice, manganese being the main decolouriser available in Late Antique and Byzantine glass-making. However, manganese oxide below the conventional limit of intentional addition (1 wt% MnO according to Brems et al. (2012)), as found at Classe, suggests a certain degree of recycling. The two sites of Aquileia (Tito Macro and Bestie Ferite) show similar characteristics, suggesting a very low extent of recycling, while in the assemblage of Classe we can hypothesise that the Levantine samples underwent some recycling, that is consistent with the secondary working activity of the site.

Série 3.2

The final composition to be discussed, corresponding to the so-called *série 3.2* group, includes groups FC/3 from Tito Macro (Maltoni et al. 2016), CL/3 from Classe (Maltoni et al. 2015) and AQ/3 from Bestie Ferite (Gallo et al. 2014). It is a relatively rare Mn-decoloured composition, which, when identified, is recorded in Late Antique assemblages dated mainly around the fifth century CE. The main distinctive traits of this compositional group are very low alumina (usually below 2 wt% Al_2O_3), high soda and in some cases high iron, and the presence of manganese. The chemical composition of this glass reflects the relatively pure mineralogical composition of the sand employed for the primary production, rich in silica and poor in aluminium-bearing minerals (as potassium-feldspars), similar to that employed in the early Roman glass-making; on the basis of the chemical composition, Foy and co-authors (2003) hypothesise a Syro-Palestinian provenance, although in a different coastal segment with respect to Levantine 1, however, more recent studies (Schibille et al. 2017) suggest the Egyptian origin of this composition, although the precise locations of sand supply, that are different from that of HIMT glass, are unknown. *Série 3.2* glass is very well represented in Classe and in Tito Macro, less represented in the Bestie Ferite assemblage and relatively rare in the archaeometric literature: apart from the assemblages analysed in the present work, samples of this group are recorded in the Mediterranean basin both as vessels (Foy et al. 2003; Rehren and Cholakova 2014) and mosaic tesserae (Silvestri et al. 2011b). The presence of chunks of *série 3.2* composition from Classe and Aquileia Tito Macro should be noted, as they prove that this composition was actively traded as raw glass and locally worked.

Links between types and compositional groups

Investigating the links among compositional groups, types and sites, it is necessary to note that the two Aquileian assemblages have a higher degree of comparability than Classe in terms of forms, having in common the beakers Isings 106, 109, 116, the goblets Isings 111 and the bottles Isings 104 (Table 9.1). The degree of comparability between Classe and the Aquileian sites is lower due to their different functions (consumption sites for Aquileia and productive site for Classe), as already detailed in the section 'Sites'. A few types were analysed from both the Domus of Tito Macro and Classe: beakers Isings 96, 106 and 109 and goblets Isings 111. The only types in common among all the three assemblages are therefore the goblets Isings 111 and the beakers Isings 106 and 109, although with a very different relative abundance (Table 9.1). Investigating the possible relations between form and composition, some links were found: bottle Isings 104 (available only in Aquileia Tito Macro and Bestie Ferite) seem to be predominantly made with HIMT glass; cups Isings 96 (from Classe and Aquileia Tito Macro) are made with Levantine 1 or HIMT glass, but not with *série 3.2* glass; the stemmed goblet Isings 111 is reported in HIMT and *série 3.2* in all three assemblages, while Isings 111 made in Levantine 1 glass are only reported in the Bestie Ferite assemblage.

The preferential use of specific composition for certain types may be related to different factors, from the colour of the glass to its cost, and it may have been influenced by the availability and the regularity of supply. It is also possible that different compositions (differing in colour or price) were used to satisfy the needs of different segments of the glass market. Unfortunately the different ratios of the few common forms do not allow a full interpretation of the links between type and composition, and further studies will help to shed light on this topic. However, it is useful to underline that the three assemblages have a pattern of glass compositions and vessel forms that suggest a dating before the sixth century CE, although this indication is not fully supported by the available archaeological data.

Isotope analysis

The chemical analysis of the glass finds from Aquileia and Classe highlighted the similarity between the materials from the two cities in terms of glass compositions. The discovery of specific characteristics and the homogeneity of certain groups (as for instance HIMT and HIT) in the two cities raises questions about the provenance of the glass and the possible locations of supply.

Isotope analyses, and Sr and Nd in particular, has proved to be a valuable tool to trace the provenance of the raw materials of glass, giving information on the carbonatic fraction and the heavy-non quartz fraction of the sand, respectively (see, for instance, Degryse et al. 2009 and references therein). Isotope analyses were conducted on a selection of finds from Tito Macro, Bestie Ferite and Classe, selecting the samples on the basis of their chemical composition, giving preference to those with lower evidence of recycling, avoiding the intentionally coloured samples and selecting, when possible, raw glass and glass-working indicators. A total number of 50 samples were chosen and full analytical results are given in: Maltoni et al. (2015) for Classe, Gallo et al. (2015) for Aquileia-Bestie Ferite and Maltoni et al. (2016), for the Aquileia-Tito Macro samples.

All analysed samples have an absolute content of Sr of about 400–600 ppm, that is indicative of glass produced with coastal sands rich in shells. The isotopic ratio of strontium is always lower than that of modern oceanic sea water ($^{87}Sr/^{86}Sr = 0.7092$) (Figure 9.5a) and, although the samples are well distributed between the value of modern oceanic water and that typical of continental limestone (0.7080) (Freestone et al. 2009), the samples of Levantine 1 and *série 3.2* composition have a higher Sr isotope ratio with respect to HIMT. Despite the generally low levels of Sr isotope ratio in HIMT, the use of continental limestone as a primary source of carbonates in these samples can be excluded, as their absolute content of Sr is markedly higher than the expected value of 100–150 ppm (Brems et al. 2013a). Therefore, taking into account the geochemical evidence of the higher contents of certain elements (magnesium, titanium, and iron) in HIMT than other groups (Table 9.2), the lowest values of $^{87}Sr/^{86}Sr$ (Figure 9.5a) in HIMT samples suggest that in these samples Sr is introduced also by minerals rich in Fe, Mg and Ti with low isotopic ratios other than carbonates, such as for instance amphiboles and pyroxenes.

On the basis of the chemical and isotopic evidence, HIMT glass is hypothesised to be of Egyptian provenance, where coastal sands are strongly influenced by the contribution of the Nile, while Levantine 1 is hypothesised to be of Syro-Palestinian origin, where coastal sands are rich in shells. *Série 3.2* glass, originally considered as a Syro-Palestinian primary group (Foy et al. 2003), was more recently interpreted as of Egyptian provenance (Schibille et al. 2017). The three groups here identified are therefore hypothesised to be of eastern Mediterranean origin, and this is confirmed by the low negative value of εNd, that is between –3.5 and –5.5 in all the analysed samples (Figure 9.5b). When comparing

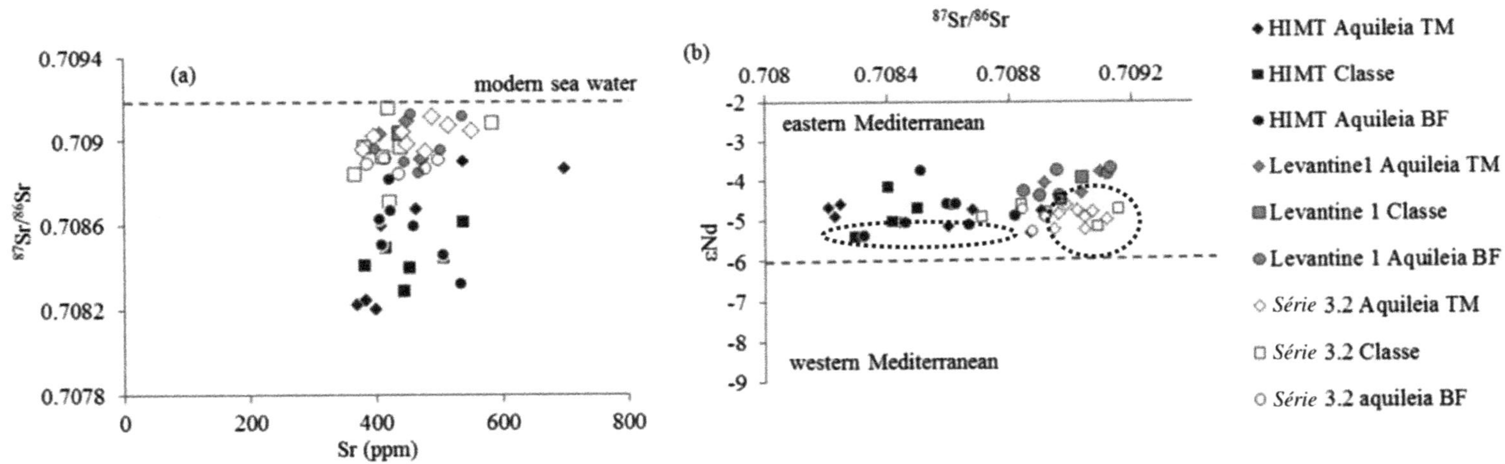

Figure 9.5 Binary diagrams of the isotopic data. (a) Sr vs $^{87}Sr/^{86}Sr$; (b) εNd vs $^{87}Sr/^{86}Sr$. Dotted lines represent $^{87}Sr/^{86}Sr$ of modern sea water (Brems et al. 2013a and references therein) and εNd value that discriminates eastern and western Mediterranean sand (Brems et al. 2013b and references therein) in Figures 5a and 5b, respectively. In Figure 5b dotted ellipses represent the compositional fields of Levantine 1 (right) and HIMT (left) glass as reported in Degryse (2014). Raw isotopic data from Maltoni et al. 2015 for Classe; Gallo et al. 2015 for Aquileia Bestie Ferite; Maltoni et al. 2016 for Aquileia Tito Macro.

the present samples with those reported in the literature for Late Antique and Byzantine glass (Freestone et al. 2003; Degryse et al. 2008; Degryse 2014; Freestone et al. unpublished manuscript), a minor difference is found: the previously published samples have slightly more negative values (between –6 and –5 as εNd), which is still consistent with the eastern Mediterranean sediments, but could indicate a small difference in the location of supply.

Another interesting trend is found when Levantine 1 and *série 3.2*, are compared (Figure 9.5b): despite the similarity in their Sr isotope signal, the two compositions have a small difference in their εNd values that reflect a different geochemical origin of the sand, as already suggested on the basis of their chemical composition.

Conclusions

The present work addresses the circulation of glass during Late Antiquity in north Adriatic Italy. It considers the two major harbours of the timespan under investigation, Classe and Aquileia, in a comparative perspective. The chemical and isotope analyses, performed with comparable techniques characterised by high standards of precision and accuracy, allowed comparisons to be made between the assemblages from the two cities and with the reference groups, already published in the literature.

During the fourth–sixth century CE the two cities of Classe and Aquileia were supplied by similar trade routes and the same glass compositions, with comparable chemical features, were imported and locally shaped.

All the three assemblages (Classe, Aquileia-Tito Macro and Aquileia-Bestie Ferite) are dominated by HIMT glass. Glass of this type found in this area shows specific compositional features with very high iron, titanium, alumina and manganese, opening the way to the hypothesis of preferential trade routes between specific primary production locations and the north Adriatic area. Levantine 1 and *série 3.2* glass were also identified, although with different internal distributions. The glass-working workshop of Classe seems to have been regularly supplied by fresh glass of HIMT and *série 3.2* compositions, while Levantine 1 was probably less available. A general scarcity and absence of chunks of the Levantine 1 compositional type at Tito Macro and Classe, suggest a possible difference in the patterns of trade and consumption compared to the Bestie Ferite assemblage. This may be related to a small difference in dating or other unknown reasons.

The existence of a chunk and some vessels of intentionally coloured HIT glass demonstrates that glass-colouring took place also at the primary stage of production, at least for this specific Late Antique composition, and that HIT blue glass was traded in the form of chunks in Aquileia.

The existence of a link between certain typologies and specific glass compositions was investigated, and some indications were given, but further studies and more data are required to confirm the identified trends.

As expected for glasses of the above-mentioned compositions, on the basis of the isotopic composition, all analysed samples are consistent with an eastern Mediterranean provenance. However, the present study revealed some interesting trends that shed more light on glass circulation during the Late Antique periods: an Egyptian provenance is supported for HIMT while the Syro-Palestinian provenance is supported for Levantine 1; *série 3.2* composition, originally considered as a Syro-Palestinian provenance, has a slightly different isotope signal with respect to the others groups and this suggests the exploitation of different sand sources, probably of Egyptian provenance, although different from those of HIMT glass.

In summary, the combination of isotopic and chemical data supports the hypothesis of an eastern Mediterranean origin for the Late Antique glass here analysed, which may be produced in few primary workshops located on the Syro-Palestinian and Egyptian coasts and then imported to the northern Adriatic area in the form of chunks. The secondary working activity in the area of Aquileia and Classe is confirmed and the centralised production model is fully supported for Late Antiquity.

References

Augenti, A. and Cirelli, E. 2010. 'Classe: un osservatorio privilegiato per il commercio della tarda antichità'. In *LRCW 3: Late Roman Coarse Wares, Cooking Wares and Amphorae in the Mediterranean: Archaeology and Archaeometry*, edited by S. Menchelli, S. Santoro, M. Pasquinucci and G. Guiducci, 605–15. Oxford: Information Press.

Augenti, A. and Cirelli, E. 2012. 'From Suburb to Port: The Rise (and Fall) of Classe as a Centre of Trade and Redistribution'. In *Rome, Portus and the*

Mediterranean. (Archaeology Monographs of the British School at Rome), edited by S. Keay, vol. 21, 205–21. Oxford: Oxbow Books.

Bertacchi, L. 1987. 'La produzione vetraria aquileiese nelle sue fasi più antiche'. In M Mirabella Roberti (ed.) *Vita sociale, artistica e commerciale di Aquileia romana*, 419–26. Udine: Arti Grafiche Friulane.

Bonetto, J. and Ghedini F. 2014. 'Vitruvio ad Aquileia. La casa ad atrio dei Fondi ex Cossar'. In *Vitruvio e l'Archeologia*, edited by P. I. Clini, 49–64. Venezia: Marsilio.

Brems, D., Degryse, P., Hasendocks, F., Gimeno, D., Silvestri, A., Vassilieva, E., Luypaers, S. and Honings, J. 2012. 'Western Mediterranean Sand Deposits as a Raw Material for Roman Glass Production'. *Journal of Archaeological Science* 39: 2897–907.

Brems, D., Ganio, M., Latruwe, K., Balcaen, L., Carremans, M., Gimeno, D., Silvestri, A., Vanhaecke, F., Muchez, P. and Degryse, P. 2013a. 'Isotopes on the Beach, Part 1: Strontium Isotope Ratios as a Provenance Indicator for Lime Raw Materials Used in Roman Glass-Making'. *Archaeometry* 55: 214–34.

Brems, D., Ganio, M., Latruwe, K., Balcaen, L., Carremans, M., Gimeno, D., Silvestri, A., Vanhaecke, F., Muchez, P. and Degryse, P. 2013b. 'Isotopes on the Beach, Part 2: Neodimium Isotopic Analysis for the Provenancing of Roman Glass-Making'. *Archaeometry* 55: 449–64.

Brill, R. H. 1988. 'Scientific Investigations of the Jalame Glass and Related Finds'. In *Excavations at Jalame: Site of a Glass Factory in Late Roman Palestine*, edited by G. Davidson Weinberg, 257–94. Columbia: University of Missouri Press.

Buora, M., Mandruzzato, L. and Verità, M. 2009. 'Vecchie e nuove evidenze di officine vetrarie romane ad Aquileia'. *Quaderni Friulani di Archeologia* XIX: 51–8.

Calvi, M. C. 1968. *I vetri romani del museo di Aquileia*. Aquileia: Associazione Nazionale per Aquileia.

Ceglia, A., Cosyns, P., Nys, K., Terryn, H., Thienpont, H. and Meulebroeck, W. 2015. 'Late Antique Glass Distribution and Consumption in Cyprus: A Chemical Study'. *Journal of Archaeological Science* 61: 213–22.

Cirelli, E. 2007. 'Ravenna e il commercio nell' Adriatico in età tardoantica'. In *Felix Ravenna.La croce, la spada, la vela: l'alto Adriatico fra V e VI secolo. Catalogo della mostra*, edited by A. Augenti and C. Bertelli, 45–50. Milano.

Cirelli, E. 2014. 'Typology and Diffusion of Amphorae in Ravenna and Classe Between the 5th and the 8th Centuries AD'. In *Late Roman Coarse Wares, Cooking Wares and Amphorae in the Mediterranean: Archaeology and Archaeometry. Proceedings of the 4th International Conference*, edited by N. Poulou-Papadimitriou, E. Nodarou and V. Kilikoglou, 541–52. Oxford: Archaeopress Publishers of British Archaeological Reports.

Conte, S., Chinni, T., Arletti, R. and Vandini, M. 2014. 'Butrint (Albania) Between Eastern And Western Mediterranean Glass Production: EMPA and LA-ICP-MS of Late Antique and Early Medieval Finds'. *Journal of Archaeological Science* 49: 6–20.

Crowfoot, G. M. and Harden, D. B. 1931. 'Early Byzantine and Later Glass Lamps'. *The Journal of Egyptian Archaeology* 17: 196–208.

Degryse P. (ed.) 2014. *Glass-Making in the Greco-Roman World. Results of the Archglass Project*. Leuven: Leuven University Press.

Degryse, P., Schneider, J., Lauwers, V. and Brems, D. 2008. 'Sr-Nd isotopic Analysis of Glass from Sagalassos (SW Turkey)'. *Journal of Cultural Heritage* 9: e47–9.

Degryse, P., Schneider, J., Lauwers, V., Waelkens, M., Muchez, P. and Ganio, M. 2009. 'Radiogenic Isotopes in the Provenance Determination of Raw Materials: A Case of Lead and Glass Recycling at Sagalassos (SW Turkey)'. *JONAS: Journal of Nordic Archeological Science* 16: 15–23.

Degryse, P. and Shortland, A. J. 2009. 'An Inaugural Lecture to the Society: Trace Elements in Provenancing Raw Materials for Roman Glass Production'. *Geologica Belgica* 16: 135–43.

Foster, H. E. and Jackson, C. M. 2009. 'The Composition of "Naturally Coloured" Late Roman Vessel Glass from Britain and the Implications for Models of Glass Production and Supply'. *Journal of Archaeological Science* 36: 189–204.

Foster, H. E. and Jackson, C. M. 2010. 'The Composition of Late Romano-British Colourless Vessel Glass: Glass Production and Consumption'. *Journal of Archaeological Science* 37: 3068–80.

Foy, D. 2000. 'Un atelier de verrier à Beyrouth au début de la conquête islamique'. *Syria* 77: 239–90.

Foy, D., Vichy, M. and Thirion-Merle, V. 2003. 'Caractérisation des verres de la fin de l'Antiquité en Méditerranée occidentale: l'émergence de nouveaux courants commerciaux'. In *Actes du colloque de l'Association Française pour l'Archéologie du Verre Aix en Provence*, edited by D. Foy and M. D. Nenna, 41–85. Aix-en-Provence: Monique Mergoil.

Freestone, I. C. 1994. 'Chemical Analysis of Raw Glass Fragments'. In *Excavation at Carthage: The Circular Harbour, North Side, the Site and Finds Other than Pottery (*British Academy Monographs in Archeology), edited by H. R. Hurst, vol. II, 290. Oxford: Oxford University Press.

Freestone, I. C., Degryse, P., Shepherd, J., Gorin-Rosen, Y. and Schneider, J. (unpublished manuscript) 'Neodymium and Strontium Isotopes Indicate a Near Eastern Origin for Late Roman Glass in London'.

Freestone, I. C., Gorin-Rosen, Y. and Hughes, M. J. 2000. 'Primary Glass from Israel and the Production of Glass in Late Antiquity and the Early Islamic Period'. In *La Route du Verre. Ateliers Primaires et Secondaires du Second Millènaire av. JC au Moyen Age*, edited by M. D. Nenna 65–83. Lyon: Maison de L'orient Mediterranéen.

Freestone, I. C., Greenwood, R. and Gorin-Rosen, Y. 2002. 'Byzantine and Early Islamic Glassmaking in the Eastern Mediterranean: Production and Distribution of Primary Glass'. In *Hyalos-Vitrum-Glass. History, Technology and Conservation of Glass in the Hellenic World*, edited by G. Kordas, 167–74. Athens: Glasnet.

Freestone, I. C., Jackson-Tal, R. E. and Tal, O. 2008. 'Raw Glass and the Production of Glass Vessels at Late Byzantine Apollonia-Arsuf, Israel'. *Journal of Glass Studies* 50: 67–80.

Freestone, I. C., Leslie, K. A., Thirlwall, M. and Gorin-Rosen, Y. 2003. 'Strontium Isotopes in the Investigation of Early Glass Production: Byzantine and Early Islamic Glass from the Near East'. *Archaeometry* 45, 19–32.

Freestone, I. C., Wolf, S. and Thirlwall, M. 2005. 'The Production of HIMT Glass: Elemental and Isotopic Evidence'. In *Annales du 16e Congrès de l'Association International pour l'Histoire du Verre*, edited by H. E. M. Cool and M. D. Nenna, 153–7. Nottingham: Association International pour l'Histoire du Verre.

Freestone, I.C., Wolf, S. and Thirlwall, M. 2009. 'Isotopic Composition of Glass from the Levan and the South-Eastern Mediterranean Region'. In *Isotopes in Vitreous Materials*, edited by P. Degryse, J. Henderson and G. Hodgins, 31–52. Leuven: Leuven University Press.

Gallo, F., Marcante, A., Silvestri, A. and Molin, G. 2014. 'The Glass of the "Casa delle Bestie Ferite": A First Systematic Archaeometric Study on Late Roman Vessels from Aquileia'. *Journal of Archaeological Science* 41: 7–20.

Gallo, F., Silvestri, A., Degryse, P., Ganio, M. et al. 2015. 'Roman and Late-Roman Glass from North-Eastern Italy: The Isotopic Perspective to Provenance Its Raw Materials'. *Journal of Archaeological Science* 62: 55–65.

Ganio, M., Boyen, S., Fenn, T., Scott, R., Vanhoutte, S., Gimeno, D. and Degryse, P. 2012a. 'Roman Glass Across the Empire: An Elemental and Isotopic Characterization'. *Journal of Analytical Atomic Spectrometry* 27: 743.

Ganio, M., Latruwe, K., Brems, D., Muchez, P., Vanhaecke, F. and Degryse, P. 2012b. 'The Sr-Nd Isolation Procedure for Subsequent Isotopic Analysis Using Multi-Collector ICP-Mass Spectrometry in the Context of Provenance Studies on Archaeological Glass'. *Journal of Analytical Atomic Spectrometry* 27: 1335–41.

Gorin-Rosen, Y. 2000. 'The Ancient Glass Industry in Israel: Summary of the Finds and New Discoveries'. In *La Route du Verre: Atelieres primaires et secondaires du second millinaire av. J.-C. au Moyen-Age*, edited by M. D. Nenna 49–64. Lyon: Maison de l'Orient Méditerranéen.

Henderson, J., Evans, J. A., Sloane, H. J., Leng, M. J. and Doherty, C. 2005. 'The Use of Oxygen, Strontium and Lead Isotopes to Provenance Ancient Glasses in the Middle East'. *Journal of Archaeological Science* 32: 665–73.

Isings, C. 1957. *Roman Glass from Dated Finds*. Groningen and Djakarta: Wolters.

Israeli, Y. 2008. 'The Glass Vessels'. In *Archaeological Excavations at Caesarea Maritima Areas CC, KK and NN, Final Reports. Volume 1: The Objects*, edited by J. Patrick, 369–418. Israel Exploration Society, Jerusalem.

Maltoni, S., Chinni, T., Vandini, M., Cirelli, E., Silvestri, A. and Molin, G. 2015. 'Archaeological and Archaeometric Study of the Glass Finds from the Ancient Harbour of Classe (Ravenna, Italy): New Evidence'. *Heritage Science* 3: 13.

Maltoni S., Silvestri A., Marcante, A. and Molin, G. 2016. 'The Transition from Roman to Late Antique Glass: New Insights from the Domus of Tito Macro in Aquileia (Italy)'. *Journal of Archaeological Science* 73: 1–16

Mirti, P., Casoli, A. and Appolonia, L. 1993. 'Scientific Analysis of Roman Glass from Augusta Praetoria'. *Archaeometry* 35: 225–40.

Nenna, M. D. 2014. 'Egyptian Glass Abroad: HIMT and Its Market'. In *Neighbours and Successors of Rome: Tradition of Glass Production and Use in Europe and the Middle East in the Later 1st millenium AD, 183–193*, edited by D. Keller, J. Price and C. M. Jackson, 183–93. Oxford: Oxbow Books.

Paynter, S. 2008. 'Experiments in the Reconstruction of Roman Wood-Fired Glassworking Furnaces: Waste Products and Their Formation Processes'. *Journal of Glass Studies* 50: 50271–90.

Rehren, Th. and Cholakova, A. 2010. 'The Early Byzantine HIMT Glass from Dichin, Nothern Bulgaria'. *Interdisciplinary Studies* 22–3: 81–96.

Rehren, Th. and Cholakova, A. 2014. 'Glass Supply and Consumption in the Late Roman and Early Site Byzantine Site Dichin, Northern Bulgaria'. In *Neighbours and Successors of Rome: Tradition of Glass Production and Use in Europe and the Middle East in the Later 1st millenium AD, 83–94*, edited by D. Keller, J. Price and C. M. Jackson, 83–94. Oxford: Oxbow Books.

Rosenow, D. and Rehren, Th. 2014. 'Herding Cats: Roman to Late Antique Glass Groups from Bubastis, Northern Egypt'. *Journal of Archaeological Science* 49: 170–84.

Schibille, N., Sterrett-Krause, A. and Freestone, I. C. 2017. 'Glass Groups, Glass Supply and Recycling in Late Roman Carthage'. *Archaeological and Antropological Science* 9: 1223–41.

Shortland, A. J., Schachner, L., Freestone, I. C. and Tite, M. 2006. 'Natron as a Flux in the Early Vitreous Materials Industry: Sources, Beginnings and Reasons for Decline'. *Journal of Archaeological Science* 33: 521–30.

Silvestri, A. 2008. 'The Coloured Glass of Iulia Felix'. *Journal of Archaeological Science* 35: 1489–501.

Silvestri, A. and Marcante, A. 2011. 'The Glass of Nogara (Verona): A "Window" on Production Technology of Mid-Medieval Times in Northern Italy'. *Journal of Archaeological Science* 38: 2509–22.

Silvestri, A., Molin, G. and Pomero, V. 2011a. 'The Stained Glass Window of the Southern Transept of St. Anthony's Basilica (Padova, Italy): Study of Glasses and Grisaille Paint Layers'. *Spectrochimica Acta Part B: Atomic Spectroscopy* 66: 81–7.

Silvestri, A., Molin, G. and Salviulo, G. 2008. 'The Colourless Glass of Iulia Felix'. *Journal of Archaeological Science* 35: 331–41.

Silvestri, A., Tonietto, S. and Molin, G. 2011b. 'The Palaeo-Christian Glass Mosaic of St. Prosdocimus (Padova, Italy): Archaeometric Characterisation of "Gold" Tesserae'. *Journal of Archaeological Science* 38: 3402–14.

Sternini, M. 1995. 'Il vetro in Italia tra V e IX secolo d.C'. In *Le verre de l'Antiquité tardive et du haut Moyen Age: typologie, chronologie, diffusion. Association française pour l'archéologie du verre, huitième rencontre*, edited by D. Foy, 234–89. Guiry-en-Vexin: Musée archéologique départemental du Val d'Oise.

Uboldi, M. 1999. 'I vetri'. In *S. Giulia di Brescia: gli scavi dal 1980 al 1992. Reperti preromani, romani e alto medievali*, edited by G. P. Brogiolo, 271–307. Firenze: All'insegna del Giglio.

10
How clean is your (glass)house?: A Late Antique glass workshop at Pella in Jordan

Margaret O'Hea

Abstract

Between 2005 and 2013, four seasons of excavations by The University of Sydney in Area XXXII at Pella in the north Jordan Valley (Figure 10.1) have uncovered a secondary glass workshop of the late sixth or early seventh century CE. Although it has been identified as such by the presence of glass-working debris in conjunction with clear indicators of hot-working activities, the kilns themselves were made using construction techniques not previously recorded for ancient glass-working. This raises questions about what criteria might be used to identify secondary glass kilns in the Levant. Although further research on the associated artefacts is ongoing, it is nonetheless useful to provide a preliminary report on the physical remains within this four-roomed workshop.

Background

For the period between the first century BCE and the early ninth century CE, at least 15 other secondary glass workshops have already been published in the Levant. Yet of these, only four – two at Sepphoris, one each at Bet She'an in Israel and Raqqa in Syria – have yielded clear physical traces of glass-blowing kilns *in situ*. Those claimed for late fourth-century CE Jalame are problematic (Brill and Wosinski 1988, 287): while droplets, chunks, wasters and cullet fragments all certainly indicate that glass-blowing took place at Jalame, they were

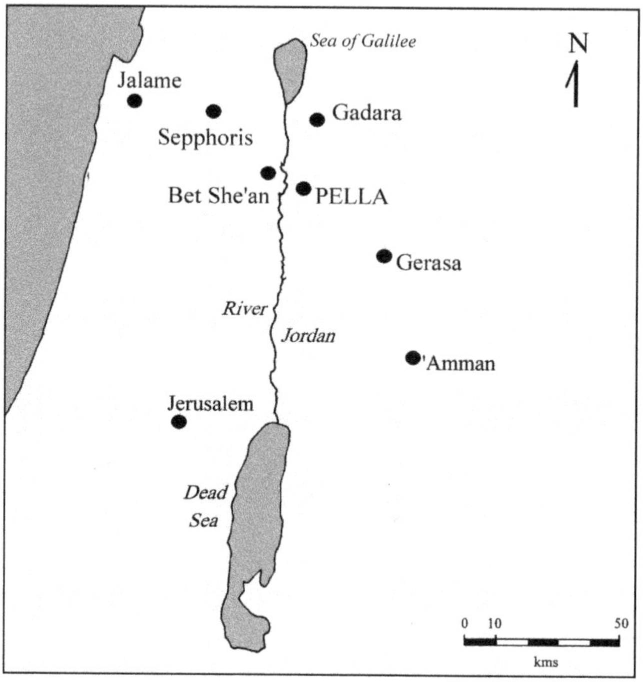

Figure 10.1 Location of Pella of the Decapolis in the north Jordan Valley.
Source: © The University of Sydney Expedition to Pella

found either in an external dump or within the matrix of tamped earth floors in adjoining rooms. The poorly preserved and heavily burnt room (*c.*2.4 × 3.6 m), which was identified as a secondary kiln (Weinberg 1988, 25–8) is much more likely to have been a primary furnace (Henderson 2007, 64). Other workshops are identified only by glass-working debris, as summarised in Goren-Rosen (2000, 56–8, 61), to which can be added Jerash, Bosra (Dussart 2000, 91–3), Gadara (el-Khouri 2012, 89) and Ramla, where fired flat bricks were found *ex situ* but with traces of vitrification (Tal et al. 2008, 81–3). Physical details of beehived glass-blowers' furnaces in antiquity are, therefore, not well represented in the homeland of glass itself.

In the East, where stone and mud-brick are the default vernacular architectural media, it is striking that the foundations of surviving kilns include 'roof tiles' or fired tile-bricks. They were retrieved from the remnants of an early Byzantine workshop at Sepphoris (Strange et al. 2006, 79), while the later fifth to sixth centuries CE workshop from the upper city yielded only bare traces of a kiln plan as indicated by a channel in the floor (Fischer 2008, 51, fig. 3.4). At Bet She'an, the collapsed contents of a kiln set against a masonry wall included fired bricks, roof tiles and sherds (Mazar and Bar-Nathan 1998, 29) in addition to the 'burnt and charred' stonework (Goren-Rosen 2000 59–60). It appears to have been destroyed by a seventh-century CE earthquake.

The five early Medieval kilns at Raqqa were semicircular constructions set into or against walls in clay-luted fired brick; the dome was presumed to have been in *pisé* (that is, packed unfired clay or clay mix). Their fronts were not well preserved, but had arched stoke-holes at the base in clay that had fired (Henderson 2007, 79–82, figs 3.42–3). Channels with square-sectioned clay walls were traced, leading from an external fire-box across the workroom floor (Henderson 2007, 81 and fig. 3.42).

Common to all three sites is the location of a kiln against a masonry wall, the use of prefired brick or tile, and of *pisé*, which had fired as a result of kiln use. Where recorded, they have a plan that indicates an opening at ground level to a fire-box from a wide stoke-hole. Foundations and debris from Western examples show some variety in form, but basically also had a wide fire-box before a wide stoke hole, used fired bricks and/or stone for walls and a clay or *pisé* dome with arched openings; a good summary is provided by Amrein (2001, 99–125).

Area XXXII, Pella kilns

Let us now turn to Pella. Since the mid-1990s, University of Sydney excavations along the southern edge of the *tell* have uncovered more than 500 m^2 of a substantial late Roman masonry building floored with mosaics. This appears to have been damaged in the late fourth or early fifth century CE. At some point thereafter – perhaps as late as *c.*600 CE – some existing wall lines were rebuilt almost from scratch, while new walls subdivided all earlier spaces. Masonry from the earlier building was reused in a haphazard fashion. A thick tamped earth floor overlay earlier mosaics in all the new rooms, and sat flush with new doorsills. Ceilings were *pisé* and reed: as with most vernacular buildings in the Levant, it would have had a flat roof. There may have been an upper floor built entirely of mud-bricks, although no staircases have been identified; certainly a great deal of mud-brick and used, domestic pottery as well as glass, metal and bone objects collapsed into rooms from above.

This repurposed building was in use long enough for some walls to be repaired and doorways blocked, as well as a second tamped floor laid down before the entire building suffered major upper structural collapse. Early seventh-century CE coins were in the latest floor matrix. Copious amounts of early mid-seventh-century CE pottery in that destruction suggests that it might be due to the earthquake of 659 CE. This seems to have wreaked similar damage in Area XXXIV on Tell Husn (Russell 1985, 47; Watson and Tidmarsh 1996, 303) and it is perhaps also responsible for the damage done to the Bet She'an workshop some 12km to the west. Although the masonry walls remained largely intact, only a few rooms were subsequently cleared out and reused until they in turn were destroyed by the major 749 CE earthquake that devastated the region (Tsafrir and Foerster 1992, 234; see also the suggestion of more than one mid-century earthquake in Walmsley 2000, 284, no. 36).

Excavations from 2005 to 2013 uncovered four interconnecting rooms in the north-western corner of the building (Figure 10.2), which are now identified as a secondary glass workshop. Here, there was no clearance or reuse after 659 CE. An interconnecting pair of long northern rooms (1 and 2) roughly 3.8 m wide each had to their south a smaller, square room (3 and 4). The only exit from this four-roomed unit must be through room 1; a doorway is visible in its western wall/baulk, and another is possible in its unexcavated northern wall. It is possible that this complex formed the north-western corner of the revamped building, but only future excavations will confirm this.

A tentative and broad phasing of these rooms is shown in Figures 10.2a–c. Kilns were present in both rooms 2 and 3 from the earliest, late sixth-century CE phase (Figure 10.2a) through to the final phase prior to collapse *c.*659 CE (Figure 10.2c). The small south-western room 4 has no internal features of any kind, but a concentration of metal artefacts – as yet unidentified – suggests that it could have been a tool store-room. Roughly two-thirds of the north-western room 1 has been excavated; although there are no remains of kilns or kiln material, a thick clay platform was lain north of its doorway into room 2, built over a low stone-walled bin or large conduit filled with glass chunks, cullet (broken, recycled glass) and a waster in the form of a blown spoon (Figure 10.3). This glass was clearly intended to go back *into* the kiln, as the waster-spoon was found with chunks, cullet and droplets from the kiln/crucible.

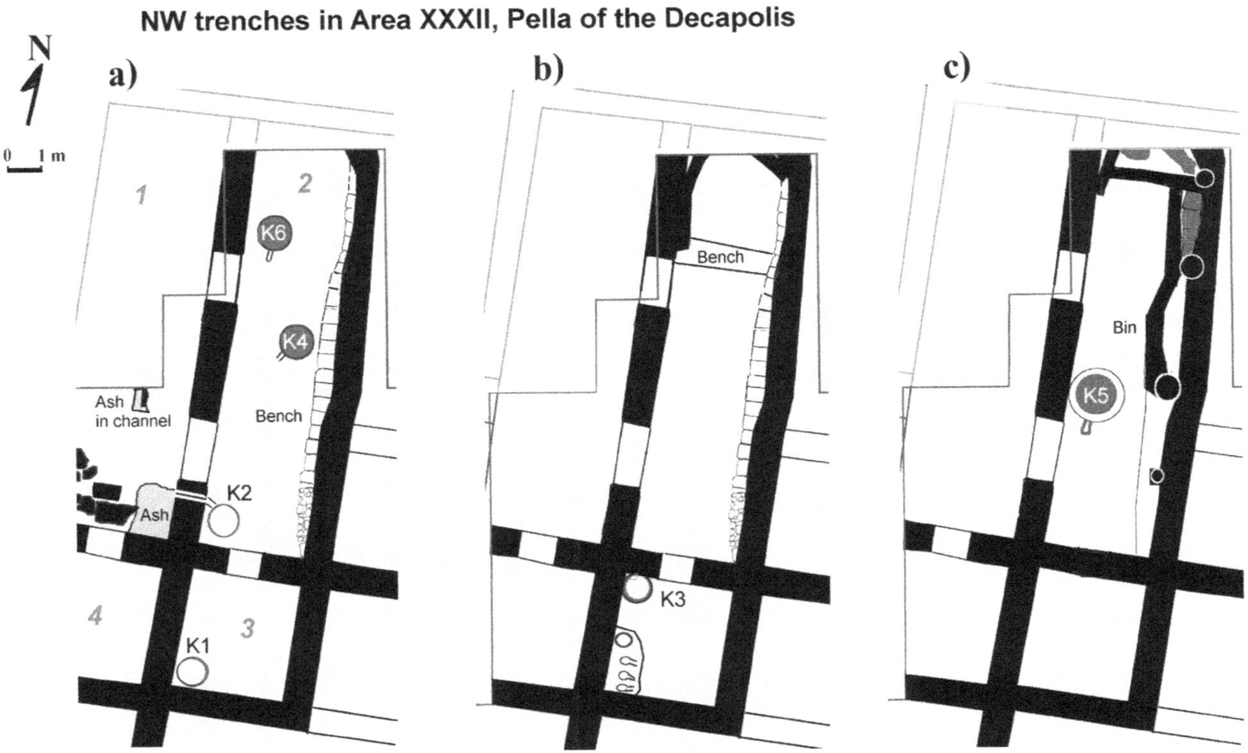

Figure 10.2 Preliminary phasing of the late Byzantine–early Umayyad glass-working complex in Area XXXII, Pella: phase 1 = 2a (*c.*600 CE), phase 2 = 2b and phase 3 = 2c (*c.*659 CE).
Source: © The University of Sydney Expedition to Pella

Figure 10.3 Glass-working chunks, droplets and waster spoon from room 1.
Source: © The University of Sydney Expedition to Pella

In the eastern suite of rooms 2–3, thick levels of ash and heat-affected material associated with both phases of tamped earth floors clearly indicate that hot-working activities took place here. Glass-working is indicated by the droplets and chunks scattered throughout this complex – in some cases, built into repairs to some walls (Figure 10.4) – while glass-blowing is indicated by the spoon and another waster from room 2 (Figure 10.5). No other hot industrial activity is indicated here.

By the end of the 2013 season, five kilns were identified in the eastern suite of rooms, and it is these that will be discussed in full here. Another two kilns – referred to here K6 and K7 – were found in the excavation of the northern end of room 2 in early 2015, but will be fully published elsewhere. Room 3 had only one kiln in any one phase, whereas the larger room 2 had two to three kilns active at any given time.

Tannur-like kilns

The surprise was that kilns K1–6 clearly differ from both known Western and Levantine glass-working kilns. Indeed, when room 3 was excavated in 2005, both this author and the entire team identified them as rather odd versions of bread ovens (*tannurs/tabuns*). Now, these are features

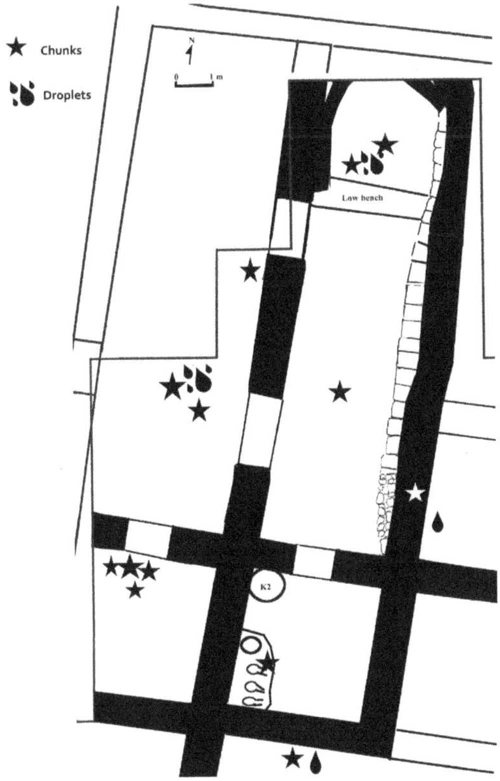

Figure 10.4 Locations of chunks (stars) and droplets (teardrops) in all phases of late sixth- to seventh-century-building at Pella.
Source: © The University of Sydney Expedition to Pella

familiar to all Levantine field archaeologists as they are found in nearly every domestic unit from the Neolithic period (Rova 2014, 126) to the modern day in some traditional villages. At Pella, the basic format was a shallow pit cut into a floor, into which a disk of pure clay was set. Onto this was placed a slightly smaller open-topped beehive oven with finished rim, made with a distinctive chaff and quartz rich clay. The base was sometimes chocked onto the wider, underlying clay bed with small stones and/or sherds. When a fire was laid inside, it self-fired the walls. A *tannur* was used until it over-fired and collapsed, at which point the ash from within spilled into the shallow depression without. Sometimes the clay base was relain and another set atop the tamped and ashy remnants of the original. *Tabuns* are, strictly speaking, *tannurs* that have a dung-fueled fire set around the outside base of the oven rather than one

Figure 10.5 Waster goblet found in stone and pisé bin, room 2 (phase 3). Source: © The University of Sydney Expedition to Pella

set within, where heat-conducting pebbles were laid instead. These are not found at Pella before the Medieval Period, nor are any found with any deliberate holes at the base for clearing ash, as is found in modern examples (Rova 2014, 125, fig. 4b): access was purely from the open but lidded top.

The Pella kilns cannot be identified as bread ovens of any kind. Six were certainly constructed in their lower half in the form and dimensions of a standard *tannur* but they have added features that are never found with ancient bread ovens (Table 10.1). The best preserved and largest *tannur*-like kiln 5 provided in 2013 the fullest set of these attributes, which were repeated with a sixth *tannur*-like kiln excavated in the northern third of room 2 in early 2015. Kilns 1 and 4 were incorporated into later clay features, and survived only to the top of their sub-floor surrounding flue, while kilns 3, 5 and now 6 were preserved in part above the finished rim of their *c.*50 cm high *tannur* walls.

The first striking feature of all six kilns is the presence of an annular, fully covered flue made of unfired yellow clay mixed with small rubble

Table 10.1 Excavated Pella tannur-like kilns and identified characteristics

Kiln ID	*Room*	*Pre-fired tiled floor*	*Curvsed tiles*	*Covered flue around*	*Flue to kiln*	*Tannur base*
K1	3	X	✓	✓	Not identified	✓
K2	1	X	X	✓	Not identified	✓
K3	3	X	✓	✓	Not identified	✓
K4	2	✓ – two sets	✓	✓	✓	✓
K5	2	✓– two sets	✓ *in situ*	✓	✓	✓
K6	2	✓ – two sets	✓ *in situ*	✓	✓	✓
K7	2	✓	X	✓	X	X

and fired tile fragments – not roof tiles, but two specific types not found elsewhere at Pella and described below. This flue entered the kiln by a hole knocked through the *tannur*-like base, and from there channelled up to the floor. Every flue was filled with very fine white to light grey ash. Only the poorly preserved example around kiln 2 was difficult to see, as it was mostly demolished and sat immediately below a yellow clay surface, thick with ash. It is unique, however, in that its flue led away from the kiln through a clay lined, square channel through the adjacent stone wall into room 1.

Second, all but kiln 2 have yielded fragments of semicylindrical fired tiles *c*.2.5 cm thick, more than 18 cm wide and 16 cm deep. They formed at least three bands of tiled domed superstructure. Some had one horizontal edge with a projecting tongue that fitted into the grooved rim of the base *tannur* below; others have a corresponding grooved edge. The highest course of tiles had a thickened, bevelled top edge, indicating a large open hole at the top of the beehive-shaped kiln. Some curved tiles were found still slotted onto the rim of the *tannur*-base of kiln 3 in room 3, while large fragments were preserved around the earlier, demolished kiln 1 in the same room. This suggests that even the earliest kilns' superstructures were made in this way. All were made in a coarse and gritty fabric that was similar to but less chaff-rich than normal *tannur* walls. In fact, they closely resemble the contemporary Coarse Red Ware (CRW) fabric that was used for storage bins and jars.

The largest kiln 5 (1.2 m diameter) dates from the last phase of activity in room 2. Its superstructure of tiles, unfired clay and small rubble had either collapsed or been pushed into its sunken base (Figure 10.6).

Figure 10.6 Half-sectioned fill of kiln 5, showing yellow clay, rubble stones and fired curved tile fragments.
Source: © The University of Sydney Expedition to Pella

Fragments from here and kiln 6 suggest that the tiled dome was faced externally with 6–8 cm of clay. Some may have also lined the interior of the tiled superstructure, but not the *tannur* base.

Third, kilns 4 and 5 in both their phases shared a trait never found in bread ovens: each had floors of flat pre-fired tiles, *c.*3 × 44 × 44 cm (Figure 10.7). Like the curved tiles, they were coarsely levigated with plenty of grit, but were fired a lighter colour and had a slipped and smoothed upper surface. All the tiled bases showed a distinctive heat pattern of heavy cracking and blackening around an unaffected central area *c.*48 cm in diameter. Since kiln 5's floor was found complete, the presence of additional flat tile fragments from the middle fill of kiln 5 suggest that they could also have been used for internal shelving, as hypothesised in Taylor and and Hill's experimental kiln (2008, 254, 258). A central stand of yellow clay and rubble would also explain the heat pattern on the floor. That said, neither tiles nor clay show anything approaching vitrification, which would be expected with a crucible support.

No clear signs of either stoke-holes or work-holes have yet been identified, although a large collapsed fragment of *pisé* found south of kiln 5 shows a funnel-shaped profile that might indicate either a chimney capping at the top of the kiln, or the side of a fire-box drawn out from the

Figure 10.7 View south-west of kiln 5 in room 2: tiled floor with heat-pattern.
Source: © The University of Sydney Expedition to Pella

external clay facing of the kiln. Like most of the clay, however, it showed only light orange burning. Nor is there any certain indication of a fire-box at floor level: at best, a semicircular patch of low, flat and burnt stones *c*.30 cm north-east of kiln 2 might be a candidate, but it is both large and relatively distant from the kiln (Figure 10.2).

Kilns 5 and 6 are well preserved because they were set up to 30 cm into their surrounding floors. The earlier kiln 6 might have had a fire-box on its southern side, but here the surrounding floor was removed by the foundation trench for a low masonry wall or bench across the room. To its south, a raised yellow clay and stone platform ran the width of the room immediately north of kiln 5. It is, therefore, likely that this kiln's glory-hole was on this side. Any putative external fire-box set into the earthen floor could only have been to its east, but it could not be traced. All that can be said with certainty is that if there had been one, it did not have a tiled floor. In room 3, faint traces of a channel cut into the floor led away from kiln 3, but again no fire-box could be traced.

What was the purpose of the enclosed flues around Pella's kilns? Kilns 3, 5 and 6 all had a circular hole (*c*.7 cm in diameter) broken low into the *tannur*-wall after its first firing. This hole led directly both into the surrounding flue and – via a short and enclosed conduit – up to the floor's surface (Figure 10.7). Given that the other three kilns were excavated as if bread ovens, and that *tannur* walls tend to fragment and collapse during excavation, a missing section would not necessarily have been noted. It would have been difficult to feed fuel into the kiln via this hole, so the likeliest explanation is that it was for bellows. Perhaps the annular flue was also meant simply to retain heat during this process. Modern models for the use of bellows in metal-working kilns assumes that they blew *down* onto a crucible (Fischer 2008, 71): if correctly identified, our bellows would at best only have blown onto its side.

The putative bellows-hole into kiln 5 lay to its south. To its north was a *c.*20 cm high clay platform, which showed no evidence of direct heat to its surface, although it was covered with ash. A reused masonry block was embedded in it and partly extended over the flue. Next to it was set the lower half of a cut-down CRW jar (Figure 10.8). This

Figure 10.8 Top view from north baulk of partially excavated clay platform north of kiln 5, room 2.
Source: © The University of Sydney Expedition to Pella

combination can be found before a gathering- or glory-hole in traditional workshops: with one foot stepped up, the blow-pipe or punty could be worked while resting against a protected thigh. Alternatively, it could have been used for marvering. Equipment could be regularly cleaned of attached hot glass by dipping into a nearby trough or bowl of cold water.

Two other architectural features are worthy of note here. Room 2 incorporated, from its start, a projecting stone bench along almost the entire eastern wall. It was thickly faced with more yellow clay at the same time as the construction of kiln 5 and its clay work platform, and a clay and stone bin was built over both the platform and the bench (Figure 10.9). The bin's floor was lined with more flat tiles and yellow clay, and inside it was a fragmentary ceramic lamp and a complete waster goblet (Figure 10.5). Another near-complete but fragmentary goblet was found below the edge of the clay-faced bench to its south, on the associated latest floor. The 2015 season revealed a companion bin further north that was solidly packed and topped with fired tiles to form a bench top. These tiles showed clear signs of applied heat, although it is possible that they were reused from an earlier kiln. No artefacts were found on this bench.

A wider and lower hot-working bench of clay over large rubble stones in room 3 is not yet attested elsewhere in excavated glass

Figure 10.9 Room 2 bin on stone bench along eastern wall (clay facing removed).
Source: © The University of Sydney Expedition to Pella

Figure 10.10 Room 3 view south: hot-working clay and stone bench.
Source: © The University of Sydney Expedition to Pella

workshops (Figure 10.10). No traces of a superstructure were identified over three shallow depressions, which were lined with fired *tannur* clay and opened out to the bench's edge. A fourth deep depression had no channel, but from its ashy fill the excavator retrieved arcs of iron rust *c.*2 cm in diameter, which could have come from blow-pipes. All the depressions were relined at least once before the room was blocked up, and the heat exposed in all of them partially fired the underlying clay benchtop itself. A single chunk of raw glass, with claw-marks from a utensil, was also found on the benchtop.

Fuel and equipment

Our palaeobotanist could not identify the fuel plants from the fine white ash in any of the first five kilns, but carbonised olive pips were excavated in early 2015 by the author from the flue of kiln 6. Olive pips are also attested at Sepphoris where Fischer (2008, 46) has plausibly argued that the fuel was olive pressings rather than olive wood. The high ash content (6–10 per cent) of this biomass fuel (www.olivketts.com/biomass.html) may in part explain the thick ashy deposits in all four rooms below that of the earthquake destruction. By contrast, timber fuels have much lower ash content (Francescato et al. 2008, 22). At Bet She'an, too, olive pips were identified in two ash piles, although these contained wasters and so were assumed to be annealing piles in the preliminary report (Goren-Rosen 2000, 59).

Crucibles found on other glass-working sites are usually simply robust, coarse ware vessels, identifiable by over-firing, vitrification and/or an inner coating of glass (for Western examples, see Price 1998, 344 and Amrein 2001, 81–85; for contemporary Jerash, Dussart 2000, 92 photo 13). The only possible remnant of a vitrified ceramic container in the Pella workshop is a tiny $2mm^2$ chip of yellow glaze from the eastern bench of room 2. Even if it is from a crucible, the absence of anything more substantial from this fully excavated room is consistent with its abandonment prior to the 659 CE earthquake. The same may be argued about the relatively few raw glass chunks retrieved and the paucity of moils. A handful of possible moils are now identified, which had originally been catalogued as heat-deformed fragments of hollow lamp stems or tubes. If the Pella workshop was abandoned at the time of the earthquake, it would also explain why there seems to have been domestic occupation above these rooms; sixth-century civic code forbade smithies and glass workshops close to private dwellings (Hakim 2001, 12; Julian of Ascalon 1851, Bk II, tit. IV, ch. 19).

Except for glass retrieved from ash-contexts, it is difficult to estimate exactly how much cullet – in the sense of recycled broken glass – might have been left scattered across the latest floors, because it is difficult to isolate from the broken glassware in the burnt collapse from above. In any case, it is reasonable to assume that an active glass-working environment would be relatively clean of glass-working debris, as Henderson (2007, loc 2185) has noted. On other sites, it is possible that recycling or sorting dumps have been scattered by post-depositional processes rather than reflecting actual scatter across a floor in use. Many small glass sherds and some droplets formed part of the matrix of floor packings – but not the surface deposits – in all four rooms as well as within the *pisé* constructions in rooms 2 and 3.

There are some fragmentary metal objects that are associated directly with the floors in these rooms. They await full cleaning and analysis but a few points can be made at this early stage. None are from room 3 with its hot-working bench, but there is a cluster of iron around the doorway between rooms 1 and 4, including a possible jacks- or shears-blade and several hemispherical small bowls from rooms 1 and 2, which might be from the end of long ladles known from early modern European illustrations (for example, Stiaffini 1999, figs 67–8). There are no certain fragments of blow-pipes or punties, other than the corrosion mentioned above from the bench in room 3.

Temperatures

The adaptation of a standard clay *tannur* to an industrial kiln does have broad antecedents in both Bronze and Iron Age metal-working in Mesopotamia (Rova 2014, 129 no. 66), and there is anecdotal evidence that traditional Indian metal-working kilns were made of common potter's clay with added quartz (Freestone 1989, 157). Nevertheless, there remains the problem of what temperatures could be reached in such kilns without showing visible signs of vitrification of the lining or indeed the walls. The upper clay luting of Pella's kilns and their tiled bases all show evidence of strong heat, which is only to be expected. Fischer's experimental mud-brick kiln reached only 482°C in its crucible, yet still managed to fire its own mud-bricks (Fischer 2008, 78).

Glass-blowing requires a crucible temperature of at least 1050°C (Brill and Wosinski 1988, 280, tables 9–12), although the temperature of a kiln's walls can be 100–300°C lower, especially if a bellows is used (Freestone 1989, 155; Fischer 2008, 70–1). Taylor and Hill's experimental glass kilns made of fired tile and *pisé* all developed vitrified interior surfaces (except where crucibles had been placed) as well as showing much glass splattering (Paynter 2008, 284–5 and fig. 13). By contrast, almost all the clay superstructures of the Pella workshop lack vitrification. One fragment of pisé from kiln 7 in room 2 has a semi-vitrified inner surface, but most do not. A tiny, amorphous lump of vitrified ceramic material was retrieved from the packing of the latest floor in the same room – a remarkably small amount for a room that contained at least four kilns over its lifetime. Another fragment of vitrified refractory material was excavated immediately *outside* the western wall of room 1

Figure 10.11 Fragment of vitrified refractory material from Trench XXXIIDD west of workshop.
Source: © The University of Sydney Expedition to Pella

(Figure 10.11). At 1.4 cm thick, it is thinner than any surviving *pisé* fragments, and the small curvature suggests it came from a crucible rather than any kiln lining.

There are also no traces at Pella of the degree of splattering noted within Bet She'an's kiln. Taylor and Hill noted that splattering derived from glass gathering and from moving portable crucibles in and out of the kiln. They also suggested that thick 'daub' found on late Roman crucibles at Hambach, Germany, might have been used to 'support the pots in position in the furnace' (Taylor and Hill 2008, 261). Something similar has been tentatively hypothesised above for our kilns with tiled floors.

Nevertheless, the lack of vitrified kiln interiors remains a serious obstacle to the identification of any of the Pella kilns as glass-blowers' furnaces. An alternative identification as perhaps annealing kilns faces the same problem, as indicated by Taylor and Hill (2008, 286). In any case, the presence of a glass droplet from the flue of kiln 6 and of small fragments of heat-affected cullet from the base of two other kilns at Pella indicates that melting of glass took place here, rather than annealing. That all the Pella kilns were freestanding separates them from the later and well-attested habit of attaching annealing ovens to hotter furnaces, but by itself cannot really help in identifying their function, either.

Another possibility is that they were used simply to add colourant to glass melt. At Lombardic Aiano-Torracia, a kiln with stone and clay walls and heat-affected *pisé* vaulted top was associated with piles of glass tesserae used to colour the glass batch. Whether for bead-making or vessel-blowing is unclear (Cavalieri and Giumlia-Mair 2009, 1026, fig. 3), but it sat in the same room as what appears to be a free-standing circular kiln, just as at the fifth- to sixth-century CE workshop at Trento (Cavada and Endrizzi 1998, 174–5). However, these Lombardic rectangular kilns lacked the characteristic flues of the Pella kilns.

It may be argued, of course, that different regions used different forms of colouring ovens. The late eighth- or early ninth-century CE *Kitab al-Durra al-Maknuna* (*Book of the Hidden Pearl*) by Jabir ibn Hayyan discussed the ways to colour glass with metallic compounds (al-Hassan 2009, 139–47). He mentioned a range of different types of ovens from a brick-making furnace (*atun*) to portable ceramic oven (*nafikh nafsihi*), but commonly specified the use of a *tannur*. For instance, in recipe 33 fol. 4b, a handled ceramic crucible was to be placed on a platform within a similarly-sized *tannur*, with fuel-hole opposite the raised crucible and another hole at the top level of said crucible to monitor the fire and for smoke (al-Hassan 2009, 144). Recipe 44 fol. 6b required burial of a crucible-pot in nearly half a metre of fuel in the base of a *tannur* that had been covered over and luted with clay (al-Hassan 2009, 146).

There are no piles of glass tesserae here at Pella that would clearly support an identification as colouring ovens; the only possible remnant of powdered mineral colourant came from a large glass flask below the earliest floor packing and so might not relate at all to our workshop. More to the point, the two wasters that must be from this workshop were naturally coloured as were all the droplets. In addition, the idea that all these *tannur*-like kilns were used solely for adding colourants would seem to suggest a level of coloured glass vessel production not found in this period either within the building or across the site as a whole.

If the lack of vitrified refractory material is taken to mean that no *tannur*-like kiln was used for glass-blowing, then where did that activity take place? The northern end of room 2 was excavated in 2015, with a large, raised semicircular kiln replete with floor tiles, heavily fired *pisé* and rubble superstructure set across the entire width of the room. It too lacks any vitrified refractory material. The only other possibility is in the north-western section of room 1, which is unlikely to be excavated in the near future. In a broad sense, however, it makes little overall difference to the current association of our *tannur*-like kilns with glass vessel production. If no such vitrified kiln lies in room 1, then the *tannur*-like kilns remain the best candidates for glass-blowing. If there *is* such a kiln here, it merely confirms that, in some way or another, the other six belonged to a secondary glass workshop.

Clearly, much work still must be done to understand how Pella's *tannur*-like kilns functioned, including compositional analysis of the chunks, recycled glass and furnace glass (droplets). Yet their close association with evidence of glass-blowing has immense implications for future identification of these workshops, including those that preceded glass-blowing itself. It is possible that Western stone and fired brick kilns might not necessarily reflect the original template for constructing a glass-blowing kiln. Pella's kilns are modifications of a very ancient hot-working technology, used for millennia in the very regions where glass vessel-making first developed. As yet, no one has with certainty identified Hellenistic or earlier glass-*working* kilns in the Levant, merely the debris associated with vessel or jewellery manufacture or with kilns linked to glass-*making* (Mallowan 1954, 77, 83). Could it be that we have been ignoring the fragmentary and humble *tannur* in the corner?

Acknowledgements

I am grateful to the Jordanian Department of Antiquities and to the project's director Dr S. J. Bourke for permission to publish this material, and to all the teams involved in the excavations. Figures 10.5, 10.6, 10.9–10.11 were photographed by B. Miller; the rest are by the author, as are the preliminary plans. All images remain the copyright of The University of Sydney Expedition to Pella. Trench supervisors were T. Adams for XXXIIAA (room 3) in 2005; R. M. Stone for XXXIIBB (rooms 1 and 4) in 2007; the author for XXXIIFF in 2011 (helped at the end of season by B. Churcher), XXXIIGG in 2013 and XXXIIHH in 2015 (all room 2). Dr P. Watson has kindly shared her preliminary dating for the pottery, but all conclusions in this chapter remain the responsibility of the author.

References

Al-Hassam, A. 2009. 'An Eighth-Century Arabic Treatise on the Colouring of Glass: *Kitazb Al-Durra Al-Maknuzna* (The Book of the Hidden Pearl) of Jazbir Ibn Hayyan (*c.*721–815)'. *Arabic Sciences and Philosophy* 19: 121–56.

Amrein, H. 2001. *L'Atelier de verriers d'Avenches. L'artisanat du verre au milieu du 1er siècle après J.–C.* Lausanne: Cahiers d'archéologie romande.

Brill, R. and Wosinski, J. 1988. 'Scientific Investigations of the Jalame Glass and Related Finds'. In *Excavations at Jalame: Site of a Glass Factory in Late Roman Palestine*, edited by G. D. Weinberg, 257–93. Columbia: University of Missouri Press.

Cavada, E. and Endrizzi, L. 1998. 'Produrre vetro a Trento. Primi indizi nei livelli tardoantico e altomedievali dell'area urbana'. In *Il vetro dall'antichità all'età contemporanea: aspetto tecnologici, funzionale e commerciali*, edited by R. La Guardia and T. Tibiletti, 173–80. Milan: AIHV.

Cavalieri, M. and Giumlia-Mair, A. 2009. 'Lombardic Glassworking in Tuscany'. *Materials and Manufacturing Processes* 24: 1023–32.

Dussart, O. 2000. 'Quelques indices d'ateliers de verriers en Jordanie et en Syrie du Sud de la fin de l'époque hellénistique à l'époque islamique'. In *La Route du verre. Ateliers primaires et secondaires du second millénaire av. J.-C. au Moyen Âge*, edited by D. Foy, 91–6. Lyon: Maison de l'Orient Méditerranée.

El-Khouri, L. 2012. 'Glass Production in the Byzantine Period (4th–7th Century) at Gadara (Umm Qais) Area W, 2011 Season of Excavation'. *Levant* 46 (1): 89–97.

Fischer, A. 2008. *Hot Pursuit: Integrating Anthropology in Search of Ancient Glass-Blowers*. Lanham: Lexington Books.

Francescato, V., Bergomi, L., Metschina, C., Schnedl, C., Krajnc, N., Koscik, K., Nocentini, G. and Stranieri, S. 2008. *Wood Fuels Handbook*. Legnaro: Italian Agriforestry Energy Association.

Freestone, I. 1989. 'Refractory Materials and Their Procurement'. In *Old World Archaeometallurgy: A Conference Proceedings from 1987*, edited by A. Hauptmann, E. Pernicka and G. Wagner, 155–62, Bochum: Deutschen Bergbau-Museums.

Goren-Rosen, Y. 2000. 'The Ancient Glass Industry in Israel: Summary of the Finds and New Discoveries'. In *La Route du verre. Ateliers primaires et secondaires du second millénaire av. J.-C. au Moyen Âge*, edited by D. Foy, 49–63. Lyon: Maison de l'Orient Méditerranée.

Hakim, B. 2001. 'Julian of Ascalon's Treatise of Construction and Design Rules from Sixth-Century Palestine'. *Journal of the Society of Architectural Historians* 60 (1): 4–25.

Henderson, J. 2007. *The Science and Archaeology of Materials. An Investigation of Inorganic Materials*. London: Routledge.

Julian of Ascalon 1851. 'De novis operibus, Lib. II. Tit. IV, 19'. In *Manuale Legum sive Hexabiblos*, edited by W. Heimbach, 246–9. Leipzig: T. O. Weigel.

Mallowan, M. 1954. 'The Excavations at Nimrud (Kalḫu), 1953'. *Iraq* 16 (1): 59–114.

Mazar, G. and Bar-Nathan, R. 1998. 'The Bet She'an Excavation Project – 1992–1994'. *Excavations and Surveys in Israel* 17: 27–36.

Olivketts Olive. 2005. Biomass for Energy. Last modified 4 May 2015. www.olivketts.com/biomass.html

Paynter, S. 2008. 'Experiments in the Reconstruction of Roman Wood-Fired Glassworking Furnaces: Waste Products and Their Formation Processes'. *Journal of Glass Studies* 50: 271–90.

Price, J. 1998. 'Glassworking'. In *The Prehistory and History of Glassmaking Technology*, edited by P. McCray, 331–48. Westerville: The American Ceramic Society.

Rova, E. 2014. 'Tannurs, Tannur Concentrations and Centralised Bread Production at Tell Beydar and Elsewhere: An Overview'. In *Paleonutrition and Food Practices in the Ancient Near East: Towards a Multidisciplinary Approach*, edited by L. Milano and F. Bertoldi, 121–70. Padua: S.A.R.G.O.N.

Russell, K. W. 1985. 'The Earthquake Chronology of Palestine and Northwest Arabia from the 2nd Through the Mid-8th Century AD'. *Bulletin of the American Schools of Oriental Research* 260: 37–59.

Stiaffini, D. 1999. *Il Vetro nel Medioevo*. Rome: Fratelli Palombi.

Strange, J., Longstaff, T. and Groh, D. 2006. *Excavations at Sepphoris, Volume I. University of South Florida Probes in the Citadel and Villa*. Leiden: Brill.

Tal, O., Jackson-Tal, R. and Freestone, I. (2008) 'Glass from a Late Byzantine Secondary Workshop at Ramla (South), Israel'. *Journal of Glass Studies* 50: 81–95.

Taylor, M. and Hill, D. 2008. 'Experiments in the Reconstruction of Roman Wood-Fired Glassworking Furnaces'. *Journal of Glass Studies* 50: 249–70.

Tsafrir, Y. and Foerster, G. 1992. 'The Dating of the "Earthquake of the Sabbatical Year" of 749 C. E. in Palestine'. *Bulletin of the School of Oriental and African Studies* 55 (2): 231–5.

Walmsley, A. 2000. 'Production, Exchange and Regional Trade in the Islamic East Mediterranean: Old Structures, New Systems?' In *The Long Eighth Century*, edited by I. Hansen and C. Wickham, 265–344. Leiden: Brill.

Watson, P. and Tidmarsh, J. 1996. 'Pella/Tall al-Husn Excavations 1993 The University of Sydney – 15th Season'. *Annual of the Department of Antiquities Jordan* XL: 293–313.

Weinberg, G. D. 1988. 'The Glass Factory and Manufacturing Processes'. In *Excavations at Jalame: Site of a Glass Factory in Late Roman Palestine*, edited by G. D. Weinberg, 24–37. Columbia: University of Missouri Press.

11

Glass supply and trade in early Islamic Ramla: An investigation of the plant ash glass

Matt Phelps

Abstract

Several questions remain concerning plant ash glass production and supply in the Near East. This chapter presents the results of LA-ICP-MS analysis of 54 samples of well-dated vessel glass excavated from seven sites in Ramla, Israel. These samples date to the eighth to twelfth centuries CE, thus enabling the study of diachronic developments in glass supply. The results identified three main compositional groups: P-1, corresponding to glass from Tyre; P-3 and P-4, corresponding to Mesopotamian/Iranian types most closely matching Nishapur Colourless and Nishapur Coloured, respectively. Compositional investigation of flux ratios (MgO/CaO and K_2O/P_2O_5) alongside Al_2O_3 and with comparison to literature groups identified three regional glass compositions: Eastern Mediterranean, Mesopotamian Type 1 and Mesopotamian Type 2. These broad regional compositions provide a framework in which future plant ash glass can be interpreted.

Sample chronology demonstrated plant ash glass to appear in the late eighth century with P-1 (Tyre glass) becoming the most abundant. Vessel context and form in conjunction with archaeological and documentary evidence suggested that a centralised production model continued to be used for this glass type until at least the twelfth century CE, with this glass likely supplied as chunks to Ramla and worked locally. This model of supply possibly also extended to Egypt and the Byzantine territories for this glass type. The vessels forming groups P-3 and P-4 were supplied using a different model, with their form and decoration instead suggesting long-distance trade of the finished vessels from

Mesopotamia/Iran during ninth to mid-eleventh century CE. This began during the Abbasid period, with the change in trade potentially stimulated by the centralisation of taxation under the Abbasid Caliphate.

Introduction

The supply of natron glass during the late Byzantine–early Islamic transition is becoming increasingly well understood (Freestone et al. 2000; Foy et al. 2003; Rehren et al. 2010; Freestone et al. 2015; Phelps et al. 2016). In a recent paper, Phelps et al. (2016) demonstrated distinct shifts in the natron glass industry of Palestine during the eighth century CE, characterised by changing recipes and production sites, new imports of Egyptian glass and the first appearances of plant ash glass. The aim of this chapter is to build on this work by investigating and characterising the plant ash glass from the important administrative centre of Ramla during the Umayyad, Abbasid and Fatimid periods. The analyses of glass vessel samples, integrated with the previously published data, is able to provide information on glass production, supply and trade. The investigation of selected literature data alongside new results enables the creation of a framework in which plant ash glass groups can be more fully examined.

Our knowledge of the plant ash glass industry in the Near East remains particularly poor. While plant ash glass has been analysed from a variety of sources, including consumption sites in Israel (Sepphoris: Fischer and McCray 1999; Caesarea: Brill 1999); Syria (Al-Hadir: Gratuze and Foy 2012); Egypt (Raya and Fustat: Kato et al. 2010a; 2010b) and production sites in Raqqa, Syria (Henderson 1999; Henderson et al. 2004) and Tyre, Lebanon (Freestone 2002), a framework of named types and model of organisation for the plant ash industry, is still lacking. While some studies have attempted to infer more general trends (Fischer and McCray 1999; Brill and Stapleton 2012; Henderson et al. 2016), they have tended to lack either the quantities of samples, the accuracy of dating or the analytical precision to enable robust conclusions to be made. Therefore, important questions still remain concerning the number of production sites, the chronology and extent of glass compositional types, the characterisation of meaningful regional compositional groups and an understanding of how the industry operated as a whole.

This chapter presents the results of the analysis of plant ash glass vessels. The samples are taken from excavated consumer sites in Ramla dating from the early eighth century until the end of the twelfth century

CE, a period generally under-represented in the literature. This data complements previously analysed natron samples from Ramla (Phelps et al. 2016). Ramla was an important, wealthy city and thus provides a broad range of local and imported vessel types. The samples are mainly diagnostic vessel fragments, well dated from controlled excavations. Careful dating and a wide time period enables change through time to be examined. Analysis was by LA-ICP-MS, a highly precise and accurate technique able to fully characterise major, minor and trace elements. The analytical data, alongside the careful use of specific comparative data from a range of nearby regions, allows the characterisation of plant ash glass types and their periods of operation, thereby enabling the investigation of specific organisation questions regarding this industry.

Methodology

The samples

New analytical results are presented for 54 plant ash glass samples. These are a sub-set of 95 analysed samples excavated from Ramla, of which the remaining 41 natron glass vessels are published in Phelps et al. (2016). This full dataset will be referred to in the discussion only. Sampling strategy and dating is detailed in Phelps et al. (2016, 58) and will only be summarised here. The samples were selected from mainly diagnostic fragments of vessel glass selected to provide a representative selection of forms and fabrics with a preference towards common utilitarian forms (e.g. bottles, bowls, lamps) rather than unique types, although some were included (e.g. horn-shaped object, RAM 4768–06). Self-coloured, de-coloured and cobalt blue vessels were selected, while other coloured vessels (e.g. emerald green) were avoided. Table 11.1 presents site information, sample number and details of associated published site and glass reports for each sampling location. Vessel information (colour, context, date) for the 54 plant ash vessels is provided in Table 11.2 (for natron glass vessels see Phelps et al. 2016, Appendix C). Vessel drawings sourced from the published glass reports (see Table 11.2) are presented in Table 11.3.

Dating was of paramount importance. Vessels were dated through form and style by the glass specialists at the Israel Antiquities Authority, of which details can be found in the glass reports (Table 11.1). These dates were further constrained using stratigraphy, context and the use of coin or pottery finds. Ramla was founded *c.* 715 CE, providing a *terminus post quem* for the contexts. The glass dated from the early eighth to

Table 11.1 Details of the Ramla sampling sites – site excavation and glass reports are shown

Site	*Permit*	*Number of samples*	*Natron/ plant ash*	*Date range*	*Excavation report*	*Glass report*
Ramla	A-3592	5	2/3	7th–11th		Gorin-Rosen forthcoming
Danny Mass Street	A-3897	8	0/8	10th–11th	Shmueli 2012, 2016	Katsnelson 2016
Ma'asiyaha Junction	A-4740	13	4/9	8th–13th	Haddad 2013	Gorin-Rosen 2013
Lod-Na'an railroad track	A-4768	11	4/7	8th–late 11th	Haddad 2010	Gorin-Rosen 2010B
Ha-Nevi'im Nursery School	A-5947	31	24/7	8th–12th	Haddad 2011	Gorin-Rosen 2011
Ha-Etzel Street	A-6297	16	2/14	8th–11th	Toueg 2013	Winter 2013
Ha-Hez Street	A-6490	11	5/6	8th–early 11th	Toueg and Torgë 2015	Winter 2015

Table 11.2 Vessel details for the plant ash glass from Ramla (dating key at base of table, permit number and glass publication shown for each site)

Sample	*Colour*	*Figure**	*Form*	*Decoration*	*Group*	*Date*
Permit A-3592: Gorin-Rosen forthcoming						
RAM 3592 04	colourless	2.6	bottle	-	P-1	4–5
RAM 3592 05	colourless	2.8	bottle	mould blown	P-1	4–5
RAM 3592 06	colourless	2.9	small bottle	wheel cut	P-3	4–5
Permit A-3897: Danny Mass Street, Katsnelson 2016						
RAM 3897 01	colourless	2.5	bottle	-	P-1	5
RAM 3897 02	colourless	2.4	jar or lamp	trail	P-1	5
RAM 3897 03	colourless	1.8	lamp with wick tube	-	P-1	5
RAM 3897 04	colourless	1.9	bottle?	wheel cut	P-3	5
RAM 3897 05	blue	1.4	elongated bottle	-	P-4	5
RAM 3897 06	colourless	2.3	bowl	tonged	P-1	5
RAM 3897 07	colourless	1.3	straight-sided beaker	-	P-1	5
RAM 3897 08	colourless with greenish tinge	2.9	bottle	engraved star of David	P-1	5

Permit A-4740: Ma'asiyaha Junction, Gorin-Rosen 2013						
RAM 4740 02	colourless	1.3	bottle	wheel cut	P-3	5
RAM 4740 04	colourless	1.2	miniature ampoule	-	P-1	5
RAM 4740 05	colourless	1.6	vessel with octagonal cross-section	mould blown	P-2a	3
RAM 4740 06	very pale greenish yellow	1.9	large thick-rimmed jar	-	P-1	6
RAM 4740 08	colourless	-	-	-	P-1	5
RAM 4740 10	colourless	-	-	-	P-1	5
RAM 4740 11	pale blue	-	-	-	P-Outlier	5
RAM 4740 12	colourless	1.4	bottle with hexagonal cross-section	facet cut	P-3	5
RAM 4740 13	colourless	1.5	vessel	facet cut	P-3	5
Permit A-4768: Lod-Na'an railroad track, Gorin-Rosen 2010B						
RAM 4768 04	colourless	22.9	bottle with hexagonal cross-section	wheel cut	P-1	4
RAM 4768 05	colourless	22.8	bottle	wheel cut	P-3	4
RAM 4768 06	colourless	22.10	unique horn-like	wheel cut	P-1	4

(*continued*)

Table 11.2 (cont.)

Sample	*Colour*	*Figure**	*Form*	*Decoration*	*Group*	*Date*
RAM 4768 08	blue	22.6	bottle	-	P-4	4
RAM 4768 09	blue	22.3	thimble-like jar	-	P-4	4
RAM 4768 10	colourless	22.7	bowl	wheel cut with geometric designs	P-3	4
RAM 4768 11	colourless	22.4	ampoule	-	P-1	4
Permit A-5947: Ha-Nevi'im Nursery School, Gorin-Rosen 2011						
RAM 5947 17	greenish yellow	15.5	cup or bowl	-	P-3	3
RAM 5947 26	greenish yellow	16.1	low bowl	-	P-1	4
RAM 5947 27	colourless	16.2	-	-	P-1	4
RAM 5947 28	pale purple	16.4	cylindrical cup with wick tube	-	P-1	6
RAM 5947 29	colourless	16.5	square bottle	wheel cut	P-3	4
RAM 5947 30	colourless	16.3	jug or juglette	-	P-1	5
RAM 5947 31	colourless	16.6	bottle	wheel cut with grooved pattern	P-3	5

Permit A-6297: Ha-Etzel Street, Winter 2013						
RAM 6297 01	colourless with greenish tinge	36.2	small bowl with flaring rim	-	P-1	4
RAM 6297 02	light greenish blue	36.3	small bowl with out-curved rim	-	P-1	4
RAM 6297 03	colourless with bluish tinge	36.4	beaker	-	P-1	4
RAM 6297 05	cobalt blue	37.3	elongated bottle	-	P-4	4
RAM 6297 07	colourless	37.8	square section bottle	mould blown	P-3	4
RAM 6297 08	colourless	37.10	inkwell	-	P-1	4
RAM 6297 09	light greenish blue	38.1	large plate with out-splayed rim	-	P-1	5
RAM 6297 10	light greenish blue	38.2	large plate with out-splayed rim	-	P-1	5
RAM 6297 11	green	38.3	large plate with out-splayed rim	-	P-1	5
RAM 6297 12	colourless with greenish tinge	38.4	large jar with out-splayed rim	-	P-1	5
RAM 6297 13	green	38.5	bowl	-	P-1	5
RAM 6297 14	light olive green	38.6	unknown vessel	-	P-1	5

(*continued*)

Table 11.2 (cont.)

Sample	*Colour*	*Figure**	*Form*	*Decoration*	*Group*	*Date*
RAM 6297 15	light greenish blue	39.1	large bottle with thickened rim	-	P-1	5
RAM 6297 16	colourless	39.3	small jar with out-splaying rim	-	P-1	5
Permit A-6490: Ha-Hez Street, Winter 2015						
RAM 6490 05	colourless with yellowish tinge	1.8	cylindrical beaker	-	P-1	4
RAM 6490 06	light green	1.11	bottle	-	P-1	4
RAM 6490 07	cobalt blue	1.14	elongated bottle	-	P-4	4
RAM 6490 08	cobalt blue	1.15	elongated bottle	-	P-4	4
RAM 6490 09	cobalt blue	-	bottle	-	P-4	4
RAM 6490 11	colourless	1.13	square section miniature bottle	mould blown	P-3	4–5

* Figure number in associated glass publication.
1 Seventh century, late Byzantine–early Umayyad.
2 Early–mid-eighth century, Umayyad.
3 Mid–late eighth century, early Abbasid.
4 Ninth century, mid-Abbasid.
5 Tenth–eleventh century, late Abbasid-Fatimid.
6 Mid-eleventh–twelfth century, Fatimid-Crusader.
4–5 Ninth–early eleventh century. Samples are spread evenly over groups 4 and 5.

Table 11.3 Drawn image or photograph of the plant ash glass vessels where available (images not to scale)

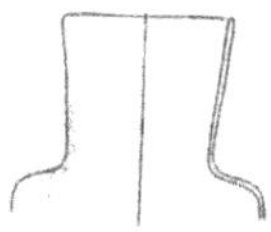	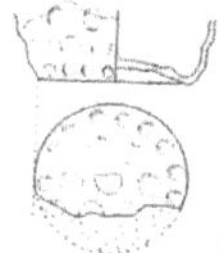	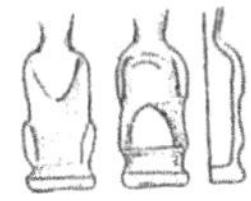	
RAM 3592-04	RAM 3592-05	RAM 3592-06	RAM 3847-01
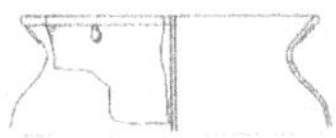	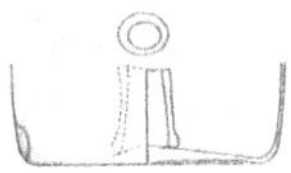	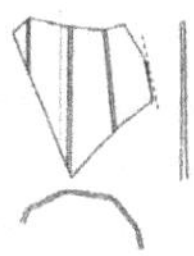	
RAM 3847-02	RAM 3847-03	RAM 3847-04	RAM 3847-05
		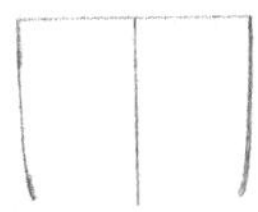	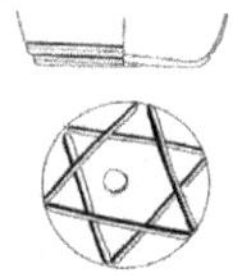
RAM 3847-06		AM 3847-07	RAM 3847-08
		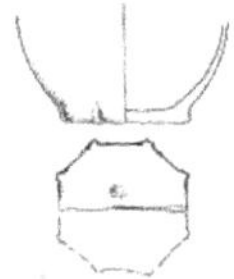	
RAM 4740-02	RAM 4740-04	RAM 4740-05	RAM 4740-06
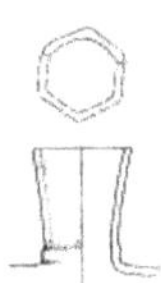	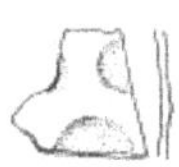	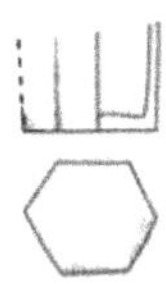	
RAM 4740-12	RAM 4740-13	RAM 4768-04	RAM 4768-05
	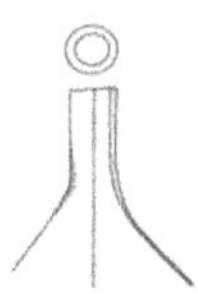		
RAM 4768-06	RAM 4768-08	RAM 4768-09	RAM 4768-10
	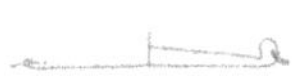		
RAM 4768-11	RAM 5947-17	RAM 5947-26	RAM 5947-27

(continued)

Table 11.3 (cont.)

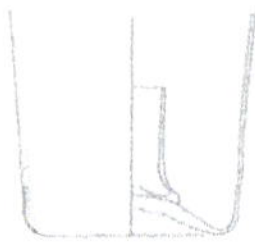 RAM 5947-28	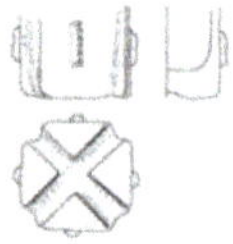 RAM 5947-29	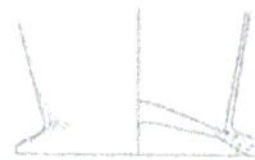 RAM 5947-30	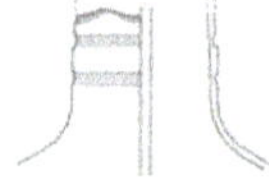 RAM 5947-31
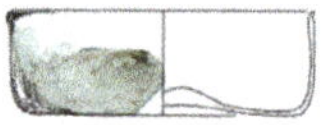 RAM 6297-01	 RAM 6297-02	 RAM 6297-03	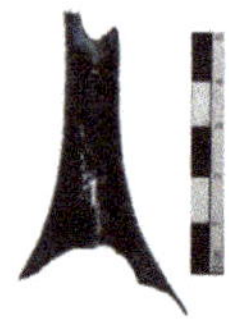 RAM 6297-05
 RAM 6297-07	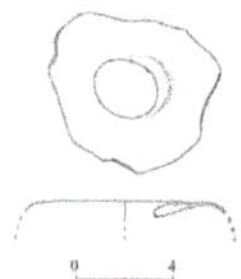 RAM 6297-08	 RAM 6297-09	
 RAM 6297-10		 RAM 6297-11	
 RAM 6297-12	 RAM 6297-13	 RAM 6297-14	 RAM 6297-15
 RAM 6297-16	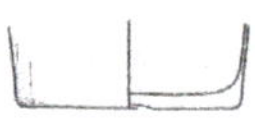 RAM 6490-05	 RAM 6490-06	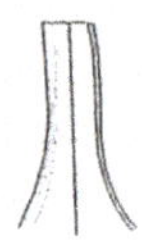 RAM 6490-07
 RAM 6490-08	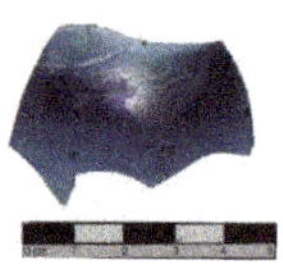 RAM 6490-09	 RAM 6490-11	

Images taken from publication reports, of which report reference and image number is given in Table 11.2.

the twelfth century CE, and were assigned to five dating brackets: late Umayyad (early-mid eighth century CE), early Abbasid (late eighth century CE), mid-Abbasid (ninth–tenth century CE), Abbasid-Fatimid (tenth–mid-eleventh century CE) and Fatimid-Crusader (mid-eleventh–twelfth century CE). While care was taken to make the dating as accurate as possible, there is a high probability of overlap between the groups, particularly with long-lived forms or where contextual information is not as precise. Five samples (two natron, three plant ash) dating to the ninth–mid-eleventh century CE were split equally between two adjacent dating categories.

The site

Ramla was founded as the new regional capital of Jund Filastin in *c.*715 CE by Caliph Sulayman (r. 715–717 CE), son of Caliph Al-Malik, while he was provincial governor (Luz 1997, 27). It replaced nearby Lod as capital (Schick 1998, 84). Ramla (Figure 11.1) was located in a densely populated and rich agricultural region. Some 15 km inland, it was situated on the crossroads between the Via Maris, connecting Damascus to Fustat, and the road linking the coast to Jerusalem, 40 km away. Its prime location meant that it was to become a large and prosperous city, excelling as a commercial centre, as well as benefitting from its administrative role. It also developed an important industrial base due to strong local agricultural production. Prominent industries included textile production, leather dyeing (Gutfeld 2010, 4) and agricultural products such as olives and fruit (Avni 2014, 177). Ramla was unique in being the only city in Palestine founded by Muslims and the first city founded in the region for 350 years (Luz 1997, 27). The city was built in a classical grid pattern centred around a core containing the White Mosque, administrative buildings and a palace. Markets lined the main streets leading to the eight city gates. The city became prosperous, particularly during the ninth and tenth centuries CE where urban expansion has been archaeologically recognised. The city reached an estimated 2.5 × 2.5 km in size at its height (Avni 2014 181–3), however, a combination of political instability, severe earthquakes in 1033 and 1068 CE and the Seljuq invasion of 1071 CE, saw the city sharply decline in the later eleventh century CE (Avni 2014 181–3). Previous investigations have identified large quantities of glass (Gorin-Rosen and Katsnelson 2005; Pollak 2005, 2007; Jackson-Tal 2008; Gorin-Rosen 2010a), with Gorin-Rosen (2010a, 250) particularly noting the rich diversity of forms and fabrics, such as the high-quality glass with cut decoration apparent in the

Figure 11.1 Map of ancient Palestine divided into the military districts of Jund Filastin and Jund al-Urdunn. Ramla is marked, as are the important city of Jerusalem and regional capital Tiberias. Glass production sites Apollonia, Bet Eli'ezer and Tyre are also labelled. Based on Avni 2014, fig. 1.3.

Fatimid period. Pollak (2007, 131) also commented on these high-quality types, suggesting some vessels were imported.

The glass used for this study is taken from seven excavated locations. These have published excavation reports shown in Table 11.1.

They were mainly salvage excavations conducted by the Israel Antiquities Authority over the last 15 years. The sites were areas of glass consumption, consisting of buildings, streets, dumps and fills, located within the confines of the old city. These sites provided generally good stratigraphy and numerous finds for dating. Each site has a Permit number (e.g. A-3592), which can be used to identify the site in the excavation literature.

Analytical procedure and data processing

Full details of the methods are published elsewhere (Phelps et al. 2016, 58–9) and only a summary is provided. Analysis was by LA-ICP-MS (laser ablation inductively coupled plasma mass spectrometry) performed at the Ernest-Babelon Laboratory, IRAMAT, Orleans, France under the supervision of Bernard Gratuze. This is a high accuracy and high precision technique allowing the quantification of 58 elements with detection limits down to 0.01 ppm depending on the element (Gratuze 2016). Glass from sites with Permits A-4740, A-4768 and A-5947 were analysed during Campaign 1 and the remaining samples during Campaign 2 (see Phelps et al. 2016, 59), each using a different ablation device but the same mass spectrometer. Calibration and quantification was performed with five reference standards, analysed periodically, as described by Gratuze (2014).

Data exploration utilised statistical and graphical techniques, with the final groupings created by means of hierarchical cluster analysis (HCA) using Ward's method performed in R (version 3.12). This method utilised the error sum of the squares with the distance between the points represented by squared Euclidian distances (see Shennan 1997, 741). Data was input as standardised variables. Results were displayed using principal component analysis (PCA).

Results

Group identification

Individual sample results are presented in Table 11.4 for major, minor and selected trace elements. Of the 95 vessels from Ramla, 54 were identified as plant ash glass based on the contents of potash and magnesia as outlined in Phelps et al. (2016, 60). Groupings within these glasses were investigated using an iterative process of hierarchical cluster analysis. This process demonstrated six major oxides to be the most effective in

Table 11.4 LA-ICP-MS data for the plant ash glass samples sorted by compositional group (wt% or ppm as labelled)

	Major and minor elements as wt%											*Trace elements as ppm*					
P-1 tyre type	Na_2O	MgO	Al_2O_3	SiO_2	P_2O_5	Cl	K_2O	CaO	TiO_2	MnO	Fe_2O_3	CoO	CuO	SrO	ZrO_2	BaO	PbO
RAM 3592 04	13.37	3.19	2.10	65.10	0.26	0.79	2.28	10.20	0.10	1.85	0.60	6.7	62	581	53	330	8.9
RAM 3592 05	13.45	3.20	2.14	64.83	0.27	0.80	2.30	10.24	0.11	1.90	0.61	5.9	62	583	53	333	8.4
RAM 3897 01	12.51	2.79	2.11	68.13	0.34	0.94	2.78	8.10	0.12	1.40	0.62	5.8	16	684	57	393	8.9
RAM 3897 02	12.11	2.34	2.15	68.11	0.32	0.91	2.72	8.92	0.09	1.65	0.53	5.1	16	687	49	385	9.1
RAM 3897 03	12.09	2.96	1.58	69.85	0.25	0.81	2.86	8.60	0.06	0.49	0.31	2.1	23	597	43	252	3.1
RAM 3897 06	12.56	2.57	2.04	69.18	0.25	0.69	2.45	9.15	0.06	0.55	0.36	2.3	18	657	40	298	6.8
RAM 3897 07	12.02	2.94	1.58	69.85	0.24	0.81	2.77	8.74	0.06	0.55	0.31	2.1	23	620	42	262	3.0
RAM 3897 08	11.77	2.78	1.79	68.43	0.34	0.93	3.19	9.37	0.09	0.69	0.46	3.3	37	1003	49	234	9.6
RAM 4740 04	13.73	2.81	1.75	67.89	0.28	0.71	2.18	9.13	0.05	0.98	0.33	3.2	15	709	32	288	12.2
RAM 4740 06	11.93	2.73	1.77	70.10	0.31	0.73	2.40	8.37	0.09	0.91	0.54	5.0	40	529	48	271	10.6
RAM 4740 08	9.81	2.92	1.78	70.37	0.32	0.62	2.19	10.47	0.08	0.83	0.46	3.7	37	731	48	283	17.5
RAM 4740 10	9.63	2.85	1.73	70.94	0.31	0.61	2.19	10.22	0.08	0.83	0.46	3.7	38	716	45	285	17.5
RAM 4768 04	13.17	3.29	1.79	67.77	0.26	0.72	2.61	9.00	0.06	0.76	0.41	2.6	14	728	35	346	10.3
RAM 4768 06	13.90	2.70	1.72	68.23	0.28	0.78	2.10	8.56	0.08	1.05	0.48	3.7	39	467	43	219	6.5
RAM 4768 11	13.60	2.71	1.68	70.09	0.27	0.82	2.61	6.74	0.08	0.85	0.43	3.1	35	437	41	198	4.2
RAM 5947 26	12.01	2.93	2.02	66.25	0.35	0.61	1.97	11.48	0.09	1.52	0.60	4.5	62	636	54	327	17.6
RAM 5947 27	12.23	3.07	1.51	69.34	0.26	0.71	2.30	9.33	0.07	0.67	0.38	2.7	37	715	39	252	7.4
RAM 5947 28	12.99	2.71	1.83	69.82	0.24	0.73	2.24	7.69	0.07	1.11	0.45	4.0	38	500	40	263	6.1

RAM 5947 30	12.05	2.95	1.58	70.80	0.24	0.73	2.20	8.31	0.06	0.59	0.34	2.0	22	696	42	251	4.9
RAM 6297 01	12.13	3.37	1.79	69.07	0.25	0.76	2.22	8.98	0.08	0.75	0.45	2.6	32	596	46	209	4.0
RAM 6297 02	12.27	3.37	1.68	68.55	0.26	0.66	2.30	9.46	0.08	0.72	0.49	14.7	59	661	53	241	82.1
RAM 6297 03	11.58	3.20	2.01	67.62	0.29	0.64	2.30	10.37	0.09	1.15	0.59	6.7	62	574	56	259	90.9
RAM 6297 08	12.18	3.02	1.99	69.90	0.23	0.81	2.05	7.67	0.11	1.25	0.67	5.0	49	438	57	232	6.4
RAM 6297 09	11.69	2.45	2.21	68.53	0.40	0.83	2.51	9.85	0.12	0.51	0.75	4.3	20	681	59	240	62.7
RAM 6297 10	12.08	2.27	1.97	69.70	0.36	0.88	2.61	7.87	0.10	1.41	0.59	5.5	16	636	53	305	8.7
RAM 6297 11	12.23	2.92	2.21	69.45	0.34	0.87	2.38	7.26	0.13	1.32	0.76	6.0	17	541	56	334	12.1
RAM 6297 12	10.64	3.19	1.87	68.85	0.28	0.58	2.35	10.36	0.07	1.19	0.47	3.6	46	671	45	262	6.9
RAM 6297 13	12.25	3.00	2.25	69.02	0.34	0.88	2.39	7.35	0.13	1.48	0.76	6.3	17	555	58	364	10.6
RAM 6297 14	11.62	2.32	2.09	68.97	0.40	0.84	2.51	9.82	0.11	0.49	0.68	3.9	18	658	58	226	38.5
RAM 6297 15	11.57	2.55	2.06	67.78	0.39	0.77	3.31	10.14	0.11	0.51	0.67	4.1	21	728	54	234	60.2
RAM 6297 16	11.52	2.46	2.28	70.36	0.35	0.87	2.11	7.41	0.12	1.61	0.76	6.7	33	592	55	358	136.1
RAM 6490 05	11.95	3.52	1.89	67.33	0.26	0.64	2.43	10.35	0.07	0.92	0.46	4.1	47	792	45	299	7.1
RAM 6490 06	12.33	3.46	2.03	66.06	0.28	0.67	2.81	10.45	0.07	1.15	0.51	23.7	76	820	45	333	59.0
Average	**12.15**	**2.90**	**1.91**	**68.67**	**0.30**	**0.76**	**2.44**	**9.09**	**0.09**	**1.02**	**0.52**	**5.11**	**35**	**643**	**48**	**284**	**23.0**
St Dev	*0.95*	*0.33*	*0.22*	*1.52*	*0.05*	*0.10*	*0.31*	*1.17*	*0.02*	*0.41*	*0.14*	*4.05*	*17.37*	*114*	*7*	*52*	*31.16*

(continued)

Table 11.4 (cont.)

	Major and minor elements as wt%											*Trace elements as ppm*					
P-2 Syrian Type	**Na_2O**	**MgO**	**Al_2O_3**	**SiO_2**	**P_2O_5**	**Cl**	**K_2O**	**CaO**	**TiO_2**	**MnO**	**Fe_2O_3**	**CoO**	**CuO**	**SrO**	**ZrO_2**	**BaO**	**PbO**
RAM 4740 05	13.34	3.06	0.97	68.45	0.38	0.88	2.57	8.55	0.07	1.20	0.38	5.3	29	589	136	148	21.9
P-3 Nishapur Colourless	**Na_2O**	**MgO**	**Al_2O_3**	**SiO_2**	**P_2O_5**	**Cl**	**K_2O**	**CaO**	**TiO_2**	**MnO**	**Fe_2O_3**	**CoO**	**CuO**	**SrO**	**ZrO_2**	**BaO**	**PbO**
RAM 3592 06	12.65	4.84	1.08	69.03	0.14	0.72	3.09	7.58	0.03	0.51	0.23	1.8	10	449	31	173	2.1
RAM 3897 04	13.10	5.39	0.83	70.18	0.10	0.71	2.96	6.09	0.05	0.25	0.23	1.8	13	522	90	77	3.1
RAM 4740 02	11.15	4.82	1.03	73.35	0.09	0.53	2.12	6.18	0.03	0.34	0.27	2.4	9	432	36	127	4.2
RAM 4740 12	13.31	4.71	1.11	71.49	0.10	0.63	2.08	5.84	0.05	0.22	0.36	2.2	8	377	50	95	4.8
RAM 4740 13	10.59	5.10	1.02	73.43	0.08	0.49	1.90	6.56	0.04	0.40	0.29	3.1	7	462	44	115	5.8
RAM 4768 05	10.55	4.66	0.94	74.16	0.10	0.62	2.32	5.87	0.03	0.43	0.23	2.1	7	401	36	114	3.3
RAM 4768 10	12.24	4.06	0.81	72.82	0.10	0.58	2.79	5.86	0.04	0.37	0.24	1.3	11	447	58	106	3.9
RAM 5947 29	12.02	4.74	1.00	72.76	0.08	0.57	2.13	5.95	0.03	0.35	0.29	2.4	7	390	37	109	4.7
RAM 5947 31	11.73	5.16	1.02	71.36	0.12	0.56	2.42	6.74	0.03	0.47	0.28	3.3	17	495	34	122	4.3
RAM 6297 07	13.23	5.47	0.82	69.66	0.12	0.69	3.24	6.27	0.02	0.21	0.17	1.9	11	479	32	91	1.9
RAM 6490 11	14.07	5.13	1.21	69.30	0.12	0.56	2.80	5.45	0.07	0.79	0.36	5.1	15	498	162	165	2.9
RAM 6490 12	11.61	5.27	0.91	71.99	0.09	0.64	2.34	6.51	0.03	0.30	0.23	2.1	9	460	41	102	1.5
RAM 5947 17	13.97	4.44	1.75	69.34	0.20	0.63	2.84	4.58	0.09	1.40	0.62	6.0	37	343	119	329	8.1
Average	**12.19**	**4.95**	**0.98**	**71.63**	**0.10**	**0.61**	**2.51**	**6.24**	**0.04**	**0.39**	**0.27**	**2.4**	**10**	**451**	**54**	**116**	**3.5**
St Dev	*1.18*	*0.40*	*0.24*	*1.79*	*0.03*	*0.07*	*0.43*	*0.70*	*0.02*	*0.32*	*0.11*	*1.37*	*8.00*	*52*	*40*	*65*	*1.79*

P-4 Nishapur Coloured	**Na_2O**	**MgO**	**Al_2O_3**	**SiO_2**	**P_2O_5**	**Cl**	**K_2O**	**CaO**	**TiO_2**	**MnO**	**Fe_2O_3**	**CoO**	**CuO**	**SrO**	**ZrO_2**	**BaO**	**PbO**
RAM 3897 05	14.42	2.73	1.83	65.00	0.23	0.62	2.25	9.60	0.13	1.03	1.60	1060	1907	745	127	244	168
RAM 4768 08	13.42	2.72	2.33	68.47	0.22	0.71	2.15	6.35	0.14	1.11	1.85	699	2176	354	141	206	144
RAM 4768 09	12.39	2.52	2.20	69.25	0.28	0.78	1.65	8.25	0.16	0.74	1.37	511	1677	484	135	214	228
RAM 6297 05	11.73	3.12	3.09	67.88	0.19	0.74	1.59	5.65	0.20	1.26	3.43	1594	6093	430	281	311	296
RAM 6490 07	13.58	3.27	1.91	65.52	0.23	0.76	1.57	7.26	0.10	2.11	2.89	1904	3877	343	30	233	79
RAM 6490 08	11.94	2.70	2.13	68.35	0.19	0.73	1.77	5.89	0.14	2.04	2.94	1942	6388	474	146	202	196
RAM 6490 09	12.90	2.70	2.42	67.48	0.19	0.79	2.30	6.52	0.16	1.37	2.22	1104	4600	365	152	302	310
Average	**12.91**	**2.82**	**2.27**	**67.42**	**0.22**	**0.73**	**1.90**	**7.07**	**0.15**	**1.38**	**2.33**	**1259**	**3817**	**457**	**145**	**245**	**203**
St Dev	*0.96*	*0.27*	*0.42*	*1.58*	*0.03*	*0.06*	*0.32*	*1.42*	*0.03*	*0.52*	*0.77*	*567*	*1972*	*140*	*73*	*45*	*82*

Note: Mean and standard deviation at base of each group. bdl = below detection limit.

separating the vessels. Three oxides (P_2O_5, MgO and CaO) are most associated with the plant ash component and the remaining oxides (Al_2O_3, Fe_2O_3, ZrO_2) are most associated with the silica component. (Fe_2O_3 was also linked to the cobalt additive, see below). Each of these components is therefore related to the regional geology in which the raw materials were formed and thus they form a suitable basis on which to meaningfully separate the glass. Some notable oxides were avoided: K_2O due to the similarity between all the samples, and TiO_2 due to its strong correlation with ZrO_2. Other trace elements were also omitted at this stage, but are discussed later.

The results of HCA are presented in Figure 11.2. This image presents 53 of the 54 samples, one sample (RAM 4740–05) forms part of a larger group P-2, and will be discussed elsewhere (Phelps et al. forthcoming). The remaining samples separate into 3 groups; P-1, P-3 and P-4. The first separation is at over dissimilarity 250 creating P-3, a mainly coherent group of 13 vessels. The second major split occurs at around dissimilarity 150. This forms the largest grouping, P-1, containing 33 samples. This group exhibits additional branching around dissimilarity 25, however, further investigation identified no justifiable separation based on composition, chronology or location, with differences probably due to natural variability in the plant ash and sand (see later). The final group is P-4, containing seven vessels, of which one sample, RAM 6297–05, appears to separate slightly from the main group. Group averages for selected major, minor and trace elements are presented in Table 11.5.

The principal component analysis image in Figure 11.3 displays how these groups relate to each other using PCs 1 and 2, which describe 52.38 per cent and 34.91 per cent of the variation respectively. The image demonstrates clear separation between the groups, with P-1 distinguished by high CaO, P_2O_5 and Al_2O_3; P-3 with high levels of MgO but low in the remaining oxides; and P-4 characterised by high amounts of Fe_2O_3, ZrO_2, and Al_2O_3.

Group identification was performed against a range of comparative data selected from a spread of geographical locations with an emphasis on sites with high-quality data, of the corresponding time periods, and from which glass compositional groups have been identified. Comparative samples included Islamic period glass from: Raqqa, Syria (Raqqa Type 1: Henderson et al. 2004; 2016); Banias, Israel (Freestone et al. 2000); Fustat, Egypt (Group 3 (A), this is a sub-set of Gratuze and Barrandon 1990 Group 3); Tyre, Lebanon (Freestone 2002); Nishapur, Iran (Nishapur Coloured and Colourless, Brill 1995) and Samarra, Iraq (Henderson et al. 2016) and Sasanian glass from Veh

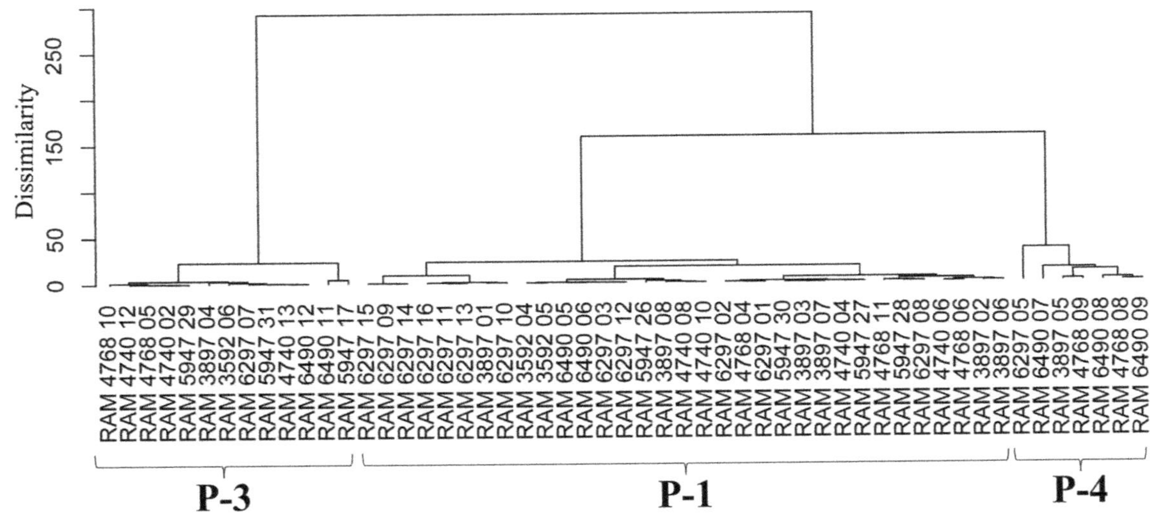

Figure 11.2 Labelled dendrogram displaying the results of the hierarchical cluster analysis by Ward's method. N = 53. Oxides used are Al_2O_3, Fe_2O_3, ZrO_2, P_2O_5, CaO and MgO.

Table 11.5 Group average and flux oxide ratios (wt% unless otherwise marked)

Group	Type	Colour†	N.		Na_2O	MgO	Al_2O_3	SiO_2	P_2O_5	Cl	K_2O	CaO	TiO_2	MnO	Fe_2O_3	CoO*	SrO*	ZrO_2*	MgO/CaO	K_2O/P_2O_5
P-1	Tyre Type[1]	Colour-less	33	**m**	**12.15**	**2.90**	**1.91**	**68.67**	**0.30**	**0.76**	**2.44**	**9.09**	**0.09**	**1.02**	**0.52**	**5**	**643**	**48**	**0.32**	**8.22**
				s.d	*0.95*	*0.33*	*0.22*	*1.52*	*0.05*	*0.10*	*0.31*	*1.17*	*0.02*	*0.41*	*0.14*	*17*	*114*	*7*		
P-3	Nishapur Colourless Type[2]	Colour-less	13	**m**	**12.19**	**4.95**	**0.98**	**71.63**	**0.10**	**0.61**	**2.51**	**6.24**	**0.04**	**0.39**	**0.27**	**2**	**451**	**54**	**0.79**	**24.42**
				s.d	*1.18*	*0.40*	*0.24*	*1.79*	*0.03*	*0.07*	*0.43*	*0.70*	*0.02*	*0.32*	*0.11*	*8*	*52*	*40*		
P-4	Nishapur Coloured Type[2]	cobalt blue	7	**m**	**12.91**	**2.82**	**2.27**	**67.42**	**0.22**	**0.73**	**1.90**	**7.07**	**0.15**	**1.38**	**2.33**	**1259**	**457**	**145**	**0.40**	**8.67**
				s.d	*0.96*	*0.27*	*0.42*	*1.58*	*0.03*	*0.06*	*0.32*	*1.42*	*0.03*	*0.52*	*0.77*	*1972*	*140*	*73*		

m = mean

s.d = standard deviation

* ppm

† most frequent colour

1 LA-ICP-MS re-analysed by Phelps and Freestone. Original publication Freestone et al. 2000 and Freestone 2002.

2 LA-ICP-MS re-analysed by Lankton (pers. comms.) using LA-ICP-MS; coloured samples removed.

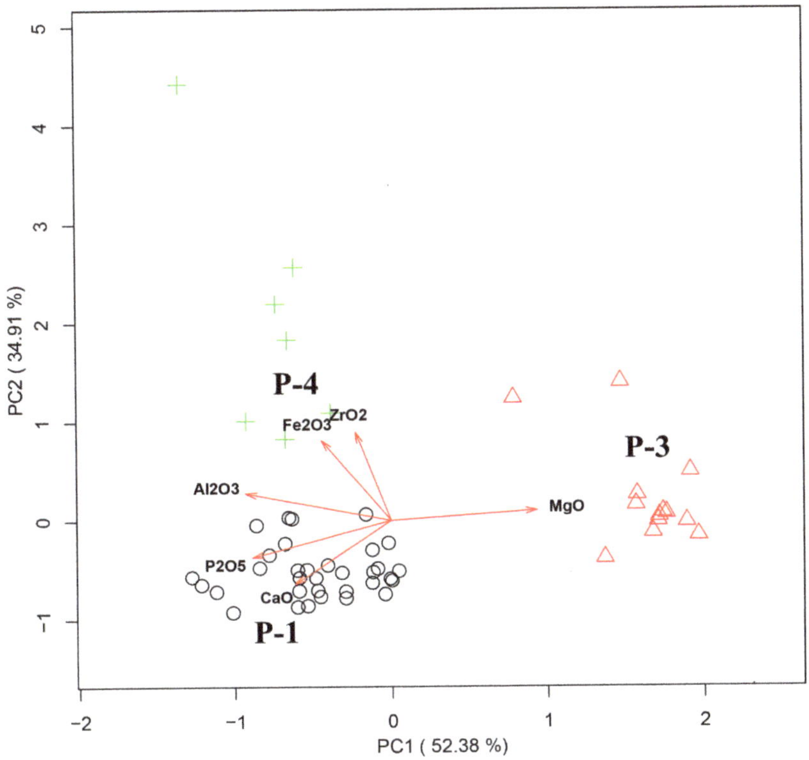

Figure 11.3 Principal component analysis bi-plot. Number of samples, names of groups and selected oxides as in Figure 11.2. Oxide weightings are marked.

Ardašīr, Iraq (Sasanian 1a, 1b and 2; Mirti et al. 2008; 2009). The data best relating to groups P-1, P-3 and P-4 is presented in Figure 11.4. P-1 conforms most closely to glass from the primary production site of Tyre dating to the tenth–eleventh century CE (Freestone 2002; unpublished data from Freestone and Phelps). While groups P-3 and P-4 display similarity to several Sasanian and Mesopotamian/Iranian Islamic glasses but are closest to the Nishapur Coloured and Colourless groups respectively. These two groups were first identified by Brill (1995), although the data used here is unpublished LA-ICP-MS data (Lankton pers. comms.).

Compositional characteristics of the groups

The composition of glass is reliant upon the raw materials: principally the flux and silica source. Natron glass is characterised mainly by its silica

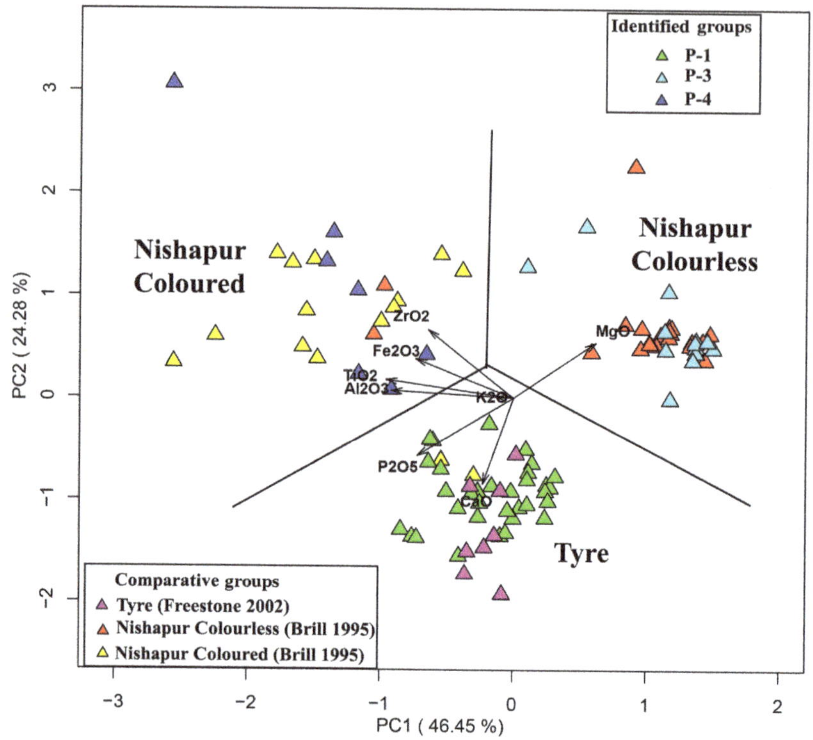

Figure 11.4 Main principle components with comparative data. Oxides used: Fe_2O_3, ZrO_2, TiO_2, Al_2O_3, K_2O, P_2O_5, CaO and MgO. Site references in key. Data sources are re-analysed LA-ICP-MS for Tyre (unpublished data from Freestone and Phelps) and Nishapur (Lankton pers. comms.).

source as defined by the mineralogy of the sand and geochemistry of the region (Freestone 2006). Plant ash glass is more complex, characterised by the silica source and also the plant ash, which is much more compositionally variable than natron. The composition of plant ash is dependent on geology and hydrology of where the plant grows (Barkoudah and Henderson 2006), on plant species (Brill 1970; Tite et al. 2006) and climate, but also on anthropogenic factors, such as the duration and temperature of ashing (Rye 1976; Tite et al. 2006) and any ash purification that may have taken place (McCray 1998). In the characterisation of the groups below, a distinction will therefore be made between the elements most related to the plant ash (e.g. Na, K, P, Ca, Mg; Barkoudah and Henderson 2006) and those most related to the silica source (e.g. Ti, Zr,

Fe, Al etc; see Degryse and Shortland 2009; Brems and Degryse 2014). The plant ash components will be used to define three broad regional types while the silica-related elements will be used to identify more localised production types where possible.

Eastern Mediterranean glass: P-1 Tyre type

The flux elements of P-1 are characterised by high CaO (9 per cent; see Table 11.5), relatively high P_2O_5 (0.3 per cent) and relatively low MgO (2.9 per cent). Figure 11.5 presents MgO/CaO against Al_2O_3 for the Ramla glasses against comparative glass taken from the eastern Mediterranean sites (Tyre, Raqqa, Banias, Fustat) and Mesopotamian/Iranian sites (Nishapur, Veh Ardašīr, Samarra). Data sources and average values for selected groups are given in Table 11.6. Figure 11.5 separates the glass into three broad regions. P-1, with its low MgO/CaO ratio (0.32; Table 11.5), falls to the left-hand side of the image alongside glass from other eastern Mediterranean sites. The MgO/CaO ratio for P-1 matches the 0.28–0.37 range given for Tyre, Raqqa Type 1, Banias and Egypt. A similar trend can be seen in the K_2O/P_2O_5 ratio, with P-1 falling within the 6.45–8.84 range of the other eastern Mediterranean glasses. Both ratios contrast with the generally higher values of the Mesopotamian/Iranian glass, although some overlap is seen with the P-4 group. It is suggested here that the glass from the eastern Mediterranean used a similar plant ash type, distinguished by its high lime content. The wide regional similarity is possibly due to geological similarities within the eastern Mediterranean, in addition to the possible use of similar plant species and potentially similar burning or ashing practises. This grouping, designated Eastern Mediterranean, demonstrates that it is possible to identify regional plant ash types.

In silica-related oxides, the vessels of P-1 very closely match the composition of the working waste and chunks analysed from the production site of Tyre (Figure 11.6), suggesting the P-1 glass to be made with the same raw materials and similar recipe, and likely sharing a production area. P-1 has relatively high alumina (1.91 per cent), while zirconia (48 ppm), titania (0.09 per cent) and iron oxide (0.52 per cent) are quite low. Figure 11.6 also indicates a spread in the TiO_2 and ZrO_2 concentrations, most likely due to natural variation in the rutile and zircon abundance in the sand. While P-1 overlaps slightly with that of Sasanian 1b group in Figure 11.6, the differences in other elements mean that P-1/Tyre glass is recognised as an exclusive group. The sands at Tyre are recognised as a mature sand, high in silica, relatively high in alumina, but

Table 11.6 Comparative data group averages and flux element ratios (data sources at base of table, wt% except for ZrO_2 in ppm)

Location	*Type*	*Date*	*N*		*Na_2O*	*MgO*	*Al_2O_3*	*SiO_2*	*P_2O_5*	*Cl*	*K_2O*	*CaO*	*TiO_2*	*MnO*	*Fe_2O_3*	*ZrO_2*	*MgO/CaO*	*K_2O/P_2O_5*
Eastern Mediterranean																		
Tyre, Lebanon*	Tyre Type	10th–11th	8	**m**	**12.85**	**3.61**	**1.81**	**65.06**	**0.33**	**0.76**	**2.26**	**11.21**	**0.09**	**1.33**	**0.54**	**52**	**0.32**	**6.85**
				sd	*1.22*	*0.26*	*0.32*	*1.65*	*0.05*	*0.11*	*0.22*	*2.15*	*0.01*	*0.67*	*0.05*	*3*		
Banias, Israel*		11th–13th	12	**m**	**11.98**	**2.4**	**1.21**	**71.65**	**0.24**	**0.86**	**1.52**	**8.59**	**0.12**	**0.83**	**0.48**	**170**	**0.28**	**6.33**
				sd	*0.57*	*0.57*	*0.62*	*1.15*	*0.04*	*0.07*	*0.35*	*0.98*	*0.02*	*0.28*	*0.1*	*38*		
Raqqa, Syria	Raqqa Type 1	8th–11th	90	**m**	**12.93**	**3.43**	**1.2**	**67.49**	**0.28**	**0.77**	**2.52**	**9.31**	**0.07**	**1.14**	**0.56**	**142‡**	**0.37**	**9.00**
				sd	*1.4*	*0.32*	*0.19*	*1.51*	*0.04*	*0.13*	*0.36*	*1.45*	*0.01*	*0.55*	*0.31*	*13*		
Fustat, Egypt§	Egypt Group 3 (A)	10th–11th	7	**m**	**14**	**2.83**	**2.24**	**66.17**	**n/a**	**n/a**	**2.26**	**9.17**	**0.17**	**1.2**	**0.85**	**96**	**0.31**	
				sd	*1.24*	*0.28*	*0.11*	*1.19*	*n/a*	*n/a*	*0.28*	*0.36*	*0.02*	*0.08*	*0.13*	*20*		
Mesopotamian Type 1																		
Veh Ardašīr, Iraq#	Sasanian 1a	3rd–7th	29	**m**	**16.01**	**4.05**	**2.28**	**60.02**	**0.31**	**n/a**	**3.32**	**6.7**	**0.18**	**0.15**	**1.09**	**305**	**0.60**	**10.71**
				sd	*1.39*	*0.43*	*0.57*	*2.52*	*0.06*	*n/a*	*0.42*	*1.03*	*0.04*	*0.42*	*0.32*	*118*		
	Sasanian 1b	3rd–7th	11	**m**	**16.02**	**4.1**	**2.19**	**60.49**	**0.27**	**n/a**	**3.41**	**6.74**	**0.13**	**0.12**	**0.91**	**64**	**0.61**	**12.63**
				sd	*1.44*	*0.43*	*0.34*	*1.76*	*0.07*	*n/a*	*0.4*	*0.83*	*0.03*	*0.25*	*0.21*	*20*		
Nishapur, Iran†	Nishapur Coloured	9th–10th	15	**m**	**15.86**	**3.76**	**3.05**	**64.68**	**0.32**	**0.76**	**2.91**	**6.78**	**0.15**	**0.39**	**1.12**	**130**	**0.55**	**9.09**
				sd	*1.63*	*1.22*	*0.83*	*2.63*	*0.08*	*0.19*	*0.5*	*1.03*	*0.04*	*0.45*	*0.2*	*42*		

Mesopotamian Type 2																	
Veh Ardašīr, Iraq[#]	Sasanian 2	3rd–7th	13	**m**	**17.43**	**7.13**	**1.62**	**58.63**	**0.13**	**n/a**	**2.8**	**5.55**	**0.09**	**0.18**	**0.6**	**71**	**1.28**	**21.54**
				sd	*1.14*	*0.93*	*0.41*	*3.16*	*0.02*	*n/a*	*0.42*	*0.88*	*0.02*	*0.21*	*0.17*	*18*		
Nishapur, Iran[†]	Nishapur Colourless	9th–10th	22	**m**	**12.53**	**4.69**	**1.17**	**71.18**	**0.12**	**0.65**	**2.45**	**6.27**	**0.05**	**0.4**	**0.37**	**73**	**0.75**	**20.42**
				sd	*1.48*	*0.57*	*0.48*	*2.52*	*0.06*	*0.08*	*0.38*	*0.67*	*0.03*	*0.2*	*0.23*	*39*		
Samarra, Iraq[‡]		9th–10th	21	**m**	**14.52**	**6.66**	**0.94**	**67.92**	**0.08**	**n/a**	**2.45**	**5.09**	**0.06**	**0.85**	**0.4**	**96**	**1.37**	**34.08**
				sd	*1.29*	*0.83*	*0.33*	*2.43*	*0.03*	*n/a*	*0.41*	*1.15*	*0.02*	*0.87*	*0.21*	*59*		

*LA-ICP-MS re-analysed by Phelps and Freestone. Original publication Freestone et al. 2000 and Freestone 2002.

§ = LA-ICP-MS, sub-set of Group 3 in Gratuze and Barrandon (1990). Mamluk dated samples omitted.

† = LA-ICP-MS re-analysed by Lankton (pers. comms.) using LA-ICP-MS; coloured samples removed

= sol ICP-MS in Mirti et al. 2008, 2009. Samples from Veh Ardašīr only.

‡ = LA-ICP-MS in Henderson et al. 2016

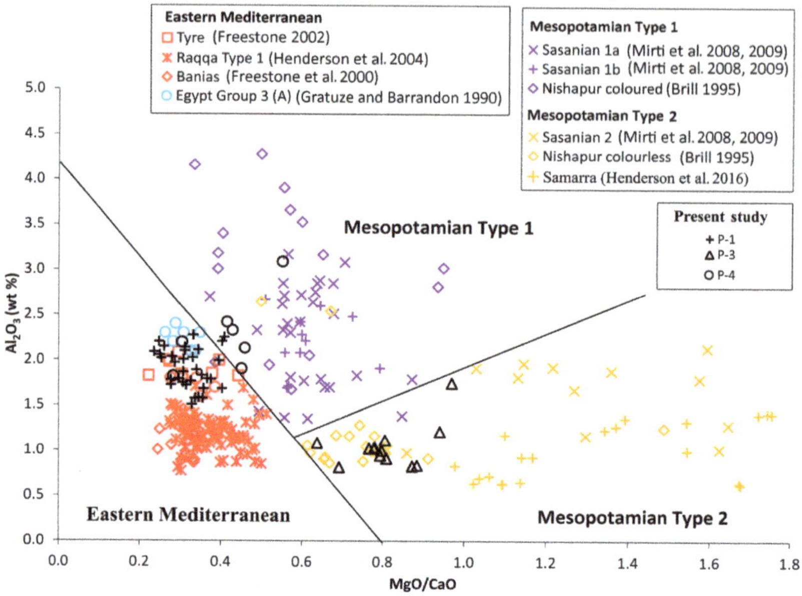

Figure 11.5 Al_2O_3 against MgO/CaO comparing the identified groups against comparative groups. The spread of vessels suggest three broad groups, which are marked and labelled. Data sources in key (further details at base of Table 11.3).

also low in lime (Freestone 2002). Literature evidence discussing glass production at Tyre notes that sand was taken from 'on the same plain' as Tyre (Carboni et al. 2003), although this location is unknown and current geological understanding of the region has shown the sands and sediments to be mainly lime rich (Beydoun 1976; Nir 1996) and therefore unsuitable for plant ash glass.

Mesopotamian Type 2: P-3 Nishapur Colourless

P-3 is a group of 13 vessels characterised by high MgO (4.95 per cent), relatively high K_2O (2.51 per cent) and low P_2O_5 (0.10 per cent) and CaO (6.24 per cent). In Figure 11.5 this group principally overlays the Nishapur Coloured glass but also a portion of the Sasanian glass from Veh Ardašīr and Islamic glass from Samarra. The flux element ratios for P-3 is 0.79 and 24.42 for MgO/CaO and K_2O/P_2O_5 respectively, this is particularly high and matches the Sasanian 2, Nishapur Colourless and Samarran groups, which have average ratios ranging from 0.75–1.35 and 20.42–34.00 respectively (Table 11.6). These groups are

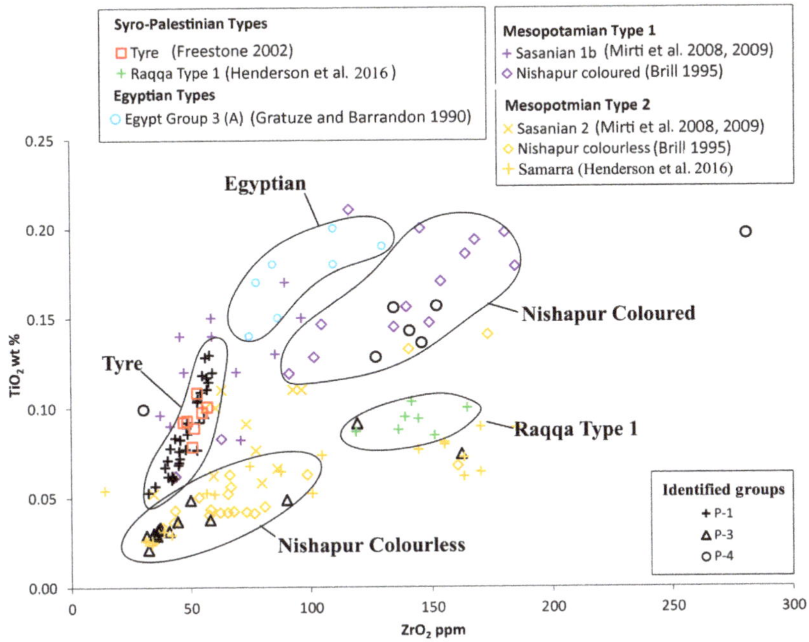

Figure 11.6 TiO_2 against ZrO_2 for the identified groups and comparative groups. Image demonstrates separation between the principal groups. Data sources in key, except Tyre and Nishapur which are re-analysed LA-ICP-MS data from Phelps and Freestone (unpublished) and Lankton (pers. comms.) respectively.

distinctly different from the eastern Mediterranean glass but also from the other Mesopotamian and Iranian glass. This flux type is designated Mesopotamian Type 2.

While the flux provides a broad compositional type, the elements related to the silica suggest finer groupings. The P-3 glass is distinct, with very low Al_2O_3 (~1 per cent), Fe_2O_3 (0.27 per cent) and TiO_2 (0.04 per cent), although ZrO_2 is slightly higher than P-1 at 54 ppm. These values suggest a clean silica source, matching Nishapur Colourless, as shown in Figure 11.6. Further matches in terms of trace elements, particularly V, Cr, Ga, Nb and Th, as well as the REE profile, can be seen in Figure 11.7, this is particularly true for Nishapur Colourless but also for Sasanian 2. The purity of the silica-source, and particularly the low concentration of alumina, led Mirti et al. (2009, 1067) to suggest the use of crushed quartz pebbles in Sasanian 2 rather than sand. As the raw materials used for P-3 are equally pure, the use of crushed quartz

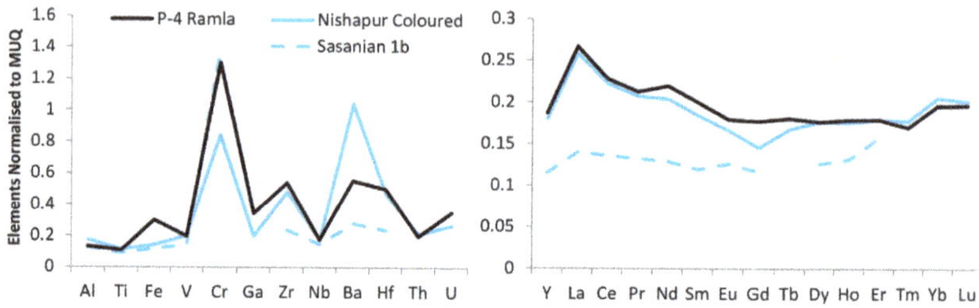

Figure 11.7 Selected trace elements (left) and REE (right) comparing P-3 to the other Mesopotamian Type 2 glass groups. Particularly similarity is seen to the Nishapur Colourless glass. Data sources as Table 11.3. Values normalised to MUQ (weathered continental crust, see Kamber et al. 2005).

is also considered possible. The vessels of P-3 and Nishapur Colourless also fall within the range of the Samarran and Sasanian 2 glass samples. The overlap is mainly with those vessels with fewer impurities, for example, those with <0.5 per cent TiO_2 and 60 ppm ZrO_2 seen in Figure 11.6. The majority of the P-3 and Nishapur Colourless glass therefore appear to be a higher purity sub-type of the Samarra glass. The higher purity glasses would likely have more value, and are thus more likely to have been traded. Overall, all these glass types show similarity in terms of flux elements, silica source oxides and the trace and REE elements, this similarity potentially suggest a shared production region. This possibility was proposed by Wypyski (2015) after identifying the resemblance between the compositions of glass from Nishapur and those from Samarra and Sasanian contexts. He suggested that glass found at Nishapur may have been traded from production sites in Mesopotamia, going on to suggest that the Nishapur Colourless type (Wypyski Type A) may have been manufactured at Samarra rather than Nishapur, as suggested by Kröger (1995, 37). The compositional similarities presented here are analogous with Wypyski's suggestion.

Mesopotamian Type 1: P-4 Nishapur Coloured

P-4 consists of 7 cobalt blue vessels. The flux elements are characterised by low CaO (7.07 per cent), common to all the Mesopotamian and Iranian glasses, which is distinctly different from the ~9 per cent found at Tyre and the eastern Mediterranean glass. MgO is lower than P-3, as is K_2O (1.9 per cent), while P_2O_5 is higher (0.22 per cent), although these oxides are somewhat similar to eastern Mediterranean values. Overall, the flux

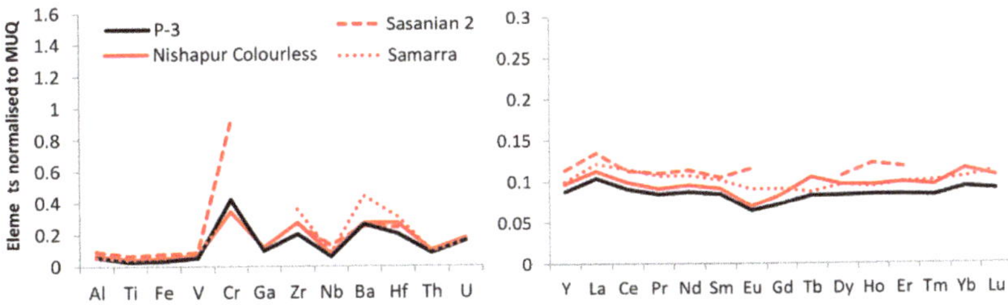

Figure 11.8 Selected trace elements (left) and REE (right) comparing P-4 to the other Mesopotamian Type 1 glass groups. Particularly similarity is seen to the Nishapur Coloured glass. Data sources as Table 11.3. Values normalised to MUQ (see Kamber et al. 2005).

element ratios are 0.4 MgO/CaO and 8.67 K_2O/P_2O_5, between eastern Mediterranean and the Mesopotamian Type 2 glass. Nishapur Coloured and Sasanian 1 (a and b) demonstrate a similar range, 0.55–0.61 for MgO/CaO and 9.09–12.63 for K_2O/P_2O_5. These groups are collectively defined as Mesopotamian Type 1 (Figure 11.5).

In silica source oxides P-4 is high in Al_2O_3 (2.27 per cent), TiO_2 (0.15 per cent) and ZrO_2 (145ppm). In Figure 11.6, close similarity is shown to the Nishapur Coloured glass, suggesting a similar region of production, while distinct from Sasanian, suggesting different raw materials but likely within the same larger geological area. The silica source for these glass types is much higher in impurities than the P-3 group, suggesting the use of sand. The trace element averages in Figure 11.8 present the close similarity between Nishapur Coloured and P-4, further enforcing the potential of a shared production region, although some individual samples, such as RAM 6297–05, do display differences that might suggest more than one production site. Less similarity is seen to Sasanian 1b, although no distinct difference in trace or REE values are observed. Wypyski suggests that between the Nishapur Colourless and Coloured types, the Nishapur Coloured vessels are more likely to have been made locally at Nishapur due to their ubiquity and lower quality, and therefore P-4 may be an Iranian type. Nonetheless, the glass could also have been traded as raw chunks and only shaped in Nishapur.

Unlike the other groups, all the vessels of P-4 are cobalt blue, averaging 1259 ppm CoO. This is not unusual, as a number of the Nishapur Coloured group originally defined by Brill (1995) are also cobalt coloured. The Co-coloured vessels contain high iron oxide (P-4 2.33 per cent), this is 1 per cent higher than the self-coloured examples of Nishapur Coloured presented in Table 11.6. This indicates that some of the iron oxide entered with the cobalt. Several other oxides are also enriched at over 2σ above the Nishapur Coloured average, these include copper (3817 ppm), manganese (1.38 per cent), nickel (291 ppm) and zinc (775 ppm). This combination of elements is suggestive of an asbolane ore (asbolite; $(Ni, Co)_{2-x}Mn^{4+}(O.OH)_4.nH_2O$; Matin and Pollard 2017) mixed with secondary iron and copper minerals. Asbolane deposits are reported from Iranian mines of Qamser near Kāshān, Iran (Kaczmarczyk and Hedges 1983, 53), however, a more recent investigation of Qamser cobalt ores identified and characterised only cobaltite (CoAsS) and erythrite ($Co_3(AsO_4)_2.8H_2O$) minerals (Matin and Pollard 2017). These had high As and do not correspond with the results here. The cobalt additive is therefore currently from an unidentified source.

Discussion

The results categorised the plant ash glass into three principal groups – Eastern Mediterranean, Mesopotamian Type 1 and Mesopotamian Type 2 – mainly based around the MgO/CaO ratio, but also differences in Al_2O_3 and K_2O/P_2O_5. Using the silica-source oxides, the glass groups were then identified into production groups: P-1, identified as a Tyre-type glass; P-3, a Nishapur Colourless type; and P-4, a cobalt-blue group conforming to the Nishapur Coloured type. A further single sample (RAM 4740–05) was of a Syrian type designated P-2, which will be discussed in a forthcoming publication. Furthermore, 41 samples of natron glasses from Ramla previously categorised in Phelps et al. (2016) were found to be mainly of an Egypt II type (Group N-3, 33 samples), similar to that first identified by Gratuze and Barrandon (1990) and Bimson and Freestone (1987). A further six samples were Levantine, of which four were Apollonia-type glass (N-1) and two (N-2) had a low soda-recipe consistent with production at Bet Eli'ezer (Freestone et al. 2000). A final two samples were of an unknown glass type.

Chronology

The chronology of the full dataset of 94 vessels sorted by compositional type is presented in Figure 11.9. The glass of the Umayyad period (early eighth–mid-eighth century CE) in Ramla consists entirely of natron glass, mainly of an Egypt II type (N-3), while a further three vessels were produced in the vicinity of Apollonia (N-1) and Bet Eli'ezer (N-2). This contrasts with the seventh century CE, in which glass supply in

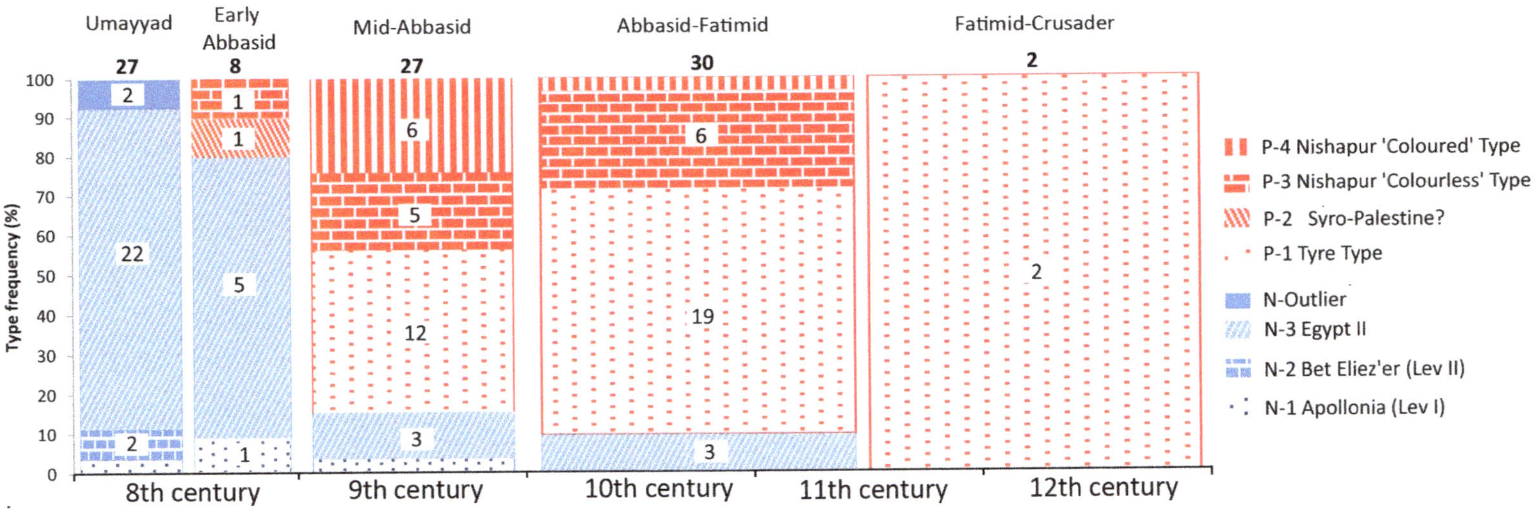

Figure 11.9 Image displaying vessel chronology sorted by compositional group. Frequency is in per cent, and x-axis is by century. Numbers at the top of each column are vessel totals, while group sub-totals are shown in areas of each column (numbers not shown in smallest segments). Natron glass in blue, plant ash glass in red. N = 94 (note RAM 6490–12, a P-3 type, removed due to insufficient dating).

Palestine was entirely dominated by glass from Apollonia (Phelps et al. 2016, 65).

The Abbasid caliphate was established in 750 CE, and from this period onwards the types of glass in Ramla alters again. Several vessels could be dated to the late eighth century CE. This period is the last in which natron glass is present in significant quantities and the first where plant ash glass is present: two samples, RAM 4740–05 and RAM 5947–17, identified as a P-2 and P-3 type respectively. In the ninth century CE plant ash glass dominates, with 12 samples of P-1 glass, five samples of P-3 and six of P-4. In the tenth–mid-eleventh century a similar picture is seen, with 19 P-1 vessels, six vessels of P-3 and P-4 as a single sample. After this date only two vessels were analysed, both of Tyre type. The low number of samples means no conclusions can be deduced for this period.

The chronology demonstrates the appearance and rise to dominance of plant ash in the Abbasid period. These types came from Tyre and Mesopotamia/Iran. The remainder of the chapter will discuss how these results effect our understanding of the models of supply (centralised vs. dispersed production) and the potential reasons for the appearance of long-distance imported glass from Mesopotamian/Iranian.

Evidence for centralised production

It is widely recognised that the Roman and Byzantine glass industries operated a centralised production model in which large quantities of raw glass was manufactured at large tank furnaces and then traded to a distributed network of smaller workshops (Freestone et al. 2002). Primary production sites have been recognised from Egypt (Nenna et al. 2005; Nenna 2015) and Israel (Gorin-Rosen 1995; 2000; Tal et al. 2004). Glass workshops (secondary production sites) from the late Byzantine–Umayyad periods have also been identified from various sites in Palestine, e.g. Bet Shean (Gorin-Rosen 2000), Apollonia (Freestone et al. 2008) and Tel Aviv (Freestone et al. 2015). However, these sites utilised natron glass and questions remain concerning the supply of plant ash glass. A recent investigation of the chemical compositions of Islamic period plant ash glass covering the eighth to fourteenth centuries CE by Henderson et al. (2016) concluded that glass was manufactured in 'production sub-zones associated with large cosmopolitan urban hubs'. They further suggested that 'decentralised production occurred over a period of *c.*800 years [in the Levant]' (Henderson et al. 2016, 142), postulating that the centralised production model had ceased use in the Levant during this time. The type of decentralised model based upon urban hubs suggested by Henderson et al. is supported by evidence from Raqqa (Henderson 1999; Henderson et al. 2004) in which primary production of localised compositional types appear alongside secondary working. Analysis of objects from Raqqa suggested this glass was then consumed locally. Glass manufactured at Raqqa, such as Raqqa Type 1, the most abundant group, is rarely mentioned from other sites and does not appear to have been traded widely, and therefore fits the model. Although, 49 vessels of a Raqqa Type 1 composition are reported from Raya, Egypt (PA-1a; Kato et al. 2010a, 1392).

The plant ash vessels analysed from Ramla demonstrate glass supply to be dominated by a single compositional type matching that made at Tyre. It suggests that supply within Ramla (and also within Palestine as a whole, Phelps et al. forthcoming) was based on imported glass from this vicinity. However, was this glass transported as chunks, which might suggest a centralised production model, or was the glass traded as vessels? The evidence for the export of chunks starts with the site of Tyre itself. Four furnaces have been excavated, dating to the tenth–eleventh century CE (Jennings et al. 2001), although the dating of the P-1 vessels suggest other furnaces were operating over a longer period of time. Estimated capacities of the furnaces suggested a combined single firing of 79 tonnes, which would equate to approximately 1/2 million 150g vessels (Aldsworth et al. 2002). Each furnace also showed signs of multiple firings. This scale of production is much too high for local use, and implies an export industry. A lack of identifiable secondary production or of working waste is also suggestive that glass was exported as chunks and not vessels. This contrasts with evidence from Raqqa but corresponds with the archaeological evidence for earlier natron glass production sites (Gorin-Rosen 2000; Tal et al. 2004; Nenna 2015).

The trade in raw glass chunks is evidenced from the Serçe Limanı shipwreck (Bass et al. 2009) dating to *c.* 1025 CE. This ship was thought to have been sailing from the Levant with a full cargo-hold before it subsequently floundered off the coast of Turkey. A portion of the cargo consisted of one tonne of cullet (broken glass) and two tonnes of raw chunk glass (Bass 2009). Compositional analysis suggested a match of some fragments to glass from Tyre, particularly the chunk glass (Brill 2009, 480), although due to differences in some elements (Mg, Na, Ca) Freestone (2002, 76) was more circumspect, finding the compositional link to Tyre inconclusive. Nevertheless, this wreck demonstrates the transport of large quantities of glass as chunks from the Levant to the Byzantine empire during the Fatimid period. Evidence of a similar trade to Egypt is provided in the Cairo Geniza. This collection of Jewish correspondence includes a legal document dating 1011 CE, which reports the sending of 37 baskets of glass (estimated at over nine tonnes) from merchants in Tyre to be sold in Egypt (Carboni et al. 2003, 143–4). The large quantity is suggestive of raw glass over vessels. Compositionally, glass of a 'Syria-Palestinian' type is noted from Raya, Egypt (Kato et al. 2010a), of which the PA-1 colourless group has a composition relatively high in alumina (1.6 per cent), and low in titania (0.06 per cent) matching that of Tyre (Phelps 2016, 346–7). 'Syro-Palestine' glass is also recognised from Samarra and Nishapur, labelled as Type D by Wypyski (2015, 132) and 'Levantine' by Henderson (Henderson et al. 2016, 142). These types again appear to match Tyre production.

Considering specifically the glass from Ramla, the vessels of P-1 consist of mainly undecorated, utilitarian wares, e.g. bottles (RAM 3592–04), lamps (RAM 3897–03) and bowls (RAM 6297–02). In addition, some of the vessels had fabrics and forms that were lower quality, signifying inferior workmanship and cheaper value. As noted by Kröger (1995, 33), it would be unlikely that such inexpensive vessels were imported, and thus were more likely made locally. The forms of vessel are similar to the mainly domestic forms represented in the N-3 glass group (Phelps et al. 2016), a glass type shown to have been traded as chunks from their finding at workshops at Tel Aviv (Freestone et al. 2015). The utilitarian forms of the P-1 group contrasts with the higher quality P-3 and P-4 vessels described below. Moreover, there is evidence for local workshops, as demonstrated from the site of Banias, Israel, dating to the eleventh–thirteenth centuries CE, although the chunk glass at this site was not of a Tyre-type glass (Freestone et al. 2000). Hadad (2005, 78) inferred the existence of local workshops at Bet Shean due to the number of unique forms of glassware identified during the Abbasid and Fatimid period.

The weight of evidence strongly suggests that the supply of the majority of glass within Ramla followed a centralised production model in which chunk glass was traded from Tyre and shaped into vessels at Ramla. Evidence further suggests large-scale movement of chunk glass to the Byzantine empire and possibly Egypt, implying that a centralised model may have extended beyond Palestine during at least the Fatimid period.

Evidence for the trade in vessels

Groups P-3 and P-4 are identified as most similar to the Nishapur glass types identified by Brill (1995). It was further suggested that these groups may have originated in Mesopotamia, as first put forward by Wypyski (2015). This was thought most likely for P-3/Nishapur Colourless (Wypyski 2015, 136), with production suggested to Samarra, and less so for P-4/Nishapur Coloured group. The compositional results presented above agree with this assessment, as does the dating of the samples to the ninth–eleventh centuries CE, which coincide with the founding and occupation of Samarra. It is also supported by additional evidence, this includes the lack of glass-working remains at Nishapur (Kröger 1995, 33) while glass-working debris has been identified from Samarra (Northedge and Falkner 1987). Moreover, there are also close similarity in form and decoration between the vessels of Nishapur and Samarra (Kröger 1995, 6, 36–7), which implies a similar origin for the glass. Kröger (1995, 6) comments that there are 'instances where the designs from the two sites seem indistinguishable'. Finally, large quantities of Mesopotamian pottery are identified from Nishapur, such as opaque white wares (see Wilkinson 1973, 179), demonstrating a trade of Mesopotamian ceramics to Nishapur. This premise is contrary to previous assessments that have suggested Nishapur as a glass-making centre (Kröger 1995, 37; Henderson et al. 2016, 142).

Typologically, the P-3 and P-4 vessels are distinct from P-1. The vessels of P-3 are composed of high-quality, clear colourless fabrics, they are almost all bottles, mainly decorated with wheel-cut designs (e.g. bowl RAM 4768–10; Figure 11.10b) or mould blown (e.g. square-shaped bottle RAM 6297–07, Figure 11.10d; see also Table 11.2). Their fabric and decoration indicates they were expensive items, suggesting they were probably imported (Gorin-Rosen 2013). The vessels of the Nishapur Colourless (Brill 1995) and Samarra Type A (Wypyski 2015, 127) groups also contain a high proportion of wheel-cut glass. It therefore appears that this glass type was either favoured for the production of wheel-cut vessels, or produced in a region specialising in wheel cutting. Furthermore, there are typological parallels between the vessels from Nishapur and Samarra and vessels found in Israel. For example, miniature bottles from Ramla (Pollak 2007, 126; Gorin-Rosen 2010a, 230) and Bet Shean (Hadad 2005, 44) and cylindrical and square-sectioned bottles from Ramla, Sepphoris and Ha-Bonim (Pollak 2007, 127) are similar to examples found from Nishapur (Kröger 1995, 88, 132, 149) and Samarra (Lamm 1928, 24, 79 and 82). In this study, similar types of miniature bottles are seen in sample RAM 3592–06 (Figure 11.10a) and RAM 5947–29 (Figure 11.10c; see Gorin-Rosen 2011, fig. 16.5). Square-sectioned bottles are demonstrated in samples RAM 6490–11 (Winter 2015, fig, 1.13) and RAM 6297–07 (Figure 11.10d; Winter 2013 fig. 37.8).

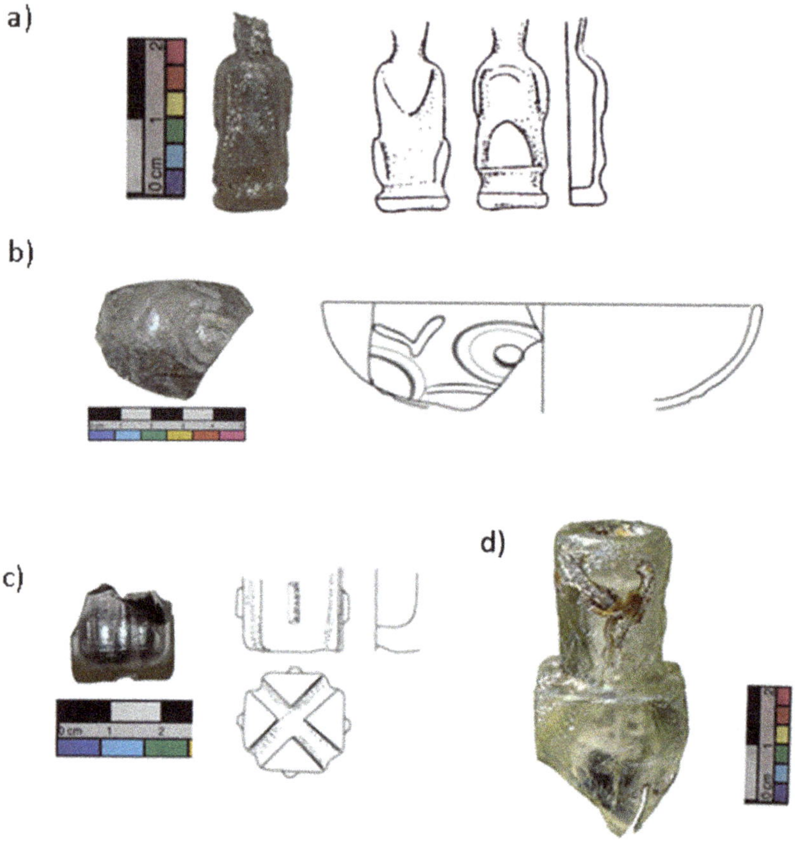

Figure 11.10 Examples of P-3 vessels: (a) RAM 3592–06, miniature bottle; (b) RAM 4768–10, bowl engraved with geometric designs; (c) RAM 5947–29, wheel-cut bottle; (d) RAM 6297–07, square-sectioned bottle. Photos by Matt Phelps. Drawings taken from published reports, see Table 11.2 for references.

The typological and decorative parallels between the vessels from Ramla and those of Mesopotamian origin coupled with the compositional similarities discussed earlier, strongly suggest the movement of vessels to Ramla, rather than raw glass. Investigating wider afield, compositional and stylistic matches have been noted to a cut-glass bottle from the Serçe Limanı assemblage made of Nishapur Colourless type glass (Brill 2009, 481), while several vessels made of a Nishapur Colourless type are also reported from Fustat (Brill 1995, 213–14). Stylistic similarities between vessels from Fustat and those from Nishapur have been observed (Kröger

1995, 9). Kato et al.'s (2010a) Group PA-2 from Raya, a collection of 40 vessels with a high proportion of wheel-cut types were similarly identified as Nishapur Colourless. Kato et al. (2010a, 1391) described the decorative designs of this group as 'Sasanian' or 'post-Sasanian', which led them to believe the glasses originated in Mesopotamia. Overall, the evidence is suggestive of a trade in decorated vessels of this glass type to Palestine and Egypt during the Abbasid and Fatimid periods.

The P-4 vessels are also distinct. They are mainly elongated bottles with flattened bodies (Figure 11.11). The bottles are cobalt blue, with examples described by Kröger as mass-produced, thin-walled and irregular (Kröger 1995, 74). They are found in large quantities in Iran and Iraq, and include thousands of fragments reported from Nishapur,

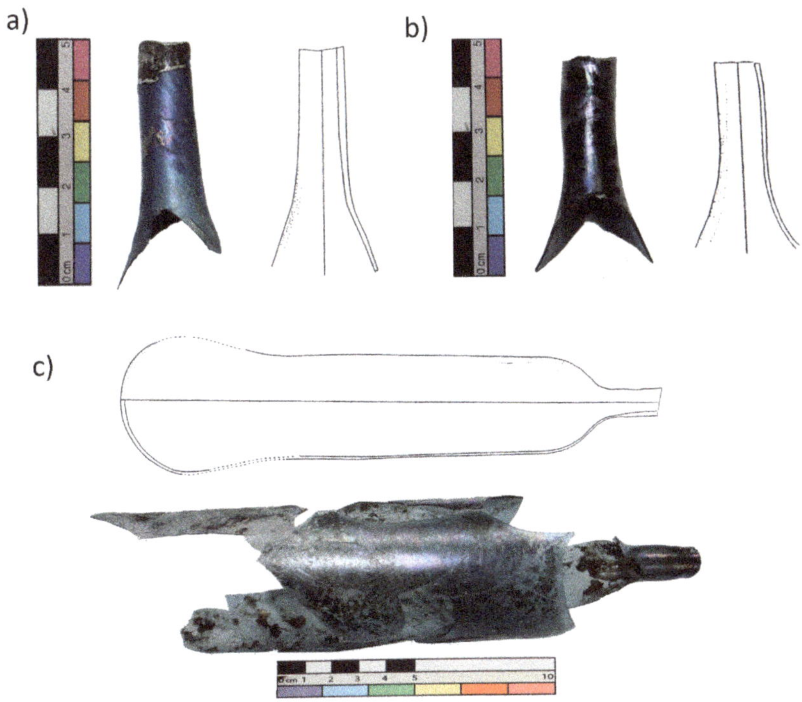

Figure 11.11 Examples of elongated bottles of P-4 composition: (a) RAM 3897–04; (b) RAM 6490–07; (c) an almost complete vessel from Caesarea (Winter pers. comms.) also of a P-4 composition is presented for comparison. Photos by Matt Phelps. Drawings taken from published reports, see Table 11.2 for references.

but also Samarra and Ctesiphon. Kröger suggested their manufacture throughout this region (Kröger 1995, 74). Examples have also been found from Israel at Ramla (Gorin-Rosen 2010a, 227); Caesarea (Pollak 2003, 228, 167) and in Egypt at Fustat (Kawatoko and Shindo 2010, Pl 9.1) and Raya (Kato et al. 2010a, fig. 2t). The composition and similarity to forms from the region of Iran and Iraq suggests production in this region, and their trade to Ramla. The relatively wide compositional spread of the P-4 group is suggestive of at least two production areas, with RAM 6297–05 possibly forming a separate production type.

For both Nishapur-type groups, bottles are the most frequent form. These were likely filled and the value of the commodity added to the vessels tradable value. Ramla was a large city, prosperous and wealthy, and thus would have been well connected to trade routes with a population rich enough to have afforded the import of these vessel types and their potentially expensive contents.

As a final point, it should be noted that several P-1 vessels also exhibited high-quality fabrics and decorations. Such examples include the engraved, bevelled hexagon shaped bottle (RAM 4768–04; Gorin-Rosen 2010b, fig. 22.9); a unique horn-like object with wheel cut decoration (RAM 4768–06; Gorin-Rosen 2010b, fig. 22.10); and a bottle with an engraved star of David on the base (RAM 3897–08; Katsnelson 2016, fig. 2.9). Therefore, while a large amount of chunk glass was likely traded into Palestine for use in local production there may have also been a trade in more highly decorated items. These could have been made in Tyre: Al-Muqaddasi, writing around 985 CE, reports Tyre as a glass-working centre specialising in wheel-cut glass (Carboni et al. 2003, 140 and 147–8), although workshops at Tyre have not yet been found. It is also possible that these glasses were worked elsewhere, and both Damascus and Aleppo have been suggested as glass-making centres in the Ayyubid period (twelfth century; Henderson 2013, 267) but may have been operating earlier. The vessels could also have been worked at as yet unidentified glass-making centres in Palestine.

Abbasid period and the growth of long-distance trade

Recent investigations have shown that in the late Byzantine and early Umayyad periods glass supply in the Levant was dominated by local Levantine compositional types (Freestone et al. 2000, 2008; Abd-Allah 2010; Rehren et al. 2010; Al-Bashaireh et al. 2016; Phelps et al. 2016). In the later Umayyad and early Abbasid periods, Egyptian-made natron glass becomes dominant, although Levantine types continued to appear. This generally localised supply of glass coincides with the prevailing understanding of trade during this period. Wickham (2004, 167) and Walmsley (2000, 322) highlight the prevalence of localised production and the redistribution of goods within the Levant during the seventh and eighth centuries CE. Wickham describes the Levant as a 'series of very localised economies'. Investigations of road networks and the sites of trade fayres agrees with this, demonstrating Syria-Palestine to have been linked by two overlapping trade zones encompassing the major cities (Binggeli 2012). This is also supported by ceramic distribution maps, which indicate movement of ceramics between 50–100 km from their production sites within Palestine, a lack of imported types is also reported (Walmsley 2012, 322). Walmsley suggested that this was due to fiscal separation of the provinces. Taxation during the Umayyad period was redistributed within regions rather than concentrating in the capital, and this may have had the effect of discouraging interregional trade (Walmsley 2000, 343).

The Abbasid period saw a number of changes. The capital was moved from Damascus to the newly founded city of Baghdad in 762 CE under caliph al-Mansur, this shifted administrative power and patronage eastwards. However, this period also saw a change to much greater centralisation of taxation. This 'fiscal unification' (Wickham 2004, 167) led to the concentration of taxed wealth in Baghdad. Much of this stemmed from the abolition of the *'ata*, the stipend paid to Muslim soldiers that came out of regional taxes (Walmsley 2000, 272; Wickham 2004, 168). The movement of wealth stimulated trade between regions and resulted in 'major transformations to the trade systems of the Islamic empire' (Walmsley 2000, 343). This encouraged demand for trade goods, principally in Baghdad, but also in large cities of the other regions. The effects of this are potentially seen in the appearance of new trade goods, such as fine Iraqi table wares and polychrome glazed wares in Palestine (Wickham 2004, 167) and can also be glimpsed in the significant amounts of decorated Mesopotamian and Iranian glassware appearing for the first time in Palestine, as demonstrated here.

Conclusion

The analysis of 54 plant ash glasses from Ramla has allowed the characterisation of three glass groups. The most abundant (P-1) is thought to have originated at Tyre, while the remaining two groups were of

Mesopotamian/Iranian origin identified as Nishapur Colourless (P-3) and Nishapur Coloured (P-4). Compositional investigation and comparisons to comparative glass from a variety of sites demonstrated that the plant ash glasses could be categorised into three broad regional types, this was principally based on their flux elements and Al_2O_3. These were named Eastern Mediterranean, which inclulded plant ash glass from Egypt, Banias, Tyre and Raqqa; and Mesopotamian Type 1 and Type 2, the former containing the lower-quality coloured glass types (Nishapur Coloured, Sasanian 1a and b) and the latter the higher-quality, colourless glass types (Nishapur Colourless, Sasanian 2 and glass from Samarra). This improved understanding of the separation of compositions within regions provides a framework within which plant ash glasses can be examined in the future.

Investigation of vessel context allowed information on glass supply to be examined. Plant ash glass appeared from the late eighth century CE and rapidly became the dominant technology. Group abundance and vessel type strongly suggested the P-1 Tyre-type glass to have been imported as chunks and shaped in Palestine, while further archaeological and documentary evidence implied the continuation of the centralised production model with this glass type until at least the twelfth century in Ramla. Chunk glass was also shown to be traded to the Byzantine empire, as seen from the Serçe Limanı, and also large quantities of glass to Egypt, as shown from documentary evidence, inferring that a centralised model was possibly also operating to a lesser extent in these regions. Examination of the Mesopotamian/Iranian glasses (P-3 and P-4) alternatively implied the importation of vessels, mainly as bottles, as suggested from their specific forms and decoration. The appearance of these vessel types as a result of long-distance trade in the ninth–eleventh centuries CE is explained within our current understanding of fiscal unification and increased centralisation of taxation following the formation of the Abbasid Caliphate, which acted to encourage inter-regional trade at this time.

Acknowledgements

This research was conducted as part of a doctorate completed at the Institute of Archaeology, UCL. The project was funded by AHRC. Additional travel to Jerusalem was paid for by the AHG (Association for the History of Glass). Access to samples and permission for sampling was provided by the Israel Antiquities Authority. Particular thanks are to be given to

Yael Gorin-Rosen for her help and guidance in sample selection and the dating of the vessels. Further thanks go to Tamar Winters and Natasha Katsnelson for providing access to their pre-publication reports and additional information concerning form and dating. Analysis of the samples was performed at IRAMAT, Orleans, with thanks to Bernard Gratuze for guidance and for allowing me use of the equipment, and also to James Lankton for help with the LA-ICP-MS and for providing new comparative data from Nishapur. Additional help with statistical analysis was provided by Mike Charlton. Thank you to Ian Freestone for his comments and suggestions, and to the referees for their useful and timely comments.

References

Abd-Allah, R. 2010. 'Chemical Characterisation and Manufacturing Technology of Late Roman to Early Byzantine Glass from Beit Ras/Capitolias, Northern Jordan'. *Journal of Archaeological Science* 37 (8): 1866–74.

Al-Bashaireh, K., Al-Mustafa, S., Freestone, I. C. and Al-Housan, A. Q. 2016. 'Composition of Byzantine Glasses from Umm El-Jimal, Northeast Jordan: Insights into Glass Origins and Recycling'. *Journal of Cultural Heritage* 21: 809–18.

Aldsworth, F., Haggarty, G., Jennings, S. and Whitehouse, D. 2002. 'Medieval Glassmaking at Tyre, Lebanon'. *Journal of Glass Studies* 44: 49–66.

Avni, G. 2014. *The Byzantine-Islamic Transition in Palestine: An Archaeological Approach*. Oxford: Oxford University Press.

Barkoudah, Y. and Henderson, J. 2006. 'Plant Ashes from Syria and the Manufacture of Ancient Glass: Ethnographic and Scientific Aspects'. *Journal of Glass Studies* 48: 297–321.

Bass, G. F. 2009. 'The Glass Cargo: A Summation'. In *Serçe Limanı, Volume 2: The Glass of an Eleventh-Century Shipwreck*, Ed G. F. Bass and J. W. Allan, 499–504. Texas: Texas A&M University Press.

Bass, G. F., Brill, R., Lledo, B. and Matthews, S. 2009. *Serçe Limanı, Volume 2: The Glass of an Eleventh Century Shipwreck*. Edited by Rachal Foundation Nautical Archaeology Series. Texas: Texas A&M University Press.

Beydoun, Z. R. 1976. 'Observations on Geomorphology, Transportation and Distribution of Sediments in Western Lebanon and Its Continental Shelf and Slope Regions'. *Marine Geology* 21 (4): 311–24.

Bimson, M. and Freestone, I. 1987. 'The Discovery of an Islamic Glass-Making Site in Middle Egypt'. In *Annales du 10e Congres de l'Association International pour l'Histoire du Verre, Madrid-Segovia*, 237–43. Amsterdam: Association Internationale Pour l'Histoire du Verre.

Binggeli, A. 2012. 'Annual Fairs, Regional Networks and Trade Routes in Syria, Sixth-Tenth Centuries'. In *Trade and Markets in Byzantium*, edited by

C. Morrisson 281–96. Washington, DC: Dumbarton Oaks Research Library and Collection.

Brems, D. and Degryse, P. 2014. 'Trace Element Analysis in Provenancing Roman Glass-Making'. *Archaeometry* 56 (S1): 116–36.

Brill, R. H. 1970. 'The Chemical Interpretation of the Texts'. In *Glass and Glassmaking in Ancient Mesopotamia*, edited by A. Oppenheim, 105–28. New York: The Corning Museum of Glass.

Brill, R. H. 1995. 'Appendix 3: Chemical Analyses of Some Glass Fragments from Nishapur in the Corning Museum of Art'. In *Nishapur: Glass of the Early Islamic Period*, edited by J. Kroeger, 211–33. New York: Metropolitan Museum of Art.

Brill, R. H. 1999. *Chemical Analyses of Early Glasses*. New York: Corning Museum of Glass.

Brill, R. H. 2009. 'Chemical Analysis'. In *Serçe Limanı, Volume 2: The Glass of an Eleventh-Century Shipwreck*, edited by G. F. Bass and J. W. Allan, 459–96. Texas: Texas A&M University Press.

Brill, R. H. and Stapleton, C. P. 2012. *Chemical Analyse of Early Glasses: Volume 3*. New York: Corning Museum of Glass.

Carboni, S., Lacerenza, G. and Whitehouse, D. 2003. 'Glassmaking in Medieval Tyre: The Written Evidence'. *Journal of Glass Studies* 44: 139–49.

Degryse, P. and Shortland, A. 2009. 'Trace Elements in Provenancing Raw Materials for Roman Glass Production'. *Geologica Belgica* 12 (3–4): 135–43.

Fischer, A. and McCray, W. P. 1999. 'Glass Production Activities as Practised at Sepphoris, Israel (37 BC–AD 1516)'. *Journal of Archaeological Science* 26 (8): 893–905.

Foy, D., Picon, M. and Vichy, M. 2003. 'Verres Omeyyades et Abbassides d'Origine Egyptienne: Les Temoignages de l'Archeologies et de l'Archeometrie'. In *Annales du 15e Congrès de l'Associaton Internationale Pour l'Histoire du Verre*, 138–43. Nottingham: Association Internationale Pour l'Histoire du Verre.

Freestone, I. 2002. 'Composition and Affinities of Glass from the Furnaces on the Island Site, Tyre'. *Journal of Glass Studies* 44: 67–77.

Freestone, I. C. 2006. 'Glass Production in Late Antiquity and the Early Islamic Period: A Geochemical Perspective'. *Geological Society, London: Special Publications* 257 (1): 201–16.

Freestone, I. C., Gorin-Rosen, Y. and Hughes, M. J. 2000. 'Primary Glass from Israel and the Production of Glass in Late Antiquity and the Early Islamic Period'. In *La Route du Verre: Ateliers Primaires et Secondaires du Second Millenaire Av. J.-C. au Moyen Age*, edited by M. D. Nenna, 65–83. Lyon: Maison de l'Orient Méditerranéen.

Freestone, I. C., Jackson-Tal, R. E. and Tal, O. 2008. 'Raw Glass and the Production of Glass Vessels at Late Byzantine Apollonia-Arsuf, Israel'. *Journal of Glass Studies* 50: 67–80.

Freestone, I. C., Jackson-Tal, R. E., Taxel, I. and Tal, O. 2015. 'Glass Production at an Early Islamic Workshop in Tel Aviv'. *Journal of Archaeological Science* 62: 45–54.

Freestone, I. C., Ponting, M. and Hughes, M. 2002. 'The Origins of Byzantine Glass from Maroni Petrera, Cyprus'. *Archaeometry* 44 (2): 257–72.
Gorin-Rosen, Y. 1995. 'Hadera, Bet Eli'ezer'. *Excavations and Surveys in Israel* 13: 42–3.
Gorin-Rosen, Y. 2000. 'The Ancient Glass Industry in Israel: Summary of the Finds and New Discoveries'. In *La Route Du Verre: Ateliers Primaires et Secondaires du Second Millenaire Av. J.-C. au Moyen Age*, edited by M. D. Nenna, 49–63. Lyon: Maison de l'Orient Méditerranéen.
Gorin-Rosen, Y. 2010a. 'The Islamic Glass Vessels'. In *Ramla: Final Report on the Excavations North of the White Mosque*, edited by O. Gutfeld, 213–64. Jerusalem: Institute of Archaeology, the Hebrew University of Jerusalem.
Gorin-Rosen, Y. 2010b. 'Ramla, Railroad Final Report: Glass'. *Hadashot Arkheologiyot – Excavations and Surveys in Israel*, 122.
Gorin-Rosen, Y. 2011. 'Ramla, Ha-Nevi'im Nursery School Final Report: The Glass Finds'. *Hadashot Arkheologiyot – Excavations and Surveys in Israel* 123.
Gorin-Rosen, Y. 2013. 'Glass Finds from the Early Islamic and Mamluk Periods at Ramla'. *'Atiqot* 75: 171–2.
Gorin-Rosen, Y. Forthcoming. *Ramla: The Glass Finds*.
Gorin-Rosen, Y. and Katsnelson, N. 2005. 'Glass Finds from the Salvage Excavations at Ramla'. *Atiqot* 49: 101–14.
Gratuze, B. 2014. 'Provenance Analysis of Glass Artefacts'. In *Modern Methods for Analysing Archaeological and Historical Glass, Volume I*, edited by K. Janssens, 311–43. Oxford: John Wiley & Sons.
Gratuze, B. 2016. 'Glass Characterization Using Laser Ablation-Inductively Coupled Plasma-Mass Spectrometry Methods'. In *Recent Advances in Laser Ablation ICP-MS for Archaeology*, edited by L. Dussubieux, M. Golitko and B. Gratuze, 179–96. Berlin/Heidelberg: Springer.
Gratuze, B. and Barrandon, J. N. 1990. 'Islamic Glass Weights and Stamps: Analysis Using Nuclear Techniques'. *Archaeometry* 32 (2): 155–62.
Gratuze, B. and Foy, D. 2012. 'La Composition des Verres Islamiques d'Al-Hadir'. *Maison de l'Orient et de la Mediterranee* 59: 139–49.
Gutfeld, O. 2010. *Ramla: Excavations North of the White Mosque*. Jerusalem: The Hebrew University of Jerusalem.
Haddad, S. 2005. *Islamic Glass Vessels from the Hebrew University Excavations at Bet Shean*. Jerusalem: The Institute of Archaeology, the Hebrew University of Jerusalem.
Haddad, E. 2010. 'Ramla, Railroad Final Report'. *Hadashot Arkheologiyot – Excavations and Surveys in Israel* 122.
Haddad, E. 2011. 'Ramla, Ha-Nevi'im Nursery School Final Report'. *Hadashot Arkheologiyot – Excavations and Surveys in Israel* 123.
Haddad, E. 2013. 'An Early Islamic-Period Roadbed in Ramla'. *'Atiqot* 75: 170.
Henderson, J. 1999. 'Archaeological and Scientific Evidence for the Production of Early Islamic Glass in Al-Raqqa, Syria'. *Levant* 31 (1): 225–40.
Henderson, J. 2013. *Ancient Glass: An Interdisciplinary Exploration*. Cambridge: Cambridge University Press.

Henderson, J., Chenery, S., Faber, E. and Kröger, J. 2016. 'The Use of Electron Probe Microanalysis and Laser Ablation-Inductively Coupled Plasma-Mass Spectrometry for the Investigation of 8th–14th Century Plant Ash Glasses from the Middle East'. *Microchemical Journal* 128: 134–52.

Henderson, J., McLoughlin, S. and McPhail, D. 2004. 'Radical Changes in Islamic Glass Technology: Evidence for Conservatism and Experimentation with New Glass Recipes from Early and Middle Islamic Raqqa, Syria'. *Archaeometry* 46 (3): 439–68.

Jackson-Tal, R. E. 2008. 'The Glass Vessels'. In *Salvage Excavation Reports. No. 5, Ramla (South): An Early Islamic Industrial Site and Remains of Previous Periods*, edited by O. Tal and I. Taxel, 166–84. Tel Aviv: Emery and Claire Yass Publications in Archaeology.

Jennings, S., Aldsworth F., Haggarty, G., Whitehouse, D. and Freestone, I. 2001. 'The Glass-Making Area on the Island Site at Tyre, Southern Lebanon'. *Bulletin d'Archéologie et d'Architecture Libanaise* 5: 219–40.

Kaczmarczyk, A. and Hedges, R. E. 1983. *Ancient Egyptian Faience: An Analytical Survey of Egyptian Faience from Predynastic to Roman Times*. Warminster: Aris & Phillips.

Kamber, B. S., Greig, A. and Collerson, K. D. 2005. 'A New Estimate for the Composition of Weathered Young Upper Continental Crust from Alluvial Sediments, Queensland, Australia'. *Geochimica et Cosmochimica Acta* 69 (4): 1041–58.

Kato, N., Nakai, I. and Shindo, Y. 2010a. 'Transitions in Islamic Plant Ash Glass Vessels: On-Site Chemical Analyses Conducted at the Raya/Al-Tur Area on the Sinai Peninsula in Egypt'. *Journal of Archaeological Science* 37 (7): 1381–95.

Kato, N., Nakai, I. and Shindo, Y. 2010b. 'On-Site Chemical Analysis of Raw and Waste Glass Unearthed in Al-Fustat Using a Portable X-Ray Fluorescence Spectrometer'. In *Artifacts of the Medieval Islamic Period Excavated in Al-Fustat, Egypt*, edited by M. Kawatoko and Y. Shindo, 17–29. Tokyo: Waseda University.

Katsnelson, N. 2016. 'Glass Finds from the Abbasid-Fatimid Periods on Danny Mass Street, Ramla'. *'Atiqot* 86: 59–67.

Kawatoko, M. and Shindo, Y. 2010. *Artifacts of the Medieval Islamic Period Excavated in Al-Fusṭāṭ, Egypt*. Tokyo: Joint usage/Research Center for Islamic Area Studies Organization for Islamic Area Studies Waseda University.

Kröger, J. 1995. *Nishapur: Glass of the Early Islamic Period*. New York: Metropolitan Museum of Art.

Lamm, C. J. 1928. *Das Glas Von Samarra (Die Ausgraungen Von Samarra, 4)*. Berlin: D. Reimer.

Luz, N. 1997. 'The Construction of an Islamic City in Palestine. The Case of Umayyad Al-Ramla'. *Journal of the Royal Asiatic Society of Great Britain and Ireland* 7 (1): 27–54.

McCray, W. P. 1998. 'Glassmaking in Renaissance Italy: The Innovation of Venetian Cristallo'. *Journal of The Minerals, Metals and Materials Society* 50 (5): 14–19.

Matin, M. and Pollard, A. 2017. 'From Ore to Pigment: A Description of the Minerals and an Experimental Study of Cobalt Ore Processing from the Kāshān Mine, Iran'. *Archaeometry* 59 (4): 731–46.

Mirti, P., Pace, M. and Malandrino, M. 2009. 'Sasanian Glass from Veh Ardašīr: New Evidence by ICP-MS Analysis'. *Journal of Archaeological Science* 36: 1061–9.

Mirti, P., Pace, M., Negro Ponzi, M. and Aceto, M. 2008. 'ICP–MS Analysis of Glass Fragments of Parthian and Sasanian Epoch from Seleucia and Veh Ardašīr (Central Iraq)'. *Archaeometry* 50 (3): 429–50.

Nenna, M. D. 2015. 'Primary Glass Workshops in Graeco-Roman Egypt: Preliminary Report on the Excavations of the Site of Beni Salama, Wadi Natrun (2003, 2005–9)'. In *Glass of the Roman World*, edited by J. Bailey, I. C. Freestone and C. M. Jackson, 1–22. Oxford: Oxbow Books.

Nenna, M. D., Thirion-Merle, V. and Vichy, M. 2005. 'Ateliers Primaires Du Wadi Natrun: Nouvelles Decouvertes'. *Annales 16e Congrès de l'Associaton Internationale Pour l'Histoire du Verre*, 59–63. Nottingham: Association Internationale Pour l'Histoire du Verre.

Nir, Y. 1996. 'The City of Tyre, Lebanon and Its Semi-Artificial Tombolo'. *Geoarchaeology* 11 (3): 235–50.

Northedge, A. and Falkner, R. 1987. 'The 1986 Survey Season at Samarra'. *Iraq* 49: 143–73.

Phelps, M. 2016. 'An Investigation into Technological Change and Organisational Developments in Glass Production between the Byzantine and Early Islamic Periods (7th–12th Centuries) Focussing on Evidence from Israel'. London, UCL (unpublished thesis).

Phelps, M., Freestone, I., Gorin-Rosen, Y. and Gratuze, B. 2016. 'Natron Glass Production and Supply in the Late Antique and Early Medieval near East: The Effect of the Byzantine-Islamic Transition'. *Journal of Archaeological Science* 75: 57–71.

Phelps, M., Freestone, I. C., Gorin-Rosen, Y. and Gratuze, B. Forthcoming. 'Plant Ash Glass in the Early Islamic Near East: Chronology, Characterisation and Origins of the Technology'.

Pollak, R. 2003. 'Early Islamic Glass from Caesarea: A Chronological and Typological Study'. In *Annales du 15e Congrès de l'Association Internationale Pour l'Histoire du Verre*, 165–70. Nottingham: Association Internationale Pour l'Histoire du Verre.

Pollak, R. 2005. 'Early Islamic Luxury Glass Vessels from Ramla – Local Production or Imported?'. *Annales du 16e Congrès de l'Association Internationale Pour l'Histoire du Verre*, 171–3. Nottingham: Association Internationale Pour l'Histoire du Verre.

Pollak, R. 2007. 'Excavation in Marcus Street, Ramla: The Glass Vessels'. In *Contract Archaeology Reports II: Excavation in Marcus Street, Ramla*, edited by M. Artzy, S. Yanklevitz and G. Tsioni, 100–33. Haifa: University of Haifa.

Rehren, Th., Marii, F., Schibille, N., Stanford, L. and Swan, C. 2010. 'Glass Supply and Circulation in Early Byzantine Southern Jordan'. In *Glass in Byzantium – Production, Usage, Analysis*, edited by J. Drauschke and D. Keller, 65–82. Mainz: Römisch-Germanisches Zentralmuseum.

Rye, O. 1976. 'Appendix 3. Khār: Sintered Plant Ash in Pakistan'. In *Traditional Pottery Techniques of Pakistan*, edited by O. Rye and C. Evans, 180–5. Washington, DC: Smithsonian Institution Press.

Schick, R. 1998. 'Palestine in the Early Islamic Period: Luxuriant Legacy'. *Near Eastern Archaeology* 61 (2): 74–108.

Shennan, S. 1997. *Quantifying Archaeology*. Iowa City: University of Iowa Press.

Shmueli, O. 2012. 'Ramla, Danny Mass Street'. *Hadashot Arkheologiyot – Excavations and Surveys in Israel* 124.

Shmueli, O. 2016. 'An Early Islamic-Period Structure on Danny Mass Street, Ramla'. *'Atiqot* 86: 118–19.

Tal, O., Jackson-Tal, R. E. and Freestone, I. C. 2004. 'New Evidence of the Production of Raw Glass at Late Byzantine Apollonia-Arsuf, Israel'. *Journal of Glass Studies* 46: 51–66.

Tite, M., Shortland, A., Maniatis, Y., Kavoussanaki, D. and Harris, S. 2006. 'The Composition of the Soda-Rich and Mixed Alkali Plant Ashes Used in the Production of Glass'. *Journal of Archaeological Science* 33 (9): 1284–92.

Toueg, R. 2013. 'Ramla'. *Hadashot Arkheologiyot – Excavations and Surveys in Israel* 125.

Toueg, R. and Torgë, H. 2015. 'Ramla, Hez Street'. *Hadashot Arkheologiyot – Excavations and Surveys in Israel* 127.

Walmsley, A. 2000. 'Production, Exchange and Regional Trade in the Islamic East Mediterranean: Old Structures, New Systems?'. In *The Long Eighth Century*, edited by I. L. Hansen and C. Wickham, 265–344. Leiden: Brill.

Walmsley, A. 2012. 'Regional Exchange and the Role of the Shop in Byzantine and Early Islamic Syria-Palestine'. In *Trade and Markets in Byzantium*, edited by C. Morrisson, 311–30. Washington, DC: Dumbarton Oaks Research Library and Collection.

Wickham, C. 2004. 'The Mediterranean around 800: On the Brink of the Second Trade Cycle'. *Dumbarton Oaks Papers* 58: 161–74.

Wilkinson, C. K. 1973. *Nishapur: Pottery of the Early Islamic Period*. New York: Metropolitan Museum of Art.

Winter, T. 2013. 'Ramla, Ha-Etzel Street – the Glass Finds'. *Hadashot Arkheologiyot – Excavations and Surveys in Israel* 125.

Winter, T. 2015. 'Appendix: The Glass Finds from Ramla, Hez Street'. *Hadashot Arkheologiyot – Excavations and Surveys in Israel* 127.

Wypyski, M. T. 2015. 'Chemical Analysis of Early Islamic Glass from Nishapur'. *Journal of Glass Studies* 57: 121–36.

12
A view from the South: Roman and Late Antique glass from Armant, Upper Egypt

Daniela Rosenow and Thilo Rehren

Abstract

47 glass vessel fragments from the Upper Egyptian town of Armant, dating to the first half of the first millennium CE, were typologically evaluated and subjected to chemical analysis. Including four samples with coloured decoration that were analysed separately from the body of the vessel, this resulted in a total number of 51 analyses. The main aim of this chapter is to learn more about this town's and the wider region's integration into the late Roman and Late Antique glass trade networks and to investigate possible similarities or differences of distribution patterns between Upper Egypt and the Nile Delta with its obvious connection to the Mediterranean Sea trade.

The analysed samples represent about 15 per cent of the total assemblage held at the Ashmolean Museum, and consist primarily of various vessel fragments consistent with fourth- to sixth-century CE shapes known from elsewhere in Egypt; only nine fragments are from vessels that on typological grounds date to the first few centuries CE, that is not later than the fourth century. Four analysed fragments are from chunks thought to represent glass-working raw material or waste. 37 analyses are of mineral natron-based soda-lime-silica glasses and match compositional groups defined in earlier studies: manganese-decolourised glass (9 fragments with 11 analyses) dominates the assemblage, followed by HIMT (9 fragments and analyses), Foy et al. (2003) *série 2.1* (8 fragments with 9 analyses), HIT (3), Egypt I (2), Levantine I (2) and antimony-decolourised glass (1). 12 pieces (13 analyses) are made of plant ash glass, falling into two groups. Only one analysis could not be assigned to any of the known compositional glass groups. Glass was worked in the town as demonstrated by fragments that can clearly be associated with secondary glass production. The pre-dominance of manganese-decolourised and plant ash-based glass over antimony-decolourised glass among the earlier finds is in contrast to what is visible in contemporary Lower Egyptian sites. Plant ash-based glass seems to have played a bigger role in the region throughout the periods represented here. Remarkable is the longevity of the use of manganese-decolourised glass, of about half a millennium based on typological dating. The almost complete absence at Armant of imported Levantine glass during late Roman/Late Antique times matches observations elsewhere in Egypt, and indicates a clear preference for the use of locally produced glass.

Introduction

The ancient city of Armant is situated *c.* 20 km south-west of Luxor on the western bank of the Nile (Figure 12.1). It goes back to the New Kingdom (mid-second millennium BCE) when it was most famous for its temple dedicated to the falcon god Monthu. The site was excavated in the 1930s by Sir Robert Mond and Oliver Humphrys Myers on behalf of the Egypt Exploration Fund (Mond and Myers 1940). During the course of the excavations, a significant number of glass fragments were discovered in the Roman and Coptic town and published by Donald Harden (Harden 1940). Several hundred glass objects were sent to the Petrie Museum of Egyptian Archaeology in London and the Ashmolean Museum in Oxford. While the Petrie Museum mainly holds bangle fragments and glass seals or weights, the Ashmolean Museum houses almost all vessel glass fragments that were sent to Britain, altogether more than 350 pieces.

The Roman to Coptic town of Armant mainly dates to the period from the middle of the third to the middle of the fifth century CE. However, a longer life span of the town is possible, as the excavators explicitly state that

> the part of the Coptic town remaining intact in the temple area was small, as most of it had been removed by *sebbakhin* (mudbrick) diggers and stone hunters. In the destroyed part of the town the pottery showed that there were certainly later levels and it is probable that later levels existed also over the part dug and planned by us.
> (Mond and Myers 1940, 36)

Figure 12.1 Map of Egypt showing the position of Armant, Alexandria and the Wadi Natrun.

Glass from Armant

Most of the glass fragments from Armant held at the Ashmolean Museum belong to vessel types that are well attested in contemporary sites in Egypt such as Ashmunein (Bailey 1998), Elephantine (Keller 2008, 2012), Kom el-Nana (Faiers 2013) and Koptos (Nenna 2000) in Middle and Upper Egypt, Bagawat (Nenna 2010) in the Kharga Oasis, Karanis (Harden 1936), Medinet Maadi (Silvano 1999) and Naqlun (Mossakowska-Gaubert 2004, 2009) in the Fayum Oasis, or Bubastis (Rosenow and Rehren 2014), Kom el-Dikka (Kucharczyk 2006b), Marea (Kucharczyk 2006a) and Marina el-Alamein (Kucharczyk 2010) in the Nile Delta. They include bowls, cups, lamps, flasks, goblets, bottles and jugs. The bowls are deep or shallow, with pad bases or stemmed bases or oval dishes, and the rim shapes include outsplayed rims, rims with flared edges going up or outfolded rims. Cups feature e.g. a pinched trail, a crimped trail, a double-fold or flared edges going up. Many pieces belong to lamps, all displaying a cracked-off rim, some of them decorated with blue blobs, and they have either a conical hollow base or ending in a blob, while only a few bases are pointed. Some fragments belong to flasks or bottles, very often showing a rim decorated with several horizontally applied thin trails of the same or a different colour such as blue, red or brown and with either a multiple coiled base ring or a slightly kicked up base with a pontil mark. Handle fragments belong to jugs similar to the aforementioned flasks or bottle-flasks. A few fragments belong to stemmed goblets or cups. Among the rarer finds are pieces belonging to types that are most common between the late first to the third centuries CE such as unguentaria, thick walled and made of dark green glass, and body fragments of cast dishes with cut decoration, an indented beaker and a jar base standing on three toes (see below). Stemmed goblets or funnel mouth bottles, on the other hand, represent types that only started occurring around the late fourth/fifth century CE and thus represent some of the youngest glass finds from Armant. The majority of the pieces are made of olive green, green or light green glass and blue/greenish glass, a number of fragments are dark blue, pinkish, purplish and brownish, while only very few are made of colourless or almost colourless glass. The vast majority of the vessels were free-blown, while only a very small amount of the material derives from cast or mould-blown vessels.

The dating of the glass vessels used for this study is necessarily tentative as it is based on the life span of the town implied by the associated find groups as well as on typological evidence, as for most fragments it is no longer possible to securely reconstruct their original find context. Glass was most likely worked at the site as there is clear evidence for secondary glass production, such as a few pieces of raw glass and glass adhering to layers of bubbly slag and to natural soil, possibly belonging to the base or walls of secondary glass production furnaces in which the raw glass was worked.

Material selection and analysis

The main aim of this chapter is to learn more about the economic integration of the Upper Egyptian town of Armant during the Roman to Late Antique periods in order to investigate possible similarities or differences of glass use and distribution patterns between Upper Egypt and the Nile

Delta with its obvious connection to the Mediterranean Sea trade and access to fresh raw glass. This study is of particular interest as the majority of available chemical data of Egyptian glass from this period so far derive from Lower Egyptian and Fayum Oasis sites and regions (Brill 1999 (Karanis), Gratuze and Barrandon 1990 (Wadi Natrun), Picon et al. 2008 (Wadi Natrun), Freestone et al. 2002 (Sinai), Foy et al. 2003 (Taposiris Magna, Tebtynis), Rosenow and Rehren 2014 (Bubastis)), while our knowledge about the integration of Middle and Upper Egypt into the Roman and Late Antique glass production and trade is very limited (but see van der Linden et al. 2009 (Elkab)).

Therefore 47 fragments of glass vessels and secondary production remains were selected for quantitative analysis, representing nearly 15 per cent of the Armant corpus held at the Ashmolean Museum. These include two cast fragments and four raw glass fragments, while the remaining pieces derive from free-blown vessels (Table 12.1). Sampling was done to include the whole range of vessel types, manufacturing methods, colours and decoration techniques represented among the glass objects in the collection. Of course, a pre-selection based on unknown criteria had already taken place by the excavators when they chose the objects being sent to Britain. However, judged by the variety of vessel types and comparative studies with contemporary sites in Egypt, one can be confident that at least a significant part of the original glass assemblage unearthed in Armant is covered in this study. Little, however, can be said about relative proportions of the different vessel types in the original assemblage.

Small pieces were chipped off the selected 47 fragments and embedded in resin blocks to expose cross sections of the glass, facilitating analysis unaffected by surface corrosion and contamination. Electron Probe Micro-Analysis (EPMA) was done at the Wolfson Archaeological Science Laboratories at the UCL Institute of Archaeology on 51 different glass samples, including four fragments with two different colours analysed separately. Of these, 30 fragments with 32 individual glass samples were also analysed by Laser-Ablation Inductively Coupled Plasma Mass Spectrometry (LA-ICPMS) at the laboratory of IRAMAT in Orleans, following established laboratory procedures. Cholakova et al. (2016) give details of both analytical methods, as well as a juxtaposition of detection limits and accuracies for the analysed elements in a soda-lime-silica matrix. The results of the two methods for oxides present at concentrations above c 1 wt% are in very close agreement; only for CaO the LA-ICPMS data were typically 5 to 8 per cent relative too high. Table 12.2 reports the measurements

Table 12.1 Catalogue of analysed samples; sorted in chronological order

number	*Inv.-no.*	*type*	*part*	*technique*	*colour*	*figure or close(st) typological parallel*	*date appr.*
Sb-dec.							
A-17	1933.1142.q	indented beaker	base	free-blown	light green	Harden 1936, pl. XV, 376	late 1st-early 4th c. CE
Mn-dec.							
A-44	1968.778.G255	plate or bowl	base	cast	light green	Harden 1940: pl. LXXXV.4	1st/2nd c. CE
A-36	1968.778.G267	jar	base	free-blown	light green	Harden 1940: pl. LXXXV.6; Harden 1936, class III	early 2nd-mid 3rd c. CE
A-10	1968.778.G326b	goblet or beaker	rim	free-blown	colourless	fig. 2.1; Harden 1936, class III or V	early 2nd-early 3rd c. CE
A-32	1968.778.G326h	cup	rim (w. crimped trail)	free-blown	olive green and blue	fig. 2.19	2th-4th c. CE
A-7	1968.778.G327b	oval dish	base	free-blown	light olive green	Harden 1936, class I	4th/5th c. CE
A-41	1968.778.G115	lamp	base	free-blown	purple	Harden 1936, pl. XVI, 457	from 4th c. CE

A-46	1968.778.G331d	lamp	base (coiled)	free-blown	light green	Harden 1936, class VI	from 4th c. CE
A-24	1968.778.G125	flask/bottle	rim	free-blown	light yellow-green	Keller 2006, type VII.54a	from 4th c. CE
A-25	1968.778.G332a	goblet or beaker	rim (w. applied trails)	free-blown	colourless and dark blue	fig. 2.14	4th-6th c. CE
PA I							
A-6	1933.1142.a	cast ribbed bowl	rim	cast	blue/green	Isings 1957, type 3a	mid 1st. C. BC-mid 1st c. CE
A-11	1933.1142.eee	unguentarium	base	free-blown	dark green	Meyer 1992, pl. 9, E	1st-3rd c. CE
A-12	1968.778.G329	bowl or beaker	base (w. applied ring)	free-blown	light brownish-pink	fig. 2.2; Harden 1936, Karanis class III	mid 3rd-mid 4th c. CE
A-42	1933.1142.vv	flask	rim and neck	free-blown	blue/green	fig. 2.4	3rd-5th c. CE
A-4	1969.307.D.I-2	raw glass fragment			green		??

(continued)

Table 12.1 (cont.)

number	*Inv.-no.*	*type*	*part*	*technique*	*colour*	*figure or close(st) typological parallel*	*date appr.*
PA II							
A-13	1968.778.G333b	jug	rim and handle	free-blown	green	fig. 2.3, Harden 1936, Karanis class XI/XII	3rd/4th c. CE
A-40	1968.778.G332c	flask	base	free-blown	turquoise	Harden 1936, Karanis class IX	3rd-5th c. CE
A-21	1968.778.G327a	bowl	(pad) base	free-blown	blue/green	Harden 1936, Karanis class III	from late 3rd c. CE
A-30	1968.778.G332d	flask	rim (w. applied trails)	free-blown	blue/green and brown	fig. 2.5; Harden 1936, Karanis class IX	from 4th c. CE
A-47	1968.778.G337a	(stemmed?) goblet?	rim	free-blown	blue/green	fig. 2.6	5th-7th c. CE
A-23	1968.778.G331a	flask/bottle	rim	free-blown	blue-green	fig. 2.17	from 5th c. CE
A-8	1968.778.G326a	flask	rim	free-blown	blue-green	fig. 2.23	from 5th c. CE
serie 2.1.							
A-3	1968.307.D-1	raw glass fragment			olive green		??
A-31	1968.778.G337	??	body	free-blown	colourless and purple		??
A-19	1933.1142.nn	flask	base (applied ring)	free-blown	light green and turquoise	fig. 2.9	late 4th/5th c. CE

A-45	1968.778.G326d	bowl	rim	free-blown	light brownish-pink	Harden 1936, Karanis class III (fold out rim)	4th/5th c. CE
A-14	1968.778.G330	(stemmed) bowl	base and stem	free-blown	olive green	fig. 2.16	late 4th-6th c. CE
A-27	1968.778.G326c	flask	rim	free-blown	light pink	fig. 2.18	late 4th-6th c. CE
A-26	1968.778.G326g	cup	rim	free-blown	olive green	fig. 2.11; Keller 2012, 485, fig. 4.4	5th/6th c. CE
A-34	1968.778.G334a	stemmed goblet	stem	free-blown	olive green	fig. 2.15	6th/7th c. CE
HIMT							
A-15	1968.778.G99	cup	rim	free-blown	dark green-blue	fig. 2.7	late 3rd-early 5th c. CE
A-2	1968.778.G306	bowl	rim	free-blown	brown-pink	Harden 1936, Karanis class III (flared edge going up)	4th/5th c. CE
A-18	1968.778.G331b	lamp	rim	free-blown	olive green	Isings 1957, type 106d	4th/5th c. CE

(*continued*)

Table 12.1 (*cont.*)

number	*Inv.-no.*	*type*	*part*	*technique*	*colour*	*figure or close(st) typological parallel*	*date appr.*
A-22	1968.778.G331c	lamp	base (coiled)	free-blown	olive green	fig. 2.10; Harden 1936, pl. XVI, 464 und 465	4th/5th c. CE
A-9	1968.778.G326f	bowl	rim	free-blown	green	Harden 1936, Karanis class III (outsplayed rim)	4th/5th c. CE
A-16	1968.778.G333a	bottle or jug	base	free-blown	dark blue	fig. 2.8; Harden 1936, Karanis class XI/XII	4th/5th c. CE
A-37	1968.778.G331e	lamp, flask or beaker	base (w. applied double ring)	free-blown	green	fig. 2.13	4th/5th c. CE
A-33	1968.778.G332b	flask	rim (w. applied trails)	free-blown	olive green	fig. 2.12; Harden 1936, Karanis class IX	4th-6th c. CE
A-28	1968.778.G326e	cup	rim	free-blown	brown	Nenna 2000, 23, fig. 9	4th-7th c. CE
HIT							
A-5	1968.778.G326i	cup	rim	free-blown	blue-green	fig. 2.20	4th-7th c. CE

A-35	1968.778.G328	(stemmed) bowl	(pad) base (criss cross décor)	free-blown	blue	Harden 1936, Karanis class III	from 4th c. CE
A-38	1968.77.G334b	(stemmed) goblet	stem	free-blown	blue	Kucharczyk 2006a, 73, fig. 3.5	6th/7th c. CE
Levantine I							
A-29	1968.778.G332e	flask	rim	free-blown	blue-green	fig. 2.22; Harden 1936, Karanis class IX	4th/5th c. CE
A-39	1969.307.D-2	raw glass fragment			blue-green		??
Egypt I							
A-20	1969.307.D.I-1	raw glass fragment			light greenish blue		??
A-43	1968.778.G121	stemmed goblet	stem	free-blown	light greenish blue	fig. 2.21	from 5th c. CE
ukn							
A-1	1933.1142.t	lamp	rim	free-blown	blue-green	Isings 1957, type 106d	4th/5th c. CE

Table 12.2 Comparison of Corning A and B composition as published (top row) and as measured (average and standard deviation of seven separate measurements done during the EPMA analysis of the Armant samples)

	SiO_2	Na_2O	CaO	K_2O	MgO	Al_2O_3	Fe_2O_3	TiO_2	Sb_2O_5	MnO	CuO	CoO	P_2O_5	Cl	SO_3	*Analytical total*
Cor A published	**66.56**	**14.30**	**5.03**	**2.87**	**2.66**	**1.00**	**1.09**	**0.79**	**1.76**	**1.00**	**1.17**	**0.17**	**0.13**	**0.10**	**0.10**	**99.53**
Cor A aver (n = 7)	66.77	14.27	5.02	2.86	2.60	0.97	1.00	0.70	1.70	1.03	1.23	0.17	0.11	0.08	0.16	99.64
StdDev	0.15	0.02	0.01	0.01	0.04	0.02	0.06	0.06	0.04	0.02	0.04	0.00	0.01	0.01	0.04	0.08
Cor B published	**61.55**	**17.00**	**8.56**	**1.00**	**1.03**	**4.36**	**0.34**	**0.09**	**0.46**	**0.25**	**2.66**	**0.05**	**0.82**	**0.20**	**0.54**	**99.98**
Cor B aver (n = 7)	62.05	16.93	8.72	1.05	1.02	4.46	0.31	0.10	0.39	0.24	2.76	0.05	0.88	0.15	0.58	100.58
StdDev	0.35	0.05	0.11	0.04	0.01	0.07	0.02	0.01	0.05	0.01	0.07	0.00	0.04	0.04	0.03	0.40

of Corning A and B reference glasses analysed by EPMA together with the Armant samples, giving all oxides as analysed by EPMA.

Results

Based on the typological assessment of the analysed objects, the assemblage spans roughly half a millennium of glass use at the site, from the BCE/CE transition to the sixth and potentially even seventh century CE. However, only 9 of the analysed fragments date not later than the fourth century CE; the remaining 38 fragments most likely date to the fourth to sixth or seventh centuries CE.

Interestingly, 12 fragments, including 4 of the 9 early fragments are made from plant ash glass, compared to only 8 of the 39 later fragments. Of the remaining assemblage, 34 fragments are mineral natron-based soda-lime-silica glasses matching compositional groups defined in earlier studies, leaving one fragment, characterised by a very high alumina content, which cannot be assigned to any known glass group.

Tables 12.3a and 12.3b present the data sorted by compositional groups in chronological order, revealing a remarkable compositional heterogeneity of the assemblage. The 12 plant ash glasses (with 13 analyses) can be divided into two groups based on their manganese content. The largest group (9 fragments with 11 analyses) of the mineral natron-based vessels are manganese-decolourised glass, while 8 fragments (9 analyses) are made of glass matching the composition of *série 2.1* of Foy et al. (2003). Another nine fragments are HIMT glass, while three fragments are made of HIT glass, two each of Egypt I and of Levantine I glass, and one fragment of antimony-decolourised glass.

The glass assemblage from Armant dates to a period when glass was an everyday commodity in the Mediterranean world. This fact is reflected in the typological range – and possibly originally large number – of glass vessel fragments discovered at the site, and with a few exceptions the majority of them derive from middle Roman to Late Antique contexts. In this respect, this Upper Egyptian glass corpus does not seem to differ considerably from contemporary Lower Egyptian assemblages, as we discuss later. However, there are a number of peculiarities regarding the detected compositional glass groups and their relative proportions that shed an interesting light on raw glass consumption patterns in a region about 800 kilometres south of the coast of the Mediterranean Sea. The following considerations are presented in a more or less chronological order of the glass groups concerned.

Table 12.3a EPMA analyses of glass samples from Armant, major and minor elements (data in wt%); sorted in chronological order

	colour	*type*	*date*	*Na_2O*	*MgO*	*Al_2O_3*	*SiO_2*	*P_2O_5*	*SO_3*	*Cl*	*K_2O*	*CaO*	*TiO_2*	*MnO*	*Fe_2O_3*	*Sum PA*
Sb decol																
A-17	l. green	indented beaker	1.-4. CE	19.6	0.51	2.18	69.2	0.04	0.33	1.15	0.57	4.83	0.13	0.02	0.65	1.12
Mn decol																
A-44	l. green	plate or bowl	1st/2nd c. CE	20.3	0.71	2.16	66.2	0.04	0.32	1.19	0.37	6.20	0.12	1.38	0.71	1.12
A-36	l. green	jar	2nd/3rd c. CE	19.7	0.42	1.92	67.6	0.04	0.35	1.03	0.41	6.34	0.07	0.90	0.60	0.87
A-10	colourless	goblet or beaker	2nd/3rd c. CE	17.6	0.41	1.74	70.5	0.04	0.28	0.95	0.38	6.52	0.07	0.91	0.44	0.83
A-32	l. olive	cup	2nd-4th c. CE	20.3	0.68	2.36	64.2	0.06	0.42	0.98	0.44	7.80	0.11	1.13	0.75	1.19
A-32	blue	cup	2nd-4th c. CE	20.5	0.70	2.37	64.1	0.07	0.42	0.97	0.45	7.61	0.13	1.00	1.00	1.22
A-7	l. olive	oval dish	4th/5th c. CE	20.1	0.63	2.28	66.1	0.06	0.44	0.89	0.47	6.90	0.09	1.32	0.73	1.15
A-41	purple	lamp	4th/5th c. CE	19.8	0.79	2.11	65.2	0.04	0.28	1.23	0.38	6.83	0.10	1.75	0.77	1.21
A-46	l. green	lamp	4th c. CE onw	20.0	0.78	2.30	64.7	0.07	0.50	0.83	0.55	7.66	0.11	1.32	0.83	1.39
A-24	l. yellow-green	flask/bottle	4th c. CE onw	19.2	0.64	2.21	68.1	0.04	0.24	1.20	0.42	5.51	0.10	1.47	0.62	1.09
A-25	colourless	goblet or beaker	4th-6th c. CE	18.4	0.75	2.41	65.9	0.10	0.37	0.91	0.67	7.27	0.11	1.82	0.99	1.51
A-25	blue	goblet or beaker	4th-6th c. CE	17.8	0.87	2.51	65.4	0.08	0.36	0.89	0.53	7.58	0.13	0.44	2.41	1.48
			Average	***19.4***	***0.67***	***2.21***	***66.2***	***0.06***	***0.36***	***1.01***	***0.46***	***6.93***	***0.10***	***1.22***	***0.90***	***1.19***

PA I																
A-6	blue-green	cast bowl	1st c. BC-1st c. CE	18.8	1.85	2.10	65.6	0.67	0.31	0.94	1.34	5.90	0.15	1.28	0.93	3.86
A-11	dark green	unguentarium	1st-3rd c. CE	14.5	3.35	1.97	64.8	1.65	0.15	0.89	2.81	6.21	0.14	2.13	1.69	7.82
A-12	l. pink-brown	bowl or beaker	3rd/4th c. CE	13.9	2.83	1.57	68.4	0.33	0.23	0.77	2.53	8.06	0.10	0.93	0.50	5.69
A-42	blue-green	flask	3rd-5th c. CE	16.8	3.13	1.75	63.8	1.28	0.28	0.84	1.79	7.47	0.12	1.21	1.31	6.20
A-4	green	raw glass fragment	??	14.7	2.16	3.21	64.5	0.48	0.46	0.40	1.86	10.21	0.26	0.28	1.66	4.49
			Average	***15.8***	***2.66***	***2.12***	***65.4***	***0.88***	***0.29***	***0.77***	***2.07***	***7.57***	***0.16***	***1.17***	***1.22***	***5.61***
PA II																
A-13	blue-green	jug	3rd/4th c. CE	17.5	1.82	2.04	64.7	0.41	0.41	0.50	1.51	8.83	0.15	0.25	1.14	3.74
A-40	blue-green	flask	3rd-5th c. CE	15.7	1.41	2.06	68.7	0.39	0.27	0.64	1.31	8.07	0.13	0.13	0.84	3.12
A-21	blue-green	bowl	3rd c. CE onw	17.3	1.51	2.11	66.3	0.32	0.28	0.79	1.27	8.26	0.16	0.27	1.02	3.10
A-30	blue-green	flask	4th c. CE onw	16.6	1.31	2.30	66.1	0.25	0.33	0.77	1.06	7.85	0.17	0.29	1.15	2.63
A-30	brown	flask	4th c. CE onw	16.4	1.79	4.47	52.2	0.80	0.18	0.46	2.22	7.76	0.41	0.23	2.77	4.80
A-47	blue-green	(stemmed) goblet	5th-7th c. CE	16.3	1.59	2.46	66.8	0.33	0.27	0.67	1.22	8.40	0.19	0.20	1.22	3.13
A-23	blue-green	flask/bottle	5th c. CE onw	16.2	1.28	2.64	64.8	0.23	0.40	0.76	0.96	7.55	0.13	0.26	1.32	2.47
A-8	blue-green	flask	5th-7th c. CE	16.0	1.44	2.16	65.9	0.30	0.32	0.83	1.21	8.01	0.14	0.35	0.94	2.95
			Average	***16.5***	***1.52***	***2.53***	***64.5***	***0.38***	***0.31***	***0.68***	***1.35***	***8.09***	***0.19***	***0.25***	***1.30***	***3.24***

(continued)

Table 12.3a (cont.)

	colour	*type*	*date*	*Na_2O*	*MgO*	*Al_2O_3*	*SiO_2*	*P_2O_5*	*SO_3*	*Cl*	*K_2O*	*CaO*	*TiO_2*	*MnO*	*Fe_2O_3*	*Sum PA*
serie 2.1																
A-3	olive	raw glass fragment	??	17.4	1.07	2.71	65.4	0.11	0.40	0.70	0.66	8.38	0.14	1.79	1.05	1.85
A-31a	purple	body sherd	??	19.6	0.87	2.21	65.8	0.13	0.40	0.19	0.78	7.20	0.11	0.81	0.70	1.78
A-31b	colourless	body sherd	??	19.4	1.13	2.45	63.3	0.18	0.47	0.82	0.79	8.20	0.12	1.56	0.90	2.10
A-19	l. green	flask	4th/5th c. CE	19.4	0.94	2.66	66.2	0.11	0.33	1.05	0.53	5.99	0.19	0.91	1.25	1.58
A-45	l. brown-pink	bowl	4th/5th c. CE	17.9	1.21	2.63	64.7	0.20	0.41	0.70	0.83	8.28	0.15	1.80	1.07	2.25
A-14	olive	(stemmed) bowl	4th-6th c. CE	18.2	1.08	2.40	65.7	0.14	0.38	0.79	0.61	7.75	0.12	1.62	0.91	1.83
A-27	l. pinkish	flask	4th-6th c. CE	16.9	1.34	2.60	64.7	0.22	0.39	0.66	0.94	8.63	0.14	2.03	1.00	2.51
A-26	olive	cup	5th/6th c. CE	18.8	1.20	2.70	63.5	0.22	0.42	0.84	0.92	7.25	0.15	1.16	2.39	2.34
A-34	olive	stemmed goblet	6th/7th c. CE	19.9	0.82	2.31	65.3	0.13	0.44	0.95	0.72	6.66	0.10	1.27	0.76	1.66
			Average	***18.6***	***1.07***	***2.52***	***65.0***	***0.16***	***0.40***	***0.74***	***0.75***	***7.59***	***0.14***	***1.44***	***1.12***	***1.99***
HIMT																
A-15	dark g/b	cup	3rd-5th c. CE	19.0	1.01	2.91	66.1	0.10	0.32	0.90	0.47	6.11	0.43	0.68	1.73	1.59
A-2	brown-pink	bowl	4th/5th c. CE	18.8	0.76	2.96	66.2	0.06	0.32	0.86	0.49	5.03	0.46	2.85	1.52	1.32
A-18	olive	lapm	4th/5th c. CE	17.1	0.95	3.30	65.6	0.10	0.23	0.85	0.43	5.13	0.45	2.48	3.31	1.48
A-22	olive	lamp	4th/5th c. CE	18.1	0.96	3.34	64.1	0.15	0.33	0.80	0.51	5.93	0.37	1.95	3.28	1.62
A-9	green	bowl	4th/5th c. CE	18.8	0.98	2.88	65.6	0.11	0.27	0.98	0.46	5.87	0.37	1.63	2.12	1.55
A-16	blue	bottle or jug	4th/5th c. CE	18.8	1.04	2.89	65.1	0.09	0.30	0.89	0.50	6.09	0.35	0.83	2.64	1.63

A-37	green	lamp, flask or beaker	4th/5th c. CE	17.8	0.92	2.72	66.0	0.12	0.27	0.91	0.47	6.11	0.31	1.76	2.53	1.51
A-33	olive	flask	4th-6th c. CE	19.4	0.96	2.96	64.2	0.12	0.28	1.13	0.37	5.47	0.38	1.36	2.87	1.44
A-28	brown	cup	4th-7th c. CE	17.5	0.90	3.11	64.2	0.08	0.28	0.75	0.59	7.16	0.45	3.12	1.76	1.57
			Average	***18.4***	***0.94***	***3.01***	***65.2***	***0.10***	***0.29***	***0.90***	***0.48***	***5.88***	***0.40***	***1.85***	***2.42***	***1.52***
HIT																
A-5	turquois	cup	4th-7th c. CE	20.2	0.87	2.63	66.7	0.05	0.34	1.11	0.39	5.62	0.46	0.18	1.41	1.31
A-35	blue	(stemmed) bowl	4th c. CE onw	18.1	0.87	2.49	67.6	0.02	0.25	1.02	0.37	6.08	0.31	0.12	1.99	1.26
A-38	blue	(stemmed) goblet	6th/7th c. CE	19.6	1.02	2.73	64.4	0.13	0.51	0.76	0.77	6.98	0.13	0.21	1.35	1.92
Lev I																
A-29	blue-green	flask	4th/5th c. CE	15.0	0.58	3.21	70.7	0.06	0.12	0.80	0.45	8.28	0.09	0.04	0.55	1.09
A-39	blue-green	raw glass fragment	??	16.7	0.57	3.15	70.6	0.11	0.18	0.96	0.56	6.41	0.13	0.04	0.72	1.23
Egypt I																
A-20	blue-green	chunk or waster	??	18.6	0.57	3.34	71.9	0.02	0.10	1.16	0.36	2.29	0.24	0.04	1.03	0.96
A-43	blue-green	stemmed goblet	5th c. CE onw	19.4	0.51	2.91	71.8	0.04	0.12	1.26	0.29	2.21	0.18	0.03	0.86	0.83
unknown																
A-1	l. blue-green	lamp	4th/5th c. CE	16.6	0.29	5.02	71.4	0.13	0.12	0.89	0.90	4.49	0.07	0.33	0.38	1.32

Table 12.3b LA-ICP-MS analyses of glass samples from Armant, trace elements (data in ppm); sorted in chronological order

	Li	*B*	*V*	*Cr*	*Co*	*Ni*	*Cu*	*Zn*	*As*	*Rb*	*SrO*	*Y*	*Zr*	*Sn*	*Sb*	*Ba*	*La*	*Ce*	*Pb*
Sb decol																			
A-17	4	218	11	10	2	4	7	19	8	5	429	5	91	2	4796	123	6	11	70
Mn decol																			
A-10	2	121	19	8	6	8	13	14	2	5	545	6	46	3	<1	202	5	9	55
A-7	3	140	25	10	6	10	24	16	3	6	619	6	65	1	<1	418	6	11	9
A-24	4	153	21	10	8	9	24	15	3	5	509	6	57	2	13	681	6	10	17
A-25	6	141	31	12	7	10	30	19	3	7	637	7	74	2	1	312	7	12	13
A-25	5	150	22	16	1989	91	1589	90	8	6	699	7	88	113	14	187	7	12	2061
PA I																			
A-6	4	211	28	19	17	18	225	39	5	6	598	5	86	31	768	254	6	10	180
A-11	3	220	40	13	18	27	20	95	1	5	678	5	64	1	14	335	6	10	42
A-12	6	96	15	9	2	14	12	26	1	21	440	5	159	0	<1	291	8	15	4
A-4	23	152	32	27	12	16	63	47	3	12	768	8	94	5	25	221	8	16	70
PA II																			
A-13	6	167	20	17	10	10	90	27	2	6	773	6	91	8	30	188	6	11	735

A-21	5	147	19	17	11	10	56	24	3	6	712	6	86	10	47	185	6	11	164
A-30	6	160	21	20	10	10	76	25	3	6	744	7	105	14	65	187	7	13	1371
A-30	6	110	51	39	38	46	5437	180	169	12	626	10	112	2848	382	214	10	19	143408
A-23	6	174	25	16	14	12	63	22	5	7	692	7	85	5	97	195	8	13	112
A-8	4	138	17	16	8	8	88	29	2	6	715	6	76	5	64	171	6	11	68
Serie 2.1																			
A-3	8	177	31	18	9	12	54	23	5	8	845	7	88	8	159	337	8	13	92
A-19	4	168	26	20	13	14	711	42	14	5	594	7	101	81	1069	256	8	13	407
A-14	7	183	30	13	7	11	41	20	4	7	781	7	75	10	69	316	7	12	73
A-27	6	167	31	14	7	15	49	28	4	8	988	7	92	6	38	310	8	14	51
A-26	6	170	53	15	16	27	69	41	14	8	717	11	88	5	27	233	12	14	84
HIMT																			
A-15	5	199	42	55	14	14	52	26	5	6	565	10	243	11	4	198	10	17	95
A-2	4	45	61	69	13	22	49	31	4	7	523	10	263	2	<1	423	9	16	18
A-18	4	207	89	59	14	36	56	51	16	6	504	13	235	1	<1	360	14	17	14
A-22	6	176	99	53	13	29	54	41	16	6	560	12	203	1	1	291	13	17	28

(continued)

Table 12.3b (cont.)

	Li	*B*	*V*	*Cr*	*Co*	*Ni*	*Cu*	*Zn*	*As*	*Rb*	*SrO*	*Y*	*Zr*	*Sn*	*Sb*	*Ba*	*La*	*Ce*	*Pb*
A-9	4	177	52	51	41	22	158	46	8	5	539	10	191	6	54	526	10	15	79
A-16	5	180	39	42	718	47	1106	43	7	5	580	9	178	28	5	212	9	15	750
A-28	6	45	70	60	14	23	70	42	5	8	759	11	275	6	<1	471	11	19	54
HIT																			
A-5	3	176	28	65	3	7	4	13	1	5	451	9	298	1	<1	126	9	16	5
Lev I																			
A-29	4	58	9	13	2	4	147	20	2	7	512	7	46	10	30	214	7	12	40
Egypt I																			
A-20	3	63	18	28	3	6	4	13	<1	4	173	7	129	1	<1	176	8	15	7
ukn																			
A-1	2	131	10	52	16	8	22	12	1	17	281	7	59	3	31	249	6	11	18

Manganese-decolourised and antimony-decolourised glass

Nine fragments are made of manganese-decolourised glass, including two decorated fragments with two analyses each. One fragment (A-44) belongs to a light green cast dish with cut decoration of oval facets and horizontal grooves and roughly dates to the first two centuries CE (Harden 1940: pl. LXXXV.4). It thus represents one of the earliest glass finds from Armant and given the life span of the town it is very likely that this piece was kept as an heirloom in the house and was in use over several generations, although the lack of a securely documented find contexts might be misleading here. The other fragments belong to free-blown vessels. A-36 is the base of a light green jar standing on three toes (Harden 1940: pl. LXXXV.6) for which a close parallel from Karanis has been discovered in contexts dating to the early second to the middle of the third century CE (see Table 12.1). A-10 is the rim of a colourless bowl or jar that on typological evidence probably dates between the early second to early third century CE (see Figure 12.2). One olive green rim of a bowl or cup is decorated with a blue crimped trail on its top (A-32, Figure 12.2.19) and dates to the second to fourth century CE. Most interestingly, this type is rather common in the Syro-Palestine region (Jennings 2006, 57, fig. 4.5.1; Keller 2006, Plate 11, type VII.19b, no. 692). Two fragments represent bases of lamps, one of the conical hollow type made of purple glass (A-41), one light green lamp base featuring an applied blob (A-46), and one light olive green pad base belongs to an oval dish (A-7). The two typologically latest pieces include a rim fragment of light yellow-green glass belonging to a flask (A-24), and a colourless rim of a beaker or goblet with blue, marvered-in trails (A-25, Figure 12.2.14), consistent with fifth- to sixth-century types.

Glass production during this early period is attested in Egypt in the Wadi Natrun and the area around Lake Mareotis (Nenna et al. 2000; Nenna 2007), and manganese-decolourised glass has been produced in the Wadi Natrun (Picon et al. 2008). However, the manganese-decolourised glass from this region (group *wna* in Picon et al. 2008) shows a distinct signature with very low levels of calcium oxide, which is not matched by the pieces from Armant, or indeed manganese-decolourised glasses found elsewhere (e.g. Silvestri et al. 2008; Rehren et al. 2015), as they all show higher levels of lime. Therefore we argue that the manganese-decolourised glass from Armant cannot be linked to the primary production furnaces in the Wadi Natrun. Instead, the town must have had a different supplier for its manganese-decolourised glass, similar

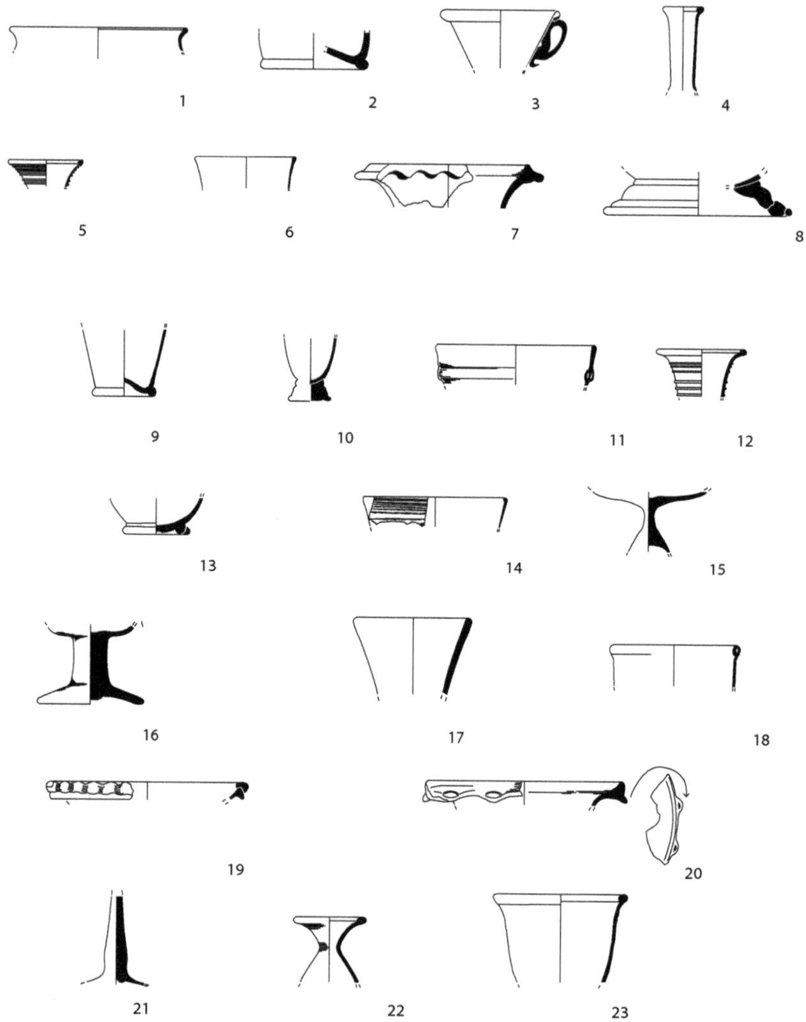

Figure 12.2 Glass vessel fragments from Armant. Scale 1:2.
Source: drawings: Daniela Rosenow, digitisation: Daniela Rosenow and Elli Petrocheilou

to that supplying the Mediterranean sites and probably situated in the Levant (Schibille et al. 2017).

Only one fragment, A-17 (Table 12.1), is made of antimony-decolourised glass. It belongs to a light green indented beaker. This type of vessel is most common during the late first to the third centuries CE, and Egyptian parallels have come to light e.g. in Elephantine (Rodziewicz 2005, Plate 3.48), Medinet Maadi (Silvano 2013, 46, fig. 4), Mons

Porphyrites (Bailey 2007, 250, fig. 8.10) or Quseir el-Qadim (Meyer 1992, Plate 8.151–66; Peacock 2011, 63, figs 7.4.44–8). Given the date of the beaker it is, together with the manganese-decolourised vessels, one of the earliest glass objects discovered in Armant. Its composition matches closely that of the Cl1/2 group from the cargo of the *Iulia Felix* (Silvestri et al. 2008), which is thought to date to the third century CE.

Compositionally, the nine manganese-decolourised fragments broadly resemble the colourless glass analysed from the cargo of the *Iulia Felix* (Silvestri et al. 2008), matching the range of minor oxide concentrations reported for CL1/1 and CL1/2 (antimony- and mixed antimony/manganese-decolourised glass, respectively). However, they do not fit either of these two groups particularly well, and a principal mismatch exists for the concentrations of decolourants, with the manganese-decolourised glass from Armant falling closer to the antimony- or mixed-decolourised glasses from the *Iulia Felix* but having manganese rather than antimony oxide as the decolourant. An overall much better match exists to the *série 3.2* of Foy et al. (2003), which they assign to glass made using the Belus sand and dating mostly to the fifth and sixth century CE. Cholakova and Rehren (Chapter 3, this volume) discuss this glass composition and its occurrence across the Roman/Byzantine empire in some more detail; suffice it here to say that the only discrepancies between the *série 3.2* glass and the manganese-decolourised glass from Armant lie in the somewhat higher alumina content of the latter, and the much earlier dating of several fragments of this composition from Armant, potentially going back to the first/second century CE.

Plant ash-based glass

Remarkably, 12 out of 47 fragments consist of plant ash-based glass, forming two sub-groups, PA I (5 fragments) and PA II (7 fragments with 8 analyses; Figure 12.3). One PA I glass is a dark green raw glass chunk (A-4) of unknown date. A-6 belongs to a blue-green pillar moulded bowl, a vessel type dating between the middle of the first century BCE and about the third quarter of the first century CE (Brun 2011) and thus, as A-44, might have been kept in a house for several generations. A-11 derives from a dark green unguentarium that, on typological evidence, dates to the first to third century CE, while A-12 (Figure 12.2.2) is the base of a deep bowl with applied base ring, made of glass with a light pinkish-brown colour. Both fragments have tentatively been dated by Harden to the third to fourth century CE (Harden 1936, classes III and XI/XII, respectively). A-42 (Figure 12.2.4) is the rim and neck of a flask, made of blue-greenish glass and possibly dating to the fourth/fifth centuries CE.

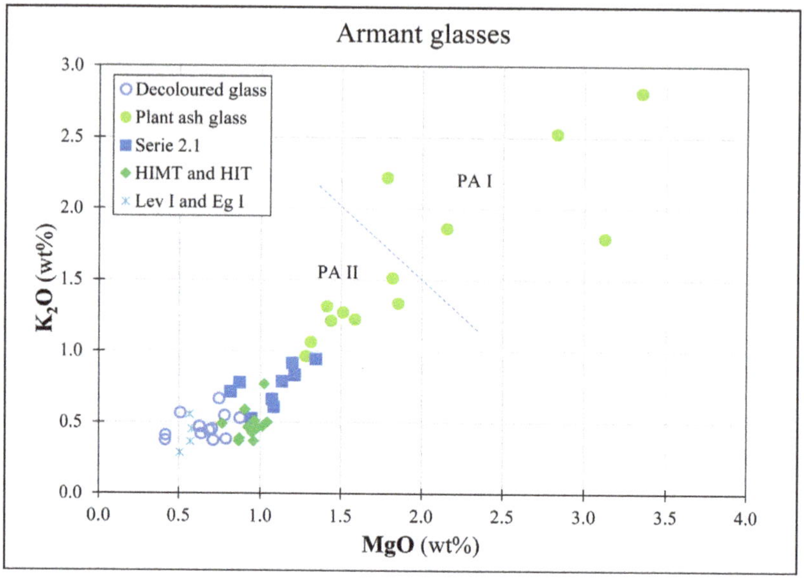

Figure 12.3 Scatter plot of MgO vs K_2O for all analysed glasses from Armant. Note the apparent continuum between the mineral natron glasses and the plant ash glasses.

Interestingly, the plant ash-based glass does not seem to be associated with a specific colour.

It is worth mentioning that among the earlier material plant ash-based and manganese-decolourised glass fragments predominate over antimony-decolourised glass. Recent research on glass from contemporary sites in Egypt such as Bubastis, Buto, Oxyrrhynchus or Saqqara has shown that antimony-decolourised glass was the more common glass composition used in Roman Egypt (Rosenow and Rehren 2014; unpublished own data), despite the fact that it was apparently considered a luxury glass in the rest of the Mediterranean world (Silvestri et al. 2008, Foster and Jackson 2010). There, Roman blue/green glass was the most widely circulated primary glass group, a composition that has so far not been detected at all among any Egyptian glass chemically analysed to date. As there are no data on glass deriving from other Roman sites in Upper Egypt it must for now remain open whether this apparent predominance of plant ash-based and manganese-decolourised glass over antimony-decolourised glass is due to the choice of glass fragments collected by the excavators, the choice of glass fragments sampled for this study, a subtle chronological difference between the assemblages from Upper and Lower Egypt available for research at the moment, or whether it truly reflects different tastes or different access and supply routes and patterns of glass usage in Lower and Upper Egypt.

PA II glasses include a blue-green pad base of a deep bowl (A-21), the rim of a blue-green funnel mouth flask with thin, horizontally applied brown trails around the rim and neck of the vessel (A-30, Figure 12.2.5), a turquoise concave base of a flask with pontil mark (A-40), a blue-green rim of a (possibly stemmed?) goblet (A-47, Figure 12.2.6), a rim and attached handle of a green/blue jug (A-13, Figure 12.2.3), a blue-green rim of a bottle (A-23, Figure 12.2.17) and an infolded rim fragment of a blue-green flask or goblet (A-8, Figure 12.2.23). These fragments seem, on the basis of typology, mostly to be of a later date than the other plant ash-based vessels (see Table 12.1).

The plant ash-(PA) based glasses are identified by their higher concentrations of magnesia, potash and phosphate compared to the mineral natron-based glasses. Using the sum of these three oxides as the main criterion, we recognise two discrete compositions: in PA I glasses the sum of these oxides is between 3.9 and nearly 8 wt%, while in PA II the sum is between 2.5 and 3.7 wt% (Figure 12.4). The separation between the two groups is not unambiguous; A-4 for instance could be assigned also to PA II, due to its low MnO content (see below), and the brown glass

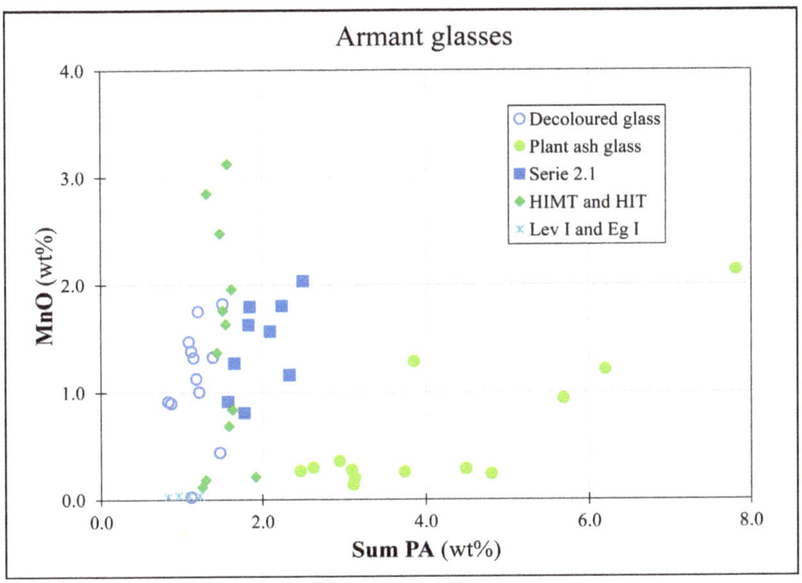

Figure 12.4 Scatter plot of the sum of the plant ash oxides ('PA'), namely K_2O, MgO and P_2O_5, vs MnO. Note the clear separation between the mineral natron and plant ash glasses in this presentation.

from sample A-30 could be assigned to PA I, based on its high potash and phosphate contents.

Using this sum of 'plant ash oxides' distinguishes much clearer between the plant ash glasses and mineral natron glasses with elevated magnesia and potash contents, such as the *série 2.1* glasses (see below), which in Figure 12.3 seem to form a continuum with the plant ash glasses. The highest value is found in the dark green unguentarium, driven partly by its extremely high phosphate content of more than 1.6 wt% P_2O_5. While this concentration is high compared to most other glass analyses, it resembles the composition of similar finds from elsewhere in Egypt (Rosenow and Rehren 2014) and beyond (Jackson and Cottam 2015). A further distinguishing criterion between the two PA groups is the concentration of manganese oxide, which in PA I averages 1.2 wt%, while in PA II it averages only 0.25 wt% and does not exceed 0.3 wt%. There appears to be also a clear chronological difference between the two glass types, with PA I giving way to PA II at some point around the fourth century CE.

The composition of the brown trail applied to the neck of vessel A-30 is remarkable. It contains about 15 wt% lead oxide and very high concentrations of alumina, iron oxide and titania, as well as half a per cent of copper. Its blue-greenish base glass composition is therefore very different from that of the applied trail, suggesting that the brown-coloured glass was procured separately from the glass used to form the vessel.

During the first half of the first millennium CE, the use of plant ash glass is rather rare west of the Euphrates (Rehren and Freestone 2015 and literature therein), and occurs only in very small amounts across the empire in Roman and Late Antique times (e.g. Brill 1991 (Sedeinga, Sudan); Henderson 1996 (Fishbourne, UK), Jackson et al. 2009 (France and Britain); Schibille 2011a (Butrint, Albania); Gallo et al. 2013 (Italy). In contrast, east of the Euphrates it was continuously used since the Late Bronze Age through to the Islamic period (Freestone 2006; Mirti et al. 2008, 2009; Simpson 2014). However, our data show that this Sasanian glass does not chemically match the material from Armant, which is lower in potassium and magnesia and thus unlikely to be an import from the East (Figure 12.5).

An earlier study of glass from Bubastis in the eastern Nile Delta (Rosenow and Rehren 2014) has already identified the ongoing use of plant ash glass there during the early first millennium CE; together with the data from Armant it seems that plant ash glass production persisted in Egypt alongside the dominant mineral natron-based glass industry, where it must be seen as a compositional glass group of at least regional

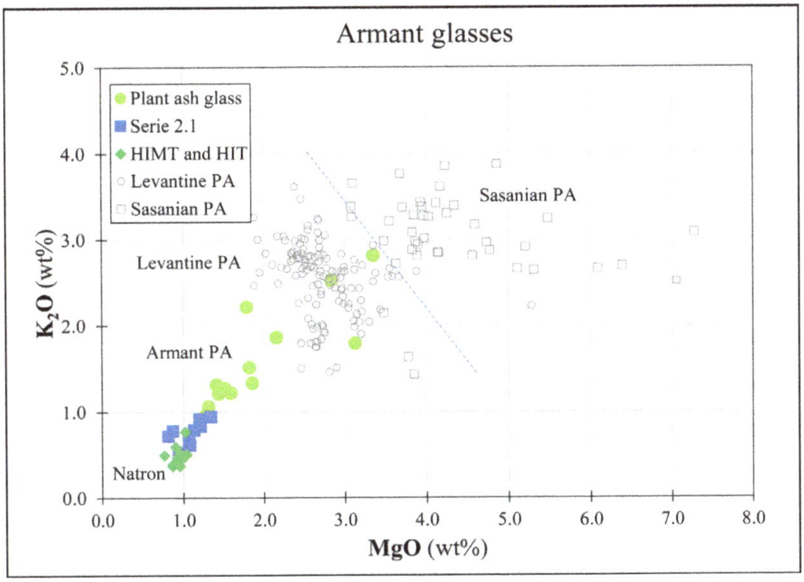

Figure 12.5 Scatter plot of MgO vs K_2O for the plant ash glasses superimposed on Mesopotamian and Sasanian glasses, demonstrating that the Egyptian plant ash glasses are not Sasanian.
Source: underlying graph modified from Freestone (2006: 204)

importance, with some export particularly of emerald green glass across the Roman empire.

Série 2.1 (Foy et al. 2003)

Eight fragments, including one bi-chrome, are made of glass closely matching the composition described by Foy et al. (2003) as *série 2.1*. It has been detected on a colourless body fragment with purple streaks in it (A-31), an olive green stemmed goblet (A-34, Figure 12.2.15), an olive green stemmed bowl (A-14, Figure 12.2.16), a light pink rim of a funnel mouth bottle (A-27, Figure 12.2.18), a single applied turquoise base ring possibly belonging to a flask made of light green colour (A-19, Figure 12.2.9), an out-folded rim of light brown-pinkish colour (A-45) and an olive green cup with double-fold (A-26, Figure 12.2.11). In addition, one olive green raw glass fragment is made of this glass composition (A-3). Based on typological evidence, the fragments date from the (late?) fourth to the sixth centuries CE. The *série 2.1* glass vessels display various colours, including pinkish, purple and colourless glass, but (light) green to olive green glass seems to be the most common one.

Glass of this composition has recently been discussed in some detail by Cholakova et al. (2016) from the lower Danube region. There, as in the material presented by Foy and co-workers, it is mostly restricted to shapes and contexts of the sixth and seventh centuries CE with only a few earlier examples, while the finds from Armant indicate that this glass composition was potentially already in use somewhat earlier (Tables 12.3a and 12.3b). In an earlier publication, we have tentatively labelled glass of this composition as 'weak HIMT' (Rosenow and Rehren 2014: 181) while stressing the need to explore its relationship to HIMT glass more fully. While a full discussion still remains to be done, the increasing availability of trace element data now allows a more detailed look at this, indicating that the 'weak HIMT' *sensu* Rosenow and Rehren (2014) comprises both *série 3.2* and *série 2.1* glass. One characteristic of the *série 2.1* composition is its relatively high strontium content compared to other mineral-natron glasses (Cholakova et al. 2016, 629), seen also among the Armant glass of this composition. The five *série 2.1* samples from Armant for which we have LA-ICPMS data have an average strontium content of 660 ppm, compared to average values of less than 510 ppm in the five analysed Mn-decolourised samples, 490 ppm in the seven analysed HIMT glasses and only about 330 ppm in the remaining analysed mineral natron glasses. Significantly, it also has a good correlation between manganese and strontium oxide (Figure 12.6). This alone already sets the *série 2.1* glass apart from the HIMT glass, as it cannot be explained as a result of simple mixing of HIMT glass with other glass compositions. On balance, we therefore favour the use of *série 2.1* over our earlier 'weak HIMT' label for glass of this composition. Unfortunately, no trace data exists at present for the Bubastis glass and it has to remain open whether there, too, we see an occurrence of *série 2.1* glass much earlier in Egypt than elsewhere.

HIMT glass

Nine glass vessels match the composition of HIMT glass, which was most likely produced on the northern coast of the Sinai Peninsula (Freestone et al. 2005) from the fourth to possibly the early sixth centuries CE. Given the chronological range of HIMT glass and its Egyptian origin it is not surprising that this group – next to the Mn-decolourised and ahead of the *série 2.1* glass – is a prominent compositional glass group within the Armant assemblage. This is also in line with analysed glass corpora from

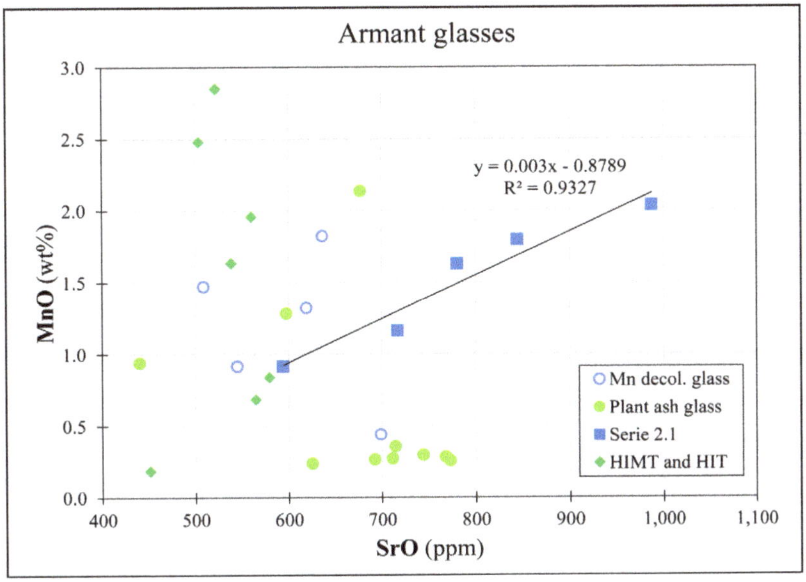

Figure 12.6 Scatter plot of SrO vs MnO, demonstrating the good correlation between the two oxides in *série 2.1* glass, but not the others.

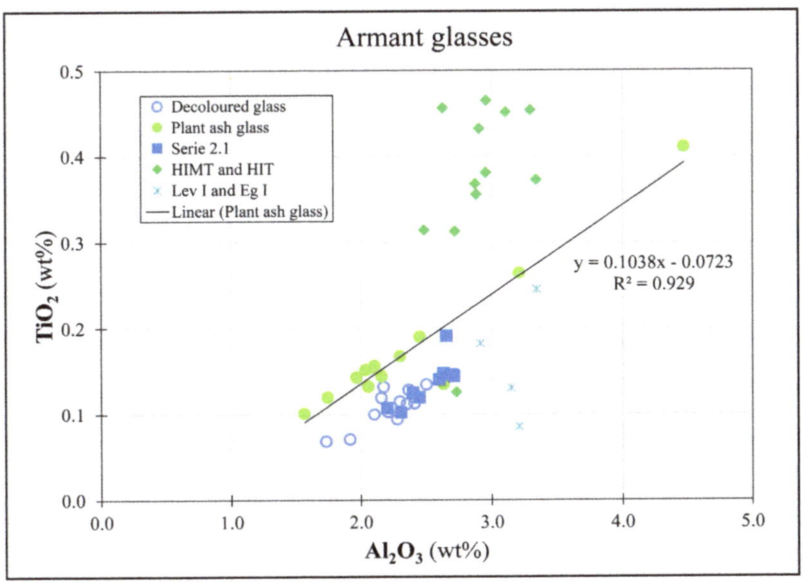

Figure 12.7 Scatter plot of Al_2O_3 vs TiO_2, demonstrating the good correlation between the two in some of the glass groups, but not all.

contemporary sites in Lower Egypt. Analysed fragments of HIMT glass vessels, all dating to the above mentioned period of HIMT glass use, include deep and shallow bowls with an outsplayed rim made of green glass (A-9), a thickened rim of brown-pinkish glass (A-2), a dark green-bluish cup with pinched trail (A-15, Figure 12.2.7), a brown cup with a flared edge going up (A-28), an olive green lamp with cracked-off rim (A-18) and an olive green lamp with coiled base (A-22, Figure 12.2.10), a funnel mouth flask with horizontally applied thin trails of the same olive green colour (A-33, Figure 12.2.12), a multiple or high coiled base ring possibly deriving from a deep blue bottle or jug (A-16, Figure 12.2.8), and a double applied base ring maybe belonging to a green lamp, flask or beaker (A-37, Figure 12.2.13). The majority of these pieces are made of green or olive green glass typically associated with this primary glass group, although a number of pieces are brown-pinkish, blue or green-bluish in colour.

The composition of the HIMT glasses conforms closely to the published analyses; the titania content averages 0.4 wt%, lime concentrations cluster closely around 6 wt%, and typical concentrations of iron and manganese oxide are around 1.5 to 3 wt% each (see e.g. the compilation of data in Nenna 2014, 178, table 18.1, first three rows).

HIT glass

Three fragments show an HIMT signature but are comparatively low in manganese oxide, with only around 0.2 wt% MnO. This glass group, dubbed HIT glass (Rehren and Cholakova 2010: 90), has come to light in a number of other places (see e.g. Maltoni et al. 2015) where it dates to the fifth and sixth centuries CE. The HIT glass fragments from Armant include a small blue pad base possibly belonging to a stemmed bowl (A-35), a blue stemmed goblet (A-38, Table 12.1) and the rim of a blue-greenish cup with pinched trail (A-5, Figure 12.2.20). All three vessel types can be dated to the late Roman/early Byzantine period. Two of the three pieces (A-35 and A-38) are intentionally coloured blue by the addition of cobalt and copper oxide with elevated levels of lead. A-5 on the other hand is blue-greenish which appears to be its natural colour. A-38 falls in its composition between HIT and *série 2.1*; its titania content is rather low for HIT glass, while its manganese oxide is very low compared to the main *série 2.1* compositions. Unfortunately, we have no trace element data for this sample to resolve this ambiguity, and have to leave it open to which of these two groups it belongs.

There is still a considerable number of questions evolving around this specific raw glass group. Its composition is close enough to HIMT glass to consider it a sub-group of the latter one. The existence of this glass group strongly indicates that manganese was not necessarily a component naturally included in the sand used to produce HIMT glass but might have been intentionally added to manipulate the colour of the glass. The intentional addition of manganese oxide in some but not all raw glass has also been seen elsewhere, in Levantine I glass with and without added Mn. Here it might be of importance that two of the three HIT glass fragments were intentionally coloured by adding copper and cobalt, resulting in a deep blue glass, and the same holds true indeed for the HIT glass fragment discovered in Classe, Italy (Maltoni et al. 2015) and a glass weight held at the British Museum from a sixth- to seventh-century CE context (Schibille et al. 2016, 12). This might be an explanation for the omission of manganese: the original intention was to produce a strongly coloured glass and the addition of a decolourant was unnecessary.

Egypt I glass

Two fragments are made of Egypt I glass, characterised by extremely low levels of calcium oxide (Table 12.3a). Both of them are light greenish-blue, A-20 being a raw glass fragment while A-43 (Figure 12.2.21) is from a stemmed goblet, which is a type of vessel most common from the sixth to the seventh century CE. Egypt I glass has been detected in relatively large amounts in two sites in the Western Delta (Rosenow and Rehren unpublished own data) and its abundance there can possibly be explained by the region's proximity to the Wadi Natrun, the alleged production region of this primary glass group (Sayre and Smith 1974, Freestone et al. 2000). Otherwise Egypt I glass is not well attested elsewhere in Egypt (but see Foy et al. 2003 for its occurrence in eighth-century Tebtynis in the Fayum) or beyond (but see Kato et al. 2009, 1704), suggesting that it was not a widely traded primary glass group.

Levantine I glass

Only two of the analysed fragments from Armant match the composition of Levantine I glass, produced in Apollonia-Arsuf/Israel (Freestone et al. 2000) and the dominating glass group used north-east of the Red Sea during the period under study here. One fragment, A-29 (Figure 12.2.22), is a rim belonging to a small flask made of blue-greenish glass dating to the fourth to seventh centuries CE. The other, A-39, is a chunk of raw glass indicating the working of this imported glass composition in Armant. The scarcity of Levantine glass is again in line with observations from contemporary sites elsewhere in Egypt (Rosenow and Rehren 2014; unpublished own data), confirming a strong preference for using raw glass produced in the country.

Unknown glass composition

Only one fragment could not be ascribed to any of the known primary raw glass groups. A-1 (Table 12.1) is the fragment of a lamp with cracked-off rim and can be dated to the fourth–sixth century CE. It has rather low magnesia (0.3 wt% MgO) and lime (4.5 wt% CaO), and is characterised by an extremely high level of alumina (5 wt% Al_2O_3) albeit not high enough to ascribe it to the high-alumina glasses discussed by Dussubieux et al. (2010).

Recycling and colouration

It is tempting to consider that fresh raw glass might not have been as readily available in Upper Egypt as it apparently has been in the northern parts of the country, and thus glass had to be recycled more often. It has been discussed elsewhere how the composition of mineral-natron glass is affected by recycling or particular working conditions (e.g. Degryse et al. 2006; Schibille et al. 2017). Jackson (1997) has pointed out that the inclusion during recycling of small amounts of coloured glass into the batch results in measureable increases in base metals such as cobalt, copper, antimony and lead; this has since been widely accepted as an indicator for recycling. Separately, Paynter (2008) was the first to document the uptake of fuel-ash oxides such as potash and magnesia into glass during extended working times; Rehren et al. (2010, 75) and Rehren and Brüggler (2015, 174) have shown this phenomenon in archaeological assemblages, where it is regularly associated with recycling.

Within the Armant assemblage, the group of plant ash glasses with low magnesia and potash concentrations (PA II) could potentially be seen as originally mineral-natron glass with increased magnesia and potash concentrations due to recycling or prolonged working. The elevated average levels of base metals such as copper (75 ppm), antimony (55 ppm) and lead (420 ppm) in many of these glasses even omitting the brown glass A-30, would support such an interpretation, as first suggested by Jackson (1997). However, the question then would be which original glass group was being recycled here, to arrive at this particular composition? Logically, this would be one or more of the dominant glass groups present in Armant – i.e. either manganese decolourised, or *série 2.1*, or HIMT. The low level of titania in the PA II glass rules out HIMT, while the similarity in most sand-derived minor oxides between PA II and *série 2.1* is striking. However, the much lower levels of manganese oxide in PA II (0.25 wt%) compared to the average in *série 2.1* (1.3 wt% MnO) makes this also highly unlikely, and also excludes manganese decolourised glass as the potential source glass. Thus, we conclude that PA II is indeed a separate glass composition, based on plant ash with relatively low levels of potash and magnesia compared to the earlier group PA I, and potentially made with the same or similar sand as *série 2.1* glass.

The available trace element data (Table 12.3b) shows that the blue decoration on A-25 (Mn decol) and the blue vessel A-16 (HIMT) are both coloured by cobalt and copper, with tin and lead also clearly elevated. The very high lead oxide content of the brown trail on the flask A-30 (PA II glass) has already been mentioned; in addition, this glass contains nearly half a per cent copper, a quarter of 1 per cent tin, nearly 400 ppm antimony and *c.*150 ppm each zinc and arsenic. Among the very early glasses was one that was decoloured by antimony. Thus, the range of base metals as potential recycling indicators is the same as elsewhere. Any discussion of elevated base metal concentrations necessarily requires a definition of concentrations present as part of the normal raw materials of the glass, primarily the sand used to make it. Here, we use relatively conservative (= high) geological threshold levels of 50 ppm for copper (100 ppm in HIMT) and lead (75 ppm in HIMT) and 25 ppm for antimony (see also Rehren and Brüggler 2015, 174 and references therein). These values are based on concentrations found in glass showing no indication for recycling from a range of sites, including primary production sites in the Levant. Using these criteria, we recognise only one fragment with recycling traces among the seven HIMT glasses for which we have trace element data, but three out of nine among the *série 2.1* fragments, two out of four PA I glasses, and all five PA II glasses. The reasons for this apparent difference in recycling rates are not immediately obvious, but could be indicative of different life histories of the individual glass compositional groups, such as the strongly coloured HIMT glass being less likely to be involved in recycling than the other, lighter-coloured glass compositions.

Discussion and conclusion

A considerable amount of glass vessel fragments came to light during excavations in the Roman and Coptic town of Armant in Upper Egypt. The majority of them belong to types associated with settlement contexts such as bowls, cups, lamps or flasks, and they primarily date to the mid-third to the mid-fifth centuries CE. Comparing this Upper Egyptian glass corpus with contemporary assemblages from Lower Egypt, several observations are of particular interest.

Secondary production remains indicate that glass vessels were manufactured at the site using HIMT glass (A-3), plant ash-based glass (A-4 and A-40), and Egypt I glass (A-20). Given the chronological range of HIMT and Egypt I glass it is safe to say that glass-working took place in Armant at least during late Roman and Late Antique times (fourth to sixth centuries CE). Both raw glass groups were most likely imported from Lower Egypt – the northern coast of Sinai peninsula (HIMT) and the Wadi Natrun (Egypt I), respectively.

While antimony-decolourised glass seems to have been the most widely circulated compositional group in Roman Lower Egypt, this glass group is here only represented by a single sample. Similarly, Levantine glass, which dominates many Late Antique assemblages outside Egypt, is only represented by two fragments, and Roman blue/green glass is entirely absent. Instead, we see here an unexpectedly prominent presence of plant ash glass, covering the entire chronological span of the site and constituting more than a quarter of all analysed finds. The remaining three quarters are mineral natron glass, dominated by three compositional groups present in about equal proportions. The earliest of these, here referred to as manganese-decolourised, is compositionally very similar to the glass group *série 3.2* of Foy et al. (2003), and differs from it primarily by its much earlier emergence in Armant. From the fourth/fifth century CE onward it coexists with the compositionally related glass *série 2.1* and the very distinct HIMT glass, both generally thought to be an Egyptian product.

The question of origin of the main glass groups at Armant is at the centre of our interest to understand the town's wider economic network. The plant ash-based glass is probably a regional product, as tentatively argued recently by Jackson and Cottam (2015, 144–5) and indicated by the relative abundance of plant ash-based glass in Armant. Plant ash-based glass production increasingly emerges as a primary source of at least regional importance in Roman and Late Antique Egypt, and we might have to consider a continuous production of this raw glass, possibly based on a technological tradition going back to the Late Bronze Age.

The origin of *série 3.2* is of major interest to us. Foy et al. (2003) established it as part of their *groupe* 3 of glass compositions, which they link to a production origin from the River Belus in Palestine. However, as pointed out recently by Cholakova et al. (2016) on the basis of trace elements and by Maltoni et al. (2016, 12–14) based on strontium and neodymium isotopic evidence, this glass composition has much more in common with other compositional groups that we consider to be most likely of Egyptian origin, such as *série 2.1*, and does not seem to have many parallels found in Syro-Palestine. We therefore consider it at present more likely to be of Egyptian rather than Syro-Palestinian origin, a view further supported by the ratio of Zr to Y, which matches the trend line for Egyptian glass given by Gratuze (2013, 214).

Of particular interest is the presence both of the manganese-decolourised glass matching the composition of *série 3.2* and of *série 2.1* glass at Armant. Outside Egypt, glass of these compositions emerges only from the fourth and the late fifth centuries, respectively, while in Armant they potentially pre-date their occurrence in Europe. In particular the second glass type is increasingly emerging as a major compositional group, from France (Foy et al. 2003: '*série 2.1*') through Serbia (Drauschke and Greiff 2010) to Bulgaria (Cholakova et al. 2016: 'sixth-century glass'), Cyprus (Ceglia et al. 2015: 'HLIMT') and Egypt (Rosenow and Rehren 2014: 'wHIMT'). In contrast, it is apparently entirely absent from the Levant, which together with its earlier emergence in Egypt than elsewhere indicates that it was indeed produced in Egypt, even though no production site has yet been identified.

In summary, the late Roman and Late Antique glass from Armant studied here is compositionally diverse, with early glasses dominated by manganese-decolourised and plant ash glass, followed from the fourth century CE by a broadly equal presence of plant ash glass, manganese-decolourised (= *série 3.2*), *serie 2.1* and HIMT glass. This change in composition over time, and the increasing reliance on regionally produced glass, matches a similar pattern seen elsewhere in the Byzantine world, as for instance in Pergamon (Rehren et al. 2015). Despite this diversity, the assemblage appears to be entirely, with the exemption of two fragments, made up of glass produced in Egypt indicating that there was barely any inter-regional exchange in raw glass between Egypt and the Levant throughout the time of the Byzantine empire.

Both the antimony-decolourised glass and Egypt I glass have come to light in Armant only in small amounts, and given the limited dataset it would be too far-fetched to deduce further conclusion about the circulation of these primary glass groups in Upper Egypt. As part of our ongoing research it is planned to sample more material from Middle and Upper Egypt as well as Sudan in order to shed more light on these regions' integration into the trade network pattern established for contemporary Lower Egypt and the Mediterranean world. Finally, one out of the 47 analysed samples cannot be assigned to any known compositional glass group. What is clear, however, is that this glass apparently never reached Lower Egypt and the Mediterranean glass trade and that we might have evidence for primary glass produced on a small scale and never intended to leave its production region and become one of the 'things that travelled'.

Acknowledgements

The research presented here was partly done while one of us (DR) was a Marie-Curie Fellow (*Glass in Late Antiquity: Science and Society*, project number 298127, FP7-PEOPLE-2011-IEF), based at the UCL Institute of Archaeology and further advanced during a period as Visiting Researcher at UCL Qatar. We thank all our colleagues from the Ashmolean Museum (Liam McNamara, Mark Norman, Daniel Bone) who have made glass samples available to us for analysis. We are also grateful for comments by Anastasia Cholakova regarding some of the glass groups and by two peer reviewers, which helped us to strengthen the chapter; any remaining errors are ours. This publication was partly made possible by NPRP grant 7-776-6-024 from the Qatar National Research Fund (a member of Qatar Foundation). The statements made herein are solely the responsibility of the authors.

References

Bailey, D. 1998. *Excavations at El-Ashmunein V: Pottery, Lamps and Glass of the Late Roman and Early Arab Periods*. London: British Museum Press.

Bailey, D. 2007. 'Glass'. In *The Roman Imperial Quarries Survey and Excavations at Mons Porphyrites 1994–1998, Volume. II. The Excavations*, edited by V. A. Maxfield and D. Peacock, 233–66. London: Egypt Exploration Society.

Brill, R. H. 1991. 'Scientific Investigation of Some Glasses from Sedeinga'. *Journal of Glass Studies* 33: 11–28.

Brill, R. H. 1999. *Chemical Analyses of Ancient Glass*. New York: Corning Museum of Glass.

Brun, J. P. 2011. 'Les objets en verre'. In *Didymoi. Une garnison romaine dans le désert Oriental d'Égypte, 1. Les fouilles et le matériel*, edited by H. Cuvigny, 215–41. Cairo: Institut français d'archéologie orientale.

Ceglia A., Cosyns, P., Nys, K., Terryn, H., Thienpont, H. and Meulebroeck, W. 2015. 'Late Antique Glass Distribution and Consumption in Cyprus: A Chemical Study'. *Journal of Archaeological Science* 61: 213–22.

Cholakova, A., Rehren, Th. and Freestone, I. 2016. 'Compositional Identification of 6th c. AD Glass from the Lower Danube'. *Journal of Archaeological Science: Reports* 7: 625–32.

Degryse, P., Schneider, J., Haack, U., Lauwers, V., Poblome, J., Waelkens, M. and Muchez, Ph. 2006. 'Evidence for Glass "Recycling" Using Pb and Sr Isotopic Ratios and Sr-Mixing Lines: The Case of Early Byzantine Sagalassos'. *Journal of Archaeological Science* 33: 494–501.

Drauschke, J. and Greiff, S. 2010. 'Chemical Aspects of Byzantine Glass from Caričin Grad/Iustiniana Prima (Serbia)'. In *Glass in Byzantium – Production, Usage, Analyses*, edited by J. Drauschke and D. Keller, 25–46. Mainz: Römisch-Germanisches Zentralmuseum.

Dussubieux, L., Gratuze, B., Blet-Lemarquand, M. 2010. 'Mineral Soda Alumina Glass: Occurrence and Meaning'. *Journal of Archaeological Science* 37: 1646–55.

Faiers, J. 2013. *Late Roman Glassware and Pottery from Amarna and Related Studies EES Excavation Memoir 102*. London: Egypt Exploration Society.

Foster, H. E. and Jackson, C. M. 2010. 'The Composition of Late Romano-British Colourless Vessel Glass: Glass Production and Consumption'. *Journal of Archaeological Science* 37: 3068–80.

Foy, D., Picon, M., Vichy, M. and Thirion-Merle, V. 2003. 'Caractérisation des verres de la fin de l'Antiquité en Méditerranée occidentale: l'émergence de nouveaux courants commerciaux'. In *Échanges et commerce du verre dans le monde antique (*Monographies Instrumentum 24), edited by D. Foy and M. D. Nenna, 41–85. Montagnac: Éditions Monique Mergoil

Freestone, I. C. 2006. 'Glass Production in Late Antiquity and the Early Islamic Period: A Geochemical Perspective'. In *Geomaterials in Cultural Heritage*, edited by M. Maggetti, and B. Messiga, Special Publications 257, 201–16. London: Geological Society London.

Freestone, I. C., Gorin-Rosen, Y. and Hughes, M. J. 2000. 'Primary Glass from Israel and the Production of Glass in Late Antiquity and the Early Islamic Period'. In *La route du verre: ateliers primaires et secondaires de verriers du second millinaire av. J.-C. au Moyen-Age*, edited by M. D. Nenna, 65–84. Lyons: Travaux de la Maison de l'Orient Méditerranéen no. 33.

Freestone, I. C., Greenwood, R. and Gorin-Rosen, Y. 2002. 'Byzantine and Early Islamic Glassmaking in the Eastern Mediterranean: Production and Distribution of Primary Glass'. In *Hyalos – Vitrum – Glass. History Technology and Conservation of Glass and Vitreus Materials in the Hellenic World, 1st International Conference, Rhodes, Greece, 1–4 April 2001*, edited by G. Kordas, 167–74. Athens: Glasnet.

Freestone, I. C., Wolf, S. and Thirlwall, M. 2005. 'The Production of HIMT Glass: Elemental and Isotopic Evidence'. In *Annales du 16e Congrès de l'Association Internationale pour l'Histoire du Verre: London, 2003*, edited by the International Association for the History of Glass, 153–7. Lochem: Association Internationale pour l'Histoire du Verre.

Gallo, F., Silvestri, A., Molin, G. 2013. 'Glass from the Archaeological Museum of Adria (North-East Italy): New Insights into Early Roman Production Technologies'. *Journal of Archaeological Science* 40: 2589–605.

Gratuze, B. 2013. 'Glass Characterisation Using Laser Ablation Inductively Coupled Plasma Mass Spectrometry Methods'. In *Modern Methods for Analysing Archaeological and Historical Glass*, edited by K. Janssens, 201–34. Hoboken, NJ: John Wiley & Sons.

Gratuze, B. and Barrandon, J. N. 1990. 'Islamic Glass Weights and Stamps: Analysis Using Nuclear Techniques'. *Archaeometry* 32: 155–62.

Harden, D. B. 1936. *Roman Glass from Karanis found by the University of Michigan Archaeological Expedition in Egypt, 1924–1929*. Michigan: University of Michigan Press.

Harden, D. B. 1940. 'The Glass'. In *Temples of Armant. A Preliminary Survey, MEES 43*, edited by R. Mond and O. H. Myers, 117–27. London: Egypt Exploration Society.

Henderson, J. 1996. 'Scientific Analysis of Selected Fishbourne Vessel Glass and its Archaeological Implications, Excavations at Fishbourne 1969–1988'. In *Chichester Excavations*, edited by B. Cunliffe, A. Down and D. Rudkin, vol. 9, 189–92. Chichester: Chichester District Council.

Isings, C. 1957. *Roman Glass from Dated Finds* (Archaeologica Traiectina 2). Groningen and Djakarta: Wolters.

Jackson, C. 1997. 'From Roman to Early Medieval Glasses – many happy returns or a new birth?'. *Annales du 13e Congrès de l'Association Internationale pour l'Histoire du Verre*, edited by the International Association for the History of Glass, 289–302. Lochem: Association Internationale pour l'Histoire du Verre.

Jackson, C. and Cottam, S., 2015. '"A Green Thought in a Green Shade": Compositional and Typological Observations Concerning the Production of Emerald Green Glass Vessels in the 1st Century AD'. *Journal of Archaeological Science* 61: 139–48.

Jackson, C., Price, J. and Lemke, C. 2009. 'Glass Production in the 1st Century AD: Insights into Glass Technology'. In *Annales du 17e Congrès de l'Association Internationale pour l'Histoire du Verre: Antwerp 2006*, edited by the International Association for the History of Glass, 150–5. Lochem: Association Internationale pour l'Histoire du Verre.

Jennings, S. 2006. *Vessel Glass from Beirut BEY 006, 007 and 045* (Berytus 48–49, 2004–2005). Beirut, Lebanon: Faculty of Arts and Sciences, American University of Beirut.

Kato, N., Nakai, I., Shindo, Y. 2009. 'Change in Chemical Composition of Early Islamic Glass Excavated in Raya, Sinai Peninsula, Egypt: On-Site Analysis

Using a Portable X-Ray Fluorescence Spectrometer'. *Journal of Archaeological Science* 36: 1698–707.

Keller, D. 2006. *Petra Ez Zantur III. Ergebnisse der Schweizerisch-Liechtensteinischen Ausgrabungen, Teil 1: Die Gläser aus Petra*. Mainz: Philipp von Zabern.

Keller, D. 2008. 'Stadt und Tempel von Elephantine – 33./34./35. Grabungbericht. Preliminary Report on the Late Roman, Byzantine and Early Islamic Glass Finds'. *Mitteilungen des Deutschen Archäologischen Instituts in Kairo* 64: 137–48.

Keller, D. 2012. 'Context, Stratigraphy, Residuality. Problems of Establishing a Chronology of Early Byzantine Glass in Southern Egypt'. In *Byzantine Small Finds in Archaeological Contexts*, edited by B. Böhlendorf-Arslan and A. Ricci, vol. 15, 477–88. Istanbul: Yayinlari.

Kucharczyk, R. 2006a. 'Late Roman/Early Byzantine Glass from the Basilica in Marea'. *Polish Archaeology in the Mediterranean* 17: 70–4.

Kucharczyk, R. 2006b. 'Late Roman/Early Byzantine Glass from the Auditoria on Kom el-Dikka in Alexandria'. *Polish Archaeology in the Mediterranean* 17: 45–53.

Kucharczyk, R. 2010. 'Glass from Houses 1 and 2 in Marina el-Alamein'. *Polish Archaeology in the Mediterranean* 19: 114–30.

Maltoni, S., Chinni, T., Vandini, M., Cirelli, E., Silvestri, A. and Molin, G. 2015. 'Archaeological and Archaeometric Study of the Glass Finds from the Ancient Harbour of Classe (Ravenna, Italy): New Evidence'. *Heritage Science* 3: 13. doi: 10.1186/s40494-015-0034-5.

Maltoni, S., Silvestri, A., Marcante, A. and Molin, G. 2016. 'The Transition from Roman to Late Antique Glass: New Insights from the *Domus of Tito Macro* in Aquileia (Italy)'. *Journal of Archaeological Science* 73: 1–16.

Meyer, C. 1992. *Glass from Quseir al Qadim and the Indian Ocean Trade*. Chicago: The Oriental Institute.

Mirti, P., Pace, M., Negro Ponzi, M. and Aceto, M. 2008. 'ICP-MS Analysis of Glass Fragments of Parthian and Sasanian epoch from Seleucia and Veh Ardašīr (Central Iraq)'. *Archaeometry* 50: 429–50.

Mirti, P., Pace, M., Malandrino, M. and Negro Ponzi, M. 2009. 'Sasanian Glass from Veh Ardašīr: New Evidences by ICP-MS Analysis'. *Journal of Archaeological Science* 36: 1061–9.

Mond, R. and Meyers, O. H. 1940. *Temples of Armant. A Preliminary Survey, MEES 43*. London: Egypt Exploration Society.

Mossakowska-Gaubert, M. 2004. 'La verrerie utilisée par des anachorètes, L'ermitage n° 44 à Naqlun (Fayyoum)'. In *Coptic Studies on the Threshold of a New Millennium, Proceedings of the 7th International Congress of Coptic Studies: Leyde, 2000*, edited by M. Immerzell and J. van der Vliet, 1443–69. Leuven: Uitgeverij Peeters en Dept. Oosterse Studies.

Mossakowska-Gaubert, M. 2009. 'Verres de l'époque Byzantine – début de l'époque Arabe (Ve-VIIIe siècle): objects provenant des eremitages en Égypte'. In *Annales du 18e Congrès de l'Association Internationale pour l'Histoire du*

Verre: Thessaloniki, edited by the International Association for the History of Glass, 357–66. Lochem: Association Internationale pour l'Histoire du Verre.
Nenna, M. D. 2000. 'Ateliers de production et sites de consommation en Égypte, Ve s. av. J.-C. VIIe s. apr. J.-C.'. In *Annales du 14e Congrès de l'Association Internationale pour l'Histoire du Verre: Venise-Milan*, edited by the International Association for the History of Glass, 20–4. Lochem: Association Internationale pour l'Histoire du Verre.
Nenna, M. D., 2007. 'Production et commerce du verre à l'époque impériale: nouvelles découvertes et problématiques'. *Facta* 1: 125–47.
Nenna, M. D., 2010. 'The Glass Vessel Decor of a Funerary Chapel in the Bagawat Necropolis, Kharga Oasis, Egypt'. In *Glass in Byzantium – Production, Usage, Analyses*, edited by J. Drauschke and D. Keller, 199–214. Mainz: RGZM.
Nenna, M. D. 2014. 'Egyptian Glass Abroad: HIMT Glass and Its Markets'. In *Neighbours and Successors of Rome. Tradition of glass production and use in Europe and the Middle East in the Later First millennium AD*, edited by D. Keller, J. Price and C. Jackson, 177–93. Oxford and Philadelphia: Oxbow Books.
Nenna, M. D., Picon, M. and Vichy, M., 2000. 'Ateliers primaires et secondaires en Égypte à l'époque gréco-romaine'. In *La route du verre: ateliers primaires et secondaires de verriers du second millénaire av. J.-C. au Moyen Âge*, edited by M. D. Nenna, 97–112. Lyon: Travaux de la Maison de l'Orient 33.
Paynter, S. 2008. 'Experiments in the Reconstruction of Roman Wood-Fired Glassworking Furnaces: Waste Products and Their Formation Processes'. *Journal of Glass Studies* 50: 271–90.
Peacock, D. 2011. 'Glass'. In *Myos Hormos – Quseir al-Qadim: Roman and Islamic Ports on the Red Sea, Volume 2: Finds From excavations 1999–2003*, edited by D. Peacock and L. Blue, 57–78. Oxford: Oxbow Books.
Picon, M., Thirion-Merle, V. and Vichy, M. 2008. 'Les verres au natron et les verres aux cendres du Wadi Natrun (Egypte)'. *Bull. l'Assoc. Francaise l'Archeol. Verre* 2008: 36–41.
Rehren, Th. and Brüggler, M. 2015 'Composition and Production of Late Antique Glass Bowls Type Helle'. *Journal of Archaeological Science: Reports* 3: 171–80.
Rehren, Th. and Cholakova, A. 2010. 'The Early Byzantine HIMT glass from Dichin, Northern Bulgaria'. *Interdisciplinary Studies (Sofia)*, 22–3, 81–96.
Rehren, Th., Connolly, P., Schibille, N. and Schwarzer, H. 2015. 'Changes in Glass Consumption in Pergamon (Turkey) from Hellenistic to Late Byzantine and Islamic Times'. *Journal of Archaeological Science* 55: 266–79.
Rehren, Th. and Freestone, I. C. 2015. 'Ancient Glass: From Kaleidoscope to Crystal Ball'. *Journal of Archaeological Science* 56: 233–41.
Rehren, Th., Marii, F., Schibille, N., Stanford, L. and Swan, C. 2010. 'Glass Supply and Circulation in Early Byzantine Southern Jordan'. In *Glass in Byzantium – Production, Usage, Analyses*, edited by J. Drauschke and D. Keller, 65–81. Mainz: RGZM.

Rodziewicz, M. 2005. 'Glass'. In *Elephantine XXVII, Early Roman Industries in Elephantine* (Archäologische Veröffentlichungen 107), edited by M. Rodziewicz, 25–8, 34–5, 81–96 and 115–22. Mainz: Zabern.

Rodziewicz, E. and Rodziewicz, M. 2005. 'Glass'. In *Elephantine XXVII, Early Roman Industries in Elephantine* (Archäologische Veröffentlichungen 107), edited by M. Rodziewicz, 25–8, 34–5, 81–96 and 115–22. Mainz: Zabern.

Rosenow, D. and Rehren, Th., 2014. 'Herding Cats: Roman to Late Antique Glass Groups from Bubastis, Northern Egypt'. *Journal of Archaeological Science* 49: 170–84.

Sayre, E. V. and Smith, R. W. 1974. 'Analytical Studies of Ancient Egyptian Glass'. In *Recent Advances in the Science and Technology of Materials*, edited by A. Bishay, vol. 3, 47–70. New York: Springer.

Schibille, N. 2011. 'Supply Routes and Consumption of Glass in First Millennium CE Butrint (Albania)'. *Journal of Archaeological Science* 38: 2939–48.

Schibille, N., Meek, A., Tobias, B., Entwistle, C., Avisseau-Broustet, M., DaMota, H. and Gratuze, B. 2016. 'Comprehensive Chemical Characterisation of Byzantine Glass Weights'. *PLoS ONE* 11 (12): e0168289. doi: 10.1371/journal.pone.0168289.

Schibille, N., Sterrett-Krause, A. and Freestone, I. C. 2017. 'Glass Groups, Glass Supply and Recycling in Late Roman Carthage'. *Archaeological and Anthropological Sciences* 9: 1223–41.

Silvano, F. 1999. 'Vetri bizantini dall'Egitto: Medinet Madi 1988'. *Catalogo delle collezione egittologiche (Universita di Pisa di Ateneo)*, 3.

Silvano, F. 2013. 'Materiali vetro e faïence dal quartiere ad ovest del *dromos* di Medinet Madi'. *Egitto e Vicino Oriente* 36: 39–62.

Silvestri, A., Molin, G. and Salviulo, G. 2008. 'The Colourless Glass of *Iulia Felix*'. *Journal of Archaeological Science* 35: 331–41.

Simpson, S. J. 2014. 'Sasanian Glass: An Overview'. In *Neighbours and Successors of Rome: Traditions of Glass Production and Use in Europe and the Middle East in the Later 1st Millennium AD*, edited by D. Keller, J. Price and C. Jackson, 200–31. Oxford: Oxbow Books.

Van der Linden, V., Cosyns, P., Schalm, O., Cagno, S., Nys, K., Janssens, K., Nowak, A., Wagner, B. and Bulska, E. 2009. 'Deeply Coloured and Black Glass in the Northern Provinces of the Roman Empire: Differences and Similarities in Chemical Composition Before and After AD 150'. *Archaeometry* 51: 822–44.

13
When things stopped travelling: Recycling and the glass industry in Britain from the first to fifth century CE

Victoria A. Sainsbury

Abstract

At the extreme north-western edge of the Roman empire, Britain's glass industry in the first half of the first millennium CE is strongly linked with its membership as a province, most raw glass being of eastern Mediterranean origin. However, the withdrawal of Roman occupation from Britain does not lead to the end of glass trade or production. Glass persisted in well past 410 CE, with new indigenous forms of both vessels and beads appearing. The assumption is that this post-Roman production relied upon a perpetually recycled store of cullet that, for the most part, was brought to Britain during its time as a member of the Roman empire.

By collating a published database of over 2,000 British glasses, dating from the first to seventh centuries CE, an attempt was made to understand how true this assumption was, as well as considering what this recycling actually meant for Britain both during and after the Roman Period. In particular, this chapter considers a subset of glasses from the first to fifth centuries CE and the relationship between trace concentrations of common glass additives, resultant from anthropogenic mixing, and geographic location, to highlight both areas of stagnation and fresh glass trade in the third to fifth centuries CE.

Introduction

The glass industry in the first half of the first millennium CE in Britain has long been considered as intertwined with its place within the Roman empire (Price and Cottam 1998; Cool 2000; Foster and Jackson 2010). Although glass vessels and beads were widespread throughout Roman Britain, it is clear that the raw material in the majority, if not the entirety, was imported (Nenna et al. 2000). The glass, originally sourced primarily from the major Levantine glass factories, arrived in Britain as vessels, raw glass and cullet, the former heading direct to consumers and the rest to be manufactured in small, probably temporary, local factories, such as have been found across England (Price 1998). For this secondary production we can then think in terms 'original production', that in which raw glass is turned into a vessel, and 'recycled production', whereby at least some part of the glass used in the secondary production is in the form of previously made glass objects and vessels.

This pattern of centralised primary and dispersed secondary (as original and recycled glass) production, common across most of Europe, is assumed to hold in England until the late fourth century CE. After this point, it has been assumed Britain's glass 'industry' lost connection with the primary production and simply relied upon a scavenging-style recycling, 'a gradually diminishing and degrading reservoir of cullet, ultimately derived from the prodigious industries of the first to fourth centuries' (Freestone and Hughes 2006, 128). However, Freestone and Hughes showed in this paper that a more complex picture is present, and that glass produced after 410 CE was still reaching Britain. This, however, is often overlooked in discussions of glass and it is still not clear how this glass is arriving. There are two main reasons for the persistence of the belief that recycling accounts for all glass in Britain; first, the historically based assumption that political and military abandonment of Britain meant the complete loss of the large-scale Roman trading networks, and thus the sourcing of fresh Levantine glass (Jackson 1996). Second, that very little glass is known from fifth and sixth centuries CE contexts in England suggesting that the reserve of cullet was nearly exhausted (Harden 1956, 1978).

Increasingly, however, this view is being modified by our updated understanding and new excavations. Sites stylistically seen as Roman are dating later (Simmonds et al. 2011) and as more early medieval settlement sites are uncovered, they are yielding more and more glass (Broadley 2011). As well as this, post-Roman trade in England was by no means over, with materials still coming from the continent and further afield (Campbell 2007). We have to begin to consider that our 'near disappearance' of glass is perhaps more related to biases than reality. With all this in mind, it is pertinent to reconsider the nature of this late glass in England. Is it predominately Roman material, recycled in later Britain or the north-western provinces? What proportion of new material is reaching Britain? How is it doing so?

One way to begin to approach this question is to consider the changes in composition of glass over time, in this case the elements of antimony and copper. Both of these elements have been shown to be of use by a variety of authors (e.g. antimony: Mirti et al. 1993; Jackson et al. 2003; Silvestri 2008; copper: Freestone et al. 2002; Foster and Jackson 2010). The copper content in colourless glass, which will be discussed below, can be used as a proxy for recycling.

This chapter shows that, when one considers large-scale trends in English glass, recycling is seen as crucial in the production of colourless glass much earlier than the early Medieval period, something long known in Roman glass studies. As such, there is perhaps more continuity exhibited in the fourth and fifth centuries CE than previously thought. As well as this, this same very early glass continues in circulation for many generations. However, alongside this material there are periodic refreshments of Mediterranean glass taking place after the Roman withdrawal. All of this can be demonstrated by considering the concentrations of copper and antimony within glass.

As well as looking at these trends chronologically, this chapter demonstrates a broad geographic relationship within these data, which implies that the areas of Britain with access to fresher glass trade are not static. All of this suggests that a more complex arrangement of glass consumption in post-Roman Britain existed than was previously thought.

Methodology

For this chapter, two elements are used as indicators of recycling, copper and antimony, with data taken from a database of Romano-British and early Medieval glasses. Programmes of analysis on glass often take place by way of a small number of fragments from a small number of single sites. These results are then compared against average group values of several well-known and well-established glass manufacture types, which have specific chronological and geographical relationships (Freestone et al. 2000; Foy and Nenna 2003; Freestone et al. 2008b; Foster and Jackson 2009). While this is deeply illustrative of particularly the potential date and/or origin of raw glass, there is increasingly a focus in archaeometric studies on the flow of material and recycling (Bray and Pollard 2012; Swift 2012; Pollard et al. 2015; Jackson and Paytner 2016). Rather than trying to work out precise provenance or glass types, this chapter is concerned with how the glass in circulation in England across time changes and how it is geographically and temporally related during the first half of the first millennium CE. This chapter used a collation of 1903 previously published first-millennium glasses from across England (Figures 13.1 and 13.2; see Appendix of Published Data for data sources included). These data are used to study the large-scale trends that are potentially related to recycling. This database was assembled as part of an ongoing doctoral thesis at the Research Laboratory for Archaeology and the History of Art, University of Oxford, concerned with the nature of glass in Britain after the Roman withdrawal. The papers collated were taken from *Archaeometry*, the *Journal of Archaeological Science*, and the *Ancient Monument Laboratory Reports*. Ongoing work is expanding this database to include all data in the publications of the *Annales du Congrès de l'Association Internationale pour l'Histoire du Verre*, as well as publications in the Rakow Library of the Corning Glass Museum.

In reality, due to the range of dates, find information and techniques used in this database, many of the data are not complete enough to be of use in this current discussion. In practice, this means that of the 1903 analyses in the database, a considerably smaller subset is used in almost any statistical study and this chapter primarily deals with antimony and copper, both of which are often unanalysed. As such, only 885 British glasses (329 of which are colourless/nearly colourless) are used in the discussions of antimony content. These are the only examples in the database that had been analysed for antimony content, as well as being datable to a single century. Similarly, only 345 colourless/nearly colourless examples are used in the copper discussions. Copper will only be discussed in glasses that are not coloured as it is commonly used deliberately as a colourant, which is what leads to the tainting of colourless glasses in recycled production.

The recycling indicators used are antimony and copper. Antimony, most probably added as stibnite (Freestone 2008), is a common decolourant and opacifier in Roman glass. It is first used in glass in the Bronze Age, but begins to fall out of common usage in the late third century CE, due to either economic or resource pressures (Jackson 2005). After this, there is no strong evidence for antimony being used in original glass production – whether or not antimony is added at primary or secondary production is still a matter of debate, though not vital for the current

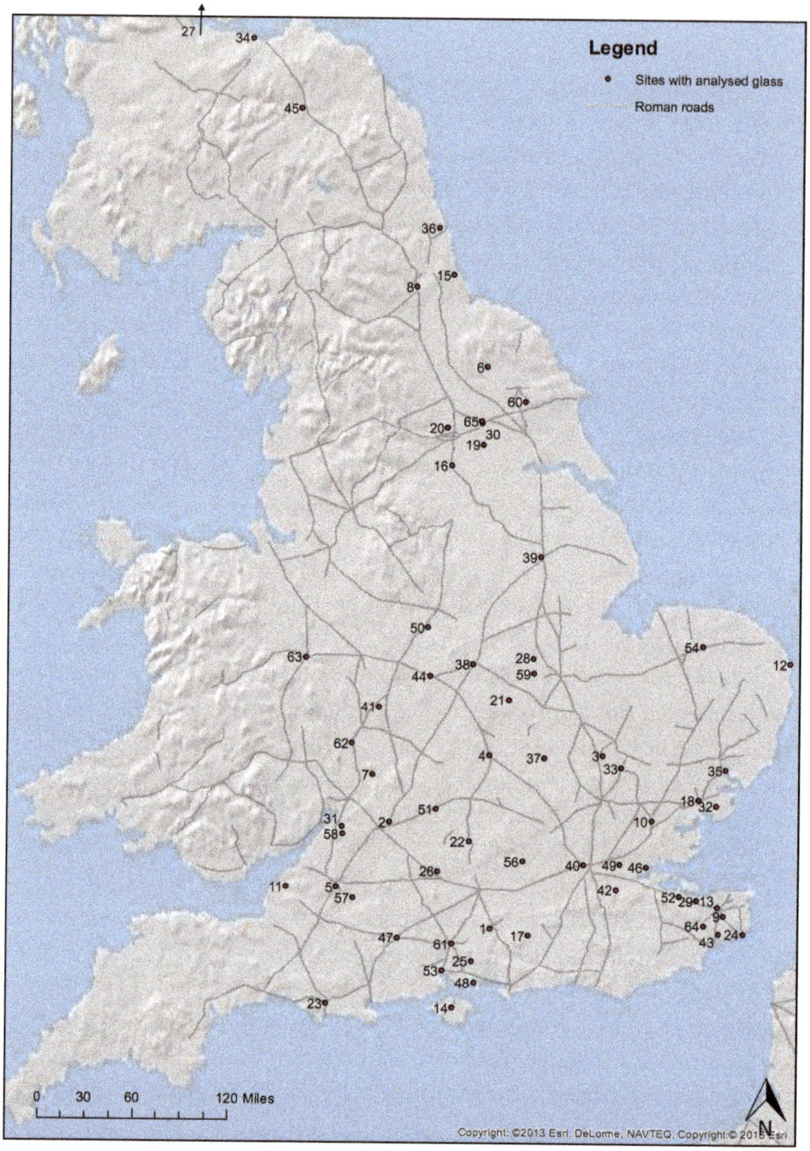

Figure 13.1 Sites with glass analysed within the database, used in this study. It should be immediately apparent that these sites, while widely spread, leave many areas unexamined.

argument. Antimony is not present above a few parts per million in either the sands/quartz pebbles, or common alkalis used for the production of first millennium CE glass (Jackson 2005). As such, the appearance of

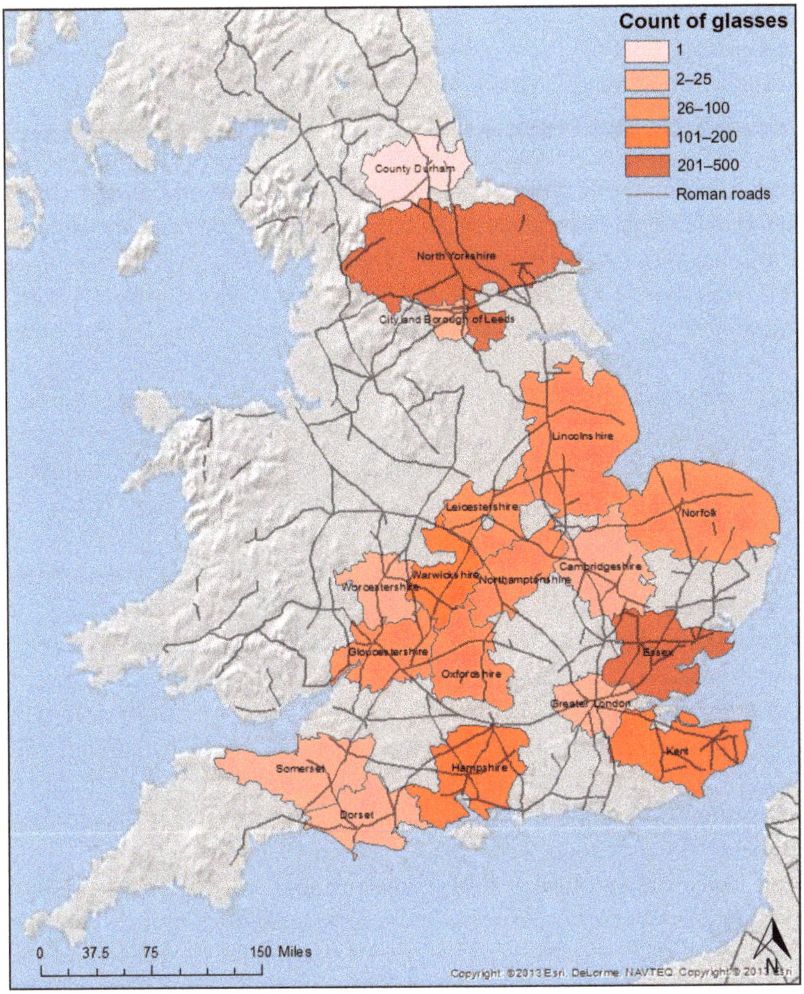

Figure 13.2 Geographic spread of first to fifth century CE analysed glass in Britain. The density of the colour demonstrates the amount of analysed glasses found in each council. North Yorkshire is predominately accounted for by York itself, and Essex, Colchester.

even 100ppm of antimony can be diagnostic of recycling if it is either present in non-opaque coloured glasses of any period *or* present in glasses post mid-third century CE – in other words, in glasses where deliberate addition is useless or in fact counterproductive. It should be noted that the term 'recycling' here is used in the broadest sense, meaning the addition of previously complete objects into vessel production. The addition of some cullet to assist production, as seen in various ethnographic glass production, is difficult to separate out and will be discounted for this chapter (for further discussions of 'recycling', see Sainsbury 2016).

Low concentrations of antimony, especially when paired with manganese glasses, can indicate recycled glass, where an antimony-free glass has greatly diluted the antimony content. This has already been demonstrated for a number of individual sites, particularly by Jackson and colleagues (Jackson et al. 2003; Baxter et al. 2005). However, what is problematic in this approach is that many glasses identified as without antimony might rather contain concentrations below the detection limit of the techniques used. For SEM-EDS, a common technique for glass, copper has detection limits of 0.1 per cent, and antimony around 0.3 per cent (Paynter 2006). This means that antimony at levels indicative of recycling cannot be identified using some analytical techniques, leading to an unavoidable under-representation of recycling. This issue is also likely encountered with copper.

As with antimony, copper is not naturally present in either glass-making sands or alkalis above 100ppm (Foster and Jackson 2010). It enters glass either through the intentional addition of copper or copper salts for colouration, or through tainted cullet. If the latter, it suggests the addition of a small amount of copper-coloured glass into a predominately colourless melt, probably as blue trails and/or blobs on predominately colourless vessels (Price 2000). This is a common decoration on Roman forms (Price and Cottam 1998). Copper is known to accumulate in repeatedly recycled Roman glass (Jackson 1996).

Both copper oxides and antimony oxides considered in this chapter have been normalised as the metal, meaning the percentage accounted for by the oxygen, has been removed. In the present work, results given by papers of previous authors were assumed correct when recording the oxide, which is mildly problematic as it often simply signifies 'any oxide'. However, due to the relative molecular weights of antimony and oxygen, the shifts seen were low. If 0.01 per cent of Sb_2O_5 is recorded, that means 0.075 per cent of antimony, whereas if 0.01 per cent of Sb_2O_3 there is 0.084 per cent antimony. For copper alloys, 0.01 per cent of Cu_2O equates to 0.089 per cent copper and for CuO, 0.080 per cent. Clearly this does introduce further uncertainty, but it is hoped that by the range of authors and papers the errors introduced will be low. Also, as we are looking at changes, rather than absolute values, this again reduces the impact of such errors.

The data is collated geographically under modern English counties. There are some issues with this, as will also be discussed later, but this method was chosen as a way to assess if there was any geographic structure within the data. Furthermore, many of the conclusions drawn from this are preliminary and should be approached cautiously. Also, this chapter focuses on the end of trade/production lines. The author recognises that many of the vessels deposited in Britain were probably not formed into vessels on the island. However, this study is concerned with the nature of the material that areas of Britain had access to, not where precisely recycling might be taking place, therefore the supply of vessels does not pose a problem.

Antimony in British glasses

By simply mapping percentages of antimony across time, it is clear that Britain relies on the recycling of earlier Levantine glass long before Roman withdrawal (Figure 13.3). A cut off of less than 0.1 per cent was used for recycled glasses, as this is a common detection limit for antimony. However, as discussed above, it is almost certain that this group represents only a proportion of the recycled glass.

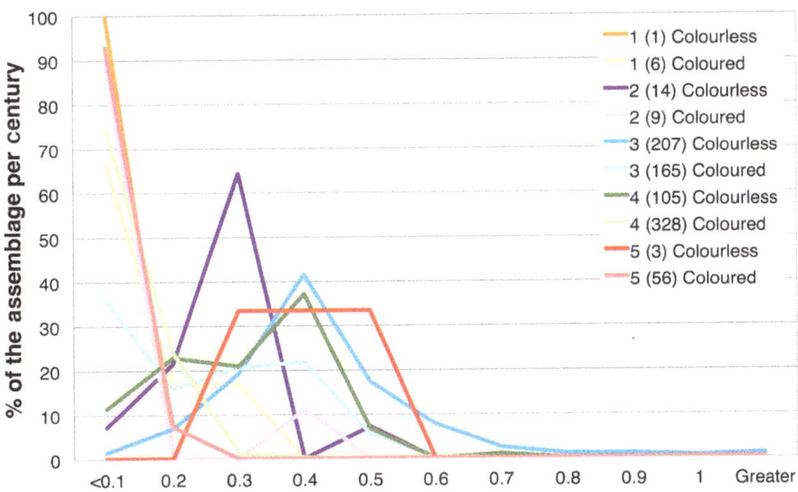

Figure 13.3 Weight per cent of antimony (Sb) in coloured and colourless British glasses used in this study. They date from the first (n: 7), second (n: 23), third (n: 372), fourth (n: 433) and fifth (n: 59) centuries CE. The first century is not commented on as the number of samples is too low. There is a slow increase in antimony over time in both coloured and colourless glasses.

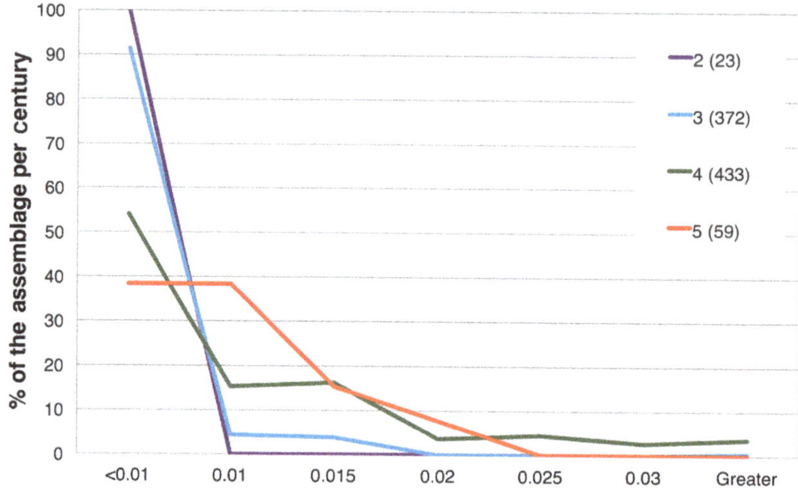

Figure 13.4 Weight per cent of copper (Cu) in coloured British glasses used in this study. They date from the second (n: 23), third (n: 372), fourth (n: 433) and fifth (n: 59) centuries CE. The second century has very low copper values, with a slow increase across the third, fourth and fifth centuries. Both the amount of copper and the percentage of the assemblage containing copper increases.

Second century CE

The second-century colourless glasses (n = 14) demonstrate an expected peak around 0.3 per cent weight of antimony. This fairly standardised composition represents the main Roman production of antimony colourless glass, as opposed to the later manganese glasses (HIMT). It is notably uniform, which when taken in context with the similarly standard but much greater sample size of the third century CE, 207 rather than 14 fragments, could imply that antimony is perhaps being added in a deliberate ratio or to a certain recipe. This is, however, slightly lower than antimony recorded outside Britain, for example, Foy Group 4, 0.63 per cent (Foy et al. 2004). It is also possible that this represents consistent careful recycling, creating a uniform signal, but we need to look beyond antimony for confirmation of this.

The coloured glasses (n = 9), except for one notable example, show little to no antimony. While this is again a very small sample set and no conclusions can be drawn, it is strikingly different from the centuries to follow. It tends to imply that either coloured glass is recycled and curated separately from colourless, or recycling is not a major feature of coloured glass produced at the time. As strongly coloured and decoloured glass is expensive to produce and glass is still of comparatively high status at this time, this could imply a desire for 'best' glass. It has been convincingly suggested that by the time of Diocletian's Edict on Maximum Pricing (301 CE), what is referred to as '*secondi*' window glass, is recycled (Whitehouse 2004). While it seems unsurprising in a modern context that recycled material is of less value, the assumption that the same is true in the past is not always valid (Sainsbury et al. 2016).

Third century CE

Moving into the third century CE, the colourless glasses (n = 207) have a slight increase in antimony, but group around 0.4 per cent weight. This apparent increase from the second century CE could be an artefact of the small sample size in the preceding century. There is a good deal of spread in the values, but there is a near normal distribution around this point, with a slight positive skew. This perhaps demonstrates a range around the 'ideal' production of 0.4 per cent, an artefact of the addition of antimony in the original production, though this is lower than analysis such as Foy's value of 0.63, and Silvestri et al.'s (2008) 0.8 per cent. However, particularly in relation to the prevalence of higher values, this could indicate recycling, which has been tainted by coloured or opaque glasses, without causing an appreciable change in colour, or dilution of higher values of antimony by mixing manganese-colourless glass, or HIMT glasses. The fact that this occurs to at least some extent will be shown later.

When the coloured glass (n = 165) itself is considered, there is clear evidence of recycling. Around 60 per cent of coloured glass contained greater than 0.1 per cent antimony. The fact that none of these glasses are opaque, or contain anywhere near the required amount of antimony for opacification, suggests that the antimony entered the glass by a recycled melt being tainted with either strongly coloured opaque glass, or with decoloured glasses. While it could be the fact that all the glass was treated with antimony, as this pattern is different from the previous century, this seems more unlikely. Also, the cost of decolourising glass and the presence of naturally coloured glass on the market seem to argue against this. The former is a known form of production, especially the use of mosaic tesserae as dye for naturally coloured or mixed glass (Cavalieri and Giumlia-Mair 2009). This pattern is a notable departure from both the preceding and proceeding centuries, where the transparent coloured glasses seem to be treated very separately from antimony decoloured or opacified glasses. Here recycling seems to be a more indiscriminate mixing, rather than like coloured glasses being carefully curated together.

Fourth century CE

In the fourth century CE the colourless glasses (n = 105) seem much as the proceeding century, but now without this higher skew but with a lower one. The peak that had been seen at 0.4 per cent in the previous century has notably diminished, with the appearance of far more of the assemblage at 0.2 per cent. While this seems to indicate standardised production again in colourless glass, it is in this period that fresh glass is no longer predominately produced with antimony. Other work has shown that British assemblages of this century tend to be very strongly dominated by HIMT glass (Jackson 2005). Taking this into account, this glass is then expected to be recycled, the consistent low antimony is more a product of continued recycling, probably with other lightly naturally colourless glasses, which would explain the negative skew. There is little antimony present in coloured glass, and only at fairly low concentrations, 0.2 per cent weight or lower.

Fifth century CE

While there are only three colourless fifth-century examples, they too are of this antimony-containing third-century CE composition, and antimony is also still present in some coloured glasses. Recycling is the only logical explanation for the coloured glass, and when considered in relation to the copper seems more likely the origin of the colourless glass as well. Although on a small scale, enduring antimony glass production cannot be ruled out at this stage.

However, antimony alone is not a significant enough marker of recycling in all of these cases. When considering this dataset alone, there is little scientific justification as to why antimony in third-century colourless glasses should be read as deliberate manufacture and fourth-century CE as recycling, so to further support this theory, trace copper also is considered.

Copper in colourless glasses

It is clear through the data amassed here that this Roman-style glass continues long past the height of Roman Britain, around 250 CE (Salway 2001). As with antimony, the second century CE shows little evidence of recycling (n = 23), with a slight increase into the third century CE (8 per cent of 372 glasses). In the fourth century CE again we see a change, 45 per cent of 433 glasses having greater than naturally explainable copper (100 ppm). By the fifth century CE, this jumps to 60 per cent of the colourless assemblage (n = 59) considered here. Not only does the number of glasses containing copper increase but also the actual weight per cent of copper increases over time. This implies either increasingly careless recycling practices, glasses deliberately coloured with copper not being recycled separately or the long-term continuous recycling of the same glass, with the continued additions of small amounts of copper coloured glass through design elements, leading to the copper slowly accumulating over time. These small elements of blue decoration on colourless glass that are popular in the Roman period remain so into the early Medieval period (Evison and Marzinzik 2008). The latter seems the most likely interpretation when this is considered in the context of the antimony. The fifth-century CE glass can thus be seen as a continuation of the same material flow.

Geographical associations

As well as looking at these patterns simply over time, any potential regional structure is of interest. Areas of increased recycling, or indeed the opposite, can highlight stagnation of external trade or the existence of notable extra-British connections. It is hoped that with the increasing massing of such evidence, we may be able to speculate further on the flow of material into and throughout Britain after the Romans.

For this preliminary study, modern county borders have been used. They are deeply problematic dividers, as they have little historical relevance at this period. However, it was chosen as a first approximation both because of the way modern archaeological data is catalogued and also for the ease of preliminary statistical analysis. It was chosen to explore whether there was any indication of structure. These data are now in the process of being considered relative to pure geographical blocks, watersheds and other more relevant historical and geomorphic factors.

Third century CE

During the third century CE, Roman Britain is relatively firmly part of the empire and its trade networks, yet recycling is still a key feature

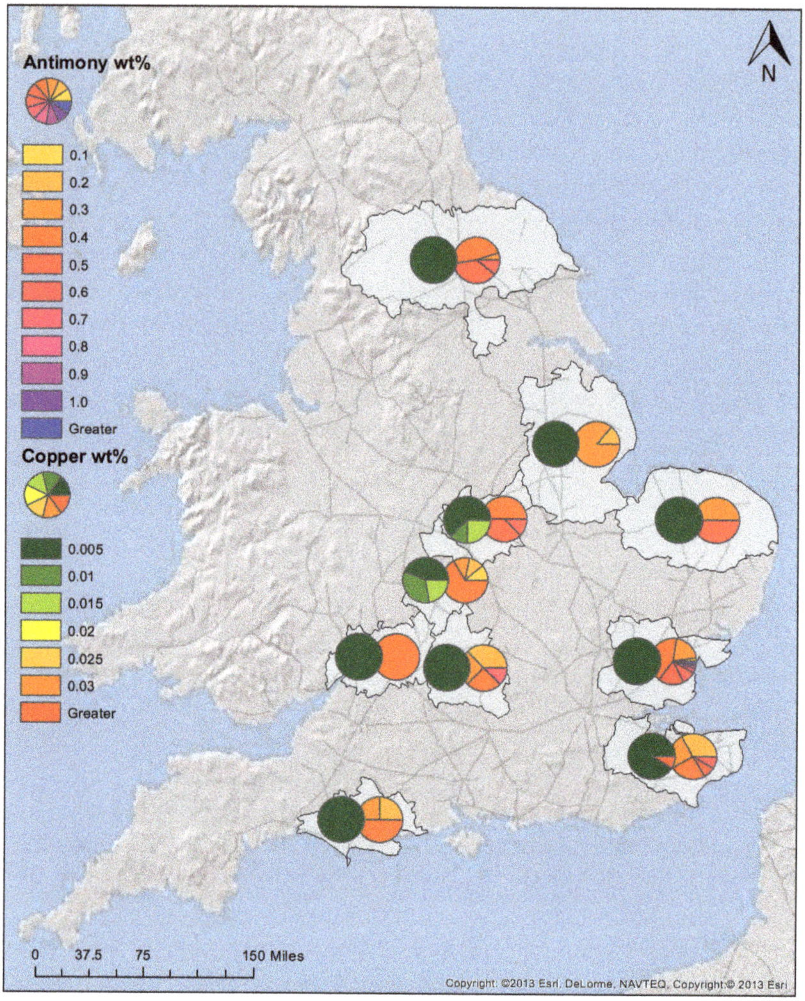

Figure 13.5 Weight percentage of antimony (Sb) and copper (Cu) in glasses across Britain in the third century CE. For antimony, the bluer the right pie chart, the more antimony. For copper, the redder the left pie chart, the more copper.

(Figure 13.5). In the Roman south-east, there is a huge variability in antimony, both in the few examples analysed from Kent (n = 12) and the many from Essex (n = 120). As we move centrally into Britain, we see an elevation of copper, but less variability in antimony (notably Warwickshire and Leicestershire). These areas seem to rely more heavily on the recycling of colourless glass. It is also worth noting that while Essex is predominately represented by Colchester, the other counties contain a range of sites, but predominately of larger settlements. Thus this difference might be more related to type of settlement than geography.

However, as we move into Yorkshire, there is no real evidence for a heavy reliance on recycling in the period. This does not mean that cullet recycling is not happening, but if it is occurring, antimony colourless glass is being carefully recycled with other antimony colourless glass, maintaining a glass with high antimony and no copper. As most of the samples are from York itself, perhaps the city either had better access to glass or more structured recycling practices. However, this is contra to the recent work done by Jackson and Paynter (2016) and it seems likely that this data must be looked at more sensitively. It seems likely York was recycling heavily, which highlights that this is merely a first attempt at integrating geography.

Fourth century CE

Moving into the fourth century CE, antimony remains high on the east coast, in a pattern similar to that seen in the central counties in the previous century (Figure 13.6). However, there is a notable increase in weight per cent of copper, which implies that much of this is recycled. However, in central and south-western Britain, this same increase in copper is instead paired with a drop in antimony, perhaps meaning there was less antimony glass available to be recycled.

It is in this century that significant historical and technological considerations should be noted. Britain experienced many troubles with its leadership and connections to the continent in the fourth century CE (Cool 2000). As well as this, antimony in the production of glass seems to either become very restricted or cease all together. When we look at the case of Britain, however, rather than this simply leading to an influx of fresh new, antimony-free glass, it seems that this new antimony-free glass simply enters the existing system. There is a continued mixing of the same antimony glass of the previous century, but with the addition of some new material, low in antimony. Ongoing research at Vrije Universiteit Brussel has suggested antimony glasses can be watered down with significant amount of the later HIMT glass while still maintaining little to no colour (Bidegaray, pers. comm.). It seems that this new glass in Britain is making more of an impact across

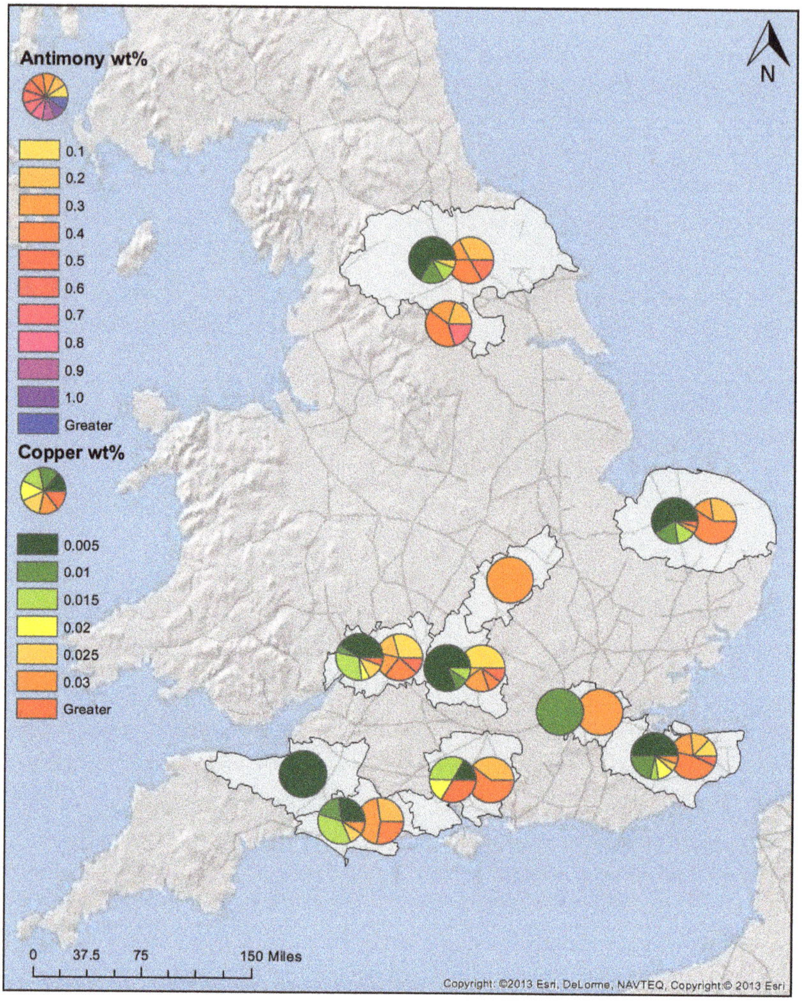

Figure 13.6 Weight percentage of antimony (Sb) and copper (Cu) in glasses across Britain in the fourth century.

the southern coast, and moving centrally, whereas the eastern coast is relying more heavily on the older antimony glass. This might be due to a more careful selection of 'truly colourless' glass for analysis (e.g. by Jackson and colleagues), as manganese-decolourised glasses usually retain some colour. Further work is being done to compare these works across analysts. Patterns in manganese also support this theory, but this will not be discussed in this chapter.

Fifth century CE

By the fifth century CE, analysis is scant. As mentioned, while this is partly to do with the decrease in glass in Britain on this period, this is often overstated. This database contains only three securely dated fifth-century CE glasses analysed for antimony, but all show above natural levels. Glass very recently analysed by the author from early Anglo-Saxon contexts at Lyminge, but not included in this study due to time

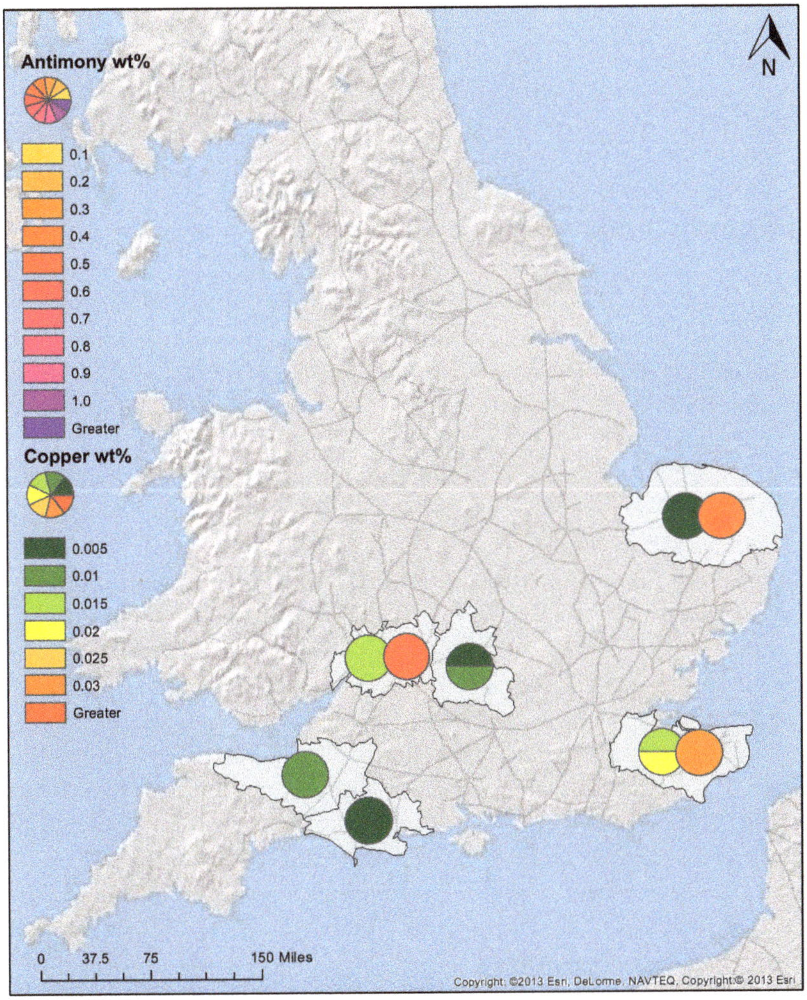

Figure 13.7 Weight percentage of antimony (Sb) and copper (Cu) in glasses across Britain in the fifth century.

constraints, shows some level of antimony in all glasses, with one colourless fragment (SF 624) showing 1700 ppm.

For this study we will concern ourselves only with those analysed for copper, of which there are still only 13 fragments (Figure 13.7). Still, all counties covered, except Kent, show evidence of fresh, low copper glass entering a system of enduring antimony-tainted glass. The copper, while often present, is routinely lower than in the preceding century. While this is only a small sample size, so conclusions must be tentative, it implies that fresher glass is reaching Britain in the fifth century CE. Whether directly, or slowly and incrementally through France is not clear, but it is clear that England is not as heavily dependent on old material as assumed. This agrees well with conclusions presented in Freestone and Hughes (2006) and Freestone et al. (2008a).

Summary and conclusions

While this is by no means a conclusive account, this chapter nonetheless demonstrates the usefulness of reconsidering the huge amounts of existing compositional data of first-millennium glass, and furthermore, in considering the glasses in the context of their temporal and spatial distribution. These broad-brush approaches, while not an answer to all problems, can highlight the patterns of compositional shift across time and space, giving structure to how a material as mutable as glass flowed across multiple centuries.

In this particular case, the circulation of glass in Roman and early Anglo-Saxon England, can be a vital tool for analysing how connected Britain, or specific areas of England, were to the wider Roman and Mediterranean worlds. While the extension of this work is continuing, looking at the direct connections with such patterns across the north-western provinces, for the problem at hand, the initial patterns imply a heavy reliance on glass recycling, across all periods, but with subtle variations. This reliance is hardly surprising, both in the wider Roman context and also Britain's distant geography, particularly in the centre of the island it seems crucial. However, rather than simply stagnating after the Roman withdrawal, the supply was clearly periodically refreshed with large injections of new glass.

With these first basic geographic separations, it seems that glass was likely first entering along the south-eastern coast, before being traded and recycled more centrally. It might even tentatively be suggested that the glass has a more eastern focus in the second and third centuries CE, shifting more centrally down the southern coast in the fourth and fifth centuries CE though this is yet to be fully explored.

In the first quarter of the first millennium CE, when Britain was under comparatively consistent Roman control, the recycling of glass was a key but not the sole part of the industry and production of the glass that ended up in Britain. Moving towards the middle of the first millennium CE, it is clear this same situation continues into the first beginnings of kingdom formations in the fifth century CE.

Acknowledgements

I would like to extend my thanks to the two referees for their invaluable comments, and to Ian Freestone, who helped greatly improve this chapter from its original incarnation.

Appendix of published data

Baxter, M. J., Cool, H. E. M., Heyworth, M. P. and Jackson, C. M. 1995. 'Compositional Variability in Colourless Roman Vessel Glass'. *Archaeometry* 37 (1): 129–41.

Baxter, M. J., Cool, H. E. M. and Jackson, C. M. 2005. 'Further Studies in the Compositional Variability of Colourless Romano-British Vessel Glass'. *Archaeometry* 47 (1): 47–68.

Bayley, J. undated. *Qualitative Analysis of Some Saxon Glass Beads from Dover, Kent. Ancient Monuments Laboratory Report (Old Series) 3635*. Swindon: English Heritage.

Bayley, J. undated. *The Analysis of Some Medieval Red Glass. Ancient Monuments Laboratory Report (Old Series) 4183*. Swindon: English Heritage.

Foster, H. E. and Jackson, C. M. 2009. 'The Composition of "Naturally Coloured" Late Roman Vessel Glass from Britain and the Implications for Models of Glass Production and Supply'. *Journal of Archaeological Science* 36 (2): 189–204.

Foster, H. E. and Jackson, C. M. 2010. 'The Composition of Late Romano-British Colourless Vessel Glass: Glass Production and Consumption'. *Journal of Archaeological Science* 37 (12): 3068–80.

Freestone, I. C., Hughes, M. J. and Stapleton, C. P. 2008a. 'The Composition and Production of Anglo-Saxon Glass'. In *Catalogue of Anglo-Saxon Glass in the British Museum*, edited by V. I. Evison, 26–46. London: British Museum.

Heyworth, M. 1987. *Examination and Analysis of Glass Beads from Wakerley. Ancient Monuments Laboratory Report 241/87*. Swindon: English Heritage.

Jackson, C. M. 1992. 'A Compositional Analysis of Roman and Early Post-Roman Glass and Glass-Working Waste from Selected British Sites'. Unpublished thesis, University of Bradford.

Jackson, C. M. 1996. 'From Roman to Early Medieval Glasses – Many Happy Returns or a New Birth?'. *Annales du 13e Congrès de l'Association Internationale pour l'Histoire du Verre*, edited by the International Association for the History of Glass, 289–302. Lochem: Association Internationale pour l'Histoire du Verre.

Jackson, C. M. 2005. 'Making Colourless Glass in the Roman Period'. *Archaeometry* 47 (4): 763–80.

Mortimer, C. 1991. *Chemical Analysis of Fragments from Two Early Saxon Glass Vessels, from Carisbrooke Castle, Isle of Wight. Ancient Monuments Laboratory Report 22/91*. Swindon: English Heritage.

Mortimer, C. 1992. *X-Ray Fluorescence Analysis of Early Anglo-Saxon Glass Beads from Market Lavington, Wiltshire. Ancient Monuments Laboratory Report 30/92*. Swindon: English Heritage.

Mortimer, C. 1995. *Analysis of a Fragment of Decorated Saxon Vessel Glass from Westminster Abbey, London. Ancient Monuments Laboratory Report 51/9*. Swindon: English Heritage.

Mortimer, C. 1996a. *Compositional and Structural Analysis of Glass Beads from Barrington Anglo-Saxon Cemetery, Cambridgeshire. Ancient Monuments Laboratory Report 76/96*. Swindon: English Heritage.

Mortimer, C. 1996b. *Compositional and Structural Analysis of Glass Beads from Mucking Anglo-Saxon Cemeteries, Essex. Ancient Monuments Laboratory Report 60/96*. Swindon: English Heritage.

Mortimer, C. and Baxter, M. J. 1996. *Analysis of Samples of Colourless Roman Vessel Glass from Lincoln. Ancient Monuments Laboratory Report 44/96*. Swindon: English Heritage.

Paynter, S. 2006. 'Analyses of Colourless Roman Glass from Binchester, County Durham'. *Journal of Archaeological Science* 33 (8): 1037–57.

Tennent, N. H., McKenna, P., Lo, K. K. N., McLean, G. and Ottaway, J. M. 1984. 'Major, Minor, and Trace Element Analysis of Medieval Stained Glass by Flame Atomic Absorption Spectrometry'. *Archaeological Chemistry* III: 133–50.

Wilthew, P. undated. *Examination and Analysis of the Glass Beads from Alton, Hampshire. Ancient Monuments Laboratory Report (Old Series) 465*. Swindon: English Heritage.

References

Baxter, M. J., Cool, H. E. M. and Jackson, C. M. 2005. 'Further Studies in the Compositional Variability of Colourless Romano-British Vessel Glass'. *Archaeometry* 47 (1): 47–68.

Bray, P. J. and Pollard, A. 2012. 'A New Interpretative Approach to the Chemistry of Copper-Alloy Objects: Source, Recycling and Technology'. *Antiquity* 86 (333): 853–67.

Broadley, R. 2011. *Lyminge Glass: Assessment Report*. Reading: University of Reading.

Campbell, E. 2007. *Continental and Mediterranean Imports to Atlantic Britain and Ireland, AD 400–800*. York: Council for British Archaeology.

Cavalieri, M. and Giumlia-Mair, A. 2009. 'Lombardic Glassworking in Tuscany'. *Materials and Manufacturing Processes* 24 (9): 1023–32.

Cool, H. E. M. 2000. 'The Parts Left Over: Material Culture into the Fifth Century'. In *The Late Roman Transition in the North* (BAR British Series 299), edited by T. Wilmott and P. Wilson, 47–65. Oxford: Oxford University Press.

Evison, V. I. and Marzinzik, S. 2008. *Catalogue of Anglo-Saxon Glass in the British Museum*. London: British Museum.

Foster, H. E. and Jackson, C. M. 2009. 'The Composition of "Naturally Coloured" Late Roman Vessel Glass from Britain and the Implications for Models of Glass Production and Supply'. *Journal of Archaeological Science* 36 (2): 189–204.

Foster, H. E. and Jackson, C. M. 2010. 'The Composition of Late Romano-British Colourless Vessel Glass: Glass Production and Consumption'. *Journal of Archaeological Science* 37 (12): 3068–80.

Foy, D. and Nenna, M. D. 2003. *Échanges et Commerce du Verre dans le Monde Antique* (Monographies Instrumentum 24). Montagnac: Editions Monique Mergoil.

Foy, D., Thirion-Merle, V. and Vichy, M. 2004. 'Contribution à l'étude des verres antiques décolorés à l'antimoine'. *Revue d'archéométrie* 28: 169–77.

Freestone, I. C. 2008. 'Pliny on Roman Glassmaking'. In *Archaeology, History and Science: Integrating Approaches to Ancient Materials*, edited by M. Martinón-Torres and Th. Rehren, 77–100. London: UCL Press.

Freestone, I. C., Gorin-Rosen, Y. and Hughes, M. J. 2000. 'Primary Glass from Israel and the Production of Glass in Late Antiquity and the Early Islamic Period'. In *La Route du Verre*, edited by M. D. Nenna, 65–83. Lyon: Maison de l'Orient et de la Méditerranée.

Freestone, I. C. and Hughes, M. J. 2006. 'The Origins of the Jarrow Glass'. In *Wearmouth and Jarrow Monastic Sites, edited by* R. Cramp, vol. 2, 147–55. Swindon: English Heritage.

Freestone, I. C., Hughes, M. J. and Stapleton, C. P. 2008a. 'The Composition and Production of Anglo-Saxon Glass'. In *Catalogue of Anglo-Saxon Glass in the British Museum*, edited by V. I. Evison and S. Marzinzik, 26–46. London: British Museum Press.

Freestone, I. C. Jackson-Tal, R. E. and Tal, O. 2008b. 'Raw Glass and the Production of Glass Vessels at Late Byzantine Apollonia-Arsuf, Israel'. *Journal of Glass Studies* 50: 67–80.

Freestone, I. C., Ponting, M. and Hughes, M. J. 2002. 'The Origins of Byzantine Glass from Maroni Petrera, Cyprus'. *Archaeometry* 44 (2): 257–72.

Harden, D. B. 1956. *Glass Vessels in Britain and Ireland, AD 400–1000*. London: Methuen.

Harden, D. B. 1978. 'Anglo-Saxon and Later Medieval Glass in Britain: Some Recent Developments'. *Medieval Archaeology* 22: 1–24.

Jackson, C. M. 1996. 'From Roman to Early Medieval glasses – Many Happy Returns or a New Birth?'. *Annales du 13e Congrès de l'Association International Pour l'Histoire du Verre*, edited by the International Association for the History of Glass, 289–302. Lochem: Association Internationale pour l'Histoire du Verre.

Jackson, C. M. 2005. 'Making Colourless Glass in the Roman Period'. *Archaeometry* 47 (4): 763–80.

Jackson, C. M., Joyner, L., Booth, C. A., Day, P. M., Wager, E. C. W. and Kilikoglou, V. 2003. 'Roman Glass-Making at Coppergate York? Analytical Evidence for the Nature of Production'. *Archaeometry* 45 (3): 435–56.

Jackson, C. M. and Paynter, S. 2016. 'A Great Big Melting Pot: Exploring Patterns of Glass Supply, Consumption and Recycling in Roman Coppergate, York'. *Archaeometry* 58 (1): 68–95.

Mirti, P. Casoli, A. and Appolonia, L. 1993. 'Scientific Analysis of Roman Glass from Augusta Praetoria'. *Archaeometry* 35 (2): 225–40.

Nenna M. D., Picon M. and Vichy M. 2000. 'Ateliers primaire et secondaires en Egypt à l'époque gréco-romaine'. In *La Route du Verre*, edited by M. D. Nenna, 65–83. Lyon: Maison de l'Orient et de la Méditerranée.

Paynter, S. 2006. 'Analyses of Colourless Roman Glass from Binchester, County Durham'. *Journal of Archaeological Science* 33 (8): 1037–57.

Pollard, A. M., Bray, P., Gosden, C., Wilson, A. and Hamerow, H. 2015. 'Characterising Copper-Based Metals in Britain in the First Millennium AD: A Preliminary Quantification of Metal Flow and Recycling'. *Antiquity* 89 (345): 697–713.

Price, J. 1998. 'The Social Context of Glass Production in Roman Britain'. In *The Prehistory and History of Glassmaking Technology*, edited by P. McCray, 331–48. Westerville, OH: The Amercian Ceramic Society.

Price, J. (ed.) 2000. *Glass in Britain and Ireland, AD 350–1100. Occasional Paper: The British Museum*. London: British Museum Press.

Price, J. and Cottam, S. 1998. *Romano-British Glass Vessels: A Handbook. Practical Handbook in Archaeology, Volume 14*. York: Council for British Archaeology.

Sainsbury, V. A., Bray, P. and Pollard M. 2018. *Mutable Objects, Places and Chronologies* (in press).

Salway, P. 2001. *The Roman Era: The British Isles, 55 BC–AD 410*. Oxford: Oxford University Press.

Silvestri, A. 2008. 'The Coloured Glass of Iulia Felix'. *Journal of Archaeological Science* 35: 1489–1501.

Silvestri, G., Molin, G. and Salviulo, G. 2008. 'The Colourless Glass of Iulia Felix'. *Journal of Archaeological Science* 3: 331–41.

Simmonds, A., Anderson-Whymark, H. and Norton, A. 2011. 'Excavations at Tubney Wood Quarry, Oxfordshire, 2001–2009'. *Oxoniensia* 76: 105–72.

Swift, E. 2012. 'Object Biography, Re-Use and Recycling in the Late to Post-Roman Transition Period and Beyond: Rings Made from Romano-British Bracelets'. *Britannia* 43: 167–215.

Whitehouse, D. 2004. 'Glass in the Price Edict of Diocletian'. *Journal of Glass Studies* 46: 189–91.

14
Things that travelled: A review of the Roman glass from northern Adriatic Italy

Alberta Silvestri, Filomena Gallo, Sarah Maltoni, Patrick Degryse, Monica Ganio, Antonio Longinelli and Gianmario Molin

Abstract

The present chapter summarises the results of an ongoing research project, developed during the last decade at the University of Padova and carried out, until now, on 260 samples of Roman glass coming from various sites (Adria, Aquileia, *Iulia Felix*) in north Adriatic Italy. A combined approach, geochemical and archaeological, was employed to investigate the type and the provenance of raw materials used, and to fill a gap in the knowledge of consumption of glass in an area which, thanks to its strategic position, played a central role in trade during Roman time. The majority of the samples are silica-soda-lime glass in composition and produced with natron as flux, although some soda ash glass samples here named as NE-I/Soda Ash group, all intentionally coloured, have also been identified. In the case of natron glass, five compositional groups (NE-I/Sb-Colourless, NE-I/Mn-Colourless, NE-I/Sb-Mn-Colourless, NE-I/unintent-Coloured, NE-I/intent-Coloured) are distinguished, suggesting various sources, production technologies or degrees of recycling. The isotopic data suggest that the primary production of the Roman glasses from northern Adriatic Italy likely took place in the eastern Mediterranean, although alternative hypotheses are possible.

Introduction

Glass may be considered a 'precious' material, due to its properties, both aesthetic and functional (e.g., transparency, lustre, colour, chemical resistance). Glass was initially used for decorative purposes (e.g., beads, necklaces) and later became functional (e.g., tableware, containers for transporting food, window panes, mosaic tesserae). In particular, the Roman period saw a prodigious use of glass in domestic and funerary contexts, primarily for the production of vessels, although mosaic tiles and window panes were also made. Roman glass generally falls within certain compositional ranges for major elements ($SiO_2 \cong$ 65–71 wt%; $Na_2O \cong$ 15–18 wt%, $CaO \cong$ 6–7 wt%, $Al_2O_3 \cong$ 2.00–2.60 wt%, $Fe_2O_3 \cong$ 0.30–0.90 wt%), as testified by the abundant archaeometric literature (e.g. Nenna et al. 2000; Foster and Jackson 2009; Foster and Jackson 2010; Gliozzo et al. 2013). The majority of Roman glasses are blue-green or *aqua* (Price and Cottam 1998), without the intentional addition of colouring or decolouring elements; on the other hand, both deeply coloured and clear colourless glasses were popular in certain periods: deeply coloured glasses (black, purple, blue, emerald green, amber) were particularly fashionable in early Roman times, while clear colourless glass was in demand during the late first–third century CE (Price and Cottam 1998). Obtaining a truly colourless glass was not easy in preindustrial times: it required pure (i.e., low iron) sand and a strong control on firing conditions; nevertheless, a slight tinge was almost impossible to avoid, therefore antimony or manganese could be added to the glass batch in order to mask the undesired colour of the natural-occurring iron. So far, many studies have been carried out on unintentionally coloured and/or colourless Roman glass from the Mediterranean basin and northern Europe (e.g. Mirti et al. 1993; Aerts et al. 2003; Foy et al. 2003; Foy et al. 2004; Paynter 2006; Arletti et al. 2008; Foster and Jackson 2009; Arletti et al. 2010; Foster and Jackson 2010; Gliozzo et al. 2013; Rosenow and Rehren 2014; Jackson and Paynter 2016), but little attention has been paid to findings from north Adriatic Italy, which, thanks to its strategic location between the eastern Mediterranean and continental European areas, played a central role in trade during the Roman period. In this context, the present work summarises the results of a systematic study on Roman glasses from northern Adriatic Italy, developed during the last decade at the Departments of Geosciences and Cultural Heritage of the University of Padova and still in progress. Aims of the study are: (1) characterisation of raw materials and production technologies employed in glass circulating in the northern Adriatic area during the Roman period; (2) study of the provenance of raw materials; and (3) comparison between analysed samples and coeval glass found in the Mediterranean basin, in order to clarify main commercial routes and to advance hypotheses on production models for the period of interest.

Materials and methods

In the present study, 260 samples from three sites are considered and discussed: (1) 57 samples, mainly from the first–second centuries CE, housed in the Archaeological Museum of Adria (Rovigo, Italy), one of the most important ports in the northern Adriatic area from the sixth century BCE until the second century CE (Bonomi 1996; Gallo et al. 2013); (2) 30 samples, mainly dated from the first to third century CE, found in the *domus of Tito Macro* (known also as *domus of Fondi Ex Cossar*) in Aquileia, one of the main archaeological sites of north-eastern Italy during Roman and Late Roman periods (Bonetto and Ghedini 2014; Maltoni et al. 2016); (3) 173 samples, found in the *Iulia Felix*, a ship wrecked in the northernmost section of the Adriatic Sea and dated to the first half of the third century CE (Toniolo 2007; Silvestri et al. 2008; Silvestri 2008). The majority of the selected types are composed of tableware (i.e., cups, plates, bottles and beakers), made of transparent glass naturally coloured in pale blue, pale green or pale yellow, but colourless and intentionally coloured glasses are also represented. The assemblage also includes two pieces of glass-working waste from Adria and Aquileia, blue and colourless, respectively. A full list of the samples subdivided by site, colour and macro-type is reported in Table 14.1. It should be emphasised that the *domus of Tito Macro* has a very complex stratigraphy and, only for this particular site, the dating of each fragment is assumed as coincident with the widest accepted chronological range of the archaeological form. Therefore, notwithstanding some types, such as the beakers Isings 106, and 109, the cup Isings 117, the bottle Isings 104 and the goblet Isings 111 are dated from the fourth to eighth century CE (Maltoni et al. 2016), they are here included due to their chemical composition.

Major and minor elemental bulk chemistry was determined by X-Ray Fluorescence (XRF) for those samples of sufficient weight (≥700 mg) for this technique. The instrument was a Philips PW 2400, equipped with a Rh tube with a rated capacity of 3 kW (60 kV/125 mA max.). The XRF analyses allowed determination of 27 elements (Si, Na, Ca, Al, K, Mg, Fe, Ti, Mn, P, V, Cr, Co, Ni, Cu, Zn, Ga, Rb, Sr, Y, Zr, Nb, Ba, La, Ce, Nd, Pb), excluding Cl, S, Sn and Sb, which were checked by Electron Probe Micro-Analysis (EPMA). Instrumental parameters, analytical conditions and standards used for quantitative analysis were the same as reported by Silvestri et al. (2011). The major and minor element concentrations of samples, with weights not sufficient

Table 14.1 Full list of the samples considered in the present study subdivided by site, colour and macro-type

	Sites			
	Adria	*Aquileia*	*Iulia felix*	
Colour	*Number*	*Number*	*Number*	*Total*
Unintent. coloured	16	4	88	**108**
Colourless	8	22	85	**115**
Intent. coloured	33	4	-	**37**
Total	**57**	**30**	**173**	**260**
Macro-types	*Number*	*Number*	*Number*	*Total*
Cup	31	11	25	**67**
Plate	5	-	30	**35**
Bottle	7	2	118	**127**
Beaker	1	13	-	**14**
Jar	9	-	-	**9**
Ewer	3	-	-	3
Goblet	-	3	-	3
Glass-working waste	1	1	-	**2**
Total	**57**	**30**	**173**	**260**

for XRF analysis, were determined by EPMA. The instrument used for quantitative analysis was a CAMECA SX50, equipped with four wavelength-dispersive spectrometers (WDS). The detailed analytical conditions, properly selected for glass analysis, and the detection limits are given in Silvestri and Marcante (2011). Laser Ablation Inductively Coupled Plasma Mass Spectrometry (LA-ICP-MS) was applied as a complementary technique to XRF and EPMA to measure trace element concentrations of the Adria glasses. The probe was composed of an Elan DRC-e mass spectrometer coupled to a Q-switched Nd:YAG laser source (Quantel Brilliant). The analytical conditions, precision, accuracy and detection limits of LA-ICP-MS measures are detailed in Silvestri and Marcante (2011).

In order to make inferences on provenance of glass, 66 samples were selected for the analysis of strontium and neodymium isotopes, and 95 for oxygen isotope. The selection was carefully conducted, in order to represent the various archaeological types, colours and the different compositional groups identified and detailed in Silvestri et al. (2008), Silvestri (2008), Gallo et al. (2013) and Maltoni et al. (2016).

After a suitable sample preparation for Sr and Nd analysis (Ganio et al. 2012b), all Sr and Nd isotope ratios were obtained using a Thermo Scientific Neptune Multi Collector Inductively Coupled Plasma Mass Spectroscopy (MC-ICP-MS), equipped with a micro-flow PFA-50 Teflon nebuliser and running in static multi-collection mode. The operating parameters and the analytical protocol adopted are given in Gallo et al. (2015).

Oxygen isotope measurements were performed according to the well-established technique of high-temperature fluorination and detailed in Silvestri et al. (2010) and Gallo et al. (2015).

Results and discussion

Chemical data and the compositional groups identified

The complete chemical data of 260 glass samples, subdivided by site, are reported in Silvestri (2008), Silvestri et al. (2008), Gallo et al. (2013) and Maltoni et al. (2016). The chemical data are here discussed in a comparative perspective, in order to identify compositional groups related to specific raw materials and/or production technologies, and to provide further insights on the consumption of glass in northern Adriatic Italy during the Roman period.

All the samples are silica-soda-lime glass in composition and the majority of them have been produced using natron as flux, although six samples from Adria and one from the *Iulia Felix* shipwreck (defined as Outlier in Silvestri 2008), here named as NE-I/Soda Ash group, show higher contents of MgO, K_2O (Figure 14.1) and P_2O_5, suggesting the addition of a soda-rich plant ash as flux. It is worth noting that these samples are all strongly coloured: four of them are emerald green, one is dark green, one black and one blue. The presence of soda ash glass in Roman assemblages is rare. Natron was the major flux used in the Mediterranean area and Europe from the middle of the first millennium BCE to the ninth century CE (Sayre and Smith 1961). However, some authors have observed that high potassium/magnesium/phosphorous compositions are frequent in glasses of particular colours, such as emerald green, "peacock" and black, but the reasons of this have yet to be clarified, although useful insights on Roman black and emerald green glasses are reported in Ceglia et al. (2014) and Jackson and Cottam (2015), respectively.

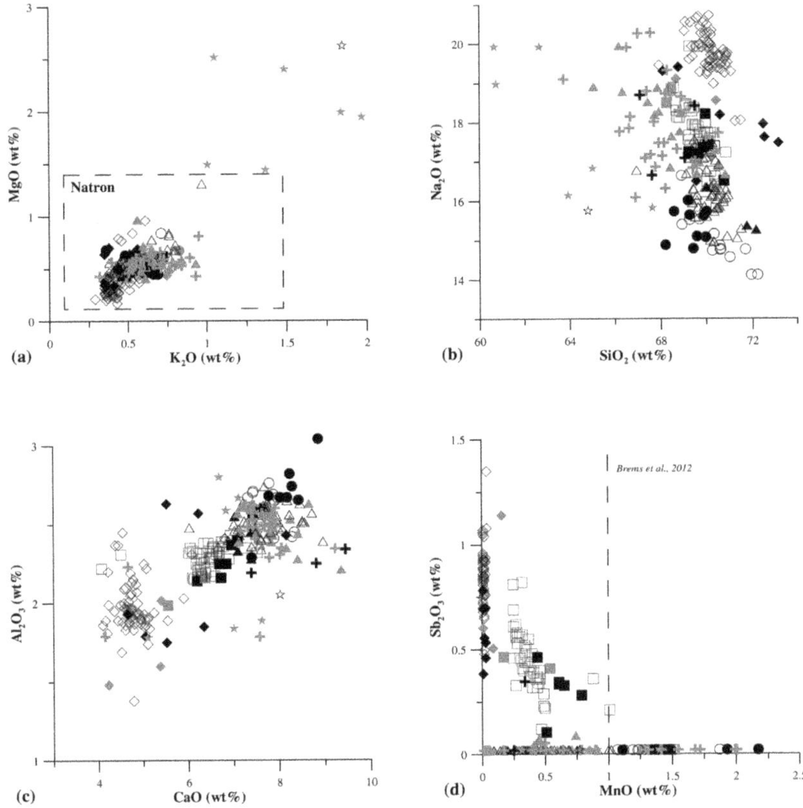

Figure 14.1 MgO *versus* K_2O (a), Na_2O *versus* SiO_2 (b), Al_2O_3 *versus* CaO (c), Sb_2O_3 *versus* MnO (d) bi-plots of glass samples from northern Adriatic Italy, subdivided by compositional groups: NE-I/Sb-Colourless (diamond), NE-I/Mn-Colourless (circle), NE-I/Sb-Mn-Colourless (square), NE-I/unintent-Coloured (triangle), NE-I/intent-Coloured (cross); NE-I/Soda Ash (star). Different colours refer to the site of provenance of samples (black: Aquileia; grey: Adria; white: *Iulia Felix*). Note that in (c) Outliers 3 from Adria, belonging to NE-I/intent-Coloured group, is not plotted for sake of clarity, due to its very high alumina content (Al_2O_3 = 4.29 wt%), and that in (d) the dotted line refers to the threshold value for intentional addition of manganese (Brems et al. 2012). Raw chemical data from Maltoni et al. 2016 for Aquileia; Gallo et al. 2013 for Adria; Silvestri 2008 and Silvestri et al. 2008 for *Iulia Felix*).

Two main compositional groups may be distinguished in the natron glass of the present assemblage: 'NE-I/Colourless', comprising samples with a variable amount of decolourisers (antimony and/or manganese)

Table 14.2 Average chemical composition and standard deviation for compositional groups discussed in the present chapter. Major and minor elements expressed in weight per cent of oxides (wt%). Total number of samples for each group (N) and number of samples, subdivided by site (AD = Adria; AQ = Aquileia; IF = *Iulia Felix*), for each group also shown

	NE-I/Sb-Colourless			*NE-I/Mn-Colourless*			*NE-I/Sb-Mn-Colourless*			*NE-I/unint-Coloured*			*NE-1/intent-Coloured*			*NE-I/Soda Ash*		
wt%	*N = 75*			*N = 24*			*N = 51*			*N = 72*			*N = 31*			*N = 7*		
	AD = 3	*AQ = 7*	*IF = 65*	*AD = 1*	*AQ = 9*	*IF = 14*	*AD = 2*	*AQ = 6*	*IF = 43*	*AD = 18*	*AQ = 4*	*IF = 50*	*AD = 27*	*AQ = 4*	*IF = 0*	*AD = 6*	*AQ = 0*	*IF = 1*
SiO_2	70.19	±	0.85	69.96	±	1.03	69.69	±	0.57	69.76	±	1.25	67.92	±	1.32	63.64	±	2.50
Na_2O	19.53	±	0.82	15.31	±	0.77	17.71	±	0.76	16.60	±	1.03	17.96	±	1.09	17.62	±	1.91
CaO	4.92	±	0.62	7.88	±	0.40	6.40	±	0.55	7.69	±	0.55	7.48	±	1.13	6.91	±	0.92
Al_2O_3	1.98	±	0.22	2.63	±	0.15	2.28	±	0.09	2.49	±	0.10	2.48	±	0.40	2.23	±	0.44
K_2O	0.42	±	0.08	0.54	±	0.11	0.58	±	0.04	0.58	±	0.13	0.66	±	0.15	1.51	±	0.39
MgO	0.38	±	0.16	0.56	±	0.10	0.57	±	0.05	0.58	±	0.13	0.55	±	0.08	2.06	±	0.48
Fe_2O_3	0.40	±	0.14	0.33	±	0.19	0.48	±	0.04	0.43	±	0.13	0.71	±	0.44	1.26	±	0.32
TiO_2	0.07	±	0.03	0.07	±	0.01	0.09	±	0.01	0.07	±	0.02	0.06	±	0.04	0.17	±	0.06
MnO	0.02	±	0.02	1.41	±	0.27	0.41	±	0.16	0.47	±	0.23	0.58	±	0.66	0.73	±	0.37
Sb_2O_3	0.81	±	0.16	<0.04			0.43	±	0.15	<0.04			0.09	±	0.13	<0.04		
P_2O_5	0.03	±	0.01	0.12	±	0.04	0.11	±	0.02	0.14	±	0.05	0.12	±	0.05	0.83	±	0.38
SO_3	0.29	±	0.04	0.15	±	0.04	0.25	±	0.04	0.16	±	0.08	0.24	±	0.09	0.26	±	0.13
Cl	1.44	±	0.13	1.16	±	0.16	1.22	±	0.10	1.22	±	0.13	1.36	±	0.28	1.33	±	0.29

and 'NE-I/Coloured', comprising the naturally coloured and intentionally coloured samples. On the basis of the colouring/decolouring elements, the above compositional groups are further divided into subgroups, named NE-I/Sb-Colourless, NE-I/Mn-Colourless, NE-I/Sb-Mn-Colourless, NE-I/unintent-Coloured, NE-I/intent-Coloured. The average composition and standard deviation of each group for major and minor elements are reported in Table 14.2.

The *NE-I/Sb-Colourless group* is composed of 74 vessels (31 cups, 23 plates, 15 bottles, 5 beakers) from the three sites here considered and 1 working waste from Aquileia. The main chemical feature of this group is the high antimony content (Sb_2O_3 = 0.81 ± 0.16 wt%) without manganese; other characteristics are high silica (70.19 ± 0.85 wt%) and soda (19.53 ± 0.82 wt%), low lime (4.92 ± 0.62 wt%) and relatively low (although variable) alumina (1.98 ± 0.22 wt%) (Table 14.2 – Figure 14.1). Samples of the 'antimony colourless' composition are frequently recorded in the archaeometric literature (Sayre and Smith 1961; Foy et al. 2004; Baxter et al. 2005; Jackson 2005; Paynter 2006; Huisman et al. 2009; Foster and Jackson 2010; Ganio et al. 2012a; Rosenow and Rehren 2014; Jackson and Paynter 2016). The Sb-based decolourisation of glass, typical of the first–third centuries CE, is more efficient than the one based on manganese; in addition, while helping gas bubbles escape from the melt, antimony also worked as a refining agent and aided the transparency and clearness of the final object. These could be some of the reasons of the choice of Sb-glass for high-status glass vessels, such as *diatreta*, cameo-cut and other cut-decorated vessels (e.g. Jackson 2005; Foster and Jackson 2010; Jackson and Paynter 2016). Nevertheless, Sb-decoloured glass was not only reserved for the production of very high-status objects, as demonstrated by the large assemblages published in the past, which report the presence of abundant undecorated tableware made with Sb-colourless glass. This evidence is also confirmed by the present assemblage, where high- and low-status vessels are included. Comparisons among the published data from Great Britain (Jackson 2005; Foster and Jackson 2010; Jackson and Paynter 2016), France (Foy et al. 2004; Ganio et al. 2012a), Egypt and Tunisia (Foy et al. 2004; Rosenow and Rehren 2014) and the present assemblage show that the largest part of the Sb-decoloured samples are characterised by low-alumina content, generally below 2.0 wt%, suggesting that a pure sand, rich in silica and poor in feldspars and accessory minerals, was exploited for their production. Only a few British and Egyptian samples (Foster and Jackson 2010; Rosenow and Rehren 2014; Jackson and Paynter 2016) contain high alumina levels (between 2.20 and 2.50

wt%), similar to five 'high-alumina' samples from Aquileia and *Iulia Felix*. If we consider the major elements and neglect Mn and Sb, the mean composition of the above high-alumina subgroup fits the general compositional patterning of the unintentionally coloured Roman glasses rather than that of the majority of Sb-colourless. Such uncommon composition could derive from recycling different glass compositions, although this hypothesis is hard to support, due to the absence of manganese, in the above samples. Therefore, a different location of primary production that employed impure sand, naturally poor in manganese, could be hypothesised. This picture is further complicated by the chronology of antimony technology, which is supposed to have a rapid decline in the fourth century CE (Jackson and Paynter 2016), which does not coincide perfectly with the dating of two types from Aquileia included in the present group, i.e., the beaker Isings 109 and the cup Isings 117 dated at the fourth century CE (Figure 14.2). The possibility that Sb colourless glass recycled in later times preserved its 'pure' composition without contamination is difficult to support. It is more likely that Sb-decoloured glass did not disappear suddenly from the market, and Sb-decoloured and Late Antique compositions coexisted in Aquileia in the fourth century CE. For more details on Late Antique glass from Aquileia see Maltoni et al. (Chapter 9, this volume). Finally, as regards the single glass-working waste from Aquileia detected in this group, it testifies to the presence of some kind of secondary working of Sb-colourless glass in the area, but, in view of its sporadic finding and in absence of archaeological dating, it is not possible to define whether it derives from an occasional or a regular activity, nor to collocate this activity in a time scale.

The *NE-I/Mn-Colourless group* is composed of 24 vessels (4 cups, 13 bottles, 5 beakers, 2 goblets) from the three sites here considered. This group is characterised by very high manganese (MnO = 1.41 ± 0.27 wt%), in the absence of antimony; other common characteristics are low soda (15.31 ± 0.77 wt%), high lime (7.88 ± 0.40 wt%), and relatively high alumina (2.63 ± 0.15 wt%) (Table 14.2 – Figure 14.1). The very high manganese content, coupled with a very high MnO/Fe_2O_3 ratio (above 3 in all the samples of the present group), is fully consistent with the intentional addition of manganese, whose threshold value was recently increased to 1 wt% MnO by Brems et al. 2012. Mn-Colourless glasses from northern Adriatic Italy are close in composition to the more common unintentionally coloured glasses, although they show lower soda and relatively higher lime and alumina contents. Comparisons with literature data from Great Britain (Jackson 2005; Foster and Jackson 2010; Meek 2013; Jackson and Paynter 2016), France (Nenna et al.

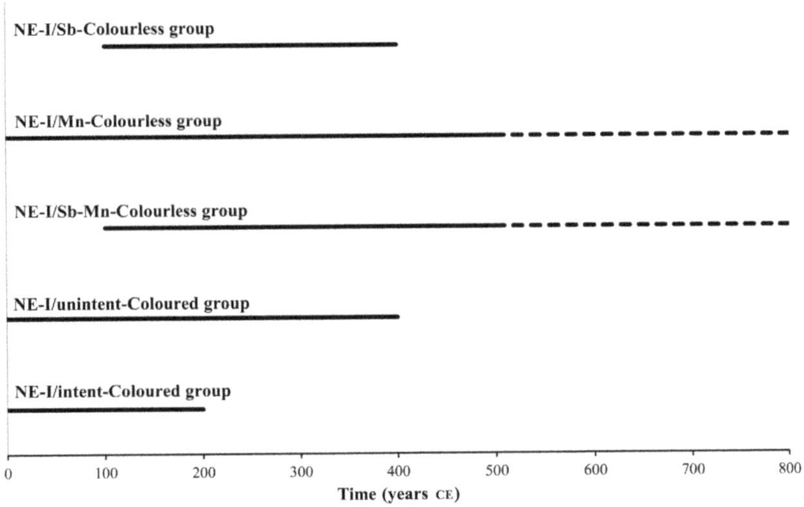

Figure 14.2 Chronology during which NE-I/Sb-Colourless, NE-I/Mn-Colourless, NE-I/Sb-Mn-Colourless, NE-I/unintent-Coloured and NE-I/intent-Coloured groups were circulated in north-eastern Italy. Dotted lines indicates the possibility that NE-I/Mn- and NE-I/Sb-Mn-Colourless groups continued to circulate until the eighth century CE, these compositions being identified in goblets Isings 111 from Aquileia, whose accepted chronological range is from fifth to eighth centuries CE.

1997; Foy et al. 2003; Ganio et al. 2012a) and Morocco (Gliozzo et al. 2013) show that this composition is quite common, although high manganese glass samples with high lime, high alumina, high soda (e.g., Foster and Jackson's 2010 group 2b) and with low lime, low alumina, high soda (e.g., Meek's 2013 group 2a and Foster and Jackson's 2010 group 2a) appear from the fourth century onwards, as reported in Jackson and Paynter (2016).

Finally, it is interesting to note that some samples of the NE-I/Mn-Colourless group from Aquileia (i.e., the beaker Isings 109, the bottle Isings 104 and the goblet Isings 111) are dated to a wide chronological range (Figure 14.2), which, once again, is not fully consistent with the chronology of the Mn-decoloured Roman glass. In addition, what seems surprising is that, as in the case of Sb-decoloured glass, Roman glass made it almost unmodified to Late Antiquity and early Medieval times, preserving the 'purity' of its chemical composition. It is possible, although hard to prove, that large quantities of early Roman raw chunks were still available in the fourth–fifth century CE in Aquileia (when considering the vessels as locally shaped) or in the place of origin of the objects (when considering the objects as imported). Another possibility is that this high-lime, high-manganese, low-soda composition derives from a specific primary production that continued its activity throughout the fourth–fifth century CE. What is evident is that in the current assemblage and in the majority of the literature where this composition is documented, manganese was added to a glass batch that slightly differs from the common unintentionally coloured glass composition and is closer at some points (lime, alumina, soda, manganese content) to the Levantine 1 production (Freestone et al. 2000), that started to circulate in the eastern Mediterranean in the fourth century CE and dominated the glass market in the sixth–seventh century CE.

The *NE-I/Sb-Mn-Colourless group* is composed of 51 vessels (41 bottles, 5 cups, 2 plates, 2 beakers, 1 goblet) from the three sites here considered. The main feature of this group is the presence of both manganese ($MnO = 0.41 \pm 0.16$ wt%) and antimony ($Sb_2O_3 = 0.43 \pm 0.15$ wt%). Apart from the decolouring elements, these samples are within the compositional ranges of the common unintentionally coloured glass: high SiO_2 (69.69 ± 0.57 wt%), Na_2O (17.71 ± 0.76 wt%), CaO (6.40 ± 0.55 wt%), Al_2O_3 (2.28 ± 0.09 wt%), Fe_2O_3 (0.48 ± 0.04 wt%) and very low titania (0.09 ± 0.01 wt%) (Table 14.2 – Fig 14.1). The presence of mixed Sb + Mn glasses is frequent in large Roman assemblages (e.g., Jackson 2005; Foster and Jackson 2010; Jackson and Paynter 2016). Jackson (2005) interpreted them as an intermediate decolouring technique, although later studies (Silvestri et al. 2008; Foster and Jackson 2010; Jackson and Paynter 2016) interpreted those glasses as recycled, due to the fact that the presence of both decolourisers was not necessary and probably unintentional. Antimony decolouring was efficient and did not require the addition of manganese; conversely, manganese decolouring is efficient only when the manganese/iron ratio is very high ($MnO/Fe_2O_3>2$, as reported in Silvestri et al. 2005). The mixed Sb + Mn samples usually have manganese in low concentrations when compared to iron; therefore the addition of low quantities of antimony would have almost no benefit. In addition, the samples belonging to the NE-I/Sb-Mn-Colourless group show intermediate compositions between the NE-I/Sb-Colourless and NE-I/Mn-Colourless groups (Table 14.2 – Figure 14.1), supporting the idea that the glasses with both manganese and antimony represent mixtures of two end-member types (i.e., Sb-colourless and Mn-colourless glass) rather than the result of adding different amount of antimony and manganese to a single glass type, as also observed by Freestone (2015) for the *Iulia Felix* assemblage.

The intermediate composition is also probably a consequence of the selection criteria of cullet for recycling, when the intention of glassmakers is to produce colourless glass. The selection is likely based on cullet macroscopic colour, with a preference for colourless fragments, which are more probably ascribed to Sb-colourless and Mn-colourless glass from the chemical viewpoint. When these colourless cullets were remelted together, a colourless glass containing both antimony and manganese, added unintentionally, should be produced, although the present assemblage demonstrates that the remelting procedures do not ever result into a truly colourless glass. This is the case of some samples from the *Iulia Felix* (all the group Ic1b and some samples from Ic1a and Ic2b, as reported in Silvestri 2008), which are included in this group due to their chemical composition, although macroscopically they show a slight tinge. The chronology of the NE-I/Sb-Mn-Colourless group is also quite interesting: it was in circulation in northern Adriatic Italy from the second to the fifth century CE, suggesting that from the fourth century glass obtained by recycling and 'new' Late Antique compositions (Maltoni et al. Chapter 9, this volume) coexisted in the considered area. In the present group, the occurrence of one goblet Isings 111 from Aquileia, dated typologically from the fifth to eighth century CE, allows us to extend its diffusion until the eighth century CE (Figure 14.2), although this actually remains only an hypothesis, due the absence of other stratigraphic data, for better constraining the date of the goblet and, consequently, of the group.

The *NE-I/unintent-Coloured group* is composed of 72 vessels (52 bottles, 16 cups, 3 jars, 1 beaker) from the three sites here considered, dated from the first to the fourth century CE (Figure 14.2). They are homogeneous in composition with high silica (69.76 ± 1.25 wt%), medium soda (16.60 ± 1.03 wt%) and alumina (2.49 ± 0.10 wt%), and relatively high lime (7.69 ± 0.55 wt%). They are also characterised by low manganese (MnO = 0.47 ± 0.23 wt%) and no antimony (Table 14.2 – Figure 14.1). In this group, the only colouring element is iron; the content of manganese is too low to be considered as intentionally added (i.e., below 1 wt% in all samples) and it is rather introduced with sand or recycling. This group is consistent with the compositional field of 'typical' silica-soda-lime Roman unintentionally coloured glass, suggesting the use of similar raw materials. The extraordinarily consistent composition of Roman glass from different sites in western Europe has already been noted by many authors and led to the hypothesis of a common origin for this type of glass of the entire empire (Nenna et al. 1997; Foy et al. 2003; Silvestri et al. 2005; Silvestri 2008).

The *NE-I/intent-Coloured group* is composed of 31 samples (14 cups, 6 jars, 5 bottles, 3 ewers, 1 beaker, 1 plate and 1 glass chunk) from Adria and Aquileia, blue, purple and amber in colour. The blue and amber samples are attested in both sites, the purple ones only in Adria. This group, dated from the first to second century CE (Figure 14.2), shows a quite homogeneous composition in terms of silica (67.92 ± 1.32 wt%), soda (17.96 ± 1.09 wt%), lime (7.48 ± 1.13 wt%) and alumina (2.48 ± 0.40 wt%) (Table 14.2 – Figure 14.1), which is consistent with the field of 'typical' silica-soda-lime Roman unintentionally coloured glass, except for three blue samples from Adria, defined as Outliers 1, 2 and 3 in Gallo et al. (2013). The outliers are characterised by lower lime (CaO = 4.15–4.66 wt%) with respect to the blue glasses (CaO = 7.43–9.22 wt%), suggesting a sand poorer in calcite. Outlier 3 also shows the highest alumina contents of all the natron glasses (Al_2O_3 = 4.29 wt%), indicative of raw material very rich in feldspars. Further considerations about the three blue outliers can be found in Gallo et al. (2013).

The various colours (blue, purple and amber) differ in their colouring and related elements. The *blue* glasses total 15 and are characterised by high iron (Fe_2O_3 ranged from 0.50 to 1.77 wt%), copper (340–1730 ppm) and cobalt (210–1740 ppm), all positively correlated, indicating that they were intentionally added to the glass from a similar source. Cobalt is probably the main colouring element, since its absorption coefficient is higher than that of copper and iron (Mirti et al. 2002; Gliozzo et al. 2010), and possible sources may be trianite ($2CoO_2 \cdot CuO \cdot 6H_2O$) and skutterudite (Co, Fe, Ni)As_3 (Henderson 1985), although further studies are required to constrain better the type of cobalt source.

In the five *purple* glasses from Adria, manganese was employed as a colourant, as these samples have high MnO contents (1.8 ± 0.2 wt%). However, it is interesting to note that the purple samples show manganese contents and a manganese/iron ratio comparable to those of the NE-I/Mn-Colourless group, but different colours. This is a further demonstration that the final colour of the glassware is the result not only of the chemical composition of the batch in terms of iron and manganese content, but also of the redox conditions in the kiln, as described in Bingham and Jackson (2008). The use of manganese as a colourant in purple and pink glass has been well documented since the Iron Age (Tite et al. 2008) and its presence in Roman glass is frequent (Arletti et al. 2006; Jackson et al. 2006). Wad, an ore composed of manganese oxides/hydroxides, often of poor crystallinity, with small quantities of psilomelane [$(Ba,H_2O)_2Mn_5O_{10}$], is indicated as a possible source of manganese (Silvestri 2008). This hypothesis is supported by the positive correlation between Ba and Mn. Only one sample, AD-V-2, clearly differs from other purple glasses for its higher barium and iron (Ba = 1277 ppm and Fe_2O_3 = 1.13 wt%; Gallo et al. 2013), perhaps suggesting other raw materials as a source of manganese.

Amber glasses are 11 in total and form a very homogeneous group, which shows the lowest contents of iron and manganese (Fe_2O_3 = 0.31 ± 0.03 wt%; MnO = 0.03 ± 0.01 wt%). Except for iron, no other discernible colouring elements were revealed, so that the amber tint is probably due to the presence of Fe^{2+} ions and Fe^{3+}- S^{2-} complex, which formed when the glass was melted in strongly reducing conditions, produced by altering the furnace atmosphere and/or the addition of carbon to the batch (Schreurs and Brill 1984; Green and Hart 1987; Jackson et al. 2006). Comparisons to amber glass reported in literature are difficult because of the scarcity of published data. However, some amber glasses were published from a secondary workshop of the mid-first century CE from Lyon (Nenna et al. 1997) and show comparable compositions, suggesting that this colour is the product of high technological skill and strict control on the raw materials and furnace conditions.

Isotopic data and implications for provenance of glass

To trace the provenance of the raw materials employed in primary production, important information can be obtained from the isotopic composition of the glass combined with the chemical data. In this study, isotopic compositions of strontium, neodymium and oxygen are obtained on a selection of samples from all the compositional groups, described in the previous section. Full isotopic datasets are published in Silvestri et al. (2010), Ganio et al. (2012a), Degryse (2014) and Gallo et al. (2015); here the most valuable insights obtained by isotopic data on Roman glass from the northern Adriatic area are reported.

The $^{87}Sr/^{86}Sr$ ratios of the majority of the Roman glass samples from northern Adriatic Italy range between 0.70884 and 0.70916 (Figure 14.3a), independent from site and compositional group, and are close to the ratio of present-day seawater ($^{87}Sr/^{86}Sr$ = 0.7092). Along with their high Sr contents (Sr = 413 ± 83 ppm), this suggests that the source of strontium was marine shell and consequently that beach sands were most likely used.

Some samples show clearly different Sr isotopic signatures. In particular, the lower Sr signature of NE-I/Mn-Colourless group can be

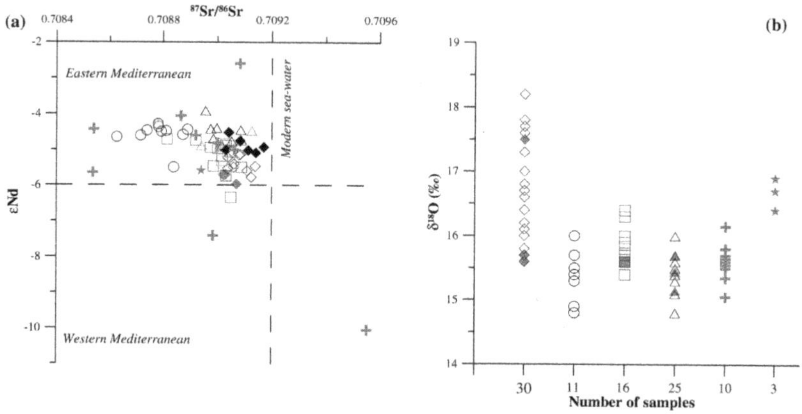

Figure 14.3 Strontium isotope ratio ($^{87}Sr/^{86}Sr$) *versus* εNd (a) and $\delta^{18}O$ (VSMOW) values (b) of glass samples from northern Adriatic Italy, subdivided by compositional groups: NE-I/Sb-Colourless (diamond), NE-I/Mn-Colourless (circle), NE-I/Sb-Mn-Colourless (square), NE-I/unintent-Coloured (triangle), NE-I/intent-Coloured (cross); NE-I/Soda ash (star). Different colours refer to the site of provenance of samples (black: Aquileia; grey: Adria; white: *Iulia Felix*). Note that in (a) dotted line at $^{87}Sr/^{86}Sr=0.7092$ refers to ratio of modern sea-water, and that the line at εNd= –6 refers to threshold value for discriminating eastern from western Mediterranean provenance. Number of analysed samples for each group also shown in (b). Raw isotopic data from Gallo et al. 2015 for Adria and Aquileia; Degryse 2014, Ganio et al. 2012a and Silvestri et al. 2010 for *Iulia Felix*.

stressed. This variation could be explained by the fact that sand is not the only source of strontium in glass, but also Mn-bearing raw material, added as decolourant, introduces strontium in the batch, and consequently modifies the $^{87}Sr/^{86}Sr$ ratio (Ganio et al. 2012a; Gallo et al. 2015). However, the 'inhomogeneous' Sr signature in the two purple Adria samples, belonging to NE-I/intent-Coloured group (sample AD-V-4 with $^{87}Sr/^{86}Sr$ = 0.70854 and AD-V-2 with $^{87}Sr/^{86}Sr$ = 0.70955, Figure 14.3a), seems to be indicative of the use of more than one type of Mn-bearing raw material, as also hypothesised on the basis of chemical compositions (Gallo et al. 2013; Gallo et al. 2015).

The majority of Roman glass from the northern Adriatic area show εNd values between –4.0 and –6.0, although higher and lower values are also measured (Figure 14.3a). Relationships between isotopic composition and compositional groups are not observed. Therefore the large spread in this isotopic composition may indicate the use of multiple sand sources or, alternatively, an intense recycling of glass with different primary origins and thus different signatures.

The εNd values of the majority of the Roman glasses from the northern Adriatic area are very similar to those of the majority of first–fourth centuries. CE glass published in literature, and also to the known fourth- to eighth-century CE primary production centres in the Levant (εNd = –4.0 to –6.0, Degryse 2014). This suggests an analogous provenance, i.e., the eastern Mediterranean. It should be stressed here that two glasses dating to the first century CE from Adria, one purple (sample AD-V-2) and one blue (sample AD-B-6), belonging to the NE-I/intent-Coloured group, show relatively low εNd values (εNd = –10.04 and –7.41 in AD-V-2 and AD-B-6, respectively – Figure 14.3a). These signatures are inconsistent with any published data from sediments or raw glass in the eastern Mediterranean but correspond well to the range in isotopic values of beach and deep-sea sediments from the western Mediterranean, from the Italian peninsula to the French and Spanish coasts, and from north-western Europe (Degryse and Schneider 2008; Brems et al. 2013). Comparisons between the Nd isotopic and trace element patterns of the two above Adria glasses and possible sand sources led us to hypothesis that pretreated sand from the Campanian littoral, location mentioned by Pliny the Elder in his *Naturalis Historia*, may be a suitable raw material. This actually remains only a speculation due to the low number of compared samples and the absence of further data on sand sources from other areas of western Mediterranean (Gallo et al. 2015).

The majority of the Roman natron glasses from northern Adriatic Italy show fairly homogeneous $\delta^{18}O$ values, ranging between 15.1‰ to 16.2‰ (VSMOW), with a mean value of 15.6‰ ± 0.3, except for the NE-I/Sb-Colourless group having $\delta^{18}O$ value significantly higher with respect to the other compositional groups (Figure 14.3b). A greater addition of natron as flux, very positive in isotopic composition, in the NE-I/Sb-Colourless group, which led to a higher percentage of sodium in the final glass may explain their systematically heavier isotopic values (Silvestri et al. 2010). In addition, it should be underlined that, notwithstanding the overlap, the samples belonging to NE-I/Sb-Mn-Colourless group have intermediate $\delta^{18}O$ values between the NE-I/Sb-Colourless and NE-I/Mn-Colourless groups (Figure 14.3b), and this may be a further confirmation of the hypothesis that these samples were produced by recycling/mixing of these two basic compositions. It is also interesting to note that the two Roman samples from Adria with 'exotic' neodymium signature (AD-V-2, AD-B-6), indicative of a western Mediterranean provenance of raw materials, are perfectly indistinguishable on the basis of oxygen isotopes data. A possible explanation of this evidence may come from the similarity in oxygen isotopic composition of probable raw materials (siliceous-calcareous sand), which, in addition to the same flux (natron) in similar ratios, make the glass samples isotopically indistinguishable (Gallo et al. 2015).

The NE-I/Soda Ash group shows higher $\delta^{18}O$ values than the majority of the Roman natron glasses, except for NE-I/Sb-Colourless group (Figure 14.3b). Taking into account that the addition of ash did not contribute isotopically heavy oxygen and the $\delta^{18}O$ of glass essentially reflects the silica source (Silvestri et al. 2010), the higher $\delta^{18}O$ of the Adria soda ash glass may reflect the use of a different silica source, although further analyses on Roman soda ash glass are required to clarify this point.

Conclusions

The combined approach, involving chemical, isotopic and archaeological data, proved a powerful mean to clarify type and provenance of raw materials and production technologies of the Roman glass found in northern Adriatic Italy, and to fill the void of knowledge on the consumption of glasses in the area of interest of the present study.

The majority of the samples are silica-soda-lime glass in composition and produced with natron as flux, although some soda ash samples, all intentionally coloured, have also been identified. In the case of natron glass, five compositional groups (NE-I/Sb-Colourless, NE-I/Mn-Colourless, NE-I/Sb-Mn-Colourless, NE-I/unintent-Coloured, NE-I/intent-Coloured) are distinguished, suggesting various sources, production technologies or degrees of recycling. In general, no close relationships were noted among compositional groups, types and/or sites, although the absence of intentionally coloured glass in the cargo of *Iulia Felix* underlines the careful selection of glasses meant for recycling in Roman times. In addition, it is worth noting that dependence on bulk composition has been observed for some intentional colours, such as emerald green and amber. Exceptions are the blue glasses, which are the only ones showing a certain variability in bulk chemistry, although their chromophore agent is always the same (cobalt), suggesting technological homogeneity in colouring techniques. The NE-I/Sb-Colourless and NE-I/Mn-Colourless groups may be considered two compositional end-members, obtained by sand of high purity, poorer in calcite and feldspars and with high natron/sand ratio in the first case, and by less pure sand, i.e., higher in calcite and feldspars, and with low natron/sand ratio in the second. This not only suggests that different sources and/or production technologies may have been exploited during the Roman period, but also that the raw materials were intentionally and carefully selected in the workshops devoted to the production of colourless glass.

Isotopic data, particularly those related to Sr and Nd isotope ratios, proved to be a powerful tool to source primary glass-making and suggest an eastern Mediterranean origin for the samples from northern Adriatic Italy, although the existence of other primary glass producers located in the western Mediterranean cannot be completely excluded. However, the number of samples with these 'exotic' compositions is low, and further isotopic analyses on Roman glass need to shed light on this interesting topic.

In conclusion, the present work provides an interesting picture of the different compositional groups that were circulating throughout the Roman world and particularly those reaching northern Adriatic Italy, which confirms its role of 'outpost' in the western Mediterranean trades.

Acknowledgements

The authors thank the *Soprintendenza per i Beni archeologici del Friuli Venezia Giulia* and the *Soprintendenza per i Beni archeologici del Veneto* for authorising the present study. They are also grateful to J. Bonetto and A. Marcante (*Dipartimento dei Beni culturali, Università di Padova*) for providing Aquileia glass samples, A. Toniolo (Scientific Committee *Iulia Felix*) for providing *Iulia Felix* glass samples, and S. Bonomi and G. Gambacurta for providing Adria glass samples, together with their archaeological support. This work was carried out with the financial support of 'PRIN 2004' (grant no. 2004041033; title: 'Science of ancient materials derived from geo-materials: basic geoscience knowledge applied to the study of metals and glassy materials') and 'PRIN 2009' research projects (grant no. 2009MC8FA8; title: 'Continuity and discontinuity in glass production technology in the north Adriatic area from the ninth century BC to the fourteenth century AD').

References

Aerts, A., Velde, B., Janssens, K. and Dijkman, W. 2003. 'Change in Silica Sources in Roman and Post-Roman Glass'. *Spectrochimica Acta Part B: Atomic Spectroscopy* 58: 659–67.

Arletti, R., Dalconi, M. C., Quartieri, S., Triscari, M. and Vezzalini, G. 2006. 'Roman Coloured and Opaque Glass: A Chemical and Spectroscopic Study'. *Applied Physics A* 83: 239–45.

Arletti, R., Vezzalini, G., Benati, S., Mazzeo Saracino, L. and Gamberini, A. 2010. 'Roman Window Glass: A Comparison of Findings from Three Different Italian Sites'. *Archaeometry* 52: 252–71.

Arletti, R., Vezzalini, G., Biaggio Simona, S. and Maselli Scotti, F. 2008. 'Archaeometrical Studies of Roman Imperial Age Glass from Canton Ticino'. *Archaeometry* 50: 606–26.

Baxter, M. J., Cool, H. E. M. and Jackson, C. M. 2005. 'Further Studies in Compositional Variabilities of Colourless Romano-British Vessel Glass'. *Archaeometry* 47: 47–68.

Bingham, P. A. and Jackson, C. M. 2008. 'Roman Blue-Green Bottle Glass: Chemical–Optical Analysis and High Temperature Viscosity Modelling'. *Journal of Archaeological Science* 35: 302–9.

Bonetto, J. and Ghedini, F. 2014. 'Vitruvio ad Aquileia. La casa ad atrio dei Fondi ex Cossar'. In *Vitruvio e l'archeologia*, edited by P. Clini, 49–64. Venezia: Marsilio.

Bonomi, S. 1996. *I vetri antichi del Museo Archeologico Nazionale di Adria, Corpus delle Collezioni Archeologiche del Veneto 2.* Venezia: Comitato Nazionale Italiano AIHV.

Brems, D., Degryse, P., Hasendocks, F., Gimeno, D., Silvestri, A., Vassilieva, E., Luypaers, S. and Honings, J. 2012. 'Western Mediterranean Sand Deposits as a Raw Material for Roman Glass Production'. *Journal of Archaeological Science* 39: 2897–907.

Brems, D., Ganio, M., Latruwe, K., Balcaen, L., Carremans, M., Gimeno, D., Silvestri, A., Vanhaecke, F., Muchez, P. and Degryse, P. 2013. 'Isotopes on the Beach, Part 2: Neodymium Isotopic Analysis for the Provenancing of Roman Glass-Making'. *Archaeometry* 55: 449–64.

Ceglia, A., Nuyts, G., Cagno, S., Meulebroeck, W., Baert, K., Cosyns, P., Nys, K., Thienpont, H., Janssens, K. and Terryn H. 2014. 'A XANES Study of Chromophores: The Case of Black Glass'. *Analytical Methods* 6: 2662–71.

Degryse, P. 2014. *Glass Making in the Graeco-Roman World: Results of the ARCHGLASS Project*. Leuven: Leuven University Press.

Degryse, P. and Schneider, J. 2008. 'Pliny the Elder and Sr-Nd Isotopes: Tracing the Provenance of Raw Materials for Roman Glass Production'. *Journal of Archaeological Science* 35: 1993–2000.

Foster, H. E. and Jackson, C. M. 2009. 'The Composition of "Naturally Coloured" Late Roman Vessel Glass from Britain and the Implications for Models of Glass Production and Supply'. *Journal of Archaeological Science* 36: 189–204.

Foster, H. E. and Jackson, C. M. 2010. 'The Composition of Late Romano-British Colourless Vessel Glass: Glass Production and Consumption'. *Journal of Archaeological Science* 37: 3068–80.

Foy, D., Thirion-Merle, V. and Vichy, M. 2004. 'Contribution à l'étude des verres antiques décolorés à l'antimoine'. *Revue d'Archéométrie* 28: 169–77.

Foy, D., Vichy, M. and Thirion-Merle, V. 2003. 'Caractérisation des verres de la fin de l'Antiquité en Méditerranée occidentale: l'émergence de nouveaux courants commerciaux'. In *Actes du colloque de l'Association Française pour l'Archéologie du Verre*, edited by D. Foy and M. D. Nenna, 41–85. Aix en Provence: Monique Mergoil.

Freestone, I. C. 2015. 'The Recycling and Reuse of Roman Glass: Analytical Approaches'. *Journal of Glass Studies* 57: 29–40.

Freestone, I. C., Gorin Rosen, Y. and Hughes, M. J. 2000. 'Primary Glass from Israel and the Production of Glass in Late Antiquity and the Early Islamic Period'. In *La Route du Verre: Atelieres primaires et secondaires du second millinaire av. J.-C. au Moyen-Age*, edited by M. D. Nenna, 65–83. Lyon: Travaux de la Maison de l'Orient Méditerranéan.

Gallo, F., Silvestri, A., Degryse, P., Ganio, M., Longinelli, A. and Molin, G. 2015. 'Roman and Late-Roman Glass from North-Eastern Italy: The Isotopic Perspective to Provenance Its Raw Materials'. *Journal of Archaeological Science* 62: 55–65.

Gallo, F., Silvestri, A. and Molin, G. 2013. 'Glass from the Archaeological Museum of Adria (North-East Italy): New Insights into Early Roman Production Technologies'. *Journal of Archaeological Science* 40: 2589–605.

Ganio, M., Boyen, S., Fenn, T., Scott, R., Vanhoutte, S., Gimeno, D. and Degryse, P. 2012a. 'Roman Glass Across the Empire: An Elemental and Isotopic Characterization'. *Journal of Analytical Atomic Spectrometry* 27: 743–53.

Ganio, M., Latruwe, K., Brems, D., Muchez, P., Vanhaecke, F. and Degryse, P. 2012b. 'The Sr-Nd Isolation Procedure for Subsequent Isotopic Analysis Using Multi-Collector ICP-Mass Spectrometry in the Context of Provenance Studies on Archaeological Glass'. *Journal of Analytical Atomic Spectrometry* 27: 1335–41.

Gliozzo, E., Santagostino Barbone, A. and D'Acapito, F. 2013. 'Waste Glass, Vessels and Window-Panes from Thamusida (Morocco): Grouping Natron-Based Blue-Green and Colourless Roman Glasses'. *Archaeometry* 55: 609–39.

Gliozzo, E., Santagostino Barbone, A., D'Acapito, F., Turchiano, M., Turbanti Memmi, I. and Volpe, G. 2010. 'The *Sectilia* Panels of Faragola (Ascoli Satriano, Southern Italy): A Multi-Analytical Study of the Green, Marbled (Green and Yellow), Blue and Blackish Glass Slabs'. *Archaeometry* 52: 389–415.

Green, L. and Hart, F. 1987. 'Colour and Chemical Composition in Ancient Glass: An Examination of Some Roman and Wealden Glass by Means of Ultraviolet-Visible-Infra-Red Spectrometry and Electron Microprobe Analysis'. *Journal of Archaeological Science* 14: 271–82.

Henderson, J. 1985. 'The Raw Materials of Early Glass Production'. *Oxford Journal of Archaeology* 4: 267–91.

Huisman, D. J., Groot, T. D., Pols, S., Van Os, B. J. H. and Degryse, P. 2009. 'Compositional Variation in Roman Colourless Glass Objects from the Bocholtz Burial (the Netherlands)'. *Archaeometry* 51: 413–39.

Jackson, C. M. 2005. 'Making Colourless Glass in the Roman Period'. *Archaeometry* 47: 763–80.

Jackson, C. M. and Cottam, S. 2015. '"A Green Thought in a Green Shade": Compositional and Typological Observations Concerning the Production of Emerald Green Glass Vessels in the 1st Century AD'. *Journal of Archaeological Science* 61: 139–48.

Jackson, C. M. and Paynter, S. 2016. 'A Great Big Melting Pot: Exploring Patterns of Glass Supply, Consumption and Recycling in Roman Coppergate, York'. *Archaeometry* 58: 68–95.

Jackson, C. M., Price, J. and Lemke, C. 2006. 'Glass Production in the 1st Century AD: Insight into Glass Technology'. In *Annales du 17e Congrés de l'Association International pour l'Histoire du Verre*, edited by K. Janssens, P. Degryse, P. Cosyns, S. Caen and L. Van't dack, 150–5. Antwerp: Association International pour l'Histoire du Verre.

Maltoni, S., Silvestri, A., Marcante, A., Molin, G. 2016. 'The Transition from Roman to Late Antique Glass: New Insights from the *Domus of Tito Macro* in Aquileia (Italy)'. *Journal of Archaeological Science* 73: 1–16.

Meek, A. 2013. 'Gold Glass in Late Antiquity: Scientific Analysis of the British Museum Collection'. In *New Light on Old Glass: Recent Research on Byzantine Mosaics and Glass*, edited by C. Entwistle, 121–30. London: The British Museum.

Mirti, P., Casoli, A. and Appolonia, L. 1993. 'Scientific Analysis of Roman Glass from Augusta Praetoria'. *Archaeometry* 35: 225–40.

Mirti, P., Davit, P. and Gulmini, M. 2002. 'Colourants and Opacifiers in Seventh and Eighth Century Glass Investigated by Spectroscopic Techniques'. *Analytical and Bioanalytical Chemistry* 372: 221–9.

Nenna, M. D., Picon, M. and Vichy, M. 2000. 'Ateliers primaires et secondaires en Ègypt à l'époque gréco-romaine'. In *La Route du Verre: Atelieres primaires et secondaires du second millinaire av. J.-C. au Moyen-Age*, edited by M. D. Nenna, 97–112. Lyon: Travaux de la Maison de l'Orient Méditerranéen.

Nenna, M. D., Vichy, M. and Picon, M. 1997. 'L'atelier de verrier de Lyon, du Ier siècle après J.-C., et l'origine des verres "romains"'. *Revue d'Archéométrie* 21: 81–7.

Paynter, S. 2006. 'Analyses of Colourless Roman Glass from Binchester, County Durham'. *Journal of Archaeological Science* 33: 1037–57.

Price, J. and Cottam, S. 1998. *Romano-British Glass Vessels: A Handbook* (Practical Handbooks in Archaeology). York: Council for British Archaeology.

Rosenow, D. and Rehren, Th. 2014. 'Herding Cats: Roman to Late Antique Glass Groups from Bubastis, Northern Egypt'. *Journal of Archaeological Science* 49: 170–84.

Sayre, E. V and Smith, R. W. 1961. 'Compositional Categories of Ancient Glass'. *Science* 133: 1824–6.

Schreurs, J. W. H. and Brill, R. H. 1984. 'Iron- and Sulfur-Related Colors in Ancient Glasses'. *Archaeometry* 26: 199–209.

Silvestri, A. 2008. 'The Coloured Glass of *Iulia Felix*'. *Journal of Archaeological Science* 35: 1489–501.

Silvestri, A., Longinelli, A. and Molin, G. 2010. '$\delta^{18}O$ Measurements of Archaeological Glass (Roman to Modern Age) and Raw Materials: Possible Interpretation'. *Journal of Archaeological Science* 37: 549–60.

Silvestri, A. and Marcante, A. 2011. 'The Glass of Nogara (Verona): A "Window" on Production Technology of mid-Medieval Times in Northern Italy'. *Journal of Archaeological Science* 38: 2509–22.

Silvestri, A., Molin, G. and Pomero, V. 2011. 'The Stained Glass Window of the Southern Transept of St. Anthony's Basilica (Padova, Italy): Study of Glasses and Grisaille Paint Layers'. *Spectrochimica Acta Part B: Atomic Spectroscopy* 66: 81–7.

Silvestri, A., Molin, G. and Salviulo, G. 2005. 'Roman and Medieval Glass from the Italian Area: Bulk Characterization and Relationships with Production Technologies'. *Archaeometry* 47: 797–816.

Silvestri, A., Molin, G. and Salviulo, G. 2008. 'The Colourless Glass of *Iulia Felix*'. *Journal of Archaeological Science* 35: 331–41.

Tite, M., Pradell, T. and Shortland, A. J. 2008. 'Discovery, Production and Use of Tin-Based Opacifiers in Glasses, Enamels and Glazes from the Late Iron Age Onwards: A Reassessment'. *Archaeometry* 50: 67–84.

Toniolo, A. 2007. '"Pallentia solphurata fractis permutat vitreis". Il carico di rottami del relitto di Grado'. In *Atti delle XI Giornate Nazionali di Studio, Il Vetro dell'Alto Adriatico*, edited by D. Ferrari and A. M . Visser Travagli, 57–69. Imola (Bo): Editrice La Mandragora.

15

Patterns in production: The Wilshere Collection of gold-glass examined

Susan Walker, Andrew Shortland and Julian Henderson

Abstract

Recent scientific examination by HH-XRF of the Wilshere Collection of late Roman gold-glass at the Ashmolean Museum, Oxford, is presented in this chapter. The results have thrown up questions of assignation of certain glasses to four groups (1, 2, 3 and 3X), each defined by the agent or agents used to decolour the raw glass from which the objects were made: two such problems of assignation are discussed here. Two clearly defined groups (3 and 3X) comprise glass decoloured with a mixture of agents: while Group 3 contains glass evidently recycled from Groups 1 and 2, Group 3X is notably variable in composition and surely represents a different workshop practice. Finally, the rise to prominence of Peter and Paul, patron saints of Rome, is clearly seen in the decoration of recycled glass (Group 3), widely regarded as the latest group within the sequence.

Introduction and methodology

The Wilshere Collection of gold-glass, marble sarcophagi and funerary inscriptions was purchased from Pusey House Oxford by the Ashmolean Museum in 2007 (Vickers 2011). A catalogue raisonné is now published, which presents the collection in the light of new archival and scientific research (Walker 2017). For a recent overview of gold-glass, including experimental manufacture and scientific analysis, the latter by Andrew Meek, the reader is referred to the catalogue of the British Museum's collection (Howells 2015). The present author takes a narrower view than some previous scholars of the purpose of gold-glass bowls, arguing that a significant number were commissioned for funerary feasts (Meredith 2015 and Walker 2017 offer recent overviews).

The British Museum's collection of ancient gold-glass has been catalogued by iconographical type (Howells 2015: 71–145). However, with regard to establishing the morphology and chemistry of the glass, iconography was not considered as a significant marker of sub-types. Instead, these have been identified by observing variance in craftsmanship: gold-leaf worked with fine, precise incisions simulating brushwork; trailed gilt inscriptions; cut and engraved gold-leaf left unprotected (on a plaque as opposed to a vessel); protected cut and engraved gold-leaf with and without evidence for shading (Howells 2015: 22–40). While not disputing the significance of such markers of relative value, analysis of the Ashmolean's collection also appears to show developments in iconography that may be related to the chemistry of the glass, notably in the choice of decolourant (see below 'The rise of Saints Peter and Paul'). The choice of added enamel colours to highlight key features of the gold-leaf decoration also appears to be related to the use of decolourant (see below 'General observations').

Scientific examination of the sandwich gold-glass vessel bases and wall medallions in the Ashmolean's collections was undertaken by Andrew Shortland and Kelly Domoney, using portable hand-held X-ray fluorescence (HH-XRF) analysis. The examinations were carried out on an Oxford Instruments X-Met 5100, running quantitative empirical calibration. Elements analysed in this process are aluminium, silicon, calcium, titanium, iron, cobalt, nickel, copper, zinc, antimony and lead, although it should be noted that only antimony and manganese were used to group the glasses as described in this chapter. The other results are included here for their value as a comparison to other published work. It should be noted that glass of this type could be expected to contain around 20 per cent soda and 0.5–1.0 per cent magnesia. However, the portable XRF used is an air path device and low energy X-rays are attenuated in this air gap. This means that low atomic number elements (such as sodium and magnesium) cannot be detected. The methodology followed was identical to that in Scott et al. 2012a and 2012b, where an empirical calibration was developed and tested specifically for the analysis of soda lime silicate glasses. In all 35 pieces of gold-glass were examined, with readings or samples taken from the inner and outer layers of glass (Table 15.1). Here, the inner layer refers to the vessel wall, which also served to protect the gold-leaf decoration applied to the outer layer, the latter comprising the separately blown base of the vessel. One gold-glass (AN2007.39) did not have an accessible, definitively ancient surface to apply HH-XRF.

Further analyses were carried out on these glasses by laser ablation-inductively coupled plasma mass spectrometry (LA-ICP-MS) (AN2007.8 and 37) and Patrick Degryse analysed a sample from one base, AN2007.26, by isotopic analysis. In 1987 10 clear inner layers of small gold-glass medallions with coloured outer layers from the same collection were analysed by Julian Henderson for Dr Marlia Mango of the University of Oxford (now numbered as AN2007.17, 18, 21, 22, 28, 29, 30, 32, 34, 39). These results remain unpublished, but they, and the mounted samples, were kindly provided for the present programme of research. The electron microprobe-wavelength dispersive X-ray spectrometry analyses were repeated by LA-ICP-MS and showed excellent agreement with the 1987 results, adding the greater detail possible with the low detection limits of the ICP-MS technique.

In this chapter, only the results of the HH-XRF analysis are discussed, the other analyses being the subject of further papers.

Results

Table 15.1 tabulates the results of all the HH-XRF examinations. The results show that the composition of all the clear gold-glass examined was consistent with being made from soda-lime-silica glass, although sodium could not be detected. This is what would be expected from Roman glass that uses natron as a flux. This was the standard means of producing glass in the Roman and Late Antique world. Gold-glass in both the Ashmolean and the British Museum collections was intentionally decoloured, thereby counteracting the iron in the sand used in the primary production of glass, which imparts a bluish-green hue; the resulting raw glass is more or less colourless. The results of HH-XRF examination shows the Ashmolean's collection of gold-glass fall within known compositional groups defined by the use of specific decolouring strategies: the use of antimony alone, manganese alone or a mixture of the two, the last most likely reflecting the use of recycled glass (Foster and Jackson 2010; Meek 2015, 31).

Group 1 (two analyses from a single object) is glass decoloured with antimony only and Group 2 (15 objects) is glass decoloured with manganese only. Group 3 (nine objects), colourless, represented in Figure 15.1 with empty or filled triangles, is glass decoloured with a mixture of antimony and manganese, the cascade of readings suggesting that vessels within this group were made of glass recycled from Groups 1 and 2. The colourless glass of Group 3X (eight objects, colourless inners and

Table 15.1 HH-XRF results (wt% oxide)

Sample	*Colour*	Al_2O_3	SiO_2	*CaO*	TiO_2	*MnO*	Fe_2O_3	*CoO*	*NiO*	*CuO*	*ZnO*	Sb_2O_5	*PbO*
Group 1: Natron glass, Sb decoloured													
2007.38 (inner)	colourless	4.3	65	6.2	0.04	0	0.38	BDL	BDL	BDL	BDL	0.32	0.04
2007.38 (outer)	colourless	4.1	67	6.5	0.04	0	0.37	BDL	BDL	BDL	BDL	0.33	0.04
Group 2: Natron glass, Mn decoloured													
2007.5 (outer)	colourless	3.2	63	8.2	0.04	0.6	0.4	BDL	BDL	BDL	BDL	BDL	BDL
2007.20 (inner)	colourless	3.3	66	8.2	0.04	0.9	0.43	BDL	BDL	BDL	BDL	BDL	BDL
2007.20 (outer)	colourless	2.4	57	7.9	0.04	0.9	0.41	BDL	BDL	BDL	BDL	BDL	BDL
2007.25 (inner)	colourless	3.8	61	8	0.04	1.4	0.45	BDL	BDL	BDL	BDL	BDL	BDL
2007.25 (outer)	colourless	3.6	58	7.8	0.04	1.3	0.44	BDL	BDL	BDL	BDL	BDL	BDL
2007.36 (inner)	colourless	4.4	63	8.5	0.05	1	0.48	BDL	BDL	BDL	BDL	BDL	BDL
2007.36 (outer)	colourless	4.5	62	8.3	0.05	1.4	0.5	BDL	BDL	BDL	BDL	BDL	BDL
2007.9 (inner)	colourless	2.6	60	7.7	0.04	0.7	0.38	BDL	BDL	BDL	BDL	BDL	BDL
2007.9 (outer)	colourless	2.1	53	7.4	0.04	1	0.36	BDL	BDL	BDL	BDL	BDL	BDL
2007.40 (inner)	colourless	4.7	48	7.6	0.06	1	0.48	BDL	BDL	BDL	BDL	BDL	BDL
2007.40 (outer)	colourless	4.6	55	8.1	0.06	1.2	0.44	BDL	BDL	BDL	BDL	BDL	BDL
2007.33 (inner)	colourless	2.9	63	8.8	0.05	1.1	0.44	BDL	BDL	BDL	BDL	BDL	BDL

(continued)

Table 15.1 (cont.)

Sample	*Colour*	Al_2O_3	SiO_2	*CaO*	TiO_2	*MnO*	Fe_2O_3	*CoO*	*NiO*	*CuO*	*ZnO*	Sb_2O_5	*PbO*
2007.33 (outer)	colourless	3.1	64	9.1	0.05	1.1	0.47	BDL	BDL	BDL	BDL	BDL	BDL
2007.6 (inner)	colourless	4	58	7.8	0.05	1.1	0.44	BDL	BDL	BDL	BDL	BDL	BDL
2007.6 (outer)	colourless	3.6	62	8.4	0.05	1.1	0.43	BDL	BDL	BDL	BDL	BDL	BDL
oldfield.44 (inner)	colourless	2.6	58	9.3	0.05	1.4	0.45	BDL	BDL	BDL	BDL	BDL	BDL
oldfield.44 (outer)	colourless	3.3	63	9.3	0.05	1.5	0.44	BDL	BDL	BDL	BDL	BDL	BDL
2007.10 (inner)	colourless	3	61	9.7	0.05	1.5	0.48	BDL	BDL	BDL	BDL	BDL	BDL
2007.10 (outer)	colourless	3	66	9.6	0.05	1.7	0.52	BDL	BDL	BDL	BDL	BDL	BDL
2007.13 (inner)	colourless	3	63	8.1	0.04	1.3	0.49	BDL	BDL	BDL	BDL	BDL	BDL
2007.13 (outer)	colourless	3	55	7.7	0.05	1.6	0.45	BDL	BDL	BDL	BDL	BDL	BDL
2007.30 outer	colourless	2.2	43	5.9	0.02	0.64	0.31	BDL	BDL	BDL	BDL	BDL	BDL
2007.34 inner	colourless	4.8	43	5.6	0.04	0.79	0.34	BDL	BDL	BDL	BDL	BDL	BDL
2007.31 (inner)	colourless	4	61	6.7	0.13	1.4	0.95	BDL	BDL	BDL	BDL	BDL	BDL
2007.31 (outer)	colourless	3.7	63	6.8	0.11	1.3	0.98	BDL	BDL	BDL	BDL	BDL	BDL
2007.23 (inner)	colourless	3.4	63	6.6	0.07	1	0.75	BDL	BDL	BDL	BDL	0.08	BDL
2007.23 (outer)	colourless	4.5	59	8.9	0.03	0.9	0.54	BDL	BDL	BDL	BDL	BDL	BDL
2007.23.repair	colourless	3	61	6.9	0.14	1.4	1	BDL	BDL	BDL	BDL	BDL	BDL

Group 3: Natron glass, Mn + Sb decoloured													
2007.24 (inner)	colourless	4	53	6.4	0.06	0.9	0.54	BDL	BDL	BDL	BDL	0.15	BDL
2007.24 (outer)	colourless	3.6	65	7.2	0.05	0.9	0.67	BDL	BDL	BDL	BDL	0.15	BDL
2007.27 (outer)	colourless	2.7	60	6.8	0.06	1	0.59	BDL	BDL	BDL	BDL	0.13	BDL
2007.27 (inner)	colourless	3.4	62	7.1	0.07	1	0.66	BDL	BDL	BDL	BDL	0.14	BDL
2007.7 (inner)	colourless	2.7	62	6.6	0.06	1	0.68	BDL	BDL	BDL	BDL	0.12	BDL
2007.7 (outer)	colourless	4.5	60	6.1	0.04	0.7	0.59	BDL	BDL	BDL	BDL	0.16	BDL
2007.11 (inner)	colourless	6.1	58	6	0.05	0.7	0.68	BDL	BDL	BDL	BDL	0.16	BDL
2007.11 (outer)	colourless	2.3	64	6.6	0.06	0.8	0.65	BDL	BDL	BDL	BDL	0.19	BDL
2007.19 (inner)	colourless	2	56	7.3	0.09	0.8	0.71	BDL	BDL	0.02	BDL	0.24	0.04
2007.19 (outer)	colourless	2.4	62	7.3	0.07	0.7	0.71	BDL	BDL	0.03	BDL	0.26	0.04
2007.15 (ring)*	colourless	5.5	58	6	0.04	0.36	0.55	BDL	BDL	0.04	BDL	0.4	0.07
2007.35b (inner)	colourless	5.9	62	5.4	0.06	0.44	0.74	BDL	BDL	0.03	BDL	0.29	0.05
2007.35b (outer)	colourless	6.8	56	5.2	0.05	0.48	0.83	BDL	BDL	0.11	BDL	0.28	0.11
2007.35a (inner)	colourless	4.1	64	6.6	0.06	0.54	0.7	BDL	BDL	0.03	BDL	0.28	0.05
2007.35a (outer)	colourless	5	57	5.6	0.07	0.6	0.88	BDL	BDL	0.11	BDL	0.27	0.11
2007.42 (inner)	colourless	5.1	59	5.6	0.05	0.46	0.74	BDL	BDL	0.03	BDL	0.27	0.05
2007.42 (outer)	colourless	6	54	5.7	0.07	0.6	0.79	BDL	BDL	0.12	BDL	0.26	0.11

(*continued*)

Table 15.1 (cont.)

Sample	*Colour*	Al_2O_3	SiO_2	*CaO*	TiO_2	*MnO*	Fe_2O_3	*CoO*	*NiO*	*CuO*	*ZnO*	Sb_2O_5	*PbO*
Group 3X: Natron glass, Mn + Sb decoloured inners, coloured outers													
2007.14 (inner)	colourless	4.9	54	8.1	0.04	0.9	0.46	BDL	BDL	BDL	BDL	0.94	BDL
2007.16 (inner)	colourless	3	65	7	0.04	0.4	0.57	BDL	BDL	BDL	BDL	0.73	0.08
2007.21 (inner)	colourless	2.9	66	7.2	0.05	0.4	0.6	BDL	BDL	0.04	BDL	0.47	0.08
2007.22 (inner)	colourless	3.3	68	6.9	0.05	0.7	0.58	BDL	BDL	BDL	BDL	0.7	0.04
2007.18 (inner)	colourless	3.9	60	7	0.07	0.99	0.66	BDL	BDL	0.02	BDL	0.11	0.04
2007.28 (inner)	colourless	2.9	72	7	0.05	0.4	0.56	BDL	BDL	BDL	BDL	0.44	0.07
2007.29 (inner)	colourless	3.8	75	7.3	0.05	0.43	0.59	BDL	BDL	BDL	BDL	0.82	0.08
2007.32 (inner)	colourless	3.3	67	7.3	0.07	0.78	0.85	BDL	BDL	0.04	BDL	0.58	0.05
2007.17 (inner)	colourless	2.7	64	6.4	0.04	0.15	0.4	BDL	BDL	BDL	BDL	0.44	0.1
2007.16 (outer)	blue	2.8	67	7.3	0.09	1	1.1	0.12	BDL	0.16	BDL	1.5	0.28
2007.21 (outer)	blue	7	56	5.9	0.06	0.03	2.16	0.13	BDL	0.31	BDL	0.66	0.07
2007.22 (outer)	blue	11.7	54	4.9	0.03	0.25	0.86	BDL	BDL	0.14	BDL	1.65	0.16
2007.18 (outer)	green	4	64	7	0.07	0.59	2.47	BDL	BDL	0.82	0.07	0.1	0.21
2007.28 (outer)	blue	2.6	74	7.3	0.05	0.4	1.36	0.09	BDL	0.2	BDL	0.67	0.17
2007.29 (outer)	blue	3.9	62	6.5	0.08	0.8	1.1	0.12	BDL	0.16	BDL	1.33	0.26
2007.32 (outer)	blue	4	63	7.2	0.07	0.52	1.13	0.08	BDL	0.16	BDL	1.7	0.43
2007.17 (outer)	blue	3.8	50	6.1	0.12	0.05	1.56	0.1	BDL	0.28	BDL	0.55	0.05

Note: BDL = below detection limit, * foot ring of the vessel, picked out with an attached ring of glass

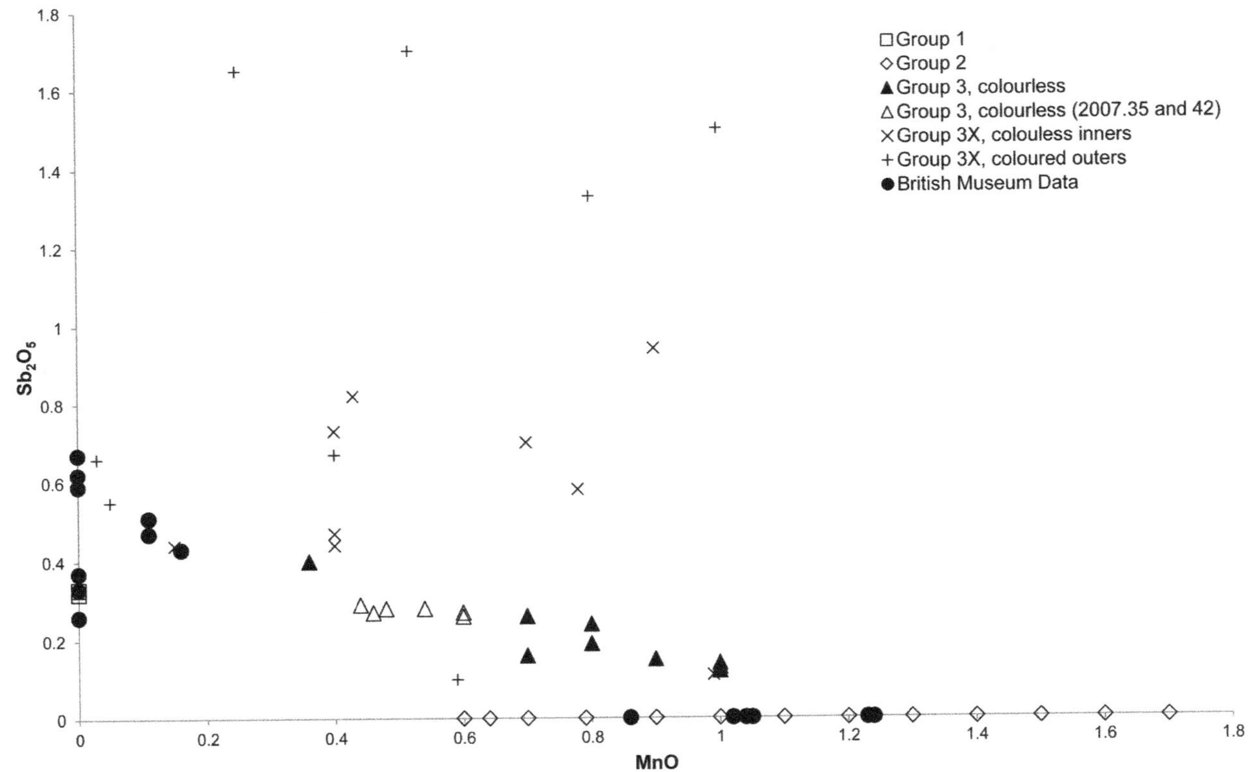

Figure 15.1 Scatterplot of HH-XRF results for Sb_2O_5 and MnO.
Source: British Museum data is taken from Meek (2015)

coloured outers) also comprises glass decoloured with a mixture of antimony and manganese. However, in this group the readings are highly variable, indeed, so random that they cannot be considered the result of systematic recycling.

As the composition of Roman glass is highly consistent, it is reasonable to compare the results with those obtained from glass recovered from stratified archaeological contexts. This suggests that antimony was used earlier than manganese, and the Group 3 glasses are of later date (Jackson 2005; Foster and Jackson 2010; Schibille et al. 2012). Iconographical developments within the gold-leaf decorative schemes support this relative chronology (see further below). However, Group 3X, is iconographically close to Group 2, and a different explanation must be sought for the variable mix of decolourants. The unifying factor within this group is the use of coloured glass outer layers, whether for inlay or for the diminutive medallions set into the walls of shallow bowls. We may be seeing here the work of specialised glass makers, who deliberately mixed decolourants.

Despite the emergence of clearly definable groups, all the glasses have at least traces of both elements. The question therefore placed, is how much of the second element (manganese in Group 1 and antimony in Group 2) is necessary to move the glass from this group to Group 3 – a mixture of the decolourants? To establish this, the first object discussed below (AN2007.38) was undoubtedly decoloured with antimony (Group 1), while the second (AN2007.17) could be assigned to Group 1 or to Group 3.

The base of a clear glass chalice (AN2007.38, Figure 15.2b) is decorated only with a toast in Greek transliterated into Latin to a man called Heraclides, enjoining him to drink and live. HH-XRF examination produced results from inner and outer glass layers at 0.32 per cent Sb_2O_5 and manganese below detection limits (Figure 15.1), making it part of Group 1, glass decoloured with antimony alone. This is one of a group of similar bases of chalices decorated in gold-leaf with text and no images, most held in the collections of the Vatican Museum and not yet analysed (Morey 1959, nos 20, 22–4 and 445, the latter now in the Metropolitan Museum of Art, New York).

Although the British Museum's collection of gold-glass vessel fragments does not include any inscribed chalices as described above, the results of SEM-EDX and XRF analysis suggest the existence of other types of gold-glass decoloured with antimony only (Meek Type 1 in Meek 2015, 32–9). These variants differed from the main body of surviving gold-glass vessel fragments, being multi-layered, often with a coloured outer layer, with shaded, powdered, 'brushed' or trailed decoration. Other sub- groups within Type 1 comprised plaques with the more familiar cut and engraved gold-leaf decoration left unprotected by a covering layer of glass, and protected vessels with shaded cut and engraved gold-leaf decoration (Meek 2015, 33).

Analysis of Roman glass with archaeological context indicates that antimony was the earliest of the decolourants in use, and stylistic analysis of the British Museum's gold-glass decoloured with antimony only also suggests a date early in the sequence of late antique gold-glass, in the late third or early fourth century CE (Jackson 2005; Foster and Jackson 2010; Meek 2015, 38). It is likely, then, that the chalice base AN2007.38 belongs early within the sequence of gold-glass.

Another fragment in the Wilshere collection (AN2007.17, Figure 15.2b) presents more of an interpretative problem. Here the results of HH-XRF give a slightly higher level of antimony (0.44 per cent Sb_2O_5) than AN2007.38 (Figure 15.2a, 0.32 per cent Sb_2O_5) but in this instance a small amount of manganese is also present (0.15 per cent MnO). The question arises of defining the class of this fragment, which formed part of a flat plaque of clear glass set on a blue outer layer, with

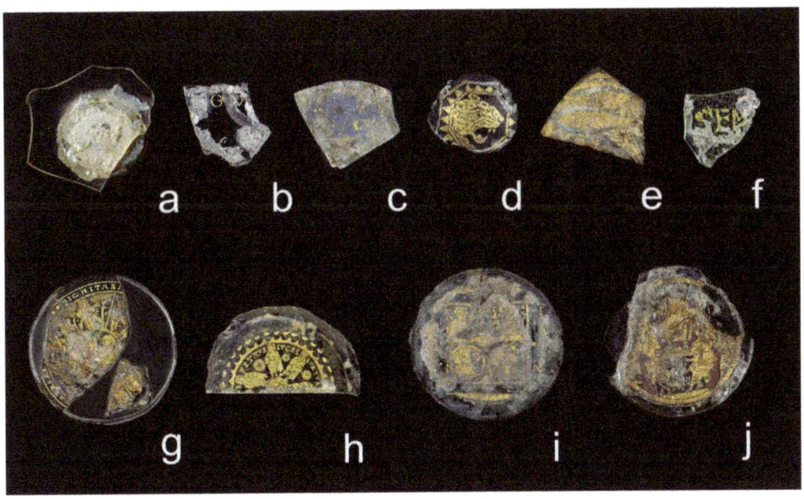

Figure 15.2 Selected gold-glass objects discussed in the text
(a) AN2007.38, 7.2 cm wide × 2.7 cm high; (b) AN2007.17, 2.2 × 2.0 cm; (c) AN2007.14, 3.5 × 2.7 cm; (d) AN2007.29, 2.0 × 1.9 cm; (e) AN2007.23, 5.5 × 4.3 cm; (f) AN2007.31, 2.3 × 1.8 cm; (g) AN2007.35/42, 11 cm diameter; (h) AN2007.10, 9.3 cm diameter; (i) AN2007.7, 2.8 × 2.5 cm; (j) AN2007.11, 9.3 cm diameter (not to scale).
Source: © Ashmolean Museum, University of Oxford

three gold-leaf letters – [N]OM – surviving near the edge. Should it be classed with Group 1 (glass decoloured with antimony only) or Group 3 (glass decoloured with a mixture of antimony and manganese)?

One of the pieces analysed by SEM-EDX at the British Museum presents a markedly similar result (BM S.317, 0.43 per cent Sb_2O_5 and 0.16 per cent MnO: Meek 2015, 35). However, this has been included within Type 1, glass decoloured with antimony only. AN2007.17 is relatively low in iron oxide (0.40 per cent Fe_2O_3) and alumina (2.7 per cent Al_2O_3); however, though the iron oxide readings match those of the British Museum's group, the alumina reading is higher: the respective results for S.317 are 0.37 per cent FeO and 1.76 per cent Al_2O_3. S.317 belongs to the group described above of vessels made of a single, unprotected layer of unusually pure glass. Howells (2015, 101–3, no. 17) notes that the very fragmentary glass, hitherto reconstructed as a shallow bowl, is actually a flat plaque with an estimated diameter of 19 cm. Like S.317, AN2007.17 is completely flat, and the lettering corresponds closely to the style of the flat, colourless glass plaque in the Vatican Museum decorated with a brushed and shaded image of a pagan deity, widely regarded as being of third-century CE date (Morey 1959, no.13). The gold-leaf decoration of British Museum S.317 is also very close to the protected cut and engraved dish AN2007.35/42 Figure 15.2g, with narratives of personal salvation drawn from the Old and New Testaments radiating around the missing centre of the disc. However, the Wilshere dish was composed of recycled glass and appears to come relatively late within the chronological sequence (see further below). S.317 was placed whole in a cist grave in the cemetery at Ursulagartenstrasse, Cologne, Germany. Within the cist were the burned bones of a woman, other glass and objects of jet, dated to the late third to mid-fourth centuries CE (Howells 2015, 101).

On balance, then, on the basis of its glass composition and its form, the date of AN2007.17, like AN2007.38, is likely to be early within the sequence of gold-glass. Small amounts of manganese (less than 0.2 per cent MnO) may be tolerated within any definition of gold-glasses decoloured with antimony only, if there are also stylistic and technical arguments for assigning the glass an early date.

A similar problem of assignment to one group or another besets the interpretation of a multi-layered, flat fragment of clear glass (AN2007.23, Figure 15.2e): the outer layer and a repair to it fall at different points along the horizontal axis defining glass decoloured with manganese only (respectively 0.9 per cent and 1.4 per cent MnO), while the inner layer, at 1 per cent close to the manganese reading for the outer layer, contains a small amount of antimony (0.08 per cent

Sb_2O_5). Like AN2007.17, this object is flat, its profile and decoration anomalous within the corpus of gold-glass (Walker 2017). The gold-leaf decoration represents a scene of fishing, with barbed hook and tong-like net set within a (possibly river delta) landscape dominated by a pair of large fish, of which the upper was to be caught with the tackle. Apart from the story of Jonah, the act of fishing does not feature within the Christian gold-glass repertoire (Dölger 1928). Very probably commissioned for secular purposes, the gold-glass plaque or inlay was cut down to focus upon the two fish, a well-known feature of Christian iconography. In the process of re-cutting, most likely for reuse within a Christian funerary environment, a repair was made to the outer layer. With regard to the glass chemistry, it is reasonable to assign this object with a complex history to Group 2, gold-glass decoloured with manganese alone. A small amount of cullet was probably introduced when the upper layer was made, leading to greater variation than the norm for this group.

Gold-leaf glasses with coloured outer layers: questions of recycling

Some gold-glass shows evidence for the use of a mixture of antimony and manganese in the decolouring process. This has been interpreted as evidence for recycling (see above); the question arises of whether the recycled material was drawn from earlier gold-glass vessels. That interpretation may be supported for vessels with clear bases decorated with gold-leaf (Figure 15.1, Group 3 colourless, where the gradual cascade of results falls well within the range of Groups 1 and 2, gold-glass products decoloured with either element used singly). Within this group, the amount of variation to be expected within a single vessel made of recycled glass is shown by the results for AN2007.35/42 (Figures 15.1 and 15.2g). Here the variation is stronger in the level of manganese introduced to the mix; the levels of antimony are fairly constant.

Nonetheless, a question arises concerning the formation of some members of Group 3X (Figure 15.1). In these gold-glasses the gold-leaf pictorial decoration – there is no text – is set on a coloured outer layer of glass and covered by a clear inner layer. Most, but not all, pieces are small, circular medallions that once decorated the walls of vessels (see Figure 15.2d for example). Within this group only two clear inner layers fall close to each other (AN2007.21 and 28); the other examples, both inner and outer layers, show very disparate readings, most lying far from each axis of the graph (Figure 15.1). The random results are not the product of recycling glass within the workshop, for which a gently cascading pattern is clearly visible (see above and Figure 15.1, Group 3 colourless), but apparently represent the casual use of available glass with as a consequence very little evidence for workshop relationships. It has been suggested that the medallions were not regarded as high-status objects and are likely to be late within the dating sequence for gold-glass (Meek 2015, 36 with fig. 12). Nonetheless the biblical vignettes represented in the gold-leaf decoration of the medallions with coloured outer layers recall those appearing in glasses decoloured with manganese alone (Group 2: e.g. AN2007.9, 13). They do not compare so well with the saints and martyrs decorating the glasses of Group 3, with the partial exception of AN2007.35/42, in which biblical scenes of salvation are combined with dominant, named figures of Peter and Paul.

The rise of Saints Peter and Paul

A particularly striking result of the analysis of the gold-glass from the Wilshere Collection is the close association of dominant images of Saints Peter and Paul on clear gold-glass bases with mixed decolourants, and therefore most likely produced from recycled glass (Group 3 colourless, Figure 15.1). In AN2007.10 (Figure 15.2h), part of the base of a glass decoloured with manganese alone (Group 2), Peter appears with Saint Luke and the martyred pope Sixtus, with no distinction of scale or position between the figures. However, where they appear on Group 3 clear glass bases, Peter and Paul assume key positions within the overall narrative of the gold leaf scenes. AN2007.7 (Figure 15.2i) has them watching over the martyred popes Julius and Sixtus; in AN2007.11 (Figure 15.2j), they flank the figure of Christ, who gives them the Word; below them sit the subordinate figures of Timothy, Sixtus, Simon and Florus. In AN2007.12, Peter and Paul are crowned by Christ, and in AN2007.35/42 (Figure 15.2g), they face each other within a central medallion, their busts placed below a chi-rho symbol. This development is surely a reflection of the growing prominence of Peter and Paul, who in the later fourth century CE became the leading patron saints of Rome (Grig 2004).

This clear result implies a possible historical support for the relative chronology of gold-glass, the recycled glass appearing latest in the sequence. However, as with the inscribed chalices, further analysis is needed of gold-glass in other major collections to be certain of the development.

Some general observations

Group 2, glass decoloured with manganese alone, is, perhaps unexpectedly, the largest group of clear gold-glass vessels represented within the Wilshere Collection: in the fourth century AD, when so much material was recycled, one might have expected a larger number of recycled glasses. In another sense Group 2 may represent the greatest extent of fourth-century CE gold-glass production at Rome, in that it includes the widest range of products, not all of which were necessarily destined for primary funerary use or veneration of the martyrs. Flat glass used to make inlay or plaques is represented by AN2007.14 and 23 (Figures 15.2c and 15.2e, respectively); AN2007.30 (Figure 15.3) came from a perfume flask or jug, while AN2007.31 (Figure 15.2f) is an inscribed sherd from a vessel of otherwise unknown form, possibly used in Christian liturgy.

Group 3 includes some gold-glass of exceptional quality (Figures 15.2j, 15.4a and 15.4b: AN2007.11, 24 and 27), showing that

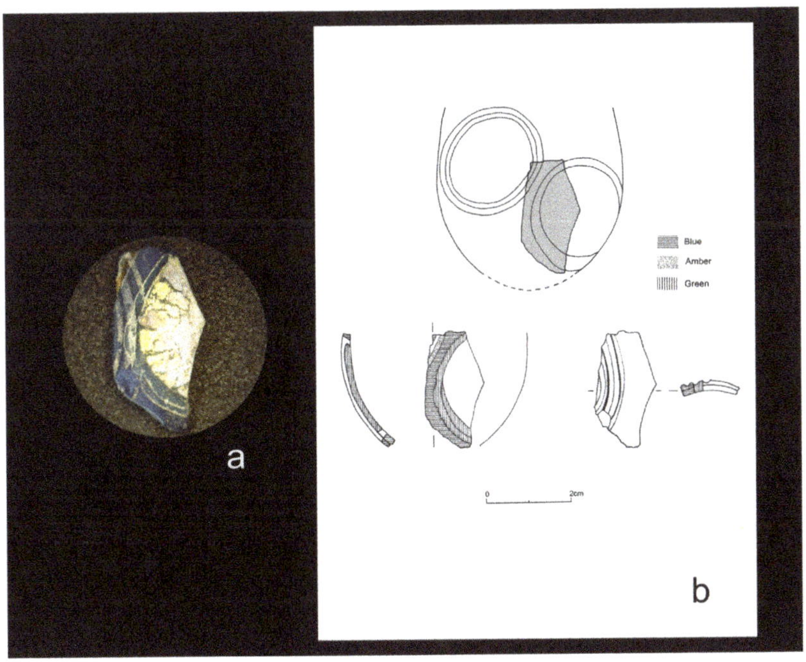

Figure 15.3 AN2007.30 (a) micrograph of fragment; (b) line drawing reconstruction of original shape and design of object.
Source: © Ashmolean Museum, University of Oxford; drawing by Yvonne Beadnell, 2012

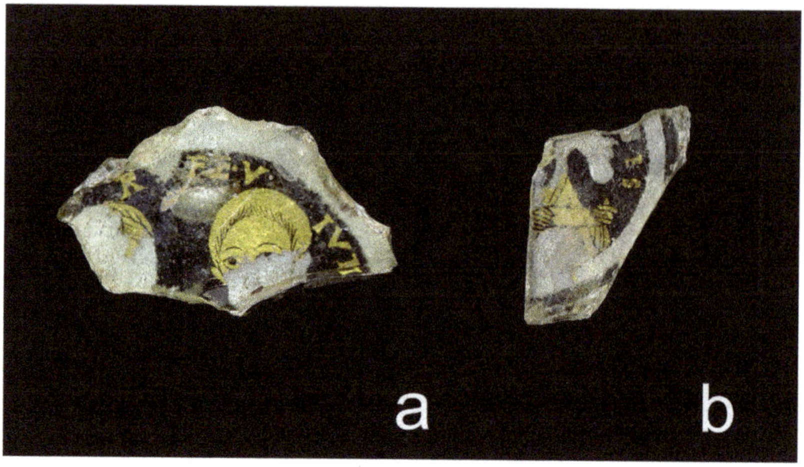

Figure 15.4 High-quality gold-glass objects made of recycled glass (a) AN2007.24, part of a medallion, 3.9 × 2.4 cm; (b) AN2007.27, part of the base of a small cup, 5.0 × 2.3 cm.
Source: © Ashmolean Museum, University of Oxford

the skills of the gold-leaf engraver and painter were not tied to supplies of fresh glass, and that the quality of design and execution of the gold-leaf decoration reflected the nature of the commission and the wealth and status of the purchaser, rather than representing a progressive decline over time. Nonetheless, the supply of enamelled paint seems to have changed with the move to using recycled glass, on which only red and black are seen, the glass of Group 2 supporting a wider range of colours including blue, green and white (e.g. Figure 15.2c, h (Group 2); j (Group 3)).

These observations are of considerable potential significance to our understanding of the production of gold-glass. It is hoped that future analysis of other collections will provide a wider spectrum of comparable material, allowing the application of these observations to a broader range of surviving Late Antique gold-glass.

References

Dölger, F. J. 1928. *Ichthus: Das Fisch-Symbol in frühchristlicher Zeit: Ichthus als Kürzung der Namen Jesu: Iesous Christos Theou Uios Soter*. 2nd edition Münster in Westfalen: Aschendorffschen Verlagsbuchhandlung.

Foster, H. E. and Jackson, C. 2010. 'The Composition of Late Romano-British Colourless Vessel Glass: Glass Production and Consumption', *Journal of Archaeological Science* 37, 3068–80.

Grig, L. 2004. 'Portraits, Pontiffs and the Christianisation of Fourth-Century Rome', *Papers of the British School at Rome* 72: 203–30.

Howells, D. T. 2015. *A Catalogue of the Late Antique Gold Glass in the British Museum* (British Museum Research Publication 198). London: British Museum Press.

Jackson, C. 2005. 'Making Colourless Glass in the Roman Period', *Archaeometry* 47(4): 763–80.

Meek, A. 2015. 'The Scientific Analysis of the British Museum's Gold-Glass Collection'. In *A Catalogue of the Late Antique Gold Glass in the British Museum* (British Museum Research Publication 198), edited by D. T. Howells, 30–40. London: British Museum Press.

Meredith, H. 2015. 'Engaging Mourners and Maintaining Unity: Third- and Fourth-Century Gold-Glass Roundels from Roman Catacombs'. *Religion in the Roman Empire* 1: 219–41.

Morey, C.R. 1959. *The Gold-Glass Collection of the Vatican Library, with Additional Catalogues of Other Gold-Glass Collections.* Vatican City: Biblioteca Apostolica Vaticana.

Schibille, N., Degryse, P., O'Hea, M., Izmer, A. and Vanhaecke, F., McKenzie, J. 2012. 'Late Roman Glass from the "Great Temple" at Petra and Khirbet et-Tannur, Jordan – Technology and provenance'. *Archaeology* 54 (6): 997–1022.

Scott, R., Braekmans, D., Brems, D. and Degryse, P. 2012a. 'Danger: High Voltage! The Application of Handheld X-Ray Fluorescence (HH-XRF) to Experimental Glass: Pitfalls and Potentials'. In *Proceedings of the 39th International Symposium for Archaeometry*, edited by R. Scott, D. Braekmans, M. Carremans and P. Degryse, 268–73. Leuven: Leuven University Press.

Scott, R. B., Shortland, A. J., Degryse, P., Power, M., Domoney, K., Bryen, S. and Braekmans, D. 2012b. 'The Analysis of In-Situ 17th-Century Painted Glass from Christ Church Cathedral, Oxford'. *Glass Technology-Part A* 53: 65–73.

Vickers, M. 2011. 'The Wilshere Collection of Early Christian and Jewish Antiquities in the Ashmolean Museum, Oxford'. *Miscellanea Emilio Marin, sexagenario dicata. Kačić, Acta provinciae SS. Redemptoris Ordinis Fratrum Minorum in Croatia* 42: 605–14.

Walker, S. (ed.) 2017. *Saints and Salvation: Charles Wilshere's Collection of Gold-Glass, Sarcophagi and Inscriptions in the Ashmolean Museum, University of Oxford*. Oxford: Ashmolean Museum.

Index

CPSIA information can be obtained
at www.ICGtesting.com
Printed in the USA
BVHW091344300520
580561BV00022B/805

9 781787 351189